Palgrave Socio-Legal Studies

Series Editor
Dave Cowan
School of Law
University of Bristol
Bristol, UK

The Palgrave Socio-Legal Studies series is a developing series of monographs and textbooks featuring cutting edge work which, in the best tradition of socio-legal studies, reach out to a wide international audience.

Editorial Board
Dame Hazel Genn, Professor of Socio-Legal Studies, University College London, UK
Fiona Haines, Associate Professor, School of Social and Political Science, University of Melbourne, Australia
Herbert Kritzer, Professor of Law and Public Policy, University of Minnesota, USA
Linda Mulcahy, Professor of Socio-Legal Studies, University of Oxford, UK
Carl Stychin, Dean and Professor, The City Law School, City University London, UK
Mariana Valverde, Professor of Criminology, University of Toronto, Canada
Sally Wheeler, Dean of Australian National University College of Law, Australia

More information about this series at
http://www.palgrave.com/gp/series/14679

Nick Gill · Anthony Good
Editors

Asylum Determination in Europe

Ethnographic Perspectives

Editors
Nick Gill
College of Life and Environmental Sciences
University of Exeter
Exeter, UK

Anthony Good
University of Edinburgh
Edinburgh, UK

Palgrave Socio-Legal Studies
ISBN 978-3-319-94748-8   ISBN 978-3-319-94749-5 (eBook)
https://doi.org/10.1007/978-3-319-94749-5

Library of Congress Control Number: 2018946177

© The Editor(s) (if applicable) and The Author(s) 2019. This book is an open access publication.

Open Access This book is licensed under the terms of the Creative Commons Attribution 4.0 International License (http://creativecommons.org/licenses/by/4.0/), which permits use, sharing, adaptation, distribution and reproduction in any medium or format, as long as you give appropriate credit to the original author(s) and the source, provide a link to the Creative Commons license and indicate if changes were made.

The images or other third party material in this book are included in the book's Creative Commons license, unless indicated otherwise in a credit line to the material. If material is not included in the book's Creative Commons license and your intended use is not permitted by statutory regulation or exceeds the permitted use, you will need to obtain permission directly from the copyright holder.

The use of general descriptive names, registered names, trademarks, service marks, etc. in this publication does not imply, even in the absence of a specific statement, that such names are exempt from the relevant protective laws and regulations and therefore free for general use.

The publisher, the authors and the editors are safe to assume that the advice and information in this book are believed to be true and accurate at the date of publication. Neither the publisher nor the authors or the editors give a warranty, express or implied, with respect to the material contained herein or for any errors or omissions that may have been made. The publisher remains neutral with regard to jurisdictional claims in published maps and institutional affiliations.

Cover credit: © Tom Wagner/Alamy Stock Photo

This Palgrave Macmillan imprint is published by the registered company Springer Nature Switzerland AG
The registered company address is: Gewerbestrasse 11, 6330 Cham, Switzerland

We dedicate this book to people who have been forced to flee their homes and start again elsewhere.

Acknowledgements

We would first like to thank the contributors to this volume, for their important work, ethnographic flair and attention to detail. We are especially grateful to Sarah Craig and Karin Zwaan for augmenting the collection with their insights from a legal perspective. We are grateful to Dave Cohen, the book series editor, as well as the anonymous reviewers of the volume who provided useful feedback. We would also like to acknowledge the editorial and production teams for Palgrave MacMillan, including Aléta Bezuidenhout, Stephanie Carey, Poppy Hull, Subasree Sairam and Josie Taylor.

The idea for the book was formed at a workshop at the University of Exeter, UK, on the 8th and 9th January 2015, organised in large part by Rose Ferraby, and funded by the University of Exeter. Later in the production process Amanda Schmid-Scott and Julia Gill both carried out editorial work on the manuscript, for which we are extremely grateful.

The book has benefitted from a productive intellectual environment generated by an inspiring set of post-doctoral researchers at the University of Exeter, including Jennifer Allsopp, Andrew Burridge, Daniel Fisher, Melanie Griffiths, Jessica Hambly, Nicole Hoellerer, Natalia Paszkiewicz and Rebecca Rotter.

We acknowledge financial support from the Economic and Social Research Council (grant number ES/J023426/1), the European Research Council (grant number StG-2015_677917, acronym ASYFAIR) and the University of Exeter. We are enormously grateful to our families and to others who have supported us in countless ways.

Contents

1 **Introduction** 1
   Nick Gill and Anthony Good

2 **Legal Overview** 27
   Sarah Craig and Karin Zwaan

Part I   Actors

3 **The "Inner Belief" of French Asylum Judges** 53
   Carolina Kobelinsky

4 **"It's All About Naming Things Right": The Paradox of Web Truths in the Belgian Asylum-Seeking Procedure** 69
   Massimiliano Spotti

5 **The World of Home Office Presenting Officers** 91
   John R. Campbell

6 **Asylum Procedures in Greece: The Case of Unaccompanied Asylum Seeking Minors** 109
   Chrisa Giannopoulou and Nick Gill

x   Contents

Part II Communication

7 Why Handling Power Responsibly Matters: The Active
   Interpreter Through the Sociological Lens   133
   Julia Dahlvik

8 Communicative Practices and Contexts of Interaction in the
   Refugee Status Determination Process in France   155
   Robert Gibb

9 Narrating Asylum in Camp and at Court   175
   Matilde Skov Danstrøm and Zachary Whyte

10 Interactions and Identities in UK Asylum Appeals: Lawyers
   and Law in a Quasi-Legal Setting   195
   Jessica Hambly

Part III Decision-Making

11 What Do We Talk About When We Talk About Credibility?
   Refugee Appeals in Italy   221
   Barbara Sorgoni

12 Making the Right Decision: Justice in the Asylum
   Bureaucracy in Norway   241
   Tone Maia Liodden

13 Taking the 'Just' Decision: Caseworkers and Their
   Communities of Interpretation in the Swiss Asylum Office   263
   Laura Affolter, Jonathan Miaz and Ephraim Poertner

14 Becoming a Decision-Maker, or: "Don't Turn Your Heart into
   a Den of Thieves and Murderers"   285
   Stephanie Schneider

15 Conclusion   307
   Nick Gill

Index   319

Notes on Contributors

Dr. des. Laura Affolter is a Postdoctoral Researcher at the Institute of Social Anthropology in Bern. She obtained her Ph.D. from the University of Bern in 2017. In her dissertation "Protecting the System: Decision-Making in a Swiss Asylum Administration", she examined everyday processes of decision-making in the first level of the Swiss asylum procedure. She thereby focused on the regularities of asylum decision-making: on the shaping of patterns of practice and on decision-makers' institutional socialisation.

Dr. John R. Campbell is Reader in the Anthropology of Africa and Law, based in Department of Anthropology and Sociology at the School of Oriental and African Studies, London. Between January 2007 and January 2009, he undertook fieldwork research funded by an ESRC Grant (RES-062-23-0296) entitled *Refugees and the Law: An Ethnography of the British Asylum System*. This research sought to follow refugees from Eritrea and Ethiopia who were seeking asylum in the UK. He has written *Nationalism, Law and Statelessness: Grand Illusions in the Horn of Africa* (2014; Routledge) and *Bureaucracy, Law and Dystopia in the United Kingdom's Asylum System* (2017, Routledge).

Sarah Craig is a Senior Lecturer in Public Law at the University of Glasgow. She has a background in legal practice and has conducted research on access to justice, human rights and on immigration and asylum law and procedures for a range of funding bodies. She is a member of the Law Society of Scotland's Immigration and Asylum Sub-Committee.

Dr. Julia Dahlvik holds a Ph.D. in sociology from the University of Vienna. She has research interests in migration, asylum, law, society and organisations. She was awarded the Dissertation Prize for Migration Research from the Austrian Academy of Sciences in 2012 and the ÖGS Dissertation Prize from the Austrian Sociological Association in 2015. She is a researcher and lecturer at the University of Applied Sciences in Vienna (FH Campus Wien), Department of Public Management.

Matilde Skov Danstrøm holds an M.Sc. in Anthropology from the University of Copenhagen. Her master's thesis examined how asylum lawyers represent asylum seekers and how asylum motives are assessed in the Danish asylum system. Her research interests revolve around asylum, development, migration and trafficking. She has worked as research assistant in the Migration Unit at the Danish Institute for International Studies and is currently head of section at the Danish Centre against Human Trafficking anchored in the National Board of Social Services.

Dr. Chrisa Giannopoulou received her Ph.D. from the Department of Balkan, Slavic and Oriental Studies in the University of Macedonia, Thessaloniki, Greece in December 2015. Her thesis focuses on the survival strategies of separated asylum-seeking children in Greek reception centres. She is currently conducting her postdoctorate research supervised by the University of the Aegean, Department of Geography in Mytilene, Lesvos. Her work and research experience also include victims of trafficking and regular migrants in Greece.

Dr. Robert Gibb is a lecturer in sociology at Glasgow University. With A. Good, he conducted research on asylum processes in France and the UK. His current research, also funded by the AHRC, focuses on the multilingual working practices of a range of actors involved in the refugee status determination process in Bulgaria.

Dr. Nick Gill is Professor of Human Geography at the University of Exeter, UK. He is a political geographer whose work focuses on issues of justice and injustice, especially in the context of border control, mobility and its confiscation, incarceration and the law. His books include *Carceral Spaces: Mobility and Agency in Imprisonment and Migrant Detention* edited with Dominique Moran and Deirdre Conlon (Ashgate, 2013) and *Nothing Personal? Geographies of Governing and Activism in the British Asylum System* (Wiley-Blackwell, 2016). His current European Research Council funded research project, ASYFAIR, examines court spaces, access to justice and the consistency of asylum determination in Europe.

Dr. Anthony Good is Emeritus Professor of Social Anthropology at the University of Edinburgh. His overseas field research focuses on South India and Sri Lanka. He has acted as expert witness in over 600 asylum appeals involving Sri Lankan Tamils and has done ESRC and (with Robert Gibb) AHRC-funded research on the asylum processes in France and the UK. Books include *Anthropology and Expertise in the Asylum Courts* (Routledge, 2007) and (with Daniela Berti and Gilles Tarabout) *Of Doubt and Proof: Ritual and Legal Practices of Judgment* (Ashgate, 2015).

Dr. Jessica Hambly is currently a Postdoctoral Research Fellow on Professor Nick Gill's ASYFAIR project at the University of Exeter. Previously, she worked as a Research Associate on the Citizenship and Law Project at the University of Bristol and as an adviser with Legal Centre Lesbos. Jess has a background in law, with an LLB from King's College London, a BCL from the University of Oxford, and an M.Sc. in Socio-legal Studies from the University of Bristol. Her Ph.D., awarded in 2017 by the University of Bristol, was a socio-legal study of advocates in asylum appeals.

Dr. Carolina Kobelinsky is a Tenured Research Fellow of the French Centre for Scientific Research (CNRS) and member of the Laboratory for Ethnography and Comparative Sociology at the Université Paris Nanterre. She has worked on issues related to asylum in France and her current research focuses on the death of migrants at Europe's southern borders and questions the violence of EU policies towards immigration.

Dr. Tone Maia Liodden currently works as a Researcher at the Work Research Institute at the Oslo Metropolitan University. She received her Ph.D. in sociology from the University of Oslo. In her doctoral thesis, she explores how asylum decision-makers reach a sense of conviction about the outcome in a context of uncertainty and how organisational factors affect the conditions of doubt and discretionary reasoning. Her research interests include sociology of law, decision-making, bureaucracy and migration.

Dr. Jonathan Miaz is a Postdoctoral Researcher at the Center of Migration Law and at the Laboratory for the Study of Social Processes at the University of Neuchâtel. He is part of the National Center of Competence in Research—"The Migration-Mobility Nexus". Jonathan holds a Ph.D. in Political Science from the University of Lausanne and from the University of Strasbourg. In his dissertation—"Asylum policy and Sophistication of Law. Bureaucratic Practices and Legal Mobilizations for the Migrants in Switzerland (1981–2015)"—he analyzed the Swiss asylum policy, focusing on the force of the law and on its production by street-level actors' practices. His thesis is based on an ethnographic study combining fieldworks (observations and interviews) in the administration and in legal defence organizations.

Dr. des. Ephraim Poertner has successfully defended his Ph.D. in Human Geography from the University of Zurich. In his doctoral thesis, he examines the ways in which asylum is governed in the Swiss public administration. Drawing on observant participation, interviews and conversations in the Swiss asylum office as well as case files and other institutional documents, he traces the governmental arrangements and practices of case-making in which applicants' lives become recorded in terms of asylum. Ephraim's research interests lie in the fields of asylum and migration governance, public administration, legal and political geography.

Stephanie Schneider is a Ph.D. Researcher at the Department of Social Sciences at the University of Siegen. Her dissertation project is an empirical investigation of contestations around "good work" and efforts at professionalising frontline asylum administrative practices in Germany. It is situated in the context of the research project "The European Field of Asylum Administrations" funded by the German Research Foundation in the framework of the research unit "Horizontal Europeanization" (FOR1539). Stephanie's research interests lie in the fields of political sociology, sociology of law and public administration, and of space and borders.

Dr. Barbara Sorgoni is Associate Professor in the Department of Culture, Politics and Society at the University of Turin, Italy. She has written extensively on issues related to the history of Italian anthropology in colonial times and on social, affective and sexual relations between citizens and subjects in Italian colonial Eritrea. Her recent research interests include ethnographic observation of policies and practices inside reception centres for asylum seekers in northern Italy, and of refugee status determination procedures at first instance and appeal level.

Dr. Massimiliano Spotti is an Assistant Professor at the Department of Culture Studies of Tilburg University as well as Deputy Director of Babylon—Center for the Study of Superdiversity, at the same institution. His current research line, entitled Asylum 2.0, aims at investigating the implication of the web and of social media for doing asylum seeking in an era of superdiversity. Further, he has widely published on issues of identity construction and citizenship in institutionalised and non-institutionalised learning environments. Together with Ofelia Garcia and Nelson Flores, he has co-edited the Oxford Handbook of Language and Society (OUP, 2017).

Dr. Zachary Whyte is an Associate Professor at the Centre for Advanced Migration Studies (AMIS), University of Copenhagen, working with asylum seekers and refugees in Denmark and beyond. He is interested in the intersections of transnationality, state practices, uncertainty and everyday life. He has pursued numerous academic and advisory projects working with asylum seekers and refugees, local communities, as well as state, municipal, private and civil society actors. His current research is on asylum camp spaces and mobility.

Dr. Karin Zwaan is the Academic Coordinator of the Centre for Migration Law, Faculty of Law, Radboud University Nijmegen. She holds a Master's (Utrecht University) and a Ph.D. (Radboud University Nijmegen) in Law (on the use of the so-called safe third country exception). Her research focuses on asylum law, including the use of expert evidence in the refugee status determination procedure. Her recent research is on the safe country of origin concept and on the application of this concept in Dutch asylum decision-making.

List of Figures

Fig. 1.1	Total number of asylum applications, first instance decisions and final decisions for EU-28 countries, and percentage of positive first instance and final decisions, 2008–2017	8
Fig. 1.2	Chart showing variability in regular asylum procedures among 17 EU member countries and 3 non-members	13
Fig. 5.1	Home office asylum and immigration instructions and rules (May 2013)	93

1

Introduction

Nick Gill and Anthony Good

Asylum as a Moral Panic

In his introduction to the third edition of *Folk Devils and Moral Panics*, Stanley Cohen (2002: vii–xxvi) gives fresh examples of 'moral panics' that arose in the 30 years following the first appearance of his book; one of these examples concerns refugees and asylum seekers. He characterises such panics as focused on issues that are actually new forms of older worries and concerns, and in these terms the 'asylum panic' is understood as a particular manifestation of a long-running, perhaps immemorial, fear of strangers or outsiders (Simmel 1976). Indeed, the policy approaches of European governments display both of the classic responses to outsiders identified by Zygmunt Bauman (1997). 'Anthropophagy'—'devouring' strangers and 'metabolically transforming them into a tissue indistinguishable from one's own' (ibid.: 18)—is evident in the long running penchant for 'assimilationist' strategies towards immigration in various European countries (Vertovec and Wessendorf 2010). At the same time 'anthropoemy'—'vomiting' out strangers and 'banishing them from the limits of the orderly world' (Bauman

N. Gill (✉)
University of Exeter, Exeter, UK
e-mail: n.m.gill@exeter.ac.uk

A. Good
University of Edinburgh, Edinburgh, UK
e-mail: A.Good@ed.ac.uk

1997: 18)—has been vividly exemplified in recent years by the erection of new barriers. Hungary, for example, faced with the receipt of significantly more first-time asylum applications in the first half of 2015 than in previous years, famously constructed a wire fence along its 175-kilometer border with Serbia in order to deter new entries (Migration Policy Centre 2016), resulting in the onward migration of thousands of rejected would-be immigrants.

Cohen (2002) suggests, however, that the moral panic surrounding asylum is 'crucially different' (ibid.: xxiii) from his other examples of moral panics, including those surrounding benefit cheats, paedophiles and high school massacres. Rather than being focused on 'specific newsworthy episodes' (Cohen 2002: xxiii), the moral panic about asylum seekers has been long drawn-out, characterised by a 'virtually uninterrupted message of hostility and rejection' (ibid.: xxii). Asylum is a rare example of a moral panic that is chronic rather than acute in nature. Tyler (2013) dates the more or less continuous moral panic about Britain as a 'soft touch' for criminals and bogus refugees to the early 1990s. Similarly, talk of 'crisis' in France dates back to at least the mid-1980s, when annual numbers of asylum claims trebled within a few years (Legoux 1995: xxiii).

Cohen also argues that the moral panic surrounding asylum is 'more overtly political than any others' (Cohen 2002: xxiii). For example, although the 1951 Refugee Convention is a recognition of the special moral claims of refugees, as persons suffering persecution because of their beliefs or ethnicity, the political purpose of the Convention has altered significantly since its inception. Despite the popular impression that it safeguards refugees, its continued observance is a paradoxical confirmation of the legitimacy of immigration controls more generally in modern liberal democracies.

Furthermore, the asylum issue is deeply contested as a result of an inherent contradiction between the need for Western states to portray themselves as representing shared communities with common values, including recognition of basic human rights such as the right not to suffer persecution; and the discretionary right assumed by modern states to decide who can enter and reside in their territory. This tension accounts for what Gibney (2014) terms the 'schizophrenic response' (n.p.) of European states, whereby they 'continue to embrace asylum but spurn the asylum seeker' (n.p.) and offer protection only grudgingly. It has also resulted in the occasional eruption of pro-asylum voices from various quarters over the last two decades, and especially since the summer of 2015, which gives the asylum issue a particularly disputed feel (see Conlon and Gill 2015).

This contestation relates to what Goodwin-Gill conceptualises as two competing models for approaching refugee issues: a model that focuses on the need to treat every individual asylum applicant on their own merits; and an instrumental security model that emphasises control of refugees on the basis of the balance between the perceived risks they pose and the opportunities they offer to receiving countries (2001: 14–15). This book is full of examples wherein particular administrative and legal systems display one, and sometimes both, of these tendencies.

The Asylum System 'in Crisis'

One manifestation of this schizophrenia is the repeated invocation of the trope of 'crisis' in relation to asylum. Thus, the 'refugee crisis' that dominated European political attention in 2015–2016—provoked largely by the unusually large numbers of people entering Europe in flight from the Syrian conflict—was a particularly intense form of the moral panic that has surrounded the questions of asylum and immigration more generally over the last few decades. This 'crisis' is commonly portrayed, by politicians and in the media, using either fluvial or animal metaphors, such as likening the arrival of asylum seekers to a 'flood', 'tide', 'torrent' or 'wave' that threatens to 'swamp' the recipient society (Charteris-Black 2006: 570–572), or alternatively likening it to a 'stampede, 'flock' or 'swarm' of arrivals with a similar potential to overwhelm receiving countries. Both types of metaphor are clearly dehumanising, but they also both employ a rhetorical ruse in relation to the notion of disaster. On the one hand, immigration itself is represented as a 'natural' disaster (Charteris-Black 2006). This view implicitly relieves liberal democracies of their own responsibilities for the immigration pressures they experience: responsibilities rooted in the often invisible 'systemic violence' (Žižek 2009: 8) of global capitalism, historical exploitation, unequal trading relationships and neo-colonialism of which they are a part. On the other hand, immigration *systems* are portrayed as the disaster: bureaucrats are typically portrayed as inept and inadequate to the task of responding effectively to the challenges migration poses.

This elision of asylum *as* crisis—whereby asylum seekers are seen as cultural, economic, or security threats; and asylum *in* crisis—whereby the administrative systems for controlling the numbers of applicants, deciding on the validity of their claims, and deporting those whose claims are deemed to be false, are seen as inadequate—'serves as an important mechanism in the reproduction of dominant asylum discourse' (Moore 2010: 145). Specifically, it affords the opportunity to project the supposed disaster of migration onto an evidently disastrous administration. This slippage is extremely expedient politically because it provides a particularly direct way for sensationalist media and opposition parties to portray the 'crisis' as stemming from the incompetence of politicians. The obvious subtext is that the challenging political party will provide a more competent administration by being more efficient and, typically, more exclusionary. Over time this configuration of 'crisis', political critique and policy response results in an inexorable ratchetting up of immigration controls as power either swaps hands between parties who make increasingly bold and ambitious promises about control whilst in opposition, or as incumbent parties become more exclusionary in order to hold on to power.

This discourse of crisis can also be linked to distrust, political alienation and the rise of the political right in Europe in recent years (see *New York Times* 2017). Paying attention to why large sections of liberal society have turned towards right-wing, immigration-restricting parties in recent years is crucially important for understanding the development of immigration and asylum law. Working class, low skilled voters in many Western economies are facing unemployment, falling real wages, rising personal debt and a mismatch between their own skills and those required by largely tertiary and quaternary industrial economies. The rise of right wing populism in the United States and Britain, for example, has been driven by structural changes in their economies that have rendered this social group disillusioned and feeling politically unrepresented (Ford and Goodwin 2014). Similarly in much of continental Europe, the economic difficulties of the late 2000s, including the sovereign debt crisis that erupted at the end of 2009, produced rising unemployment levels, fuelling right wing sentiments and increasing pressure on politicians to restrict numbers of immigrants, including asylum seekers and refugees (Greven 2016). Although radical right–wing parties are once again 'a force to be reckoned with' (Akkerman et al. 2016: 3), the most notable feature of the right-wing parties that have benefitted from these developments is their strengthened *mainstream* appeal; policies and rhetoric that might once have been considered radically right-wing are becoming more acceptable and politically potent.

The issue of refugee migration to Europe played a part in the United Kingdom Independence Party's (UKIP) successful campaign for Britain to vote to leave the EU in 2016 for instance, which involved poster images of refugees making their way on foot across the Balkans alongside the caption 'Breaking Point: The EU has Failed us all', a tactic which opponents interpreted as 'exploiting the misery of the Syrian refugee crisis in the most dishonest and immoral way'.[1] Moreover, those governments that welcomed

---

[1]Yvette Cooper, British Member of Parliament, quoted in The Huffington Post (Hopkins 2016).

the most refugees in 2015, such as Germany and Sweden, have faced harsh criticism from sections of their electorates in the following years as racial tensions, poverty among incumbent populations and the fear of terrorism nurtured a backlash of anti-refugee sentiment. In consequence, attention has gradually turned towards measures to contain refugee flows in Turkey or other locations closer to the source of the migratory movements.

As in many other contexts the term 'crisis', which was 'once a signifier for a critical decisive moment', has 'come to be construed as a protracted historical and experiental condition' (Roitman 2013: 2; see also Agamben 2005). Its widespread use, says Roitman, subordinates particular events, in all their singularity and uniqueness, to a 'generic logic' that seems 'self-explanatory' (2013: 3). Its use also inevitably entails explicit or implicit judgments about what a normal state of affairs would look like: 'crisis compared to what?' (ibid.: 4). In the case of asylum in Western Europe this may be the situation at the height of the Cold War, when asylum seekers came mostly from the Soviet Bloc and 'each one constituted a vote for the political system of the West and a reproach to that of the East' (Schuster 2003: 190). Consequently almost all such refugees were granted asylum with very little individual scrutiny, reinforcing the presumption that they must, therefore, 'have been authentic refugees fleeing authentic persecution' (Legoux 1995: xxiii). Use of crisis discourse also, importantly, legitimates and supports the redistribution and extension of state power (Strasser 2016: 48; Klein 2007; Mountz and Heimstra 2014), allowing the adoption of measures of governance that would otherwise seem excessively authoritarian (Buzan et al. 1998: 21–23).

In the Cold War period security threats were commonly presented as political or military in character, and the entity posing the threat was a state or some supra-national grouping like 'the Soviet Bloc'. The focus was on material factors such as the scale of a state's military capacity. More recently, however, it has become common to identify threats in economic, environmental and health-related contexts too as part of a pandemic of anxieties that seem to accompany modern everyday life (Furedi 2002; Pain and Smith 2008; Beck 1992). Popular understanding of the consequences of migration is an important form of this heightened sense of social fear. Furthermore, when a strong state response is seen as the antidote to the fearful condition in question, it becomes in the interests of state bureaucrats, as well as their contracted agencies, to confirm and reproduce the sense of unease that provokes an appeal to them (Bigo 2002; see also Isin 2004). From this perspective the increasingly common tendency among politicians to identify refugees and migrants as, on the one hand, threats to the 'culture' or 'identity' of the indigenous population and, on the other, as posing criminal or terrorist threats to citizens' personal safety and security, is unsurprising (Huysmans 2000: 751).

The constructivist approach to securitisation pioneered by the Copenhagen School of Security Studies foregrounds the performative aspects of security discourse. Buzan et al. define securitisation as a perlocutionary 'speech act'—whereby some particular issue is 'presented as an existential threat, requiring emergency measures and justifying actions outside the normal bounds of political procedure' (1998: 23–24)—that is accepted as valid by its target audience. In other words, securitisation is the inter-subjective process whereby a phenomenon like migration becomes a security issue, not because it necessarily poses an actual or significant threat, but because it is successfully presented as doing so.

During the post Cold War era of the 1990s and early 2000s, immigration was one area wherein securitisation 'opened up a number of discursive opportunities to correlate terrorism with immigration, thereby helping to legitimise practices and technologies in migration control that were usually reserved for emergencies' (Boswell 2007: 589; see Buzan et al. 1998: 23–26; Huysmans 2000). Here it is helpful to distinguish analytically between securitisation as framed in political discourse and securitisation as manifest in administrative action (Boswell 2007: 591). Unlike in the United States, it is at this latter level in particular, argues Boswell, that securitisation has been most apparent in Europe. Furthermore, rather than counter-terrorism practices having been incorporated into practices of migration control, the process has been rather the reverse, namely that tools developed in furtherance of migration policy, such as databases on foreign nationals, airline passenger lists, and frontier passport controls, 'have been harnessed in order to enhance the surveillance of suspected or potential terrorists' (2007: 601).

In short, for all the reasons identified above, national and supra-national legal and administrative structures for processing and assessing asylum claims, and controlling or deporting those who make them, have been portrayed on the one hand as increasingly important to the economic and social well-being, and even the physical safety, of citizens; and on the other, as grossly inadequate and inefficient, and in urgent need of root and branch reform. In such circumstances it is remarkable that so little empirical research has been carried out into how these structures actually operate in practice. The great bulk of the research that has been done on administrative and legal systems of asylum determination falls under the heading of legal studies rather than social science and is thus primarily normative rather than critical in its stance. The present volume seeks to help remedy these lacunae.

The 'Refugee Crisis' in Perspective

The crisis rhetoric surrounding asylum seeking in Europe was exacerbated by the civil war in Syria, compounded by the human rights abuses perpetrated by the self-styled Islamic State (IS) in Syria and Iraq. These had resulted in the deaths of over 250,000 people by mid-2015 (BBC 2016) and produced one of the largest human migration events in history. Around 11 million people were forced to leave their homes and seek safety between the beginning of the civil war in March 2011 and mid-2016 (www.syrianrefugees.eu 2016). It is well known that attempts to reach Europe often end in tragedy, underscoring the lengths to which migrants have been forced to go to find safety. 3700 people lost their lives in the Mediterranean in 2015, and over 4900 died in the same way in 2016 (IOM 2016). The risk of dying along this route was estimated at one in 269 arrivals in 2015 and one in 88 (one in 47 between Libya and Italy) in 2016 as migrants turned to more perilous routes and smugglers resorted to more dangerous tactics in an attempt to avoid heightened border controls (UNHCR 2016a).

Yet for all the crisis talk about refugees in Europe, it is notable that the vast majority of Syrians affected by the violence in their country sought safety either within Syria itself or within Turkey, Lebanon, Jordan, Egypt and Iraq. It is estimated that 6.6 million Syrians were internally displaced within Syria, and a further 4.8 million sought safety in the region, between March 2011 and the end of 2016 (www.syrianrefugees.eu 2016). Despite this, the United Nations High Commission for Refugees (UNHCR) had received only just over half of the required aid needed to respond to the humanitarian needs of the displaced in mid-2016. This shortfall contributed to inadequate living conditions in refugee camps and cities[2] in the region around Syria. For its part, the European Union received 1.18 million applications for asylum from Syrians between April 2011 and September 2016 (UNHCR 2016b). Although this helps to explain the substantial increase in total asylum claims received by the European Union illustrated in Fig. 1.1 it is only a fraction of the total numbers displaced.

Indeed, as Moreno-Lax (2017a) demonstrates in her comprehensive analysis of EU asylum law, although there is a right to asylum enshrined in EU law, the EU is highly active in curtailing access to this right. This is achieved through a panoply of pre-border, extra-territorial and preemptive

---

[2]Koizumi and Hoffstadter (2015) note that many of the world's refugees live in urban areas rather than dedicated camps, posing distinctive policy challenges that are only belatedly beginning to be addressed.

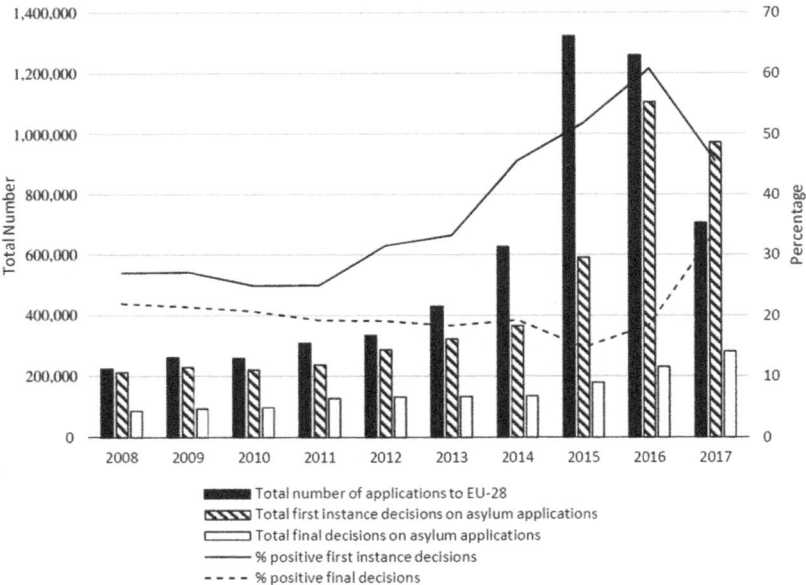

Fig. 1.1 Total number of asylum applications, first instance decisions and final decisions for EU-28 countries, and percentage of positive first instance and final decisions, 2008–2017
Sources Eurostat 'Asylum and first time asylum applicants'—annual aggregated data (rounded)—tps00191, 'First instance decisions on asylum applications by type of decision—annual aggregated data'—tps00192, and 'Final decisions on applications by citizenship, age and sex Annual data (rounded)'—migr_asydcfina, all at http://ec.europa.eu/eurostat/data/database (accessed 21 June 2018). 'Positive' decisions include Geneva Convention, humanitarian, subsidiary and temporary protection status. *Note* what are referred to as final decisions in the graph are decisions taken by administrative or judicial bodies in appeal or in review and which are no longer subject to remedy. The true 'final instance' may be, according to the national legislation and administrative procedures, a decision of the highest national court. However, these statistics refer to what is effectively a final decision in the vast majority of all cases: i.e. that all normal routes of appeal have been exhausted

measures, including offshore border checks, outsourced visa processing, privatised pre-boarding controls, and maritime interdiction. These 'remote control' activities effectively limit access to asylum in Europe and introduce a fundamental inconsistency between the lofty aspirations of the Union as articulated by its commitment to asylum, effective judicial protection and non-refoulement (that is, a commitment to not return anyone to a situation in which they will face persecution), and the practical barriers that asylum seekers face in attempting to access Europe.

It should also be noted in the context of the development of the preemptive, extraterritorial controls that Moreno-Lax (2017b) describes, that the rising death toll in the Mediterranean is part of a broader and longer-term escalation in the number of migrants dying in and *en route* to Europe. The European Network against Nationalism, Racism, Fascism and in Support of Migrants and Refugees (UNITED) has kept a 'list of deaths' since 1993, which includes reported deaths that have occurred as a result of European border militarisation, asylum laws, poor accommodation conditions, detention, deportations and carrier sanctions. It stood at 22,394 on 19 June 2015 (UNITED 2015), roughly two months before the publication of the photograph of the dead body of Alan Kurdi, the drowned toddler whose death ignited a renewed round of moral panic surrounding the "refugee crisis" in Europe.

Asylum determination—meaning the process of reaching a decision on a claim for international protection on the grounds of asylum—has long played an important role in European politics, but during 2015 and 2016 it rose in prominence as the refugee issue took centre stage. Figure 1.1 charts the number of applications, first instance decisions and final decisions reached on asylum claims to Europe between 2008 and 2017, as well as the percentage of positive first instance and final decisions.[3] First instance decisions refer to decisions on asylum claims usually made by a government official in the country of asylum. Where asylum seekers receive a negative decision on their first instance claim, they have the right to appeal, in European countries at least, either through legal or administrative means depending on the country in question. The decision on appeal is usually[4] the final decision on an application and Fig. 1.1 illustrates how significant these final decisions are. In 2011 for example, the number of final decisions reached through appeal totaled over half the number of initial decisions, underscoring how indispensable appeal processes are to the overall decision-making system.

Figure 1.1 reveals various facets of the politics surrounding European asylum determination. Firstly, the volume of decisions, both first instance and final, increased markedly between 2008 and 2016, as indicated by the striped and white bars respectively. Over that period the volume of final

---

[3] It is worth noting that because of the time it takes to administer asylum claims, many first instance decisions made in 2016 will have concerned applications received in 2015 or earlier, and many final decisions made in 2016 will have concerned applications made even earlier. The same point could be made for the other years shown.
[4] Unless there are specific matters of law that can be appealed to higher courts.

decisions more than doubled and the volume of initial decisions more than quadrupled. An expansion of this scale and pace in any decision-making system is likely to introduce challenges in terms of staff stress and turnover, resources and training (see for example, Sorgoni, this volume, who describes an increase from ten Territorial Commissions in Italy—which examine initial asylum claims—to 45 between 2010 and 2016). Secondly however, this rapid acceleration in decision-making lagged behind the increase in the number of applications (the black bars). In 2008 there was virtual parity between the number of new applications received and the number of first instance decisions made, but for every subsequent year before 2017 this parity was not restored. This led to criticism that the European asylum determination system is ill-equipped to cope with rapid increases in applications. It has also produced delays for applicants, which have been associated with mental ill health by various studies (Laban et al. 2005; Coffey et al. 2010). From the perspective of decision-makers, the period from 2008 to 2016 therefore constituted something of a perfect storm: an extremely rapid increase in decision-making frequency coupled with a demoralising generation of backlogs, delays and associated criticisms.

The plotted lines in Fig. 1.1 reveal another interesting development in asylum determination in Europe: the divergence between the rate of success at first instance and the rate of success at the point of a final decision between 2010 and 2016. During this period the rate of success at first instance more than doubled, from around 25% to over 60% (illustrated by the solid line in Fig. 1.1). During the same period the rate of success on appeal declined however (the dashed line), falling below 20% in 2011 and remaining there until 2016. There are various possible explanations for this development. It may be that the first instance procedure improved in terms of its ability to detect legally well-founded[5] claims. This could help to explain why the appeal system was less likely to deliver positive decisions on asylum claims: because fewer claims that reached this stage are legally well founded. Alternatively however, it could mean that decision makers at the appeal stage simply *perceived there to be* an improvement in the ability to detect well founded claims at the initial stage, because the proportion of claims granted at the initial stage had risen. Appeal stage decision-makers might reason that if a claim has not been granted at the initial stage when so many other claims are, there must be something wrong with many of the

---

[5]Although it is necessary at this point in our argument to talk about 'well-founded claims' the discussion elsewhere in the introduction makes it clear that we perceive serious shortcomings in what the law asserts a well-founded claim to be.

applications that reach them. What this reasoning misses, however, is the possibility that there may simply be more legally well-founded claims overall. If this is true, there is a risk that the increase in first instance positive decisions is misinterpreted by appeal stage decision makers as a signal that first stage procedures have improved in their ability to detect well-founded claims, when in fact there may have been no such improvement and therefore no particular reason for appeal decision makers to be more conservative.

By 2017 the system seemed to be catching up again: the total number of first instance decisions exceeded the number of new claims for the first time during the period shown in Fig. 1.1 for instance. But if criticism about slowness and delays was not enough, the asylum determination system has also drawn objections based on its inconsistent treatment of claimants over the same period (for example AIDA 2013). International law dictates that refugees can only be recognised as such if they fulfil the specific definition set out in Article 1(A)2 of the 1951 Geneva Convention, as modified by the accompanying 1967 Protocol, namely that a refugee must be someone who:

> owing to well-founded fear of being persecuted for reasons of *race, religion, nationality, membership of a particular social group or political opinion*, is outside the country of his nationality and is unable or, owing to such fear, is unwilling to avail himself of the protection of that country. (italics added)

Yet none of these five italicised 'Convention reasons' are precisely defined, either in the Convention itself or in the UNHCR *Handbook* that provides guidance on its application,[6] nor are the key notions of 'well-founded fear' and 'persecution'. Consequently these have all been subjected to legal interpretation by a whole range of national courts across Europe and beyond, not always with congruent results.

What is more, both first instance and appealed decision-making across the countries of Europe have in practice been approached in very different ways reflecting the different legal cultures and political circumstances of the member countries. This results in uncomfortable geographical anomalies both in the rate of ostensibly similar refugee claims that are recognised and granted refugee status (or another form of positive status such as humanitarian status, subsidiary or temporary protection status), and in the procedural approach that different countries take to asylum determination.

---

[6]UNHCR (1979, Annexes updated 2011). *Handbook and Guidelines on Procedures and Criteria for Determining Refugee Status*. Available at: http://www.unhcr.org/uk/publications/legal/3d58e13b4/handbook-procedures-criteria-determining-refugee-status-under-1951-convention.html [Accessed 31 July 2016].

The proportion of Syrian asylum seekers who were awarded some form of positive status in 2015 was 97% in the EU-28 as a whole for example, but particular countries deviated significantly. For instance, Hungary, Italy and Romania each awarded some form of positive status in fewer than 60% of cases.[7] In the same year, the recognition rate of Afghans—the second most common nationality of asylum claimants to Europe after Syrians[8]—varied from 78, 83 and 96% in Austria, France and Italy to 16, 14 and 5% in Hungary, Romania and Bulgaria, respectively.[9]

International inconsistency is also evident procedurally. Figure 1.2 illustrates the variability in procedures among 17 member countries of the EU as well as three non-members,[10] based on surveys carried out by the European Council for Refugees and Exiles (ECRE) in 2017.

As can be seen from Fig. 1.2, procedural inconsistency is evident in relation to whether or not time limits apply to asylum claims, whether asylum seekers have access to free legal assistance on appeal against a negative decision in practice, the use of video-conferencing and the degree to which appeals are suspensive[11] and judicial, among other things. In fact, there is only unambiguous uniformity of approach concerning three out of the 12 procedures shown.

If inconsistencies between countries are not troublesome enough, individual countries also often have more than one legal process through which asylum claims can be determined, typically including both a regular process and a fast-track process for applications that are deemed to be easier to determine or less likely to be well-founded. The proliferation of different processes introduces complexity and inconsistencies within countries as well as across them. Greece, for example, has at least five proceedures including the regular procedure, border procedure, fast-track border procedure, accelerated procedure and Dublin procedure (Asylum Information Database 2018). The current form of the fast-track border procedure has been made possible by the European Union's application of

---

[7]Statistics refer to first instance decisions only. Eurostat table migr_asydcfsta, 'First instance decisions on applications by citizenship, age and sex Annual aggregated data (rounded)'. Available at: http://ec.europa.eu/eurostat/data/database; published 6 June 2018 [Accessed 22 June 2018].

[8]Eurostat (2016). *Asylum Statistics*. Available at: http://ec.europa.eu/eurostat/statistics-explained/index.php/Asylum_statistics; published 20 April 2016 [Accessed 6 January 2017].

[9]Statistics refer to first instance decisions only. Countries that delivered fewer than 100 first instance decisions are discounted. Eurostat table migr_asydcfsta, 'First instance decisions on applications by citizenship, age and sex Annual aggregated data (rounded)'. Available at: http://ec.europa.eu/eurostat/data/database; published 6 June 2018 [Accessed 22 June 2018].

[10]The 17 European Union (EU) Member States comprise Austria, Belgium, Bulgaria, Croatia, Cyprus, France, Germany, Greece, Hungary, Ireland, Italy, Malta, Netherlands, Poland, Spain, Sweden and the United Kingdom, and the three non-EU countries are, Serbia, Switzerland and Turkey.

[11]If an appeal is suspensive then a deportation will not be carried out until it is completed.

1 Introduction 13

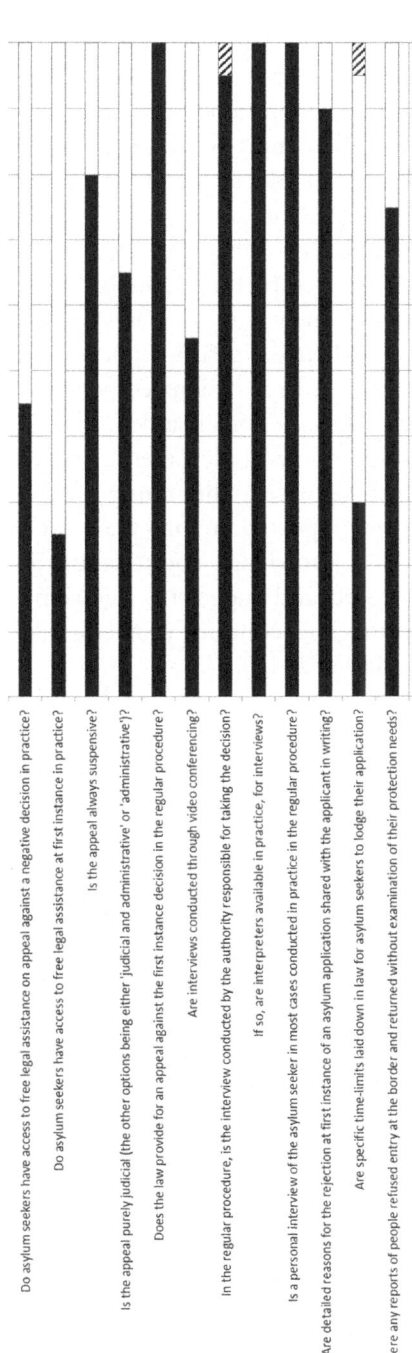

Fig. 1.2 Chart showing variability in regular asylum procedures among 17 EU member countries and 3 non-members

Note For the questions 'Do asylum seekers have access to free legal assistance on appeal against a negative decision in practice?' and 'Do asylum seekers have access to free legal assistance at first instance in practice?' the 'No' count includes the response 'With Difficulty'. For the question 'Are there any reports of people refused entry...?' reports include NGO reports, media, testimonies, etc. For the question 'Are interviews conducted through video conferencing?' the 'Yes' count includes responses 'Frequently' and 'Rarely'. More procedures were surveyed but it was not possible to illustrate them in this format. *Source* Asylum Information Database managed by ECRE. Available at: http://www.asylumineurope.org/reports%20 (Accessed September 2018) the concept of hotspots to migration in 2015,[12] which allows various European agencies to 'assist' countries that are receiving 'disproportionate migratory pressures' in order to help them 'fulfil their obligations under EU law' (European Commission 2015; see also Giannopoulou and Gill, this volume). This innovation, 'supersedes the national in favour of hybrid, super-national governance' via a process of what has been called 'super-state' formation (Painter et al. 2017: 259). In conjuction with the EU-Turkey deal that came into force in 2016 to facilitate the assessment of asylum claims received by the EU in Turkey, the fast-track border procedure has generated an 'extremely truncated asylum procedure with fewer guarantees' (Greek Council for Refugees 2017: n.p.), effectively turning the Greek Eastern Aegean islands that have been designated hotspots into sites of containment and deportation back to Turkey (Tazzioli and Garelli 2018).

Under these conditions asylum interviews undertaken by officials working for the European Union have been reportedly different to those conducted by Greek officials. Cases have been reported in practice where European Asylum Support Office experts lack knowledge about countries of origin, lack cultural sensitivity, employ closed and suggestive questions, use repetitive questions akin to interrogation, and conduct unnecessarily exhaustive interviews (Greek Council for Refugees, 2017).

The assessment of vulnerability is often crucial to which legal track is taken by an asylum application. In Greece for example, if an applicant is considered to be vulnerable then their application can be transferred out of the fast track border procedure. But deciding on what constitutes vulnerability is itself highly variable and, in the absence of conceptual clarity, can depend upon who is making the assessment (AIDA 2017). The definition of vulnerability employed by the member countries of the European Union varies markedly: although most recognize being a child, being an unaccompanied child, being disabled, being a victim of torture and being pregnant as forms of vulnerability only a subset recognize being a victim of human trafficking, serious illness, mental disorders, lack of legal capacity and post traumatic stress disorder as forms of vulnerability (AIDA 2017: 16).

One of the most contested and protracted areas of controversy in relation to the consistency of procedures used to determine refugee status in Europe, and more broadly to ensure common standards for the treatment of asylum seekers and refugees, concerns the Common Europe Asylum System (CEAS), a series of directives intended to harmonise the procedures and standards of member countries, both at the first instance stage of their claim and during their appeal.

---

[12]The 'EU introduced the term "hotspots" in policy conversations addressing crime and natural disasters, long before its deployment in the field of migration' (Tazzioli and Garelli 2018: 6).

Although hailed as a milestone on the road to integration in Europe, the system has been roundly critiqued, largely on the basis of its widely acknowledged inability to ensure a harmonious approach to asylum seeker protection and refugee claim determination as the number of applications the EU received increased markedly in 2015. So prominent was the CEAS's failure to unite the countries of Europe at the height of the increase in asylum claims in 2015 that the European Union hurriedly sought to strengthen and reform it via a series of additional measures proposed in mid-2016, including turning a series of its 'directives' into 'regulations': in other words rendering them binding obligations on member states rather than merely suggestions. The politics and legal significance of these developments is central to the issue of asylum determination in Europe, and is discussed more extensively in the next chapter.

Legal and Ethnographic Approaches to Asylum

The statistics and charts provided above hint at the extent and complexity of the contradictions and tensions within the European asylum system, as well as the extraordinary degree of discretion available both to countries and individual decision makers within the broad rules set out by the Union. There are a number of existing comparative studies of European asylum systems, both in the scholarly literature (Joly 1996; Cherubini 2014; Guild and Minderhoud 2011); and in reports or web-sites curated by NGOs, such as the excellent interactive online resources made available by ECRE through their Asylum Information Database.[13] Generally, however, these are written from a legal standpoint rather than the ethnographic perspective adopted in this volume.

There are important differences between the doctrinal study of law and the approach favoured by ethnographers (Kandel 1992), partly because, as Twining neatly puts it, 'judges have a duty to *decide*... scientists and historians mainly *conclude*' (Twining 2006: 53, italics added). Doctrinal legal scholarship is fundamentally normative, both because its subject-matter is focused on norms, and because it generally locates itself within the legal paradigm, studying law in relative isolation from its social and political context (Anders 2015: 413).[14] Legal scholars are concerned with teasing out the 'correct interpretations of general legal abstractions' in particular cases (hence the emphasis in legal education on the study of written judgments, at least in common

---

[13]Available at: http://www.asylumineurope.org/ [Accessed 6 January 2016].
[14]There are exceptions to this, such as the critical legal studies movement, and of course socio-legal studies constitutes a very different approach to studying the law.

law traditions), and with 'philosophical reflections on what and how law should be' (von Benda-Beckmann 2008: 94). By contrast, the ethnographic approach to law is descriptive, and inherently comparative and relativistic.

The knowledge and forms of reasoning that characterise the formal legal systems of European states are highly esoteric, having diverged from everyday, lay understandings as a concomitant of professionalisation. However, while ethnographers do of course need to understand the legislative and administrative frameworks within which legal actors operate, these are neither their starting nor their finishing point. They approach lawyers or bureaucrats just as they would any other exotic group, trying through prolonged and detailed observation of their daily practices to understand their distinctive modes of thought and the practical actions that express these, or sometimes depart from them. Their analyses seek to set these concepts and practices within a broader socio-cultural context; unlike doctrinal academic lawyers, their ultimate analytical vantage point is located outside the legal paradigm itself. In fact the laws and judgments associated with hegemonic, state-sponsored legal systems are studied no differently from 'folk systems' of law underwritten by religious or traditional authorities (von Benda-Beckmann 2008: 97; see also Good 2015, 2017).[15]

As that last comment implies, ethnographies of law are almost always concerned with situations of legal pluralism in one or more of the senses identified by Moore (2001). First, states themselves are internally complex, and their institutions compete for legal authority, as with the very different migration policies and aspirations of the Westminster and Scottish governments in the UK.[16] Second, the state may preside over diverse legal systems applying only to specific sub-sections of its population, as with the different family law systems for Hindus and Muslims in India (Solanki 2011); this has been labelled 'weak legal pluralism' (Griffiths 1986). Third, the state legal system may be partly implemented by non-state bodies (privately-run asylum detention centres, for example). Fourth, the state legal system vies with the legal systems of other states in supra-national arenas like the CEAS, or with international law vis-a-vis global institutions like UNHCR. Fifth, 'strong legal pluralism' arises when the state is enmeshed with 'non-governmental, *semi-autonomous social fields* which generate their own… obligatory norms to which they can induce or coerce compliance' (Moore 2001: 107; italics added).

Moore's notion of a 'semi-autonomous social field' has proved crucial for clarifying studies of legal pluralism. She does not see such fields as necessarily corresponding to particular social groupings. Rather, a social field is defined:

---

[15]Where formal state law is concerned ethnographers should avoid the 'expertise-trap' of simply accepting what legal experts write about it (von Benda-Beckmann 2008: 101).

[16]Available at: http://www.centreonconstitutionalchange.ac.uk/news/holyrood-and-westminster-could-diverge-immigration [Accessed 12 December 2016].

by a processual characteristic, the fact that it can generate rules and coerce or induce compliance to them… The independent articulation of many different social fields constitutes one of the basic characteristics of complex societies. (Moore 1978: 57–58)

So despite their capacities to generate rules and enforce conformity, such fields can only do so within limits; they are only *semi*-autonomous because they co-exist with, and are affected by, other semi-autonomous social fields that serve to set limits upon their own powers of enforcement. Moore gives the example of the garment industry in New York City, where formal legislation relating directly or indirectly to garment production, such as banking law and labour law, operates alongside the quasi-legal regulations of non-state bodies like trade unions and manufacturers' associations, and less formal rules growing out of 'the interplay of the jobbers, contractors, factors, retailers, and skilled workers in the course of doing business with each other' (Moore 1973: 728). Governments, of course, seek to regulate the social fields within their state boundaries—by means of legislation, for example. But legislation often fails to achieve its intended aims, or has unplanned or unexpected consequences, because it is not introduced into a vacuum, but into a situation that already contains complex sets of social arrangements and obligations, that may distort or even defeat its intended purpose.

We could make a case for how asylum exemplifies each of the sorts of legal pluralism Moore outlines, but her fourth and fifth senses seem particularly pertinent. Asylum clearly exemplifies legal pluralism in the fourth of Moore's senses listed above, for instance. Thus, although the United Kingdom—for example—was an early signatory of both the *1951 United Nations Convention Relating to the Status of Refugees*, and the subsequent *1967 Protocol* that made it less narrowly focused on the specific circumstances prevailing after the end of the Second World War, these were not formally incorporated into UK law until the coming into force of the *1993 Asylum and Immigration Appeals Act*. Since then immigration and asylum have been subject to a growing body of UK national legislation, beginning with the *1971 Immigration Act* and added to at an increasingly frantic pace over the past two decades. They are also regulated by the *Immigration Rules*, a hugely complex body of quasi-legislative regulatory material that has undergone even more frequent modification.[17] To a large extent, both the plethora of primary legislation, and the rapidly-changing *Immigration Rules*

---

[17]https://www.gov.uk/guidance/immigration-rules/immigration-rules-part-11-asylum [Accessed 31 July 2016].

reflect repeated attempts by the state to place yet more national restrictions upon the rights supposedly guaranteed by the international Convention.

Asylum also displays the characteristics of Moore's fifth sense of legal pluralism, 'strong legal pluralism'. Asylum procedures involve complex interactions between different professional actors (administrators, judges, lawyers, doctors and other 'experts', public service interpreters, and so on), regulated in complex ways by national and international legislation; by the rules of procedure developed by or for different bureaucracies or court systems; by the ethical codes of the professional bodies to which these actors belong; and by the unwritten conventions that have arisen through their day-to-day interactions. In addition, these procedures centre on would-be refugees from all over the world, and each asylum applicant carries with them their own 'legal consciousness' (Merry 1990), generally not reflecting any prior experience or understanding of the national legal system within which their claim is being decided.

In short, European asylum systems are prime examples of 'strong' legal pluralism in which, as Griffiths puts it, 'the 'law' which is actually effective on the 'ground floor' of society is the result of enormously complex and… unpredictable patterns of competition, interaction, negotiation, [and] isolationism' (1986: 39). It is hard to imagine how anything other than an ethnographic approach could hope to successfully disentangle processes of such complexity.

Approaching Asylum Determination Ethnographically

This present collection comes at a crucial time for Europe, when the European Union is consolidating its attempts to implement the Common European Asylum System; when mainland Europe is receiving unusually large numbers of people displaced by violence in the Middle East; when efforts to exteriorise border controls have heightened; and when the consequences for migration patterns of Britain's expected exit from the European Union are still almost entirely unclear. It represents the fruits of years of detailed in-person observations of the often obscured legal and administrative processes by which asylum claims are decided. In what follows, a legal overview of the CEAS (Craig and Zwaan) precedes sections on the diverse actors involved, the means by which they communicate, and the ways in which they make their decisions on a daily basis.

The section on actors covers judges, first instance decision making officials, government legal representatives, and child asylum applicants. We employ the concept of 'actors' because it throws into relief two elements of these processes. Firstly, when considering the whole machinery of asylum determination the concept of actors helps to make clear the diversity of people involved in making determination processes happen. Determination is not something that is simply conceived and executed by legal elites and politicians—for some people involved in the system of determination it is a daily *practice*, with all the connotations of work, routine, habits and norms that this entails. Secondly, the concept of actors emphasises the agency that each of these people can have within the process of determination. When examined in detail, asylum determination is not simply the application of a set of legal rules to particular cases in a social, economic and cultural void. Rather, the wide range of people involved in determination can each, in their specific ways, also affect the course that the determination takes, for example via their emotional involvement, their bodily comportment, their language and their interactions. As such each of the actors we might identify as being involved in asylum determination is capable of *acting upon* that process, however subtly. A focus on the actors involved in determination therefore offers an antidote to the emphasis on either legal doctrine or outcome in legal studies. There are, in fact, more actors involved in determining an asylum appeal than might be imagined, from solicitors, barristers and judges, to caseworkers, clerks, security personnel, police, youth workers and a range of 'experts', not to mention applicants themselves. The mechanics of asylum determination therefore have their own sociology, involving rivalries, alliances, and competing cultures and discourses. Ethnographic analysis of courts, reception centres, tribunals and the back-offices of immigration decision making is ideally suited to examine these phenomena.

In her chapter on the challenges of judging asylum claims, for example, Carolina Kobelinsky critically reflects on the intractable dilemmas that judges face, and the prominent role of personal convictions and emotions in determining life or death cases, drawing on 14 months of ethnographic fieldwork conducted at the French Court of Asylum. Massimiliano Spotti's analysis of credibility assessments in the Belgian determination system examines how a second crucial set of actors—the immigration officials charged with making decisions about asylum claims at first instance—valorise particular forms of factual truth that often bear little relation to the lived histories of asylum seekers, but which can nevertheless lead to life-threatening forms of identity misrecognition. John Campbell's work on presenting officers who put forward the legal case against asylum seekers on behalf of the British Home Office during tribunal appeal hearings offers a rare glimpse of the fractious and obscured sociology of a world that is made insular by the adversarial nature of the British legal process. And Chrisa Giannopoulou and Nick Gill take advantage of the street-level perspective offered by an ethnographic approach to report on the tensions between vulnerability and agency in the context of asylum seeking children in the Greek system of reception centres and camps.

The second section of the book turns to the pivotal issue of communication during the asylum determination process. Communication in asylum cases is frequently inadequate to the task. In particular, the tension between the global processes that produce asylum seekers and refugees and the national and local contexts in which understanding about them circulates, produces the ideal conditions for mutual incomprehension and misunderstanding (Blommaert 2009). Language in asylum claim determination

> is dominated by frames that refer to static and timeless (i.e., uniform and national) orders of things. So while asylum seekers belong to a truly global scale of events and processes, the treatment of their applications is brought down to a rigidly national scale, a very modernist response to postmodern realities. This creates many problems—problems of justice, to name just one category. It also lays bare some of the threads of the fabric of globalization—the paradox between transnational processes and national frames for addressing them, for instance. (Blommaert 2009: 415)

These tensions give rise to both constraints over the means of expression and instances of misinterpretation and miscommunication. When communicative mistakes are made in this arena people's lives are put at stake, so it is difficult to think of an area in which clear and effective communication is more important. The diversity of languages involved in processes of asylum claim determination, however, render the area extremely challenging from the perspective of the practical necessity for good quality, reliable and professional interpretaters and translators. With all these difficulties in mind, the chapters in this section underscore the unerring serendipity and unreliability of communication even in grave contexts such as asylum determination.

Julia Dahlvik's analysis of the Austrian Federal Asylum Office, for instance, argues that the role and power of interpreters in the administrative asylum procedure is so extensive that renewed attention should be given to professional ethics governing their conduct. Relatedly, Robert Gibb's analysis of asylum interviews and appeals in France settles upon the metaphor of 'power struggle' to capture the ways in which communication is contested within these settings. Matilde Skov Danstrøm and Zachary Whyte corroborate the gravity of communication in the Danish asylum system, by not only highlighting the pivotal role of narrative in asylum appeal processes but also the way in which the inability to 'perform' narratives convincingly can endanger just asylum decisions. Finally, Jessica Hambly examines the work of judges in asylum appeals in the British context from a fresh perspective. Rather than concentrating on their (mis)use of discretion, she examines the non-legal forms of interaction and relationships that judges form with those around them in the course of their work. This approach understands judging as not only a legal act of decision making, but a complex social process of communication and competition between actors, organisations, and institutions.

The third section focuses squarely on the issue of decision making on asylum claims by judges and administrative officials. In all the chapters in this section, the subjectivities of the legal process of decision making are in evidence. For example, drawing on analysis and observation of 230 Italian asylum appeal decisions, as well as interviews with judges, Barbara Sorgoni focuses on the critical concept of credibility, arguing that internal consistency of asylum claims is given too much weight in the deliberations of legal officials in the absence of alternative criteria. Similarly, Tone Liodden finds that Norwegian asylum decision makers tend to turn towards 'equal treatment' of claims in the absence of evidence and other criteria upon which to base their decisions, with important implications for the kinds of justice practised in asylum determination. For Laura Affolter, Jonathan Miaz and Ephraim Poertner working in the Swiss context, the key issue is how self-understandings of their official roles inform what asylum system decision makers do and how they understand and enact 'justice'. And Stephanie Schneider, in her work on the German asylum system, underscores the dilemmas facing system bureaucrats in an environment that overtly pursues productivity but delegates the responsibility for quality onto individuals.

Overall, the contributors offer a series of contextually rich accounts that move beyond doctrinal law to expose the gaps and variances between policy and legislation as they are written down and as they are practised. Not only do they provide empirical depth and innovative insights regarding particular countries but they are also adeptly theorised. What is more, through their proximity and juxtaposition, the contributions offer the reader a comparative perspective covering ten European countries.

Although the contributors write variously from sociological, anthropological, geographical and linguistic disciplinary perspectives, they are united in adopting an ethnographically-based methodological approach. Through this rich empirical and multi-disciplinary lens, they capture the current, contested reality of claiming asylum in Europe, laying bare the confusion, improvisation, inconsistency, complexity and uncertainty inherent to the process. Their fusion of empirical insights, ethnographic approaches, theoretical reflections and legal subject matter offers a series of windows onto a complex and obfuscated area of law that is nevertheless central to foundational debates about the viability of the European Union and the moral obligations that Western developed states owe to outsiders seeking protection. Most fundamentally, this book addresses the need to find out how, precisely, claims for international protection under asylum law from some of the most marginalised people in the world are being handled.

References

Agamben, G. (2005). *State of Exception*. Chicago and London: University of Chicago Press.

Akkerman, T., de Lange, S. L., & Rooduijn, M. (Eds.). (2016). *Radical Right-Wing Populist Parties in Western Europe: Into the Mainstream?* London: Routledge.

Anders, G. (2015). Law at Its Limits: Interdisciplinarity Between Law and Anthropology. *The Journal of Legal Pluralism and Unofficial Law, 47*(3), 411–422.

Asylum Information Database. (2017). *The Concept of Vulnerability in European Asylum Procedures*. European Council on Refugees and Exiles. http://www.asylumineurope.org/sites/default/files/shadow-reports/aida_vulnerability_in_asylum_procedures.pdf. Accessed 5 Mar 2018.

Asylum Information Database. (2018). *Types of Procedures: Greece*. Greek Council for Refugees. http://www.asylumineurope.org/reports/country/greece/asylum-procedure/general/types-procedures. Accessed 5 Mar 2018.

Bauman, Z. (1997). *Postmodernity and Its Discontents*. Cambridge: Polity Press.

Beck, U. (1992). *Risk Society: Towards a New Modernity*. New Delhi: Sage.

von Benda-Beckmann, F. (2008). Riding or Killing the Centaur? Reflections on the Identities of Legal Anthropology. *International Journal of Law in Context, 4*(2), 85–110.

Bigo, D. (2002). Security and Immigration: Toward a Critique of the Governmentality of Unease. *Alternatives: Global, Local, Political, 27*, 63–92.

Blommaert, J. (2009). Language, Asylum and the National Order. *Current Anthropology, 50*(4), 415–441.

Boswell, C. (2007). Migration Control in Europe After 9/11: Explaining the Absence of Securitization. *Journal of Common Market Studies, 45*(3), 589–610.

British Broadcasting Corporation [BBC]. (2016, March 11). *Syria: The Story of the Conflict* [online]. Available at: http://www.bbc.co.uk/news/world-middle-east-26116868. Accessed 4 Jan 2017.

Buzan, B., Wæver, O., & de Wilde, J. (1998). *Security: A New Framework for Analysis*. Boulder, CO: Lynne Rienner.

Charteris-Black, J. (2006). Britain as a Container: Immigration Metaphors in the 2005 Election Campaign. *Discourse and Society, 15*(5), 563–581.

Cherubini, F. (2014). *Asylum Law in the European Union*. London: Routledge.

Coffey, G. J., Kaplan, I., Sampson, R. C., & Tucci, M. M. (2010). The Meaning and Mental Health Consequences of Long-Term Immigration Detention for People Seeking Asylum. *Social Science and Medicine, 70*(12), 2070–2079.

Cohen, S. (2002). *Folk Devils and Moral Panics: The Creation of the Mods and Rockers* (3rd ed.). London and New York: Routledge.

Conlon, D., & Gill, N. (2015). Editorial: Interventions in Migration and Activism. *ACME: An International E-Journal for Critical Geographies, 14*(2), 442–451.

European Commission. (2015). *The Hotspot Approach to Managing Exceptional Migration Flows*. https://ec.europa.eu/home-affairs/sites/homeaffairs/files/what-we-do/policies/european-agenda-migration/background-information/docs/2_hotspots_en.pdf. Accessed 5 Mar 2018.

Ford, R., & Goodwin, M. (2014). Understanding UKIP: Identity, Social Change and the Left Behind. *The Political Quarterly, 85*(3), 277–284.

Furedi, F. (2002). *Culture of Fear: Risk Taking and the Morality of Low Expectation*. New York and London: Continuum.

Gibney, M. (2014). Asylum: Principled Hypocrisy. In B. Anderson & M. Keith (Eds.), *Migration: A COMPAS Anthology*. Oxford: COMPAS. Available at: http://compasanthology.co.uk/. Accessed 30 Nov 2016.

Good, A. (2015). Folk Models and the Law. *The Journal of Legal Pluralism and Unofficial Law, 47*(3), 423–437.

Good, A. (2017). Law and Anthropology: Legal Pluralism and "Lay" Decision-Making. In D. Watkins & M. Burton (Eds.), *Research Methods in Law* (2nd ed., pp. 211–238). London: Routledge.

Goodwin-Gill, G. (2001). After the Cold War: Asylum and the Refugee Concept Move On. *Forced Migration Review, 10,* 14–16.

Greek Council for Refugees. (2017). *Fast-Track Border Procedure (Eastern Aegean Islands)*. European Council on Refugees and Exiles. http://www.asylumineurope.org/reports/country/greece/asylum-procedure/procedures/fast-track-border-procedure-eastern-aegean. Accessed 5 Mar 2018.

Greven, T. (2016). *The Rise of Right-Wing Populism in Europe and the United States: A Comparative Perspective Friedrich Ebert Foundation*. Washington, DC. http://www.fesdc.org/fileadmin/user_upload/publications/RightwingPopulism.pdf. Accessed 5 Mar 2018.

Griffiths, J. (1986). What is Legal Pluralism? *Journal of Legal Pluralism, 24,* 1–55.

Guild, E., & Minderhoud, P. (Eds.). (2011). *The First Decade of EU Migration and Asylum Law*. Leiden, NL: Martinus Nijhoff.

Hopkins, S. (2016). Nigel Farage's Brexit Poster Is Being Likened To 'Nazi Propaganda', Compared to Auschwitz Documentary Scene: A 'Prominent' White-Skinned Man Also Removed from Image. *Huffington Post*. Available at:

http://www.huffingtonpost.co.uk/entry/nigel-farages-eu-has-failed-us-all-poster-slammed-as-disgusting-by-nicola-sturgeon_uk_576288c0e4b08b9e3abdc483. Accessed 5 Jan 2017.

Huysmans, J. (2000). The European Union and the Securitization of Migration. *Journal of Common Market Studies, 38*(5), 751–777.

International Organisation for Migration [IOM]. (2016, December 22). *Latest Global Figures: Migrant Fatalities Worldwide*. Available at: https://missingmigrants.iom.int/latest-global-figures. Accessed 4 Jan 2017.

Isin, E. (2004). The Neurotic Citizen. *Citizenship Studies, 8,* 217–235.

Joly, D. (1996). *Haven or Hell? Asylum Policies and Refugees in Europe*. Oxford: Macmillan.

Kandel, R. F. (1992). Six Differences in Assumptions and Outlook Between Anthropologists and Attorneys. In R. F. Kandel (Ed.), *Double Vision: Anthropologists at Law* (NAPA Bulletin, No. 11, pp. 1–4). Washington, DC: American Anthropological Association.

Klein, N. (2007). *The Shock Doctrine: The Rise of Disaster Capitalism*. New York: Metropolitan Books.

Koizumi, K., & Hoffstaedter, G. (Eds.). (2015). *Urban Refugees: Challenges in Protection, Services and Policy*. London: Routledge.

Laban, C. J., Gernaat, H. B., Komproe, I. H., van der Tweel, I., & De Jong, J. T. (2005). Postmigration Living Problems and Common Psychiatric Disorders in Iraqi Asylum Seekers in the Netherlands. *The Journal of Nervous and Mental Disease, 193*(12), 825–832.

Legoux, L. (1995). *La crise de l'asile politique en France*. Paris: Centre Français sur la Population et le Développement.

Merry, S. E. (1990). *Getting Justice and Getting Even: Legal Consciousness Among Working-Class Americans*. Chicago: University of Chicago Press.

Migration Policy Centre. (2016). *Migrant Crisis*. Available at: http://www.migrationpolicycentre.eu/migrant-crisis/. Accessed 4 Jan 2017.

Moore, S. F. (1973). Law and Social Change: The Semi-autonomous Social Field as an Appropriate Object of Study. *Law and Society Review, 7*(4), 719–746.

Moore, S. F. (1978). *Law as Process: An Anthropological Approach*. London: Routledge and Kegan Paul.

Moore, S. F. (2001). Certainties Undone: Fifty Turbulent Years of Legal Anthropology. *Journal of the Royal Anthropological Institute, 7*(1), 95–116.

Moore, K. (2010). *A Cultural Study of Asylum Under New Labour*. Ph.D. thesis, Cardiff University.

Moreno-Lax, V. (2017a). *Accessing Asylum in Europe: Extraterritorial Border Controls*. Oxford: Oxford University Press.

Moreno-Lax, V. (2017b, February 7). *Accessing Asylum in Europe: Extraterritorial Border Controls*. Podcast of Public Seminar, Refugee Studies Centre. Available at: https://www.rsc.ox.ac.uk/news/accessing-asylum-in-europe-extraterritorial-border-controls-meet-refugee-rights-dr-violeta-moreno-lax. Accessed 5 Mar 2018.

Mountz, A., & Heimstra, N. (2014). Chaos and Crisis: Dissecting the Spatiotemporal Logics of Contemporary Migrations and State Practices. *Annals of the Association of American Geographers, 104,* 282–390.

New York Times. (2017, October 23). How Far is Europe Swinging to the Right? Aisch, G., Pearce, A., and Rousseau, B. https://www.nytimes.com/interactive/2016/05/22/world/europe/europe-right-wing-austria-hungary.html. Accessed 5 Mar 2018.

Pain, R., & Smith, S. (2008). *Fear: Critical Geopolitics and Everyday Life.* Farnham: Ashgate.

Painter, J., Papada, E., Papoutsi, A., & Vradis, A. (2017). Hotspot Politics—Or, When the EU State Gets Real. *Political Geography, 60,* 259–260.

Pollet, K., Soupios-David, H., & Teffera, A. (2013). *AIDA [Asylum Information Database], Not There Yet: An NGO Perspective on Challenges to a Fair and Effective Common European Asylum System, Annual Report 2012–2013.* European Council on Refugees and Exile.

Roitman, J. (2013). *Anti-Crisis.* Durham and London: Duke University Press.

Schuster, L. (2003). *The Use and Abuse of Political Asylum in Britain and Germany.* London and Portland, OR: Frank Cass.

Simmel, G. (1976). *The Stranger: The Sociology of Georg Simmel.* New York: Free Press.

Solanki, G. (2011). *Adjudication in Religious Family Laws: Cultural Accommodation, Legal Pluralism, and Gender Equality in India.* New York: Cambridge University Press.

Strasser, S. (2016). The Crises Effect: Global Moral Obligations, National Interventions, and the Figure of the Pitiful/Abused Migrant. In K. Roth & A. Kartari (Eds.), *Cultures of Crisis in Southeast Europe: Part 1: Crises Related to Migration, Transformation, Politics, Religion and Labour* (Ethnologica Balkanica 18) (pp. 47–66). Berlin: Lit-Verlag and Dr. W. Hopf.

Syrian Refugees. (2016, September). *A Snapshot of the Crisis—In the Middle East and Europe: The Syrian Refugee Crisis and Its Repercussions for the EU.* Available at: www.syrianrefugees.eu. Accessed 5 Jan 2017.

Tazzioli, M., & Garelli, G. (2018). Containment Beyond Detention: The Hotspot System and Disrupted Migration Movements Across Europe. *Environment and Planning D: Society and Space.* Early view.

Twining, W. (2006). *Rethinking Evidence: Exploratory Essays* (2nd ed.). Cambridge: Cambridge University Press.

Tyler, I. (2013). *Revolting Subjects: Social Abjection and Resistance in Neoliberal Britain.* London: Zed Books.

United Nations High Commission for Refugees [UNHCR]. (2016a). *Mediterranean Death Toll Soars, 2016 Is Deadliest Year Yet.* Available at: http://www.unhcr.org/uk/news/latest/2016/10/580f3e684/mediterranean-death-toll-soars-2016-deadliest-year. Accessed 5 Jan 2017.

United Nations High Commission for Refugees [UNHCR]. (2016b). *Syria Regional Refugee Response: Inter-agency Information Sharing Portal.* Available at: http://data.unhcr.org/syrianrefugees/regional.php. Accessed 5 Jan 2017.

UNITED. (2015). *List of 22,394 Documented Deaths of Asylum Seekers, Refugees and Migrants Due to Restrictive Policies of Fortress Europe.* Amsterdam: UNITED for Intercultural Action. Available at: http://www.unitedagainstracism.org/wp-content/uploads/2015/06/Listofdeaths22394June15.pdf. Accessed 5 Jan 2017.

Vertovec, S., & Wessendorf, S. (Eds.). (2010). *The Multiculturalism BackLash: European Discourses and Practices.* Oxford: Routledge.

Žižek, S. (2009). *Violence: Six Sideways Reflections.* London: Profile Books.

Open Access This chapter is distributed under the terms of the Creative Commons Attribution 4.0 International License (http://creativecommons.org/licenses/by/4.0/), which permits use, duplication, adaptation, distribution and reproduction in any medium or format, as long as you give appropriate credit to the original author(s) and the source, a link is provided to the Creative Commons license and any changes made are indicated.

The images or other third party material in this chapter are included in the work's Creative Commons license, unless indicated otherwise in the credit line; if such material is not included in the work's Creative Commons license and the respective action is not permitted by statutory regulation, users will need to obtain permission from the license holder to duplicate, adapt or reproduce the material.

2

Legal Overview

Sarah Craig and Karin Zwaan

Introduction

Common rules on most aspects of the asylum process are in force in the European Union (EU), building on the international refugee protection regime. This so-called EU *asylum acquis* has resulted in a "Common European Asylum System (CEAS)". EU legislation states that the CEAS is to be based on a full and inclusive application of the 1951 UN Geneva Convention relating to the Status of Refugees (Refugee Convention). The principle of non-refoulement—also included in the Refugee Convention—is the most important principle in asylum law and is laid down in several international legal instruments.[1] This principle prohibits the forced direct or

---

[1] E.g. Article 33, UN Refugee Convention; Article 3, UN Convention against Torture; Article 7, UN International Covenant on Civil and Political Rights; Article 3, European Convention on Human Rights (ECHR); Article 19(2), EU Charter on Fundamental Rights; Article 21, QD1 and QDII; and Article 5, RD.

S. Craig (✉)
University of Glasgow, Glasgow, Scotland
e-mail: sarah.craig@glasgow.ac.uk

K. Zwaan
Radboud University Nijmegen, Nijmegen, The Netherlands
e-mail: k.zwaan@jur.ru.nl

© The Author(s) 2019
N. Gill and A. Good (eds.), *Asylum Determination in Europe*,
Palgrave Socio-Legal Studies, https://doi.org/10.1007/978-3-319-94749-5_2

indirect removal of a person to a country or territory where he[2] runs a risk of being subjected to severe human rights violations.

The CEAS consists of rules to determine which State is responsible for determining a claim; to define asylum seekers' entitlements and obligations as regards their reception in Member States; to regulate the asylum procedure itself; and to determine who qualifies for international protection.

Unlike the rest of the chapters in this volume, this chapter is not empirical, but sets out the legal framework for asylum determination in Europe. Its primary purpose is to offer a reflection on and some insight into the functioning of the CEAS, with a view to creating a legal background and framework for the ethnographic chapters that follow.

International and European Law Framework

The CEAS is a fundamental part of the EU's Area of Freedom, Security and Justice (AFSJ), and its aim is to establish a fair and efficient asylum system. The CEAS consists of a legal framework covering all aspects of the asylum process, and a support agency—the European Asylum Support Office (EASO). One must bear in mind that achieving the CEAS' twofold goal of efficiency and fairness is, from a human rights perspective, a task that creates internal contradictions, in the sense that implementing efficiency may rule out fairness, and promoting fairness requires an investment of time and effort which State authorities may discourage. The task of reconciling, in individual cases, the conflicts inherent in pursuing this twofold goal falls on decision-makers and judges (see, for example, the chapters by Kobelinsky, Hambly, Affolter et al., and Liodden, this volume). As demonstrated throughout this book, not only decision-makers, but a cast of other actors also have profound influences. The substantive chapters of this book provide perspectives on the conflicts inherent in asylum decision-making and on how the actors involved attempt to resolve them, but while most of the countries discussed here participate fully in the CEAS, not all do. Two Member States (UK and Denmark) exercise opt-outs in relation to certain CEAS measures, and another two are non-EU countries (Norway and Switzerland). However, all of the countries take part in the 'Dublin regime', and have other

---

[2]Early refugee law has been 'characterized by a complete blindness to women, gender, and issues of sexual inequality' (Edwards 2010: 23). We are aware that nowadays reference would be made to 'they' instead of 'he', but as this is a legal chapter for reasons of clarity we are using 'he' if the actual legal text uses 'he'.

associations with the AFSJ. We therefore focus in this chapter on the CEAS, and on its contradictory aims and themes, because they flesh out the meaning, as well as the weakness, of international protection standards, and they also highlight the conflicts—between fairness and efficiency, and between protection and exclusion—which bedevil asylum decision-making processes in all of the countries covered here.

Since 1999, the CEAS has gone through two phases of legislation. The first culminated in 2005, and the second concluded in 2013. The first phase focused on harmonisation on the basis of common minimum standards, leading to the second, whose aim was the establishment of a single asylum procedure and a uniform status for those who are granted asylum throughout the EU, an aim which has not yet been achieved. Whereas some common EU rules in the asylum field take the form of directly binding 'Regulations', most take the form of 'Directives', which require Member States to achieve a particular result without dictating the means of achieving that result. Directives are usually transposed into national legislation. They therefore depend on national implementation for their effectiveness.

The protection of asylum seekers, refugees and those in need of subsidiary protection can be characterised as an interplay between several overlapping legal regimes. The main instruments are the 1951 UN Refugee Convention, the UN Convention against Torture, the UN Convention on Civil and Political Rights, EU law and the ECHR.[3]

Judicial scrutiny at the highest level is performed by the Court of Justice of the EU (CJEU), which has jurisdiction to consider requests for preliminary rulings from national courts, as well as dealing with appeals and other matters. The CJEU is tasked with examining the legality of EU measures, interpreting EU law, and ensuring its uniform application across the 28 EU Member States. In the implementation of this last task, the CJEU relies on national courts to apply EU law uniformly in their respective jurisdictions, albeit under the supervision of the CJEU. The CJEU is first and foremost an important actor in the protection of human rights, drawing on them as fundamental principles of EU law, and ruling on how human rights standards should be interpreted across the Member States. This Court is not to be confused with the European Court of Human Rights (ECtHR), a permanent international court set up in 1959 with jurisdiction to rule on all matters concerning the interpretation and application of the ECHR; it specialises in

---

[3]Currently, all Member States have ratified the ECHR as well as several non-EU countries and even some non-European countries.

the safeguarding of a minimum level of human rights protection among the ECHR's contracting parties. The ECtHR may receive applications from any person, group or non-governmental organisation claiming to be the victim of a violation of the rights set out in the ECHR by one of its state parties.

The terms used in European asylum law need some clarification. In daily life the terms 'migrant', 'asylum seeker' and 'refugee' are often used interchangeably, but they refer to different legal statuses. 'Migrant' is the general term for people who move from one region to another. This movement might be voluntary or because of economic hardship or other problems.[4] The term 'asylum seeker' is used for someone who has left their country to seek international protection. In EU law, international protection takes two forms. In the first place, protection as a refugee: 'refugee' refers to a person who has fled their country and cannot return because of a well-founded fear of persecution due to their race, religion, nationality, membership of a particular social group or political opinion.[5] In the second place, someone who has fled because they face serious harm[6] may qualify for international protection. Serious harm may consist of: (a) the death penalty or execution; or (b) torture or inhuman or degrading treatment or punishment of an applicant in their country of origin; or (c) serious and individual threat to a civilian's life or person by reason of indiscriminate violence in situations of international or internal armed conflict.

Situations of armed conflict and violence frequently involve exposure to serious human rights violations or other serious harm amounting to persecution or serious harm. Such persecution/serious harm could include situations of genocide and ethnic cleansing; torture and other forms of inhuman or degrading treatment; rape and other forms of sexual violence; forced recruitment, including of children; arbitrary arrest and detention; hostage taking and enforced or arbitrary disappearances. In situations of armed conflict and violence a person may be at risk of being singled out or targeted for persecution or serious harm. Equally, in such situations, entire groups or populations may be at risk of persecution, leaving each member of the group at risk. The fact that many or all members of particular communities are at risk does not undermine the validity of any particular individual's claim.[7]

---

[4]See EASO Practical Guide Evidence assessment: https://www.easo.europa.eu/practical-tools.
[5]Article 1A(2) UN Refugee Convention.
[6]Article 15 QDII. The UK and Ireland opted into the CEAS' first phase instruments, which means that they are still bound by the original QD1 and APD1. Article 15 QDI is in similar terms.
[7]See UNHCR (2016, paras. 13 and 16).

At the time of writing, the main CEAS legislation comprises the revised Dublin Regulation (Dublin III), the revised Eurodac Regulation, the Reception Conditions Directive (I or II), the Qualification Directive (I or II) and the Asylum Procedures Directive (I or II). Most of the countries whose national asylum systems provide the focus for the substantive chapters of this book participate in both phases of CEAS legislation but, as noted above, four do not. The UK chose to 'opt in' to the first phase of CEAS legislation, but then took a piecemeal approach, 'opting out' of the revised 'second phase' versions of the Reception Conditions Directive (II), Qualification Directive (II), and Asylum Procedures Directive (II), and 'opting in' to the revised Dublin Regulation (Dublin III) and the revised Eurodac Regulation (aka the Dublin system). Denmark has a long-standing 'opt-out' arrangement in relation to most CEAS measures but like the UK, it participates in the Dublin system. As already noted, Switzerland and Norway are non-EU states that participate in the Dublin system, and their position is, of course, of interest to the UK in the context of the June 2016 Brexit vote. Whether, as part of the Brexit negotiations, the UK would also seek to continue its participation in the Dublin system following its departure from the EU is something we can speculate about, especially given the UK's common interest with the rest of the EU in the security objectives of the Eurodac database, but nothing can be assumed.

The Dublin III Regulation establishes a hierarchy of criteria for identifying which EU Member State is responsible for examining an asylum seeker's claim for protection in Europe. To establish this responsibility the applicant is fingerprinted, and the information goes to the Eurodac database (Eurodac Regulation). The aim of the Dublin Regulation is to ensure that only one EU Member State is responsible for the examination of an asylum application (to deter multiple asylum claims), and to allow that State to be identified as quickly as possible. The Dublin regime permits Member States to rely on the principle of mutual trust and the presumption that all EU Member States are safe for all asylum seekers: its criteria therefore provide that most asylum seekers may be sent back to their state of entry. This leads to an unequal distribution of asylum seekers amongst EU Member States and to the Member States where most asylum seekers enter the EU, such as Greece and Italy, facing problems in managing the increasing numbers of asylum seekers arriving (Guild 2016; Costello and Mouzarakis 2014). The extreme suffering which the operation of the Dublin criteria has caused to individuals has led to landmark cases being decided by the ECtHR and the CJEU which recognised the failure of the mutual trust principle and of the presumption of safety in the Dublin regime. This case law has been codified in the Dublin

III Regulation so that it is not possible to transfer an asylum seeker to the responsible Member State where 'there are substantial grounds for believing that there are systemic flaws in the asylum procedure and in the reception conditions for applicants in that Member State, resulting in a risk of inhuman or degrading treatment'. In these circumstances, the Member State that is prevented from transferring the asylum seeker must examine the application itself.[8]

The Reception Conditions Directive[9] sets out common standards for reception conditions for asylum seekers and makes it clear that an asylum seeker is entitled to reception while their asylum claim is being determined. It sets out rules relating to housing, food, health care and employment, as well as detailed common rules governing the limited circumstances in which asylum seekers can be detained.

The Qualification Directive[10] sets out the standards to establish whether third country nationals or stateless persons[11] should be granted international protection. It defines who may be a beneficiary of international protection and describes the content of that protection. International protection may be given in the form of two different statuses, namely refugee status or subsidiary protection status.[12] Subsidiary protection aims to cover other forms of protection, as guaranteed by human rights treaties, such as the ECHR or the UN Convention against Torture. The Qualification Directive aims to harmonise eligibility criteria for international protection, and incorporates a series of rights for beneficiaries of international protection (protection against refoulement, residence permits, travel documents, access to employment, access to education, social welfare, healthcare, access to accommodation, access to integration facilities, as well as specific provisions for children and vulnerable persons). By defining and harmonising the guarantees in human rights treaties which all the countries discussed in this volume have signed up to, the Qualification Directive (QD) provides the tools for giving meaning to those guarantees.

---

[8] Article 3(2) Dublin III. This Article codifies the cases ECtHR 21 January 2011, no. 30696/09, *M.S.S. v. Belgium and Greece* and CJEU 21 December 2011, joined cases C-411/10 and C-493/10, N.S. and Others.

[9] RCDII. Denmark, and the UK are not bound by this Directive, but Ireland has opted into the RCDII (Recast Reception Conditions Directive). The UK is bound by the terms of RCDI.

[10] QDII. The UK and Ireland opted into the CEAS' first phase instruments, which means that they are still bound by the original QDI.

[11] A third country national is a national of a non-EU country.

[12] Article 2 QDII; Article 2 QD1.

The standards to guarantee access to a fair and efficient asylum system are laid out in the Asylum Procedures Directive (APD).[13] The asylum procedure is meant to establish whether a third country national should be granted international protection, and whether the asylum seeker is entitled to have his claim processed according to the procedural standards of the APD. The APD aims to ensure fair, quick and good quality asylum decisions, and also that asylum seekers with special needs (such as unaccompanied minors) receive the necessary support to make their claims. Other procedural rights include rights to a personal interview, to legal assistance, a right to appeal and the right to remain in the territory while an appeal is being determined.[14]

The Asylum Procedure: Determining Refugee— Or Subsidiary Protection Status

In EU asylum procedures the central question that must be answered is whether an asylum seeker is in need of international protection. EU law stipulates that a person qualifies for international protection if he or she is a refugee and thus fears persecution, or if they would be subjected to serious harm when returned to their country of origin.[15] Protection entails—more than anything else—the prohibition of '*refoulement*'. This prohibition is firmly rooted in international,[16] European[17] and EU[18] law, and means that a state is prohibited from sending a person (back) to a place where they could be persecuted or risk serious harm.[19] An applicant qualifies for international protection if they have a well-founded fear of being persecuted for reasons of race, religion, nationality, membership of a particular social group or political opinion in accordance with the 1951 Convention, or would face a real risk of suffering serious harm if returned to the country of origin or habitual residence. To determine an asylum application, evidence may be submitted

---

[13]APDII. The UK and Ireland opted into the CEAS' first phase instruments, which means that they are still bound by the original APD1.
[14]Articles 14, 22, 24, 46 QDII; Articles 12, 39 QD1.
[15]Article 4(3) QDII; Article 4(3) QD1.
[16]Article 33 Refugee Convention, Article 3 of the UN Convention against Torture, Article 7 UN International Covenant on Civil and Political Rights.
[17]Article 3 European Convention on Human Rights.
[18]Article 4 Charter of Fundamental Rights of the European Union.
[19]Article 15 QDII; Article 15 QDI.

by an applicant to substantiate his or her application and may also be gathered by the determining authority through its own means. Evidence may include anything that asserts, confirms, supports, refutes or otherwise bears on the relevant facts in issue.

Article 8(2) APDI (Article 10(3) APDII) requires Member States to ensure that 'decisions by the determining authority on applications for asylum are taken after an appropriate examination'. To this end, Member States should ensure that applications are examined and decisions taken individually, objectively, and impartially. Article 9(2) APDI (Article 11(2) APDII) requires that, where an application is rejected, the reasons in fact and in law are stated in the decision. The obligation to state reasons for a decision that are sufficiently specific and concrete to allow the applicant to understand why his or her application has been rejected has been framed as a corollary of the fundamental EU law principle of the right to defence.

Actors

In the asylum procedure, where refugee status determination (RSD) and subsidiary protection status determination take place many 'actors' are involved. In this volume we see as main actors asylum seekers themselves (including unaccompanied minor asylum seekers; (Chapter 6), immigration officers and decision makers (Chapters 12–14), Home Office Presenting Officers (HOPOs; Chapter 5) judges (Chapter 3), interpreters (Chapter 7) and lawyers (Chapter 10). In principle, there is an even wider cast of 'actors' than this, including clerks, security staff, witnesses, MacKenzie friends, observers of the case such as media and researchers.

Legal texts on refugee law define actors differently. From the legal perspective, we think of 'actors of persecution or serious harm' and 'actors of protection'. Actors of persecution or serious harm include: (a) the State; (b) parties or organisations controlling the State or a substantial part of the territory of the State; and (c) non-State actors, if it can be demonstrated that the state and international organisations, are unable or unwilling to provide protection against persecution or serious harm.[20] Actors of protection, protect against persecution or serious harm. These can be: (a) the State; or (b) parties or organisations, including international organisations, controlling

---

[20]Article 6 QDII; Article 6 QD1.

the State or a substantial part of the territory of the State; provided they are willing and able to offer protection.[21]

With regard to the actors in the chapters of this volume, some definitions, as well as guidance about their role and treatment are also to be found in the CEAS. Article 2(l) QDII defines an 'unaccompanied minor' as a minor who arrives on the territory of the Member State unaccompanied by an adult responsible for them whether by law or by the practice of the Member State concerned, and for as long as they are not effectively taken into the care of such a person; that includes a minor who is left unaccompanied after they have entered the territory of the Member State. Also in the APD special rules apply to asylum seeking children, and it should be borne in mind that according to preamble (33) to the APD, the best interests of the child should be a primary consideration of Member States when applying the APD, in accordance with the Charter of Fundamental Rights of the European Union and the 1989 United Nations Convention on the Rights of the Child. In assessing the best interest of the child, Member States should in particular take due account of the minor's well-being and social development, including their background.

With regard to immigration officers and decision makers, para. (16) of the preamble to the APD states that:

> It is essential that decisions on all applications for international protection be taken on the basis of the facts and, in the first instance, by authorities whose personnel has the appropriate knowledge or has received the necessary training in the field of international protection.

And in relation to HOPOs (Chapter 5), who represent the UK's Home Office at appeal hearings, para. (17) of the APD's preamble states 'In order to ensure that applications for international protection are examined and decisions thereon are taken objectively and impartially, it is necessary that professionals acting in the framework of the procedures provided for in this Directive perform their activities with due respect for the applicable deontological principles'.

The central role of judges is recognised in Article 46 APDII concerning the right to an effective remedy for challenging a negative decision.[22] Even in areas where common standards apply, there is need for judicial scrutiny

---

[21]Article 7 QDII; Article 7 QDI.
[22]Article 39 APDI.

of first instance decisions. In 2015 Hungary recognised only 10% of its asylum seekers as needing protection. The figure in Germany was 40% and it reached 65% in Italy. The differences regarding refugees from Iraq were particularly extreme. On the EU average, one in two was considered worthy of protection, in Italy almost all and in Greece only 3%—in spite of the fact that all follow the same European law. European courts have highlighted, and even heightened, the contrasting situations in different Member States. For instance, ever since the ECtHR in 2011 cited grave shortcomings in the Greek asylum process, and declared the living conditions of refugees there to be 'inhumane' (see also Giannopoulou and Gill, this volume), Germany has not sent any asylum seekers back to Greece.[23] Nor is Italy necessarily a secure third country. At the end of 2014, the human rights court decreed that the Swiss-ordered deportation of an eight-member family from Afghanistan was 'inhumane treatment'—because no assurance could be received from Italy that the children would be housed in a manner suitable to their age and that the family could remain together.[24]

Communication

The UNHCR Handbook is the authoritative source of guidance for government decision makers, and it acknowledges that some asylum seekers might be reticent with officials due to their experiences in their home country. Many are tired, anxious or feel inhibited during the interview.[25]

Communication in asylum interviews is different from everyday conversation due to at least three factors (Doornbos 2005). First, the interlocutors often do not speak the same language (van der Kleij 2015: 253). In the vast majority of cases, the officer conducts the interview with the assistance of an interpreter, employed by the Ministry of Justice, Border Agency, etc., on a sessional basis. Secondly, communication in asylum cases is a form of intercultural communication (Kälin 1986: 23). Thirdly, communication in asylum cases is a form of institutional interaction: communication within a strictly organised, often bureaucratic context (Drew and Heritage 1992). The CEAS framework acknowledges that the asylum process needs

---

[23]Judgment of the ECtHR 21 January 2011, Application no. 30696/09, *M.S.S. v. Belgium and Greece*. and CJEU 21 December 2011, joined cases C-411/10 and C-493/10, N.S. and Others.
[24]ECtHR 4 November 2014, Application no. 29217/12, Tarakhel. See also: http://www.zeit.de/gesellschaft/2016-03/european-asylum-law-refugees-turkey/seite-2.
[25]Para. 198 and 199 UNHCR Handbook.

to provide a context within which communication is possible, but it takes a pragmatic approach. Preamble (25) APDII provides that 'every applicant should have [...] the opportunity to cooperate and effectively communicate with the competent authorities so as to present the relevant facts of his or her case'. Expanding on this, Article 12 APDII specifies that providing the services of an interpreter is a basic guarantee for asylum applicants when submitting their case to the competent authorities, and Article 14 requires the competent authorities to:

> select an interpreter who is able to ensure appropriate communication between the applicant and the person who conducts the interview, in a language preferred by the applicant, unless there is another language which he or she understands and in which he or she is able to communicate clearly.[26]

Throughout this volume, and particularly in Part II, perspectives on communication build on the linguistic, cross-cultural and bureaucratic issues referred to above, and consider in detail the influence which the actors involved have on the process. They examine the provision of interpretation, the interviewing and decision-making processes, etc., and they reflect on the roles of the interpreter, applicant, decision maker, lawyer and other actors who influence the process in formal and informal ways. The interpreter's active role in communicating between applicant and decision-maker, and the implications of their ability, through their omissions and interventions, to influence the fairness (or otherwise) of the outcome of the claim come in for particular attention. These chapters capture the challenges posed to the asylum process by cross-cultural communication, and they also bring out the essentially narrative and communicative nature of the asylum process (Zahle 2005). The pragmatic approach to communication which the procedural rules of the APD take—requiring provision of an interpreter capable of ensuring 'appropriate communication'—struggles to embrace the complex communication needs that accompany the recounting of traumatic personal experiences, and as these chapters show, the rules rely heavily on the behaviour of individual interpreters and decision-makers.

---

[26]Reasonable requests that the interpreter be of the same gender as the applicant should also be complied with, and interviews with minors should be conducted in a child appropriate manner (Article 14 APDII).

Decision Making

Being recognised as a refugee or receiving subsidiary protection is vitally dependent on the legal or administrative process by which governments determine protection claims. In relation to the decision-making process, the UNHCR handbook states:

> It should be recalled that an applicant for refugee status is normally in a particularly vulnerable situation. He finds himself in an alien environment and may experience serious difficulties, technical and psychological, in submitting his case to the authorities of a foreign country, often in a language not his own. His application should therefore be examined within the framework of specially established procedures by qualified personnel having the necessary knowledge and experience, and an understanding of an applicant's particular difficulties and needs. (UNHCR 2011, para. 190)

The ECtHR has held that individuals need access to the asylum procedure as well as adequate information concerning the procedure to be followed. The authorities are also required to avoid excessively long delays in deciding asylum claims. In assessing the effectiveness of examining first instance asylum claims, the ECtHR has also considered other factors, such as the availability of interpreters, access to legal aid and the existence of a reliable system of communication with asylum seekers.[27]

Standard and Burden of Proof

The effectiveness of the right to asylum and to be protected against refoulement would be undermined if States placed too heavy a burden on applicants of establishing a well-founded fear of persecution or serious harm. As regards the *standard* of proof, the asylum seeker is expected to show that there is a 'reasonable degree of likelihood' of future persecution or that there are substantial grounds for believing that they face a real risk of serious harm. This standard is relatively relaxed: it is far lower than the criminal law standard, and even the usual civil law standard, and this suggests that proving an asylum claim should be comparatively straightforward.

---

[27]ECtHR 21 January 2011, Application no. 30696/09, M.S.S. vs. Belgium and Greece, para. 293.

Understanding why it is not straightforward requires us to consider in some detail what is involved in substantiating an asylum claim.

States are afforded extensive discretion when laying down the rules for asylum procedures regarding the burden and standard of proof. As regards the *burden* of proof, this is placed on the asylum seeker. Usually states expect asylum seekers to adduce evidence in order to substantiate their asylum claim. For many asylum seekers, it is difficult to obtain such evidence.

States will take into account different forms of evidence—including documents and other evidence—concerning the position and personal circumstances of the applicant: their nationality; the reasons for applying for asylum, including previous persecution; the situation in the country of origin; the applicant's activities in the country of refuge; and the availability of safe third countries. Medical reports, country of origin information (COI) and language analysis are also relevant in this framework.

Evidentiary Assessment

Evidentiary assessment can be defined as the primary method of establishing the facts of an individual case through the process of examining and comparing available pieces of evidence. The assessment of evidence is, in general, not regulated by international law (UNHCR 2013). The 1951 Refugee Convention does not provide for any specific provisions dealing with evidentiary assessment. Some guidance has, however, been developed in the field both in the form of the UNHCR *Handbook* (UNHCR 2011, see above) and in the UNHCR *Note on Burden and Standard of Proof in Refugee Claims* (UNHCR 1998).

As regards the assessment of evidence, the Qualification Directive constitutes the first legally binding supranational instrument of regional scope establishing what criteria the applicant needs to meet in order to qualify for international protection. The Qualification Directive relies to a large extent on international and European refugee and human rights instruments and jurisprudence.

European countries have different legal traditions and varying practices regarding evidentiary assessment. If Member States apply similar legal concepts on eligibility for international protection, but their treatment of the evidence is different, they may reach different conclusions. Asylum procedures are different from other legal procedures, due partly to the serious consequences of the decision taken, and partly to the lack of the usual means of establishing objective evidence. In most cases the asylum narrative is the main source of evidence, whereas in other types of case, there are likely to be other witnesses who can support or call into question aspects of the claimant's account. Therefore, establishing requirements for specific procedural norms for the assessment of evidence and the knowledge of these standards are essential for a fair and effective asylum decision-making process.[28] As a result, the Qualification Directive not only defines what a refugee or person needing subsidiary protection is, but it also establishes procedural norms for the assessment of evidence in asylum claims.

Procedural Norms for the Assessment of Evidence (Article 4 QDI; QDII)

Article 4 QDII[29] addresses the assessment of facts and circumstances with regard to qualification for both refugee and subsidiary protection status. Article 4(1) QDII, together with Article 4(2) QDII, stipulates that it is the duty of the Member State to assess the relevant elements of the application in cooperation with the applicant. Article 4(2) QDII lists the relevant elements required for the substantiation of an application for international protection. These consist of the applicant's statements and all the documentation at the applicant's disposal regarding his age, background (including that of relevant relatives), identity, nationality (ies), country (ies) and place(s) of previous residence, previous asylum applications, travel routes, travel documents, and the reasons for applying for international protection. Article 4(3) QDII states that the assessment of an application should be carried out on an individual basis and lists non-exhaustively some of the factors that should be taken into account. Moreover, Article 4(5) QDII states that where aspects of the applicant's statements are not supported by documentary or other evidence, those aspects shall not need confirmation when five stipulated conditions are met.[30] These conditions are:

---

[28]See also EASO (2015).

[29]The text of Article 4 is the same for QD1 and QDII, but here we refer to QDII.

[30]The terms of Article 4 QDI are the same as Article 4 QDII, and therefore, the same measures apply in the UK. UK Immigration Rules say that confirmation of the person's statements will not be needed (when the five conditions in Article 4(5) QDI noted above) are met: Immigration Rules Part 11 Asylum: Rule 339L. (339 N 'In determining whether the general credibility of the person has been established the Secretary of State will apply the provisions in s.8 of the Asylum and Immigration (Treatment of Claimants, etc.) Act 2004.').

a. the applicant has made a genuine effort to substantiate his application;
b. all relevant elements at the applicant's disposal have been submitted, and a satisfactory explanation has been given regarding any lack of other relevant elements;
c. the applicant's statements are found to be coherent and plausible and do not run counter to available specific and general information relevant to the applicant's case;
d. the applicant has applied for international protection at the earliest possible time, unless the applicant can demonstrate good reason for not having done so; and
e. the general credibility of the applicant has been established.

This provision is intended as a 'translation' of the 'benefit of the doubt' idea. The principle of the benefit of the doubt recognises the considerable difficulties that applicants and decision-makers face gathering evidence to support the claim, and that there may still be some doubt regarding the facts.[31] As the UNHCR Handbook puts it:

> After the applicant has made a genuine effort to substantiate his story there may still be a lack of evidence for some of his statements. [...] It is hardly possible for a refugee to 'prove' every part of his case and, indeed, if this were a requirement the majority of refugees would not be recognised. It is therefore frequently necessary to give the applicant the benefit of the doubt. (Para. 203)

To sum up, the principle means that, when the conditions in QD Article 4(5) are met, corroboration (confirmation) of the applicant's own statements are not required in order to 'substantiate' (prove) their claim for international protection.

Credibility Assessment

The consequence of recognising that the applicant's statements can be sufficient to establish an asylum claim is that the outcome of the claim frequently turns on the credibility of those statements. UNHCR, in the exercise of its supervisory responsibility in relation to refugee protection,

---

[31] UNHCR Handbook para. 203.

has produced guidance relevant to the assessment of credibility (UNHCR 2013), but neither the APD nor the QD explicitly or comprehensively prescribes how credibility assessment should be carried out.

So, although the international and European legal framework establishes principles and standards, it provides no predetermined structured approach for the assessment of credibility. A national approach therefore will and may be based on free evaluation of the evidence. As the substantive chapters show, the experience of asylum seekers is often that reliance on credibility does not work to their benefit, in the positive way that the benefit of the doubt principle, as discussed by Zahle (2005), suggested that it could. Instead, it works against them, and they meet a 'culture of disbelief' (see Kobelinsky, Hambly, Affolter et al, Schneider this volume).

Article 4(2) the Duty to Co-operate

The CJEU has—in a preliminary ruling—clarified the scope of application of the duty to cooperate in Article 4(2) QD. First, the court states that the assessment of facts and circumstances takes place in two separate stages. The first stage concerns the establishment of factual circumstances which may constitute evidence that supports the application, and the second stage relates to the legal appraisal of that evidence, which entails deciding whether there is a need for international protection.[32] The Member State's duty to cooperate with the applicant, according to the CJEU, is only applicable to the first stage, when the facts and circumstances are being established, and can therefore be understood as the duty to cooperate to assemble all relevant evidence that supports the application, or to cooperate with the applicant as he takes on the burden of proving the case. Cooperation does not extend to the task of *assessing* whether the applicant has shown that a real risk of persecution or serious harm on return exists, or that s/he has discharged that burden to the required standard of proof.[33] According to the CJEU the duty to cooperate means, in practical terms, that if, for any reason whatsoever,

---

[32]CJEU 22 November 2012, C-277/11, M.M. para. 64.
[33]'Not needing confirmation' suggests a relaxed burden of proof and 'cooperation' suggests a relaxed standard of proof for asylum processes compared with civil and criminal processes. 'Substantiation' therefore incorporates both the burden and the standard of proof since a claim will be substantiated if the applicant discharges the burden of proof by providing evidence to the standard required.

the elements provided by an applicant for international protection are not complete, up to date or relevant, it is necessary for the Member State concerned to cooperate actively with the applicant, at that stage of the procedure, so that all the elements needed to substantiate the application may be assembled.

The CJEU judgment is a reminder that according to the case law of the ECtHR and in international refugee law the burden of assembling all relevant information for an application does not fall exclusively upon the applicant, but is shared with the government.[34] The bureaucratic setting of asylum decision-making does not encourage cooperation, and it is unusual to expect decision makers to cooperate with evidence-gathering, as asylum decision makers are expected to do, in case such cooperation interferes with the decision maker's adjudicative role. That is why the duty to cooperate does not extend to the legal appraisal of the evidence, and the decision maker's consideration of whether, according to the standard of proof, the claim has been substantiated. There are indications in some of the chapters below of the struggles that decision-makers face as they attempt to reach a balance between cooperating with the applicant and practising the 'organised detachment' that their bureaucratic setting demands (see for example Schneider, this volume), and even national courts have placed limits on the scope of duty to cooperate.[35]

Judicial Remedies

Judicial protection is a crucial safeguard for asylum seekers. At the European level, judicial remedies are provided by the Court of Justice of the European Union (CJEU) and the ECtHR. In the absence of an international judicial remedy that States are prepared to use, and bearing in mind that the provision of the Refugee Convention permitting States to refer disputes to the International Court of Justice has never been invoked,[36] the CJEU plays a crucial role in interpreting EU asylum law. This interpreting role may

---

[34]See also UNHCR Handbook, para. 196.
[35]TN(Afghanistan)[2015]UKSC 40, [73]; MJ(Afghanistan)[2013] UKUT 253(IAC).
[36]Refugee Convention Article 38.

directly or indirectly define the standards for EU Member States (Garlick 2015: 108). But while European-level remedies contribute to the development of refugee law, they remain remote from the experience of most asylum seekers, since they usually come into play only where a case raises an aspect of EU refugee law that requires clarification, or after national remedies have been exhausted. Unsurprisingly, then, these 'high level' remedies are not addressed by any of the authors here, whose research focusses on the national level, where the roles of the state representative (Campbell, this volume), of the asylum advocate (Hambly, this volume) and of the judge (Sorgoni, this volume) are examined.

The EU system of judicial protection is based on the principle that all individuals are entitled to effective judicial protection of the rights they derive from the EU legal order. Judicial remedies in asylum cases are therefore a matter for the national courts of the Member States (Boeles et al. 2014: 411). At the national level, access to an effective remedy to challenge a negative decision must be available (Article 46 APDII; Article 39 APDI). The ECtHR has held that, in order to be effective, the appeal must be 'suspensive', meaning that appellants must be permitted to remain on the territory pending the outcome of their appeal.[37] The scope of an appeal should permit a full review (APDII Article 46), allowing not only conclusions on the law but also factual conclusions, including about credibility, to be reviewed. Further evidence can also be submitted, such as independent expert reports about the appellant's linguistic background, where the state authorities have used in-house linguistic analysis to cast doubt on this (Zwaan 2010). Information on how to appeal, details of time limits, etc., should accompany a negative decision (APDI Article 9), and appellants should also receive legal advice and interpretation services (Article 39 APDI: Article 46 APDII). As the chapters below illustrate, however, the above safeguards do not of themselves ensure effective access to the appeal right in practice, and inadequate legal representation (or none at all), poor interpretation, battle-weary judges, aggressive State representatives and the formality and technicality of the procedures can present asylum appellants with insurmountable barriers rather than access to justice. Despite these obstacles, success rates at appeal frequently run at between 20 and 30% (see Gill and Good, Kobelinsky, Campbell, Hambly, Sorgoni, all this volume; Liodden, this volume, reports a lower proportion in Norway), indicating how

---

[37]Gebremedhin v France 25389/05, ECtHR, 26 April 2007; *Abdolkhani and Karimnia v. Turkey* 30471/08, ECtHR, 22 September 2009.

important the right to appeal safeguard is for refugee protection, as well as its potential.

Final Remarks

European Union Law has many parents and foster parents (Koopmans 1991: 506), and these parents and foster parents are firmly rooted in the legal traditions of the Member States. Almost all European asylum decisions stay within national legal systems, never reaching the lofty heights of the CJEU or the ECtHR. This means that, although we now have the European Union's CEAS, national legal traditions retain considerable influence over asylum processes. We do not have space here to explore the impact which the different European legal traditions have on asylum processes, or their relationship with legal integration (Bobek 2013), but we have taken as a point of departure the legal origins approach, because we see it as an approach which looks for the correlations between legal traditions (Nicola 2016: 869). There are many correlations between the asylum systems discussed in this volume, but three deserve emphasis. First, of course, there is the correlation between the human rights standards which bind all the states studied here, and their translation into CEAS measures, as seen in the Qualification Directive Article 4 on the burden of proof to be applied in national asylum processes. Secondly, correlations of concern about national security and sovereignty are also present in asylum systems. Mechanisms to address security issues can be found in refugee law itself, and the fingerprint and other personal data collected under the EURODAC Regulation also address Member States' security concerns, as does the CEAS' home within the EU's Area of Freedom Security and Justice. This can lead to a situation where judges, rather than presenting a challenge to State authorities, might be just as likely to be discussing the merits of deferring to them, particularly where there is a climate of insecurity (Harvey 2005). At the same time, the realities of refugee status determination across Europe reflect a collective failure on the part of Member States to work in solidarity to protect refugees (Campesi 2018). This leads us to the third and final correlation. This final correlation is also the most hopeful, as it is the one between the "legality principle"—of respect for the individual and the protection of the person in the determination of asylum cases (Harvey 2005), and the evidence in this volume's ethnographic chapters of "legal consciousness", in the sense of there being actors involved in all of the asylum processes studied here who continue to struggle with concepts of justice and fairness in their routine experiences and perceptions of law in their everyday lives (Merry 1990; Cowan 2004). Long may they continue to struggle with those concepts.

References

Bobek, M. (2013). Of Feasibility and Silent Elephants: The Legitimacy of the Court of Justice through the Eyes of National Courts. In M. a.o. Adams (Eds.), *Judging Europe's Judges*. London: Bloomsbury.

Boeles, P., den Heijer, M., Lodder, G., & Wouters, K. (2014). *European Migration Law* (2nd ed.). Antwerp: Intersentia.

Campesi, G. (2018). Seeking Asylum in Times of Crisis: Reception, Confinement and Detention at Europe's Southern Borders. *Refugee Survey Quarterly, 37*(1), 44–70.

Costello, C., & Mouzarakis, M. (2014). Reflections on Reading Tarakhel. *Asiel en Migrantenrecht, 10,* 404–411.

Cowan, D. (2004). Legal Consciousness: Some Observations. *Modern Law Review, 67*(6), 928–958.

Doornbos, N. (2005). On Being Heard in Asylum Cases: Evidentiary Assessment Through Asylum Interviews. In G. Noll (Ed.), *Proof: Evidentiary Assessment and Credibility in Asylum Procedures*. Leiden-Boston: Martinus Nijhoff Publishers.

Drew, P., & Heritage, J. (Eds.). (1992). *Talk at Work. Interaction in Institutional Settings*. New York: Cambridge University Press.

EASO. (2015). *EASO Practical Guide: Evidence Assessment*. Available at: https://www.easo.europa.eu/practical-tools.

Edwards, A. (2010). Transitioning Gender: Feminist Engagement with International Refugee Law and Policy 1950–2010. *Refugee Survey Quarterly, 29*(2), 21–45.

Garlick, M. (2015). International Protection in Court: The Asylum Jurisprudence of the Court of Justice of the EU and UNHCR. *Refugee Survey Quarterly, 34,* 107–130.

Guild, E. (2016). Does the EU Need a European Migration and Protection Agency? *International Journal of Refugee Law, 28*(4), 585–600.

Harvey, C. (2005). Judging Asylum. In P. Shah (Ed.), *The Challenge of Asylum to Legal Systems*. London: Cavendish.

Kälin, W. (1986). Troubled Communication: Cross-Cultural Misunderstandings in the Asylum-Hearing. *International Migration Review, 20*(2), 230.

Koopmans, T. (1991). The Birth of European Law at the Cross Roads of Legal Traditions. *American Journal of Comparative Law, 39*(3), 493–507.

Merry, S. E. (1990). *Getting Justice and Getting Even: Legal Consciousness Among Working-Class Americans*. Chicago: Chicago Press.

Nicola, F. G. (2016). National Legal Tradition at Work in the Jurisprudence of the Court of Justice of the European Union. *American Journal of Comparative Law, 64*(3), 865–890.

UN High Commissioner for Refugees (UNHCR). (1998, December 16). *Note on Burden and Standard of Proof in Refugee Claims*. Available at: http://www.refworld.org/docid/3ae6b3338.html. Accessed 18 June 2018.

UNHCR. (2011). *Handbook and Guidelines on Procedures and Criteria for Determining Refugee Status Under the 1951 Convention and the 1967 Protocol Relating to the Status of Refugees*.

UNHCR. (2013). *Beyond Proof. Credibility Assessment in EU Asylum Systems*. Brussels.

UNHCR. (2016). Guidelines on International Protection No. 12. Guidelines on International Protection pursuant to its mandate, as contained in par. 8(a) of the Statute of the Office of the United Nations High Commissioner for Refugees.

van der Kleij, S. (2015). *Interaction in Dutch Asylum Interviews: A Corpus Study of Interpreter-Mediated Institutional Discourse*. Utrecht: LOT Publishing.

Zahle, H. (2005). Competing Patterns for Evidentiary Assessments. In Noll, G. (Ed.), *Proof, Evidentiary Assessment and Credibility in Asylum Procedures* (pp. 13–27). The Netherlands: Brill.

Zwaan, K., Verrips, M., & Muysken, P. (Eds.). (2010). *Language and Origin: The Role of Language in European Asylum Procedures: Linguistic and Legal Perspectives*. The Netherlands: Wolf Legal Publishers.

Legal Documents

APDI. (2005). Council Directive 2005/85/EC of 1 December 2005 on minimum standards on procedures in Member States for granting and withdrawing refugee status, OJ 2005, L 326, p. 13.

APDII. (2013). Council Directive 2013/32/EU of 26 June 2013 on common procedures for granting and withdrawing international protection (recast), OJ 2013, L 180, p. 60.

CJEU. (2003). Dublin I Council Regulation 343/2003/EC of 18 February 2003 establishing the criteria and mechanisms for determining the Member State responsible for examining an asylum application lodged in one of the Member States by a third-country national, OJ 2003, L 50, p. 1.

Dublin III. (2013). Regulation (EU) No. 604/2013 of 26 June 2013 establishing the criteria and mechanisms for determining the Member State responsible for examining an application for international protection lodged in one of the Member States by a third-country national or a stateless person (recast) (Dublin III Regulation), OJ 2013, L 180, p. 31.

ECHR (European Convention on Human Rights and Fundamental Freedoms). As amended by Protocols Nos. 11 and 14 supplemented by Protocols Nos. 1, 4, 6, 7, 12 and 1.

Eurodac Regulation 603/2013/EU of 26 June 2013 on the establishment of Eurodac for the comparison of fingerprints for the effective application of Regulation (EU) No 604/2013 establishing the criteria and mechanisms for determining the Member State responsible for examining an application for international protection lodged in one of the Member States by a third-country national or a stateless person and on requests for the comparison with Eurodac data by Member States' law enforcement authorities and Europol for law enforcement purposes, and amending Regulation (EU) No 1077/2011 establishing a European Agency for the operational management of large-scale IT systems in the area of freedom, security and justice (recast), OJ 2013, L 180, pp. 1.

RCDI Council Directive 2003/9/EC of 27 January 2003 laying down minimum standards for the reception of asylum seekers, OJ 2003, L 31, p. 18.

RCDII. (2013). Reception Conditions Directive 2013/33/EU of 26 June 2013 laying down standards for the reception of applicants for international protection (recast), OJ 2013, L 180, p. 96.

RD Directive 2008/115/EC of the European Parliament and of the Council of 16 December 2008 on common standards and procedures in Member States for returning illegally staying third-country nationals, OJ 2008, L 348, p. 98.

Refugee Convention relating to the Status of Refugees. (1951). United Nations General Assembly resolution 429(V) of 14 December 1950, as amended by the 1967 Protocol.

QDI. (2004). Council Directive 2004/83/EC of 29 April 2004 on minimum standards for the qualification and status of third country nationals or stateless persons as refugees or as persons who otherwise need international protection and the content of the protection granted, OJ 2004, L 304, p. 12.

QDII. (2011). Council Directive 2011/95/EU of 13 December 2011 on standards for the qualification of third-country nationals or stateless persons as beneficiaries of international protection, for a uniform status for refugees or for persons eligible for subsidiary protection, and for the content of the protection granted (recast) OJ 2011, L 337, p. 9.

Case Law

CJEU 21 December 2011, joined cases C-411/10 and C-493/10, N.S. and Others.
CJEU 22 November 2012, C-277/11, M.M.
ECtHR 21 January 2011, Application no. 30696/09, M.S.S. vs. Belgium and Greece.
ECtHR 4 November 2014, Application no. 29217/12, Tarakhel.

Open Access This chapter is distributed under the terms of the Creative Commons Attribution 4.0 International License (http://creativecommons.org/licenses/by/4.0/), which permits use, duplication, adaptation, distribution and reproduction in any medium or format, as long as you give appropriate credit to the original author(s) and the source, a link is provided to the Creative Commons license and any changes made are indicated.

The images or other third party material in this chapter are included in the work's Creative Commons license, unless indicated otherwise in the credit line; if such material is not included in the work's Creative Commons license and the respective action is not permitted by statutory regulation, users will need to obtain permission from the license holder to duplicate, adapt or reproduce the material.

Part I

Actors

3

The "Inner Belief" of French Asylum Judges

Carolina Kobelinsky

Introduction

'I was shocked to see to what extent we don't practice law here. From the legal point of view, the questions raised here are very poor.' With these words a judge expresses his initial malaise when he was appointed to the French Court of Asylum after many years working on taxation. He then develops his reasoning:

> [T]here are few technical aspects involved in decision-making. In fact, there are some thorny questions but we do not raise them, for instance, concerning the notion of nationality or of residence; but most of our decisions completely rely on the *intime conviction*.

Like many of his colleagues, he argues that the court case law is not consistent and that the domestic law—which incorporates the Geneva Convention—provides a vague and loose definition of who is a refugee The judge highlights the *intime conviction* as the key element involved in asylum adjudication. However, this notion, which could be translated as inner or deap-seated belief, does not exist in any asylum regulation or law. It just appears in the French Code of Criminal Procedure as the unique standard

C. Kobelinsky (✉)
CNRS-LESC, Nanterre, France
e-mail: carolina.kobelinsky@cnrs.fr

for ascertaining judicial truth but it is not clearly defined. Its article 353, which is read to the jurors when they leave the Assizes court to deliberate, states that:

> The law does not ask the judges and the jurors composing the Assize court to account for the means by which they convinced themselves; it does not charge them with any rule from which they shall specifically derive the fullness and adequacy of evidence. It requires them to question themselves in silence and contemplation and to seek in the sincerity of their conscience what impression has been made on their reason by the evidence brought against the accused and the arguments of his defence. The law asks them but this single question, which encloses the full scope of their duties: have you an inner belief?[1]

Inspired by the idea of 'moral proof' (Leclerc 1995), this fragment comes from the French Revolution; it was written by a lawyer and deputy at the Parliament who contributed to the Criminal Code of Brumaire year IV (Inchauspé 2015: 604). The Anglo-Saxon tradition does not base its criminal procedure on this notion of inner belief but on reasonable doubt. Evidence that is 'beyond a reasonable doubt' is the standard required to validate a criminal conviction. As with *intime conviction*, reasonable doubt is never clearly defined in British law. The US Supreme Court provides some elements of definition in a 1994 ruling:

> It is not a mere possible doubt; because everything relating to human affairs, and depending on moral evidence, is open to some possible or imaginary doubt. It is that state of the case which, after the entire comparison and consideration of all the evidence, leaves the minds of the jurors in that condition that they cannot say they feel an abiding conviction, to a moral certainty, of the truth of the charge. (Victor v. Nebraska, 511 U.S. 1, 1994)

The ambition of adjudication in common law is respect for freedom, whereas in the French tradition it is the search for truth (Inchauspé 2015). However, in both cases the goal is to reach a moral certainty based on evidence provided before the court. This paper seeks to examine the ways in which this moral certainty is reached by asylum judges who, as the chair quoted earlier, understand their task through the notion of inner belief.

The use and implications of the *intime conviction* in criminal courts has been examined by scholars from a legal perspective (Leclerc 1995; Inchauspé

---

[1]Art. 353, *Code de procédure pénale*.

2015), and more recently by psychological approaches, based among others on psychoanalysis (Ducousso-Lacaze and Grihom 2012; Jacob Alby 2015), cognitive-experiential self-theory (Esnard et al. 2013), and forensic psychology (Pham and Reveillère 2015). The present paper does not intend to engage in a debate with these different analyses but rather to provide an ethnographic approach to *intime conviction*, grounded in the way court actors bring the notion into play during their daily practices of justice. Furthermore, the argument builds on a central element relating all the literature regarding this topic: the existence of emotions at the basis of the inner belief of the adjudicator.

Drawing on data collected between 2009 and 2011, covering 14 months of ethnographic fieldwork at the French Court of Asylum,[2] in charge of examining the cases of asylum seekers rejected by the French Office for the Protection of Refugees and Stateless Persons (OFPRA), I will explore in this chapter how this *intime conviction* that the court's actors talk about so frequently (see Greslier 2007; Belorgey 2003; Valluy 2004) is fabricated, and the way it impacts on asylum decision-making. I argue that the court's actors use this notion as a way of pointing out the "subjective" elements of adjudication, such as their affects, moral values and political orientations, and thus legitimise their decisions when the legal elements seem to be lacking. I will also contend that judges' *intime conviction* cannot escape from the current suspicion economy surrounding asylum seekers and refugees.

The suspicion at work in the adjudication process, understood as a systematic attitude of distrust or disbelief towards asylum requests, is constructed in response to the political discourse and at the same time participates in its construction (Fassin and Kobelinsky 2012). Contemporary representations and practices regarding asylum are undermined by suspicion (Daniel and Knudsen 1995; Bohmer and Shuman 2008; D'Halluin 2012; Valluy 2009). Asylum, and more generally, migration, have become highly politically contested in France and elsewhere in Europe. Although many scholars have argued that the distinction between political and economic causes of exile is difficult to sustain (Castles and Miller 1993; Schuster 2003; Zolberg 1983), public discourse associates asylum seekers with "bogus refugees" who come not for political reasons but for purely economic motives.

---

[2]The material was collected from observations of public hearings, hearings behind closed doors, in-camera deliberations, and the everyday activities of rapporteurs, in charge of the in-depth examination of the cases. I also conducted interviews and had many informal conversations with judges, rapporteurs, lawyers and interpreters. The data was completed by examining a corpus of 60 rulings focused on a particular case law related to cases motivated by the sexual orientation of claimants (see Kobelinsky 2015a).

However, this distinction and the suspicion it triggers have not always been at the core of asylum policies and representations. For nearly 30 years following the establishment of the bureaucracy of asylum in 1952, most foreigners who sought the protection of France as refugees received it. Since then, the situation has reversed, and most claimants see their applications successively rejected by the OFPRA and the remedy body. By the time of my field research, in 2009, the OFPRA acceptance rate was 14.3%, and the Court's 26.6%. In 2010, it went down to 13.5 and 22.1% and in 2011, the tendency continued as the OFPRA granted protection in 11% of cases and the Court in 17.7% of appeals (CNDA 2009, 2010, 2011).

The chapter is organised as follows: in the first section, I briefly describe the different steps and actors involved in decision-making at the court. I then focus on the hearing as a crucial moment in which adjudicators scrutinise the asylum seeker trying to build their inner belief. The third section examines the emotions at play during the encounter with the claimant and its weight in decision-making. The fourth section moves from the affects to the values at the core of asylum adjudication. Eventually, I come back to the notion of *intime conviction* and its intimate connection to the moral economy of asylum.

The Appeal's Path

Decision-making in this court nowadays involves three moments or steps. When an appeal is recorded by the registry and the case file is requested from the OFPRA, the court first of all evaluates whether or not it is admissible. The court can give a direct ruling to reject certain cases due to foreclosure (i.e. when the deadline for appeal has expired). Since 2004, it can also reject cases after an initial evaluation of the well-founded-ness of the claim (i.e. when applications for re-examination do not present any new facts). During the period covered by my fieldwork, around 20% of the cases were rejected after this initial examination.[3] The other cases continued along the path to further evaluation.

The next step implies an in-depth examination of the case carried out by a rapporteur. By the time of my fieldwork the court employed approximately

---

[3]In 2009, 14.6% of the cases were rejected by *ordonnance*, direct ruling after this initial evaluation (CNDA 2009). In 2010, the percentage climbed up to 20.2% (CNDA 2010) and in 2011, the percentage of cases rejected was 22 (CNDA 2011). The tendency, in terms of cases rejected by direct ruling, still remains around 20%.

120 rapporteurs, half of whom were civil servants, the other half of whom were working on a contractual basis. Most rapporteurs are young, between the ages of 25 and 40, and a large proportion of them are women. For some this is their first professional job. Among rapporteurs, many have a law or a political science degree. To ensure good performance, in 2010 the Court set the number of cases each rapporteur must handle every year to 403. Without counting the time that it takes to draft the decisions—which is also part of the everyday activities of the rapporteurs—and the time spent at hearings, this leaves them on average a little more than half a day to prepare each report. In 2012, after a series of collective protests, the number of cases to be handled each year was reduced to 387.

The main activity of the rapporteur consists in the study of the narrative, that is the story of persecution generally co-constructed by the applicant and their legal representatives or advocate. They also examine the synopsis of the interview the claimant had at the OFPRA, and other documents provided to support the story, in order to be able to give a recommendation to the judges. Either he or she thinks protection should be granted or, on the contrary, that the appeal should be dismissed. Sometimes the rapporteur may reserve his or her judgment and does not provide any clear recommendation, based on the possibility that unclear evidence in the case might be clarified by explanations given at the hearing.

Rapporteurs consider five major elements when examining the cases: (1) its legal content, that is, the application of the Geneva Convention, Subsidiary protection,[4] and specific case law; (2) what they call the "coherence" of the narrative, which stems from its internal logic as well as from possible discrepancies between the initial story and the answers provided during the interview with OFPRA; (3) the plausibility of the story in the light of the geopolitical situation in the country of origin, which is usually called the "external logic"; (4) the accuracy of the answers, the perception of spontaneity having a significant positive value; and (5) the examination of the supplementary documents in the file (such as medical certificates, press articles, etc.). Although rapporteurs combine these elements in different ways (some of them considering the "external logic" or the "coherence" of the narrative as the most important aspect, others preferring to focus on the supplementary evidence), the recommendations they produce are all very

---

[4]The 2003 Reform of the Immigration Law introduced subsidiary protection as a protection regime which can be granted—by the OFPRA and the Court—to those who are subject to serious threats in their country. More precarious than conventional asylum, subsidiary protection requires an annually renewable residency permit.

similar both in the expressions used and the meaning of their findings. This technical expertise almost systematically leads to casting doubt on the applications, which rarely present all the elements expected by the rapporteurs. Most recommendations are then in favour of rejecting applications based on the vagueness of the story and the lack of supporting evidence.

The five elements mentioned above create a form of distance and detachment (see Schneider's chapter, this volume, for a discussion of detachment), giving an aura of "objectivity", highlighted by all the rapporteurs I interviewed, as the most important aspect of their examination. However, some of them acknowledge they do also form their recommendations on the basis of their inner belief. While discussing the evolution of the institution with reference to the introduction of permanent chair judges who work fulltime in the court—which, as I will explain more fully later, is not the case for most judges—a rapporteur with three years of experience stresses the importance of building her own personal *intime conviction*:

> The profession of rapporteur is very hybrid in its skills and tasks. And with the arrival of the permanent chairs we have to be careful not to become the secretary of chairs saying, 'do some research on this Congolese political party, on this Sri Lankan case law' [...]. We have to be able to think by ourselves and to write the report based on our inquiries and our own *intime conviction*. (Interview, rapporteur, 3 November 2009)

A rapporteur with many years of experience in the Court also admits that ultimately his recommendations are based on his *intime conviction*:

> I analyse carefully the legal elements, the geopolitical components and the evidence supporting the narrative to be the most objective I can. But, then, there is also a more general thing, I make up my mind, I try to think as if I were the person and build my inner belief. (Conversation, rapporteur, 27 November 2009)

In this excerpt, the inner belief is related to a sort of empathy of the rapporteur who "tries" to imagine what it would be like to be in the asylum seeker's situation. Although he does not put it clearly, he seems to make a distinction between the technical elements helping to provide objectivity and a more general impression, based on empathy—and in all likelihood associated with feelings and emotions—which form his *intime conviction*. Another rapporteur makes a more explicit connection between this notion and the "subjectivity" of adjudicators when she comments on the judges' way of proceeding:

> There is a very subjective part in decision-making, the *intime conviction* lies in the judges' belief in the narrative and the applicant. We [rapporteurs] tend to reduce this through our technical examination but we cannot deny there is something else at play. (Conversation, rapporteur, 19 January 2010)

The rapporteur suggests that their in-depth examination is mainly based on the technical elements mentioned above rather than on a more subjective component, thus coinciding with the rapporteurs' general discourse on their way of studying the cases, as opposed to the judges' approach to the cases.

After the presentation by the rapporteur—whatever the recommendation is—a board of three judges examines the case during a public hearing in which they confront the asylum seeker, who can be provided with an interpreter on oath, and with the advice of a legal representative.[5] The board of judges is composed of three members: a chair who is usually a magistrate from civil or criminal justice or a former member of the *Conseil d'État*; an assessor who is either a law scholar or a former officer of the United Nations High Commissioner for Refugees (UNHCR) in the field; and another assessor who is usually a mid-level bureaucrat, a former ambassador or teacher appointed by the vice president of the *Conseil d'État* at the suggestion of OFPRA's Board of Directors.[6] Until 2009, the 160 judges were all temporary appointees who convened only a few times each month. The reform enacted by the law of 20th November 2007, served to reduce the number of temporary magistrates and to recruit ten permanent judges who would be responsible for about 40% of the caseload. The goal was to address the inadequate coordination among the decision-making bodies and to work towards the standardisation of case law, specifically to thereby reduce the disparities in decisions because, according to unofficial data circulating in the institution, the admission rate varied between one in every 20 cases and one in every two depending on the chair.

During the hearing—which will be analysed in detail in the next section—the rapporteur summarises the facts pointed out by the claimant and the

---

[5]With effect from December 1, 2008, every claimant has access to a lawyer who is paid for by the state, whereas prior to that date only claimants who had entered France with a legal permit had access to legal aid.

[6]Exceptionally, three boards of judges can come together in order to evaluate cases that are referred by the chair of the court or by a panel of judges, and they will introduce a new line of judicial precedent. The issues at stake are substantial insofar as the decisions made are intended to crystallise the position of the court not only on judicial elements, but also, more generally, on political issues, whether in relation to the situation in certain countries or regarding how to deal with a set of claims with the same characteristics. These rulings are supposed to become the court's case law.

decision made by the OFPRA, presents the supporting documents and provides a recommendation. The board of judges then listens to the claimant's legal representative and asks questions to the asylum seeker. Decisions are then made during in-camera deliberations[7] after the hearing, which normally do not take more than 30 minutes for the whole set of cases (between six and 13). The rulings are posted three weeks later in the entrance hall of the court. The board of judges either overturns the OFPRA decision and grants protection, or upholds the negative evaluation in which case the dismissed person is asked to leave France within 30 days. In the case of rejection, the dismissed person has one final opportunity to request that the case be re-opened. This procedure entails applying to the Préfecture, which verifies the existence of new evidence. In this case, the OFPRA provides a certificate for re-examination and the Préfecture has to extend the residency permit. The case then passes via the OFPRA and finally back to the court, where the claimant is given a new public hearing. If this is not successful, the rejection of the application is final. The person then has 30 days in which to leave the country before the Préfecture issues an '*Obligation to Leave France*', which, after the 30 days, is a binding measure of removal and can be enforced.

Seeing or Not Seeing the Refugee

The hearing is when the board of judges meets with the asylum seeker and, for most of them, the moment in which they learn about the case. For every judge I spoke with, the encounter with the asylum seeker is considered crucial. As in any other legal proceeding, the asylum courtroom is a codified and ritualised setting, where everyone takes on a role and pursues an objective. Applicants are expected to play a role consistent with their condition—suffering victims, seasoned activists, etc. The manner in which they talk, look, and move are all very important to the way in which the adjudicators regard them and consider their claim. As Gibb establishes (this volume) even the physical space of the hearing can influence how applicants are "seen" by officials. For all of them the encounter is the very moment in which the inner belief is built. Legal aspects, documentary evidence, arrangements of objects, the 'bodily hexis' (Bourdieu 1977) of the applicant, the language skills, the knowledge (or the misreading) of the political and social situation

---

[7]In-camera means, in legal terms, that the deliberation takes place behind closed doors with only the three members of the board and the rapporteur present.

in the country of origin will merge over the course of the hearing to provide the judges with an understanding of the case and the claimant.

In asylum procedures, as historian Gérard Noiriel (1991) wrote in the early 1990s, the official's task is based on the principle that the individual is an *applicant*, that it is their job to prove their identity and legitimate right to asylum (see Craig and Zwaan, this volume, who set out how the burden of proof is laid upon the asylum seeker in European law), but that the public authorities must establish the nature and quantity of evidence needed. A policy of proof is thus established, and it has become vital to provide a body of evidence in support of an account, but it is rarely sufficient because in most cases the documents provided are inconclusive or contested and the asylum application is rejected. If the hearing appears to be a crucial moment—in which a rapporteur's recommendation of rejection could potentially be reversed—its importance reaches its peak when it comes to evaluating applications grounded on persecution related to the sexual orientation of the asylum seeker.

The specificity of these cases, as I have argued elsewhere (Kobelinsky 2015a), lies in the fact that instead of concentrating their evaluation on the evidence of persecution, the judges focus on the veracity of the claimant's homosexuality. Once this has been established, persecution no longer has to be proven. It is therefore the ascertainment of homosexuality that paves the way to the refugee status. And this seems to happen during the encounter. The judges seek to question the claimant on what they consider to be evidence of their sexuality. For instance, some judges try to test the asylum seeker's 'gay knowledge', to use the expression of one rapporteur, asking questions about gay meeting places in France. Other court actors believe it is possible to 'see' an applicant's homosexuality during the hearing, based on their appearance and attitude. 'To be honest, he didn't look gay at all', commented a rapporteur, standing in front of the coffee machine during a break between two hearings. Minutes earlier we had been listening to a young man from Pakistan who was seeking refugee status on the grounds of his persecution as a homosexual in his country of origin. Clearly, he had failed to convince them, and they suspected him—as one of the judges later told me—of not being a 'true' homosexual. Other adjudicators seem more modest about their ability to 'recognise' homosexuals during the hearing: 'It is true that sometimes their behaviour cannot be differentiated', one of them confided. 'Differentiating' and 'looking' are both terms that presume there to be obvious homosexual attributes.[8] Many judges expected at the hearings

---

[8]'Recognising' or 'seeing' the homosexuality would mean seeing the feminine side to a man or the masculine side to a woman, which refers more to issues of gender than of sexuality.

to see before them the images conveyed by the media of white, well-off, feminine men (see Morgan 2006). The young Pakistani who 'didn't look gay at all' was clearly not effeminate enough.

Claims made on the grounds of sexual orientation implicitly demonstrate the difficulties in providing evidence to support the narrative that ultimately lies in all asylum claims. They also illustrate the shift that has occurred in the test of truth, from examining the truthfulness of an account towards assessing an applicant's sincerity during the hearing. As such, it is no longer facts but people that are subject to judgment, with applicants whose claims are grounded in persecution related to their sexual orientation expected to correspond to the stereotype of a homosexual, at least during the face-to-face encounter with the judges.

Emotional Judges

In most of the observed hearings, the judges seem to show no emotion or feeling. Comments such as 'we know this story' or 'it is the tenth time we hear the same thing', are openly expressed by judges during hearings or in the deliberations, showing a sort of frustration with requests which 'are always the same'. The repetitive nature of the cases, together with the routinisation of the process of decision-making, lead to an erosion of emotions (Fassin 2001) and a form of indifference (Herzfeld 1992). However, the asylum court is an emotional bureaucracy (see Graham 2002) and sometimes the encounter with the claimant may stir up affects, which will be considered as a component of the judges' *intime conviction*. Let us consider the case of a young asylum seeker coming from the Republic of Congo:

> The clerk calls the next case and a young, rather slender woman dressed in jeans and a long black sweater, her long hair straightened and pulled back with a headband, sits trembling on a bench in front of the board of three male judges and next to her legal representative. She confirms in a feeble and almost inaudible voice to the rapporteur, who raised the question, that she does not need an interpreter. The chair asks the rapporteur to start his reading. According to the report, the brother of this 19-year-old claimant belonged to the paramilitary group known as the Ninjas and an enemy group called the Cobras wanted to exact their revenge on her. She had been repeatedly threatened and assaulted before leaving the country. Her remarks were vague and not very developed. In support of her application, the woman produced a medical certificate from a physician. In his conclusions, the rapporteur invited the asylum seeker to revisit the attacks she had endured and to explain what fears she had should she return, but he proposed that the appeal be rejected for

unsubstantiated facts. The chair then invites the lawyer to make the statement. He emphasises the paramilitary activities of the claimant's brother and violence in the village where she resided; he stresses 'her physical and psychological fragility'. After thanking the legal representative, the chair turns to the woman and says softly: 'We will not ask you many questions'. He then asks the other magistrates if they have any questions. The judge for the UNHCR asks her about her fears in the event that she should return to her country. The applicant replies that she is afraid of being raped and killed. This is the only question. The chair concludes the hearing, which lasts just 22 minutes. [Two and a half hours later, during the deliberations behind closed doors, the case is discussed:] The chair asks his colleagues: 'What is your belief (*conviction*), what do you think?' And quickly adds 'I couldn't bear to let this girl…' [he stops as if the rest of the sentence was obvious to everyone] … 'but how to draft the decision?' The judges all agree that the case should be overturned: 'She looks confused, helpless,' says the older assessor. 'No one will probably ever know what she went through', adds the assessor appointed by the UNHCR. All nod, including the rapporteur. 'I'll find something [to be the basis of the decision] and show it to you', says the rapporteur to the chair. (Fieldnotes during the hearing and the deliberations, June 2011)

In this case, the attitude of the asylum seeker seemed fundamental when it came time to form an inner belief and make a decision. She was perceived as a fragile young woman, devastated by events that, in the words of one of the judges, 'no one will probably ever know', implying that something even more dramatic might have happened—perhaps sexual assault—which she did not share in her written account. Her body language became an indicator, if not of the sincerity of her remarks, then at least of the truth of her suffering. Her young age and the lost look on her face seemed to arouse a form of empathy and a feeling of compassion in the chair as well as in the other judges, who were both used to sitting with him. The emotion felt and their desire to help this young woman allowed them to overlook the weakness of the case as noted in the report.

As in many cases I observed, in which sentiments such as admiration, compassion or esteem are at work (Kobelinsky 2015b), this one shows that the inner belief of the judges is formed, at least in part, by the perceptions and feelings produced during the hearing. Affective reactions of course depend on the dispositions of the judges towards emotion, rooted in their personal backgrounds and their distinctive social characteristics. By virtue of their history, their political ideas, and their various identities—social, sexual, gendered, etc.—judges' sensitivities may diverge. But these reactions also depend in part on the ability of applicants to elicit emotion. Those who have the support of NGOs, the lawyers who frequently argue in the court, and the individuals familiar with the bureaucratic world of asylum all know that during the hearing, as one applicant told me, 'you have to be convincing', which also implied 'moving'. This suggests that applicants sometimes implement strategies to elicit emotional responses that predispose those who experience them to support the cause being defended (Traïni 2010). This premium placed on emotion penalises less demonstrative applicants whose stories are commented on as unconvincing during deliberations.

Although they are rare, these emotions also reinforce the distinction between those who are regarded as real refugees and those who are believed to exploit the system, as the affective reactions of the judges become an indicator of the sincerity of the applicants. And because these expressions remain infrequent, it can be said that the majority of the latter—those who do not provoke particular emotions—are not real refugees just as is the case for those who do not 'look' gay when applying on the grounds of persecution based upon sexual orientation.

Asylum as a Value

As we have seen, judges attach a great importance to the hearing as they compare the file to the individual, the analysis of documents provided to the impressions produced when listening and seeing the claimant; impressions which will inform the inner belief of asylum adjudicators. But this *intime conviction* also rests on the judges'—and more broadly all the court actors—conception of asylum. For all the judges and rapporteurs I had the chance to observe and discuss with, asylum is an institution to be protected. As a permanent chair put it:

> I set up strategies to try to find the truth and form my [inner] belief. We cannot debase political asylum, we have to be cautious and study the evidence and what comes from the hearing, we cannot grant the refugee status to anyone. (Interview, chair judge, 14 October 2010)

The judge is putting forward the need to preserve the institution of asylum from any kind of abuse. In the same vein, another judge, with a background in the civil domain and sitting in the court for many years, asserted during an interview:

> I take time to ask questions, to try to understand, of course I do make mistakes, it is not easy. People make stuff up, and we try to find out what lies closest to reality in order to help the people who really need it. We need to help those who have been persecuted, and we must also uphold the Geneva

> Convention [...] Asylum is a precious instrument of protection. (Interview, chair judge, 23 November 2009)

Asylum is shaped as a valuable institution, which protects people and which in turn needs to be protected. Another judge commented during an informal conversation: 'We must guarantee this possibility to receive people who cannot live in peace in their country because they chose a different lifestyle or because they defend a different ideology. It is our duty to protect this right'. Most of the adjudicators I discussed with use almost the same words to account for their willingness to assist refugees as well as to protect the right of asylum. This was also evident in the comments made by a rapporteur who declared in an interview: 'We have a long tradition in France of protecting the persecuted, it is something very important, and our job is to contribute to that'. The emphasis on the protective dimension of the court's actions is often propounded by judges and rapporteurs whenever they explain the way in which they conceive their work. In their discourse, it also usually appears a reference to a tradition of refugee protection which they must continue. A chair admitted at the end of one hearing in which no case had been overturned: 'You can't flout the principles of asylum, you can't grant the status to just anyone, you must respect these principles handed down to us from after the war'. In every case, asylum is presented as endowed with a powerful moral burden and value which must be defended. It then seems that these demanding criteria for granting protection leads to the disqualification of most of those who apply because the more asylum becomes an idealised entity, the harder it is to establish connections among actual stories, real individuals, and this abstract institution.

The Moral Certainty of Defending Asylum

> In criminal courts, you may not make the right decision but you always base your rulings in facts, concrete data. In the asylum domain, we confront something else, we confront a narrative and you have to evaluate its credibility, and we confront a moving reality, we examine the sincerity of the applicant [...]. Asylum decision-making is not exact science, there is a portion of chance, of personality, of rigour or humanism, of affects, there is a portion of unknown [...] and from it, we wonder about the truth of the case, we form our belief. (Interview, chair judge, 23 June 2010)

With these words, a chair judge sitting in the French Asylum Court for five years, and with more than two decades of experience in criminal courts, summarises the complexity of asylum adjudication. As he points out, during the hearing, judges examine, aside from a few legal and geopolitical points, the 'sincerity' of the applicant's narrative of persecution as well as his or her attitude and reactions. 'Do you believe that?' or 'What is your belief?' are the questions often asked by the chair to the two other judges during the in-camera deliberations. This is also the question rapporteurs ask themselves when they finish reading a file. Decision-making then relies on the inner belief that the asylum seeker is telling the truth: the truth about his sexual orientation, which did not seem to be the case for the young Pakistani mentioned earlier; the truth about her suffering in the case of the young Congolese woman. More broadly, the inner belief about the claimants' *refugeeness*.

The judge also introduces, in the extract above, the affective component of decision-making. As we have seen, whether by their occasional presence or by their frequent absence, emotions are part of asylum adjudication. Moreover, emotions and cognitions are interdependent in this process (Pham and Reveillère 2015). A chair judge, with a long experience in criminal courts—where the notion of *intime conviction* comes from, as already mentioned—clearly understands and accepts this interconnection:

> I am an emotional [person] but you cannot be taken by your emotions, you have to understand them and relate them to the evidence and the situation in the country of origin [...] and there is your inner belief. But we have to be cautious, I have already said it but it is very important, we cannot grant the refugee status to anyone. (Interview, chair judge, 14 October 2010)

In this excerpt, the judge acknowledges the importance of his emotions in decision-making and asserts the need to connect them to other elements—such as the evidence provided by the claimant and what he knows about the geopolitical context in which the story takes place—in order to form his *intime conviction*. And at the same time, he also couples this notion with the value he ascribes to the refugee status when he insists on showing caution because, as he had mentioned earlier in the interview—and as quoted in the previous section—asylum cannot be 'debased'. This understanding of asylum, which as we have seen is shared by the court's actors, is intimately linked to the suspicion economy surrounding asylum seekers and refugees. In order to win the day, shape a positive belief, and be granted asylum, it is necessary to correspond to the 'archetype of a refugee' (Akoka 2011), this ideal construct of a valuable institution which needs to be protected from abuse. Adjudicators consider asylum to be not only a right or a political institution, but also a moral principle to which they must attest. The 'moral certainty' on which the judges' *intime conviction* rests is thus, above all, that of protecting refugee status from asylum seekers.

References

Akoka, K. (2011). *L'archétype rêvé du réfugié. Plein droit n° 90*. Available at: http://www.gisti.org/spip.php?article2441.
Belorgey, J. M. (2003). Le contentieux du droit d'asile et l'intime conviction du juge. *La Revue administrative, 336*, 619–622.
Bohmer, C., & Shuman, A. (2008). *Rejecting Refugees: Political Asylum in the 21st Century*. London: Routledge.
Bourdieu, P. (1977). *Outline of a Theory of Practices*. Cambridge: Cambridge University Press.
Castles, S., & Miller, M. (1993). *The Age of Migration: International Population Movements in the Modern World*. London: Macmillan.
CNDA [Cour nationale du droit d'asile]. (2009). *Rapport Annuel 2009*. Available at: http://www.cnda.fr/content/download/9080/27370/version/1/file/ra-2009.pdf.
CNDA [Cour nationale du droit d'asile]. (2010). *Rapport Annuel 2010*. Available at: http://www.cnda.fr/content/download/9079/27367/version/1/file/ra-2010.pdf.
CNDA [Cour nationale du droit d'asile]. (2011). *Rapport Annuel 2011*. Available at: http://www.cnda.fr/content/download/9078/27364/version/1/file/ra-2011.pdf.
Daniel, E. V., & Knudsen, J. (1995). *Mistrusting Refugees*. Berkeley: University of California Press.
D'Halluin, E. (2012). *Les épreuves de l'asile. Associations et réfugiés face aux politiques du soupçon*. Paris: Editions de l'EHESS.
Ducousso-Lacaze, A., & Grihom, M. J. (2012). Pour une approche psychanalytique de l'intime conviction chez les magistrats dans une affaire d'inceste. *Annales Médico-Psychologiques, 170*, 75–80.
Esnard, C., Dumas, R., & Bordel, S. (2013). Effects of the "Intimate Conviction" Instruction on the Processing of Judicial Information. *Revue Européenne de Psychologie Appliquée, 63*, 121–128.
Fassin, D. (2001). Charité bien ordonnée: Principes de justice et pratiques de jugement dans l'attribution des aides d'urgence. *Revue française de sociologie, 42*(3), 437–475.
Fassin, D., & Kobelinsky, C. (2012). How Asylum Claims Are Adjudicated: The Institution as a Moral Agent. *Revue française de sociologie (English), 53*(4), 444–472.
Graham, M. (2002). Emotional Bureaucracies: Emotions, Civil Servants and Immigrants in the Swedish Welfare State. *Ethos, 30*(3), 199–226.
Greslier, F. (2007). La Commission des Recours des Réfugiés ou "l'intime conviction" face au recul du droit d'asile en France. *Revue européenne des migrations internationals, 23*, 107–133.
Herzfeld, M. (1992). *The Social Production of Indifference: Exploring the Symbolic Roots of Western Bureaucracy*. Chicago: The University of Chicago Press, arranged by Berg Publishers.
Inchauspé, D. (2015). L'intime conviction en droit français et dans la tradition juridique anglo-saxonne. *Annales Médico-Psychologiques, 173*(7), 603–605.

Jacob Alby, V. (2015). Qu'y a-t-il d'intime dans l'intime conviction? *Annales Médico-Psychologiques, 173*(7), 591–593.
Kobelinsky, C. (2015a). Judging Intimacies at the French Court of Asylum. *PoLAR, 38*(2), 338–355.
Kobelinsky, C. (2015b). Emotions as Evidence: An Ethnographic Exploration of Hearings in the French Asylum Court. In D. Berti, A. Good, & G. Tarabout (Eds.), *Of Doubt and Proof: Ritual and Legal Practices of Judgment* (pp. 163–182). Farnham: Ashgate.
Leclerc, H. (1995). L'intime conviction du juge: norme démocratique de la prevue. *Le for intérieur, Actes du colloque AFSP/, CURAPP*, 206–213, Presses universitaires de France.
Morgan, D. (2006). Not Gay Enough for the Government: Racial and Sexual Stereotypes in Sexual Orientation Asylum Cases. *Law and Sexuality, 15*, 135–161.
Noiriel, G. (1991). *La Tyrannie du National. Le droit d'asile en Europe (1793–1993)*. Paris: Calmann-Lévy.
Pham, T., & Reveillère, C. (2015). Les intimes convictions du clinicien. Apports de la recherche en psychologie légale. *Annales Médico-Psychologiques, 173*, 597–600.
Schuster, L. (2003). *The Use and Abuse of Political Asylum in Britain and Germany*. London: Frank Cass.
Traïni, C. (2010). Des sentiments aux émotions (et vice-versa). Comment devient-on militant de la cause animale? *Revue française de science politique, 60*(2), 335–358.
Valluy, J. (2004). La fiction juridique de l'asile. *Plein Droit, 63*, 17–22.
Valluy, J. (2009). *Rejet des exiles: Le grand retournement du droit d'asile*. Bellecombe-en-Bauges: Editions du Croquant.
Zolberg, A. (1983). The Formation of New States as a Refugee Generating Process. *Annals of the American Academy of Political and Social Science, 467*, 24–38.

Open Access This chapter is distributed under the terms of the Creative Commons Attribution 4.0 International License (http://creativecommons.org/licenses/by/4.0/), which permits use, duplication, adaptation, distribution and reproduction in any medium or format, as long as you give appropriate credit to the original author(s) and the source, a link is provided to the Creative Commons license and any changes made are indicated.

The images or other third party material in this chapter are included in the work's Creative Commons license, unless indicated otherwise in the credit line; if such material is not included in the work's Creative Commons license and the respective action is not permitted by statutory regulation, users will need to obtain permission from the license holder to duplicate, adapt or reproduce the material.

4

"It's All About Naming Things Right": The Paradox of Web Truths in the Belgian Asylum-Seeking Procedure

Massimiliano Spotti

Introduction

The present paper—part of a larger ethnographic enquiry aimed at documenting and understanding the process of doing asylum seeking in the age of globalisation—deals with the process of identity (mis)recognition that has led to the rejection of an asylum-seeking application. More specifically, the paper documents two things. First, it documents the discrepancy between the story narrated by the poorly educated asylum-seeking applicant (see Danstrøm and Whyte, this volume, for a discussion of the role of narrative in asylum determination) and the type of factual knowledge sought by the officials judging the truthfulness of his identity claim. Second, it documents how the lack of factual knowledge is a product of a discrepancy in naming practices, i.e., the discrepancy between the official naming of things and places of interest drawn by the authorities from the internet—and the locally based naming of things used by the applicant. The case documented here, as well as pointing at the politics of suspicion in the asylum-seeking procedure, also serves the metonymic function of laying bare some of the torn ligaments around the bones of globalisation. It encapsulates how migratory experiences are registered into administrative prescriptive accounts of what someone should say and how someone should name things in order to give proof of identity.

M. Spotti (✉)
Department of Culture Studies, Tilburg School of Humanities and Digital Sciences, Tilburg, The Netherlands
e-mail: m.spotti@tilburguniversity.edu

Globalisation, the EU and the Diversification of Diversity

Globalisation has brought about an intensification of the worldwide mobility of goods and information, but also of human beings. Asylum-seeking is one of the by-products of this mobility and it links local happenings to (political) events occurring many miles away. The EU and the 'floods of asylum seekers' that try to reach its soil are no exception to this. Yet, the migrants who knock at the EU's doors pose a problem to border control authorities in that they cannot anymore conceptualise migrants as people engaged in a linear move 'from the rest to the West' (Hall 1992). Rather, these globalised migratory flows are at present one of the most tangible testimonies of super-diversity. That is, rather than falling into the 'ethnic minority paradigm' of an earlier era in migration studies, they embody what Vertovec terms, in its hyphenated version, the 'diversification of diversity'. That is, a process in which diversity moves beyond ethnic minority group membership and boundaries and gives way to 'an increased number of new, small and scattered, multiple-origin, transnationally connected, socio-economically differentiated and legally stratified immigrants' (Vertovec 2007: 124). It follows that present day diversity calls for all sorts of urgent interventions that Europe, its member states and their institutions will have to face. There is the question of border control at both European as well as nation-state level. Further, there is the question of nation-states confronted with obligations to their citizens in their asylum-seeking politics, policies and practices and last, there is the question of securitisation of borders that brings up issues of institutional framing of the identities of the newly arrived migrants within a regime of suspicion. In reaction to the above, the EU engages in deploying strenuous efforts to safeguard its maritime shores and territorial borders. Typical of these efforts are those measures that set up—to borrow Bigo's terminology (2008)—a 'ban-opticon', that is, a means for channeling mobilities, modulating their intensities, speed, mode of movement and coagulation through measures of surveillance. Language is also an element taken up for surveillance administered at the institutional gates of each nation-state, e.g. the testing and consequent measurement of someone's proficiency in the language of the host country (see for instance Kurvers and Spotti 2015) but also in the language of the country of origin (see for instance Spotti 2015). Shibboleths of securitisation, however, are also present once the asylum-seeking migrant manages to enter the EU. When entered, in fact, nation-state based institutional bodies are put in place with the task of gathering information about someone's history of migration and of assessing the truthfulness of his/her narratives on the basis of a search in the applicant's narrative for tangible, factual, proofs of identity. As Craig and Zwaan note (this volume), it is not only the responsibility of the asylum seeker but also the determining state to gather such evidence. These proofs of identity rest on the 'ergoic'[1] equation that, *if* you know facts X and Y, *then* you really ought to be from place Z and thus be who you claim to be.

With this backdrop in mind, the present paper focuses on a rejected asylum-seeking application in Flanders, Belgium. The story concerns an unschooled illiterate young man, whom for the sake of argument here we call Bashir, who claims to be from a particular country and more specifically from a specific city within it. The letter of rejection of his asylum-seeking application, a by-product of the bureaucratic production of textual artefacts within the Belgian asylum-seeking procedure, is our key text here. After dealing with language in intercultural and multilingual institutional encounters like the one of asylum, this chapter presents an analysis of Bashir's life story, appropriately anonymised, and of the letter of rejection that he had received from the authorities assessing his application during the time in which I was carrying out my ethnographic interpretive fieldwork. We then tease apart the motivations that led the authorities to conclude that Bashir was not the nationality that he claimed to be and, in so doing, we focus more closely on the practice of naming places and the internet. It is when the referents encounter an institutional figure, for example, a police officer enquiring about their conduct and asking for their name and proof of identity, that naming becomes a verifiable matter. A matter that brings along with itself the issue of identity as it can lead to identity (mis)recognition and dismissal. Along this line, the analysis I present confronts and compares Bashir's story and practice of naming with the information gathered by the institutional figures that are in charge of assessing his application. This is further confronted with an interview carried out with another refugee from the same country, whom I call Majid, and who is used here as *tertium comparationis* in that he knew Bashir and his case. The implications of Bashir's case—as the analysis and its interpretation point out—are both analytical and societal. They are analytical in that they display the influence of the web and its authority in the process of asylum approval and with that the discrepancy between the web-based (toponymic) knowledge that the immigration authorities expect to hear from the applicant and the local register used

---

[1]The term 'ergoic' is an adjectivisation of the latin causative conjunction *ergo* meaning in English 'therefore'.

for the naming of places. They are societal in that they show how a discrepancy between applicant and authorities in the form of knowing and naming places is taken to be a valid proof that corroborates the politics of suspicion (Bohmer and Shuman 2018) that characterise the institutional side of asylum seeking applications in present day Europe.

Asylum, Institutional Encounters and the Authority of the Web

Although nation-states across Europe have their own idiosyncratic differences in dealing with asylum seeking applications (UNHCR 2013), the sociolinguistic, sociological and discursive processes that are embedded in this procedure have already awakened the interest of several disciplines ranging from sociolinguistics to discourse studies to the sociology of transnationalism (Blommaert 2005; Marijns 2006; Fiddian-Qasmiyeh et al. 2014). For instance, among the procedures studied, there are the institutional encounters between authorities and the applicant, who has to prove the truthfulness of his migration story, of his origin, and through that give tangible proof of identity. In the gamut of organisations involved in serving asylum seekers and supporting them in their claims, we see that the encounter with the institutional reality that will have to assess their application is still central. It is the institutional environment where the interview with the applicant will take place—which functions as an extension of the nation-state authority— that imposes its language norms, literacy norms and requirements of factual knowledge upon an applicant engaged in telling his/her migration and asylum story. Straightforward as it may seem, the encounter between the authorities on the one hand and an applicant on the other gives birth to a complex sociolinguistic environment. As Jacquemet points out in his work (2011, 2013), these institutional encounters become *loci* of trans-idiomatic practices, that is, *loci* where multilingualism is the common currency and where the multilingual interactions between the authorities and the applicant are made even more complex by the digital interfaces that both applicants and authorities use during their encounter. As I show later in this text, on the side of institutional authorities, we often find the use of available web-based resources dealing with the country of origin the claimant claims to come from. On the side of the claimant, in contrast, we often find electronically mediated communication and identity profiles, e.g. through social media channels, that aim at corroborating identity claims (Huysmans 2014).

The Belgian Asylum Procedure

According to the Dublin Regulation, the asylum applications for which Belgium is responsible are transferred to the *Commissariaat General voor de Vluchtelingen en de Staatslozen* (henceforth CGVS). The CGVS, an independent administrative authority, is exclusively specialised in asylum decision-making. In a single procedure, it examines first whether the applicant fulfils the eligibility criteria for refugee status and whether they are eligible for subsidiary protection status. The CGVS holds four competences. It grants or refuses refugee status or subsidiary protection status. It decides on the admissibility of asylum applications of EU citizens, persons from a safe country of origin or persons already having obtained refugee status in an EU Member State that is still effective, and of subsequent applications. It applies cessation and exclusion clauses or revokes refugee or subsidiary protection status (including on the instance of the Minister). It confirms or rejects the refugee status of a refugee recognised in another country. Last, it rejects asylum applications for technical reasons and issues civil status certificates for recognised refugees. There is no provision in Belgian law imposing an obligation on the CGVS to take a decision within a given time in the regular procedure. Given that Bashir's case came to a resolution in 2012, it is worth looking at the regulations that were in place in Flanders and Belgium more generally during 2012, when Bashir had his institutional encounters with the CGVS.

At the beginning of 2012, the then Secretary of State for Asylum and Migration declared in the Belgian parliament that it was her intention to provide for a quick and high quality procedure that allowed applicants to have an answer within an average timeframe of 3 months at first instance or 6 months including a final decision on appeal. To achieve this, the "Last-In-First-Out" (LIFO) principle was introduced. This meant that priority was given to handling the most recent asylum applications, and the capacity of the asylum authorities was reinforced with an extra 100 (temporary) staff. This resulted in a considerable shortening of the total processing time of new asylum applications and a higher overall output that year. New applications lodged in 2012 were processed on an average of 80 calendar days. Although laudable when taking into account the backlog of older files (i.e. one or two years old), the average processing time was still 291 days at the end of 2013.

Studies that, from an ethnographic interpretive perspective, have investigated encounters between asylum seeking applicants and authorities show that language is a key feature—but not the only feature—of such institutional encounters. Rather, it always involves a communicative event that sees the production of a 'text' about the identity of the applicant. The communicative event—either through oral, written or pictographic modes of communication (see Johnston 2008: 21–41)—draws on linguistic communicative proofs, i.e., which languages do you speak? How well have you mastered them? What do you not know of that language? However, it also draws on the factual knowledge the applicant holds (Blommaert 2001: 413–449) about the place he claims to come from. The text being produced by the applicant and the authorities during the institutional encounter of the long interview therefore serves the purpose of substantiating someone's application and it does so by having the applicant match the expectations of the factual knowledge the applicant holds and can produce about the place s/he claims to come from. It is worth noting though that these encounters and the communicative events happening around the asylum adjudication do not only take place off line. Rather, as Jacquemet explains (2014: 201–202), the asylum procedure and its protagonists are part of a late-modern communicative revolution in which the technological development that grants the retrieval of information about a country or about a language spoken in a given country become tangible proofs of truthfulness, something I call here *web-truths*. In particular, examining a case of asylum in contemporary institutional realities, means that the analyst has to account for the implications brought to bear by the digitalisation of information, where digital information is overlaid, confronted and used to measure the first hand off line information presented by the applicant. It is therefore impossible to neglect that an asylum applicant, and those institutional figures called on to assess his case, cannot escape the power of technologies and the fact that these online aids hold a strong influence on the assessment of a case. Failure to recognise this can lead to disastrous consequences of communication breakdown due to intercultural havoc and identity dismissal leading to an application rejection.

Such a heavily institutionalised process of acceptance or rejection involves several stages of text production and manipulation. First, there is the text that an applicant prepares—often orally together with other asylum applicants—before the interview with the authorities. Then there is the life-story text authored by the applicant during the long interview, an institutional encounter that has as its main purpose the gathering of the applicant's migration history and motivation for filing a request for asylum. This text production process, often taking place either in a language that may serve as *lingua franca* or through the mediation of an interpreter (Inghilleri 2010), also sees the authorities involved in the entextualisation of the applicant's story into a format, that of the legal case, that fits institutional preset narrative criteria. It is then the turn of the authorities to produce a transcription of the (recorded) long interview carried out with the applicant. It is this transcription then—an interesting trans-idiomatic textual product in its own right (Jacquemet 2009)—that once assessed turns into yet another institutional text; that of an official letter, redacted for the case of Belgium in either Dutch or French, spelling out the reasons that have led either to accept or reject the application. This decision letter—in our case a letter of rejection—serves the purpose of illustrating what it means to be an asylum seeker within the globalised politics of suspicion in Belgian Flanders.

Method

This study, part of a larger ethnographic interpretive inquiry entitled *Asylum 2.0*, builds on data collected through three rounds of sites visit aimed at shedding light on what it means to do asylum seeking in an age of globalisation both on and offline. In approaching this theme, I did ethnographic interpretive fieldwork at an asylum-seeking centre in Flanders, the Dutch speaking part of Belgium. The data for this case study were collected between the 13 and the 26 October 2012, during my first field visits to the centre. My position at the centre was that of a buffer zone between the staff and the guests. In fact, when asked by the guests—asylum applicants—who I was and what exactly I was doing there, I candidly explained to them that I was engaged in writing a book about what it means to be an asylum seeker and what asylum seeking implies, and that I was there to document their daily lives. All the participants embraced my doings and none of them opted out; rather they reacted enthusiastically to being made to feel that their lives mattered and that there was somebody interested in them and their experiences. Living along with them, having breakfast with them, talking to them while drinking endless cups of sweetened Afghani tea, following their daily doings that ranged from Dutch language lessons to knitting lessons, to gym activities to simply hanging around at the centre kicking a ball about in the evenings. In other words, what I did was deep hanging out in the cultural ecology of this institutional space. The project, in its ethnographic approach, combines insights, methods and epistemological as well as ontological stances stemming from linguistic ethnography (Blackledge and Creese 2009; Blommaert 2010; Rampton and Tusting 2007; Copland and Creese 2015) and socio-culturally rooted discourse analysis (Gee 1999). In both frameworks, there is the underlying assumption that the way individuals speak as well as speak about things reflects their culturally embedded understanding and their perception of the world.

The centre, located in a formal cloister, has big rooms assigned to families and rooms assigned either to pairs of male or female individuals, on a first come first served basis. Rather than using a nationality based criterion or an ethnic grouping criterion, the director of the centre had opted—where he and his team members felt it not to be a risk—to put together people of different ethnic, linguistic and religious backgrounds. In October 2012, while I was engaged in my ethnographic fieldwork, the centre catered for 61 guests, an odd term used in the official jargon quoted by its director so to signify hospitality and inclusion (see also Gill 2016). Following the information gathered at the centre during intake talks, its guests were from the following (often pre-supposed) nationality backgrounds: 13 from Afghanistan; 12 from 'The Russian Federation'—mostly from Armenia and Chechnya—nine from West Africa; nine from Bangladesh; seven from the Democratic Republic of Congo. The remaining 11 guests originated from what have been categorised as 'other countries' (*andere herkomstlanden*) in the unofficial statistics of the centre including various African countries, China - allegedly from Tibet - Albania and Ukraine. 40 of these guests were male, 21 were female. 11 of them were unaccompanied minors, though three of them still needed to give age-proof through bone scans. Only one guest had entered the centre in 2010 while the rest had entered in 2011 or 2012. Only two guests had passed their 50s, confirming the trend that seeking asylum is mostly a practice for either unaccompanied minors or young (often male) applicants ranging from their early 20s to their late 30s. All names given in this case study are pseudonyms so as to grant participants protection and privacy, and where necessary dates and locations have been removed. My chats with them were informal although I wrote synopses of the topics and the key points we discussed. Although video recording was not possible, audio recording happened when I felt a talk I just had was particularly interesting and revealed a facet of doing asylum seeking. In that case, guests were asked whether they felt like telling me their story again while being audio recorded. Access to their files—granted by the centre director and by the applicants—has helped me shed light on the same people but this time not from their first-hand lived perspective of doing asylum but through the legal lens that investigates the applicant during the whole procedure. Here too, guests at the centre were told of my access to their procedural files and were given the opportunity to either agree or disagree with it. None of them though disagreed.

Bashir's Asylum Application

Before we enter Bashir's life story as presented to us by the authorities in their rejection of his application, we must first make a very basic point. On the one hand, Bashir's life story is a narration put together by someone who is a young adult, who has gone through violent events that have characterised his country of origin and, in particular, his family. Further, this is the story of someone who—like many other asylum applicants—was asked to produce a coherent factual narrative about his country of origin and place of living. Although this request may seem to any literate individual an easy one to match, this person has no formal schooling in any language and—on top of it all—has very limited reading and writing skills in the Latin script through which all institutional documents are mediated. On the other hand, Bashir can read the Qu'ran because he received Qu'ranic schooling. We further have to picture his life history at a time and at a place of political tensions that have had severe repercussions within his family. The texts we present and use as primary data sources are extracts taken from the letter that sums up the findings that have emerged from Bashir's narrative during the long interview in which the CGVS asked him to give evidence of his identity as a [Bashir's nationality] from [major city in Bashir's country of origin]. It was impossible for me to gain direct access to the actual interview or to the immediate transcription produced by the CGVS. This means that the object of our analysis is the letter that the applicant, Bashir, received. In the letter at hand, typewritten and signed by a representative of the Belgian immigration authorities, we find first the negative result of Bashir's application, followed by a detailed overview that reports the grounds upon which Bashir's rejection has taken place. This letter, though, is not only a document but also the product of a long and complex process of entextualisation. The letter funnels the findings that emerged during the long interview and renders Bashir's rejection indisputable in that it is based on a lack of factual knowledge. Because the asylum procedure is a matter of assessing someone's claims of origin, origin being understood as a Cartesian matter of direct matching between applicants' knowledge and their identity claims: for example, you know fact X hence you are truly from place Y, its lack has led the authorities to the conclusion that Bashir's story had to be truly false. As in every epistolary exchange, so in this one there is an addresser, i.e. the CGVS, and an addressee, i.e. the unschooled illiterate Bashir. It being in French and Bashir being illiterate in this language, the letter had to be read out to him by his roommate Majid, a young man who came from a well-educated preacher's family in Bashir's country of origin. The text of the letter sent by the authorities runs as follows:

Of XXXX[2] nationality and [ethnicity 1] ethnic origin through your mother and [ethnicity 2] through your father, you arrived on Belgian soil on XXXX and made a request next day for asylum XXXX.

You invoke the following facts in support of your asylum application:

Your father is [ethnicity 2] and your mother is [ethnicity 1]. The respective families of your parents wanted them to separate because of their different ethnicity. On XXXX, your father was stabbed by some members of your maternal family. You took your father to the XXXX hospital, but since it was late and the service was closed, the doctors made you wait until the next day. Your father died the next morning. Also since that day, you have not seen your brother who went looking for medicine for your father. During XXXX, your mother's brothers said they would kill you. You and your mother did not dare to return home and lived outside. On XXXX, your mother entrusted you to XXXX, [an official] who was your father's friend. You stayed at the home of this person until XXXX, the day you left [your country of origin]. (Rejection letter BK, fieldwork 8.10.2012)

As the passage above shows, the letter starts with Bashir's national and ethnic identity affiliation as somebody of [country] nationality. The letter further states that Bashir is offspring to a [ethnicity 2] father and a [ethnicity 1] mother. While going through the text, we see that Bashir's story serves as testimony of the profound division amongst two major ethnic groups in Bashir's country of origin, a division that is deeply entrenched in Bashir's family and in its misfortunes. Bashir's maternal side of the family was in profound disagreement with Bashir's father, and there was pressure for his parents to separate due to their ethnic backgrounds, which at the time was also associated with the political conflicts tearing apart the country. The inner family tensions had escalated to an episode of violence when Bashir's father was stabbed by his mother's siblings. After having been taken to a major hospital, in the centre of the city where this occurred, his father passed away due to the injuries received. Bashir reported that after his father's burial he got threatened by his mother's siblings. Because of this Bashir and his mother never went back to their home, and soon afterwards Bashir's mother had given him into the custody of an official who had been friendly with his father. Bashir then stayed at the official's place until he helped Bashir leave the country. His asylum application was received in Brussels and examined two and a half months later. His hearing at the CGVS took place in the

---

[2]Here and hereafter the 'XXXX's are included to protect the confidentiality of the subject.

same year. Below we find another excerpt taken from CGVS' letter of rejection that reads as follows:

> Next, while you said that you have lived all your life in the neighbourhood of XXXX, which is located in the municipality of XXXX, you were only able to mention four neighbourhoods in this municipality (see p. 14) and were not able to specify in which neighbourhood of XXXX you lived (see p. 13) although there are four: XXXX I, XXXX II, XXXX Mosque and XXXX Pharmacy. Next, you said that you slept with your mother for 10 days in a mosque, but you were unable to name it (see p. 13). Likewise, you could not give the name of any large mosque in [city] which is astonishing insofar as you say you studied the Qu'ran every day and that [a large mosque], is in front of the hospital where you claim to have taken your father (see the documents attached to your administrative file: XXXX published on XXXX.com, map from Google Maps, and article XXXX published on petitfute.com). In addition, although you could accurately quote the name of the most widespread bottled water, the currency used in [country], the [name of the governmental headquarters], the names of two mobile operators, and say what a "[specific musical instrument used in the region]" is (see pp. 15, 16), you were however unable to describe the [nationality] flag correctly or give the name of the [nationality] football team. Likewise, although you say you used to go to the market with your father (p. 7), you were not able to name it and when asked if you knew the names of the markets, you were content to answer "this is called 'in the city'" (see p. 15). Next, you said that you watched television (see p. 10), but you were unable to give the name of any [nationality] channel, saying that you watched "[same nationality] TV channels. And also movies. I listen to music" (see p. 15). He[3] then asked you if you knew the name of the large football stadium in [city], to which you answered in the negative and said that a site is currently under construction [elsewhere] (see p. 15).

The original text of the rejection letter is in French, French being the procedural language through which the authorities corresponded with Bashir. Although I could not be present at the interview, there is no indication of the presence of an interpreter, which makes me assume that the interview took place in French, this being the working language of communication

---

[3] The 'he' here could either be referring to the interviewer or to a possible interpreter that might have been present to facilitate the interview process.

between the interviewee and the authorities. This text authored by the CGVS is an evaluation as well as a response to Bashir's story. Its main aim is to point out the lack of factual knowledge and inaccuracy Bashir showed when answering the questions posed by the CGVS' officers during the long interview. The above text, in summary, takes the form of a checklist. More specifically, a checklist that recaps the information that Bashir managed and did not manage to produce and that ended up disqualifying him as someone from the country in question and more precisely from the specific city Bashir claimed to be from. Bashir's knowledge fell short when he was asked to name which of four areas he lived in.[4] This lack of knowledge was compounded by Bashir's not knowing the (official) name of any big mosque in the city, a lack of knowledge deemed astounding (*etonnant*) as Bashir claimed to have studied the Qu'ran every day, although without being specific on the whereabouts of his studies. Further, this astonishment came from the fact that a large, well-known Mosque—is located right in front of the hospital where Bashir had brought his badly beaten father (information about this mosque used by the authorities, however, is the official information available from the internet, including its official name). The link the authorities make in the text above is ergoic and runs as follows. If you really studied the Qu'ran then it means you should have studied in a mosque. Further, if you are really from the city in question you should be able to give the official name of the mosque you used to attend. Given that you cannot do so and given that—as we have retrieved from the internet—this mosque is large and well-known, then we can cast serious doubts on the truthfulness of your identity claims. The case of the naming of the mosque is of further interest because the authorities rely here on web based information that uses the official name of this mosque. The first one is a web site giving news about the country; the second is Google maps; and the third and most intriguing one, is petitfute.com—a website that gives handy tips to French speaking tourists wishing to explore far away exotic countries.

The testing of Bashir's factual knowledge that serves to prove his 'indigenousness' (or lack thereof) continues. As we read, Bashir was able to produce the name of the bottled water most sold in the country. He further was able to name the money used in the country and to explain what the specific musical instrument used in the region is, the name of at least two mobile networks operating in the country as well as the official name of the

---

[4]The city in question is divided into what we shall call wards, with each ward consisting of more than one neighbourhood.

governmental headquarters. However, he failed to describe correctly the flag, or to name an unspecified football team. The final disproof of identity was his inability to name the market where he went with his father as well as the proper name of any market in the city, where he replied "this is called 'in the city'". He further did not know the name of any national TV channels to which question Bashir responded "the [national] TV stations and also movies and listening to music", an answer that seems more apt to answer a question about his favorite pastimes. Last, he did not know the name of the big football stadium in the city. As explained in the final part of the letter, all these questions were considered manageable for someone of Bashir's age and educational level.

A Chat with Bashir's Roommate

Given that Bashir relied almost blindly on Majid, a fellow guest at the centre who is also from Bashir's country, I did hang out with them both quite often. After Bashir had left, I decided to have a chat with Majid about Bashir's rejection, as he was the one who had read the rejection letter out to Bashir because Bashir could barely read Latin script. Majid comes from a well-known Quranic preachers' family in the city in question. Majid's application—corroborated by his physical impediment—had already been approved by the CGVS. Being aware that this could also have led to the discussion of sensitive information, I obtained Majid's consent to have an informal chat with him first. After that, I asked him whether it was fine that I taped him. In what follows, I present two extracts in English from my conversation with Majid, which took place in French. The first extract deals with Majid having to speak to Bashir's mother on a mobile phone. The episode runs as follows:

Extract 1

> *Majid*: One day Bashir came into the room.
> *Max*: hm
> *Majid*: He called his mother.
> *Max*: hm
> *Majid*: So, his mother asked him whether he did his prayers
> *Max*: hm
> *Majid*: Daily
> *Max*: Yes, yes, yes
> *Majid*: He said yes (but) his mother did not trust him.

Max: Right!

Majid: He gave me [...] to reassure his mother, he gave me the phone, so I had occasion to talk to his mother, so I then I spoke to his mother. So when I spoke to his mother, she asked me directly [...].

Max: Sorry I don't understand.

Majid: She told me, my origin is [Bashir's nationality], I, I [...] I, myself, have been born in XXXX, she told me, I myself am originally from [town in the country in question].

Max: From [same town] what, you?

Majid: Yes, she told me Ah! Me too I am from [same town], which family in [same town] do you come from? Which family? The [X]'s family. So she said fine, I know them, the [inaudible], that family is well known there, and I believe you.

Max: Well known?

Majid: Well known.

Max: Okay, your family, his family?

Majid: My family.

Max: Your family.

Majid: So, we spoke, she asked me whether Bashir was doing okay and whether he said his prayers, and whether he did this while I was there, because I [inaudible] here, so I do every [inaudible]

Max: hm

In the above, although the reported speech centres around Bashir's mother making sure that her son has done his daily prayers, we see more things emerging. The mother of Bashir, who is from the country that Bashir is from, claiming to be from a town of 15,000 people over 100 kilometers away from the capital city and coming to trust Majid because of him being the son of a well known family there. The conversation unfolds as follows:

Extract 2

Max: But, but also, Bashir's language, you told me that Bashir's language is not the same as the one reported on the letter (the letter from the CGVS: MS).

Majid: No, I have said, I did not confirm that he does not come from there, I say that he does not speak the language spoken there.

Max: He does not speak the language spoken there?

Majid: Exactly, he speaks better the language of the capital, the XXXX language.

Max: Oh, yeah?

Majid: Me too, I speak better XXXX then my mother tongue, the language of my mother and of my father, because I grew up in [city], you are forced to speak that language. But I speak French well too, that's better here in Belgium.

Max: Is [it] very different from your mother's and father's language?

Majid: Yes, very different, *very* different, very very different, there is no link between my language, but the language of [inaudible], the other is the language of the market…

Max: Hm, of [tradespeople].

Majid: Yes, people who [trade].

Max: Oh right, so that is XXXX.

Majid: Yes.

Max: Okay, but, but, but, but […] but I spoke to Bashir, once or twice and his French is way different than your French.

Majid: But yes, of course, it is not the same thing, I myself have studied, I have finished my studies, Bashir has not been to school.

Max: He has not been to school?

Majid: He entered school here.

Max: Oh yeah?

Majid: Yes! I am convinced [of that: MS] because it is me, to whom he went to, when there was a letter to send or to read he asks me whether I can read it for him. He knows absolutely nothing in French.

Max: Absolutely nothing. Oh yeah?

Majid: Yes!

Max: Okay, okay, so writing is also extremely difficult for Bashir, right?

Majid: No! He cannot write!

Max: hm.

Majid: The papers are negative.

Max: Yes, I know.

Majid: There you go. For him the motivation, they have asked him how many [wards], there are in [the city in question] […].

Max: Yes, I know, I know, I have seen the report.

Majid: There you are. He started to recite the [neighbourhoods within a particular ward] and he did not understand.

Max: Right, right.

Majid: He did not understand the difference between [wards] and [neighbourhoods]

Max: He did not understand the difference, hm

Majid: Between [wards] and [neighbourhoods]. But it has only to do with the fact that Bashir has not gone to school and not because Bashir does not come from [the country in question].

Max: Hm, okay, okay.

Majid: The same thing goes for everything, the mosque, the market. The market is at the centre of town so for him that is 'town' and the mosque, well, that is one big Mosque, but there at home we call it the big mosque.

Extract 2 shows how close Bashir was to Majid, asking him to read or write letters on his behalf implied a high level of trust. Second, we discover that Bashir, because of his lack of schooling, did not know certain (basic) notions like the difference between [wards] and [neighbourhoods]. Even more interesting is Majid's insight into Bashir's language repertoire. Aside from claiming that Bashir's proficiency in French is very limited, French being the language in which the report was written and in which Bashir had decided to give his answers during the interview, we find also another interesting sociolinguistic element. That is—following Majid's own self-reported language proficiency and meta-linguistic judgement on Bashir's language repertoire—Bashir is mostly proficient in another language, a language that one who grows up in the city in question would know. This language stems from the same language family as Bashir's father's language. Although I did not have a chance to gather data on Bashir's own sociolinguistic repertoire as he had already left the centre, Bashir's reported sociolinguistic repertoire and the lack of schooling give an interesting insight into what might have gone missing with the naming of things during the interview which was fully carried out in French. Aside from the issue of the language in which Bashir was mostly proficient, it is also interesting to notice Bashir's failure to differentiate between [ward] and [neighbourhood], as well as his inability to give the proper names for the market and mosque, all things that did not surprise Majid. In Extract 2, the names Bashir gave to places like the market and the mosque—which Majid too refers to as 'the big mosque' (*la grand Mosquee*)—are reported to be common naming practices 'there at home'. Naming practices that do not match the register the CGVS' authorities draw on through their web-gathered information.

It Is All About Naming Things Right

As shown in the extract above, as well as in the letter explaining Bashir's rejection, much of the doubt cast by the authorities on Bashir's identity comes not only from his incapacity to articulate knowledge about the city in which he grew up, but also from his inability to name places correctly. Although Bashir's lack of knowledge could easily be attributed to what McDermott names inarticulateness:

> [S]ituations that organise inarticulateness are legion, and it is easy to name the most obvious occasions. Funerals, police inquiries, job interviews, class and race border encounters, tax interrogations, sex talk with children, group therapy, television interviews, and first dates - all are potential tongue-stoppers. A folk account would have it that whenever our words can be immediately consequential and long remembered, the pressure can get to us, and new heights of eloquence and new lows of inarticulateness are frequent. (McDermott 1988: 38–40)

The ambiguous relationship between names and the things they refer to, e.g., places, has been a matter of interest for linguistic anthropology for decades and it has informed inquiries into the question of whether the name of a given thing is given from the point of view of the individual or of the collective. The relationship is not just reflective: rather there are processes of enregisterment at play that construct the practice of naming as local knowledge praxis. Given that enregisterment is the sociolinguistic process through which someone establishes the desire to be recognised as a specific someone (see Agha 2003; Karrebaek 2011), we shift the analysis here from differences *between* 'languages' to differences *within* languages, e.g., 'ways of speaking', 'ways of narrating', and 'ways of naming things'. In sum, we take a close look at all those bits *within* language that make someone part of the appropriate register of belonging in that s/he narrates things the way they should be narrated and s/he names things the way they should be named. Bashir's letter exemplifies that it is not only the process of naming but within that the process of enregistering (Agha 2003: 231–235) the names of things, like a mosque, in the way the authority wishes to hear them. More specifically, the process of naming is not solely an arbitrary process of making denotational and connotational meaning match one another. Rather, the process of naming comes with a history of use (inter-textuality), as well as with a history of sociocultural evaluation and assessment (a notion termed pre-textuality by Marijns and Blommaert 2002: 13). In the case of proper names, as Agha shows (2003: 247), the speech chain structure in which the action of naming is involved serves to maintain the coupling of a name with a referent, e.g., the association of a certain name with a given person or object. The fact that a name refers to that specific person or object is, at first, something shared by those who were involved in the immediate naming ceremony, e.g., an inauguration. It is then through the process of name transmission across socio-cultural networks, that other members become acquainted with somebody's or something's proper name even though they were not present at the naming ceremony. The naming ceremony therefore produces a continuous speech chain that needs neither to be attended to or verified but that needs to be known by those who claim to belong to that network.

To link the above to my data, I refer to the different registers of naming public spaces of interest in the city in question drawn upon by the authorities and by Bashir, bearing in mind the specific reference to the naming of the mosque Bashir claimed to have attended while following Qu'ranic classes. In the case of the co-presence of a speaker, in this case an individual naming things, and of a hearer, in this case an authority figure hearing how things are named, the issue of matching register is key to understanding the breakdown reported by the authorities in this letter of rejection. Unfortunately, I could not be present at that interview nor could I get hold of the whole transcript of the interview as it was not in possession of the asylum-seeking centre. However, the text of the rejection letter reported in Fig. 1 and 2 and the counter evidence provided by Majid are both very telling. They show how Bashir repeatedly fails to match the register that is expected from him that is, the official register he should draw upon in order to have his voice recognised by the authority as indexing his indigeneity, an indigeneity embodied in the naming of things in the right way. In other words, what emerges from the letter is an act of (web-based) misrecognition in which the CGVS—an institution that clearly operates on behalf of the State—sees a lack of verification of the identity of the applicant. As Benedict Anderson states in his work on nations as imagined communities (1993), this register of talking about a nation embodies a set of prescriptions of what *the other under scrutiny* should say and know in order to have his identity match what the authorities believe that someone who is indigenous should say and know.

Conclusions

As Shannahan puts it (2015: 77), institutional interviews for asylum assessment are places where the voice of the asylum-seeking applicant—not proficient in French—finds itself confronted with the institutional voice—in French or at least in one of its vernacular varieties—produced by the officer(s) that is assessing the case. The communicative situation that unfolds is expected to follow clear patterns of questioning as well as clear patterns of understanding and answering along the institutionally favoured matrix of what is considered valid proof of 'country talk'. Consequently, the applicant does not only need to understand the language that is being spoken and what is being spoken about, but—in order to fit the institutionally held frame of valid knowledge (cf. Bohmer and Shuman 2008: 7)—must also strive to match the register used by those who are asking the questions. These registers, within the social interactions involved in the asylum interview, play a significant role in the processes of origin assessment, in that they enable the authorities to determine the applicant's identity according to the attributes of their story. As Goffman warns us:

> [W]e lean on anticipations that we have, transforming them into normative expectations, into righteously presented demands. [...] It is when an active question arises [as to whether these demands will be filled] that we are likely to realise that all along we had been making certain assumptions as to what the individual before us ought to know to be members of a society. (Goffman 1963: 2)

The letter has been analysed as a text that encapsulates a complex sociolinguistic event. Further, it has been rendered into a bureaucratic text by the authorities, that is, a text that homogenises what someone of Bashir's age and educational level is expected to know about the country he claims to be coming from. Yet as Gee reminds us:

> The fact that people have differential access to different identities and activities, connected to different sorts of status and social goods, is a root source of inequality in society. [...] Since different identities and activities are enacted in and through language, the study of language is integrally connected to matters of equity and justice. (Gee 1999: 13)

The naming register used to define markets and mosques, or everyday items like money, are models of knowledge that link naming to indigeneity, leading to the socio-cultural recognition of the applicant as someone who is telling the truth. To rage against the bureaucratic oddity that is at the core of this study is of very little use. Rather Bashir's case evaluation shows a glimpse of the valence of factual information for the assessment of identity claims in an asylum-seeking procedure (Ochs and Capps 1996: 417–419, deals with the indexical value of language). That is, the valence of Bashir's claim is based on the complex associative networks that underpin the ideological expectations of what someone who claims to be from a certain place should know about that place and in particular, how he should express this knowledge. Further, what this paper has shown is not only evidence of how the emergence of register discrepancy gives way to misrecognition of identity claims. It also shows how identity is local knowledge dependent and it challenges someone's authenticity where this authenticity is being judged by a different institutional matrix of knowledge. It is the matching or mismatching of the above that determines who may speak, what they may speak about, and, in particular, how they may speak about their own life history of migration. As in so many other domains of contemporary social life, language turns out to be a problem in the asylum procedure. The denial of its inter-lingual as well as intra-lingual complexity is a source of rather fundamental, though often invisible, injustice. The straightforward anchoring of a personal identity, a process fraught with complications even in homogeneous communities of people belonging to a single national entity, cannot and should not be taken for granted in asylum seeking procedures even when its demarcation seems to be helped by the omnipresent authority of the web.

References

Agha, A. (2003). The Social Life of Cultural Values. *Language & Communication, 23,* 231–273.

Anderson, B. (1993). *Imagined Communities: Reflections on the Origin and Spread of Nationalism.* London: Verso.

Bigo, D. (2008). Globalised (In)Security: The field and the Ban-opticon. In D. Bigo & A. Tsoukala (Eds.), *Terror, Insecurity and Liberty. Illiberal Practices of Liberal Regimes After 9/11* (pp. 10–48). Abingdon: Routledge.

Blackledge, A., & Creese, A. (2009). Meaning-Making as Dialogic Process: Official and Carnival Lives in the Language Classroom. *Journal of Language, Identity and Education, 8*(4), 236–253.

Blommaert, J. (2001). Investigating Narrative Inequality: African Asylum Seekers' Stories in Belgium. *Discourse and Society, 12*(4), 413–449.

Blommaert, J. (2005). *Discourse: A Critical Introduction.* Cambridge: Cambridge University Press.

Blommaert, J. (2010). *The Sociolinguistics of Globalization.* Cambridge: Cambridge University Press.

Bohmer, C., & Shuman, A. (2008). *Rejecting Refugees: Political Asylum in the 21st Century.* London and New York: Routledge.

Bohmer, C., & Shuman, A. (2018). *Political Asylum Deception: The Culture of Suspicion.* Cham: Palgrave Macmillan.

Copland, F., & Creese, A. (2015). *Linguistic Ethnography—Collecting, Analysing and Presenting Data.* London: Sage.

Fiddian-Qasmiyeh, E., Loescher, G., Long, K., & Sigona, N. (Eds.). (2014). *The Oxford Handbook of Refugee and Forced Migration Studies.* Oxford: Oxford University Press.

Gee, J. (1999). *An Introduction to Discourse Analysis: Theory and Method.* London: Routledge.

Gill, N. (2016). *Nothing Personal? Geographies of Governing and Activism in the British Asylum System.* Oxford: Wiley-Blackwell.

Goffman, E. (1963). *Stigma*. London: Penguin.
Hall, S. (1992). The West and the Rest: Discourse and Power. In S. Hall & B. Gieben (Eds.), *Formations of Modernity* (pp. 275–331). Cambridge: Polity Press.
Huysmans, J. (2014). *Security Unbound*. London: Routledge.
Inghilleri, M. (2010). You Don't Make War Without Knowing Why: The Decision to Interpret in Iraq. *The Translator, 16*(2), 175–196.
Jacquemet, M. (2009). Transcribing Refugees: The Entextualization of Asylum Seekers' Hearings in a Transidiomatic Environment. *Text and Talk, 29*(5), 525–546.
Jacquemet, M. (2011). Crosstalk 2.0. Asylum and Communicative Breakdowns. *Text and Talk, 31*(4), 475–498.
Jacquemet, M. (2013). Transidioma and Asylum: Gumperz's Legacy in Intercultural Institutional Talk. *Journal of Linguistic Anthropology, 23*(3), 199–212.
Jacquemet, M. (2014). Metapragmatics: Gumperz's Legacy in the Study of Language and Power. *Langage et société—John J. Gumperz: De la Dialectologie A LÁntropologie Linguistique, 4*(150), 1–166.
Johnston, B. (2008). *Discourse Analysis* (2nd ed.). Oxford: Wiley.
Karrebaek, M. (2011). "What's in Your Lunch-Box Today?" Health, Ethnicity and Respectability in the Primary Classroom. *Journal of Linguistic Anthropology, 22*(1), 1–22.
Kurvers, J., & Spotti, M. (2015). The Moving Landscape of Dutch Integration Policy: From L1 Literacy Teaching to Literacy in Dutch as Entrance Criterion to the Netherlands. In J. Simpson & A. Whiteside (Eds.), *Adult Language Education and Migration: Challenging Agendas in Policy and Practice* (pp. 175–187). Abingdon: Routledge.
Marijns, K. (2006). *The Asylum Speaker. Language in the Belgian Asylum Procedure*. Northampton, MA: St. Jerome.
Marijns, K., & Blommaert, J. (2002). Pretextuality and Pretextual Gaps: On De/Refining Linguistic Inequality. *Pragmatics, 12*(1), 11–30.
McDermott, R. (1988). Inarticulateness. In D. Tannen (Ed.), *Linguistics in Context: Connecting Observation and Understanding* (pp. 37–68). Norwood, NJ: Able.
Ochs, E., & Capps, L. (1996). Narrating the Self. *Annual Review of Anthropology, 25*(1), 19–43.
Rampton, B. J. M., & Tusting, K. (2007). Linguistic Ethnography: Links, Problems and Possibilities [Special issue]. *Journal of Sociolinguistics, 11*(5), 575–695.
Spotti, M. (2015). *Asylum Seeking, Identity Techniques and the Paradox of Web Truths*. Entry posted on Border Criminologies, Faculty of Law—University of Oxford. Available at: https://www.law.ox.ac.uk/research-subject-groups/centre-criminology/centreborder-criminologies/blog/2014/11/asylum-seeking.
UNHCR. (2013). *Global Trends 2012*. Available at: http://www.unhcr.org/globaltrendsjune2013/.
Vertovec, S. (2007). Super-Diversity and Its Implications. *Ethnic and Racial Studies, 30*(6), 1024–1054.

Open Access This chapter is distributed under the terms of the Creative Commons Attribution 4.0 International License (http://creativecommons.org/licenses/by/4.0/), which permits use, duplication, adaptation, distribution and reproduction in any medium or format, as long as you give appropriate credit to the original author(s) and the source, a link is provided to the Creative Commons license and any changes made are indicated.

The images or other third party material in this chapter are included in the work's Creative Commons license, unless indicated otherwise in the credit line; if such material is not included in the work's Creative Commons license and the respective action is not permitted by statutory regulation, users will need to obtain permission from the license holder to duplicate, adapt or reproduce the material.

5

The World of Home Office Presenting Officers

John R. Campbell

Introduction[1]

While conducting fieldwork on the British asylum system between 2007 and 2009 I was given permission by the Home Office to 'shadow'[2] and interview five Home Office Presenting Officers (HOPOs) who were attached to a London Asylum and Immigration Tribunal (AIT). This presented a rare opportunity to understand the work of an important unit of the Home Office. HOPOs were eager to talk about their work, their insights into the cases they worked on and about their training and careers. The first section provides a brief overview of the role of HOPOs and their work. In the second section I look at a first-tier asylum appeal and a second stage reconsideration appeal to illustrate how HOPOs represent the Home Secretary. The third section briefly examines the views of Immigration Judges about the work of HOPOs. Finally, I pull together the different strands of my

---

[1] Research for this paper was funded by the Economic and Social Council RES-062-23-0296.
[2] I had permission from a London Presenting Officers Unit to follow five HOPOs through a normal work day and to question them about their background, training etc. This was but one part of my fieldwork which involved extensive fieldwork in the Tribunal and the Court of Appeal.

J. R. Campbell (✉)
Department of Anthropology & Sociology, School of Oriental & African Studies, London, England
e-mail: jc58@soas.ac.uk

argument to show how the adversarial nature of asylum appeals and the structural position of HOPOs in the appeal process helps to explain why they are so elusive in the Tribunal and what their work involves.

The Role and Work of HOPOs

HOPO are junior-level civil servants who have either been recruited directly into the civil service to work as HOPOs or they have worked elsewhere in the civil service and have applied to become a HOPO. HOPOs are assigned to a 'Presenting Officers Unit' (POU) that is attached to one of thirteen Tribunals located around the United Kingdom; their task is to represent the Secretary of State for the Home Department (hereafter the SSHD) in all appeals heard by the Tribunal. The number of court/hearing rooms in a Tribunal determines the number of HOPOs assigned to a POU. At the time of my fieldwork there were two POUs in London—Islington and Feltham—which were staffed by 116 and 70 officers respectively (they were supported by 105 and 45 administrative staff, respectively).[3]

The entry requirements for a HOPO depend upon how individuals are recruited: existing civil servants need to arrange a transfer, however new recruits must possess a BA and must pass the civil service examination (all the individuals I interviewed had bachelor degrees, a few had MAs). None of the HOPOs I met had formal legal training. Salary varied with respect to their level of experience: in 2007 salaries ranged from £24,000 to £29,000 p.a. At that time the job was sufficiently interesting and the pay sufficiently good that staff turnover was not a problem.[4] The vast majority of HOPOs are in their mid- 20s or early 30s. There is a preponderance of female staff; most HOPOs have a university degree and have worked as a HOPO for three to five years (a small number have worked in the Home Office for much longer). HOPOs are drawn from a wide range of ethnic groups.

New HOPOs are eased into their jobs. They first undergo an initial ten-day classroom induction course where they are introduced to the main areas of immigration and asylum law, legislation (several major pieces of

---

[3]Information about staffing, training and POUs is taken from replies to my FOI requests dated 26 February 2007 and 23 March 2007.

[4]At various times the Home Office has not maintained staffing levels with the result that workloads have increased dramatically and an increasing number of appeals have been adjourned because IJs are reluctant to hear an appeal without a HOPO present (they are concerned that their decisions will be reconsidered).

5 The World of Home Office Presenting Officers 93

Type of Instruction and number of instructions			
Asylum Policy Instructions	39	European Casework Instructions	14
Asylum Process Guidance	18	Information Management Guidance	1
Contact Management Information	2	Nationality Instructions	101
Detention Service Orders and related instructions	77	Non-compliance with biometric registration regulations	4
Immigration Directorate Instructions	35	Operating standards for pre-departure accommodation (return of families)	1
Enforcement Guidance and Instructions	6	Statelessness Guidance	1
Entry Clearance guidance	18	Working in the UK casework instructions	3
		TOTAL	320

Fig. 5.1 Home office asylum and immigration instructions and rules (May 2013)

legislation relating to asylum and immigration law came into force prior to and during the period covered by this fieldwork), case law, Home Office policies (see Fig. 5.1) and basic advocacy skills. Training focuses on the principal types of cases which HOPOs handle: asylum and immigration appeals, bail, deportation, settlement applications and human rights appeals. Training is supposed to provide HOPOs with the basic practical skills needed to carry out their work such as cross examination, 'submission techniques' and general court etiquette. HOPOs are not tested about their knowledge at the end of the course,[5] though their performance is said to be monitored by their team manager and is reviewed after six months on the job.

At the end of the induction course HOPOs observe cases for two days before taking an 'easy' case load for six weeks while they are mentored by a senior HOPO. After four to six months they attend a three day 'consolidation course'. New staff are expected to turn to experienced staff for guidance and advice. Each POU has a library containing relevant legal texts, but more importantly HOPOs have access to a comprehensive online library and information service that provides access to case law, legislation and to HO policies, instructions etc.

The 'instructions', rules etc. summarised in Fig. 5.1 are issued by the SSHD to enhance her control over the UK border and prevent claimants from securing status (Campbell 2017: Chapters 1–2 and 8). However it is clear that the sheer number of Instructions/Rules makes it difficult

---

[5] By contrast caseworkers in immigration law firms who are responsible for taking and filing an asylum applicant's initial claim with the Home Office, are required to undergo formal training and to pass national accreditation examinations.

for Home Office case owners, entry clearance officers and HOPOs to assess asylum applications because they are not allowed to exercise any discretion in the way they interpret and apply the instructions/rules. In this context the provision of ad hoc one-day training events to update HOPOs on changes in the law and legislation are arguably inadequate, particularly since HOPOs are not required to attend or indeed pass training courses.

The AIT allocates cases to a court, and one week before the hearing the head of the POU allocates cases to individual Presenting Officers who are assigned to 'run' the cases to be heard by Immigration Judges (IJs). The number of appeals heard by an IJ—his or her 'list'—varies with respect to the number and complexity of the cases listed but averages five appeals a day (lists contain a mix of asylum and other appeals). The Home Office anticipates that a HOPO will prepare for court the day before they are expected to 'assist' an IJ (preparation time varies from about one to one and a half hours for an asylum appeal and perhaps 20–30 minutes for other types of appeal). In a similar way to how French asylum rapporteurs are allocated a quota of cases (Kobelinsky, this volume), a HOPO's case load is said to be '11 in 20' or 'eleven lists a month' (one day in court followed by one day of preparation during a calendar month)[6]: they remain with an assigned judge until the 'list' is completed. HOPOs assist IJ's; Senior HOPOs assist 'Designated Senior Immigration Judges' (DIJs) who hear more complex appeals and are responsible for managing the Tribunal.

When HOPOs enter the Tribunal about half an hour before cases are scheduled to be heard, they go to the Presenting Officer's Preparation Room where a lot of banter occurs as they chat about their work, lawyers and the judges whose court rooms they are assigned to. The elusiveness of HOPOs in the Tribunal is, I think, directly linked to their sense of belonging to 'a family'. i.e. the POU. Their constant movement between the POU and the Tribunal means that social interaction is quite limited except just

---

[6]Senior Presenting Officers (SPO's) are required to take cases in court one day out of every five. However because they are also expected to 'assist' Designated Immigration Judges on difficult cases they are frequently in court and are expected to: (a) be familiar with COIS (Country of Origin Information Service, now called Country Policy and Information Service) reports and policy statements; (b) look at applications and check them against policies; (c) help process cases swiftly by checking bundles/files; (d) write to legal representatives informing them of decisions; (e) deal with any follow-up issues from appeal cases; (f) try to ensure that appeals won't be postponed; and (g) to expedite case hearings, they are expected to pick up 'floats' (last minute cases listed for a hearing) and assist IJs to determine these appeals.

before hearings begin and during lunch when interaction is convivial and high-spirited. Individual HOPOs are appointed to liaise with other POUs and the Country of Origin Information Office based at Lunar House (in South London) and they are responsible for monitoring Home Office information and case law on specific countries of asylum, e.g., Somalia, Eritrea, Sri Lanka. At the end of each day HOPOs are expected to record basic details on each case they complete on a special database and to refer any cases of potential fraud or of wider 'intelligence interest' to the POU Intelligence Liason Officer. These reports are also used to inform the Appeals and Litigation Team (in central London) that the SSHD should seek to reconsider an IJ's decision by filing an appeal.

There is little prospect of promotion for HOPOs unless they transfer to a different post, though the individuals I spoke to enjoyed their job as 'pretend barristers' (though some female officers do not enjoy the rough and tumble of court room exchanges). Indeed many HOPOs delay entering the court room until shortly before the hearing begins in order to avoid barristers, some of whom can be quite aggressive and who attempt to corner them in an effort to find out the Home Office position on their client's appeal. Attempts to avoid legal counsel arise, I think, because HOPOs realise that their legal training (and the time they spend preparing a case) is far more limited than what is expected of experienced legal counsel (though legal counsel are *not* always well prepared either). In contrast, some young male HOPOs enjoy adversarial conflict; one told me that the UK Border Agency (UKBA)[7] is obsessed with winning cases and that POU units around the country are engaged in an informal competition to achieve the highest 'win-ratio' (see Gill 2016: Chapters 3–4 on the competitiveness among officers).[8]

HOPOs are expected to meet 'performance targets' which have expanded in recent years. In 2007 HOPOs were supposed to 'maintain' 15% of all asylum and deportation initial decisions and 20% of entry clearance initial decisions (this expectation is somewhat at odds with the fact that IJs decide appeals). By 2013 their targets were increased such that they were expected

---

[7]HOPOs worked in the UKBA at that time of my research. It was re-incorporated into the Home Office in 2013.

[8]In response to an FOI request about this, the Home Office denied knowledge of such a competition. The competition is probably based on comparing monthly performance statistics for each POU which are published by the Home Office.

to 'maintain 70% of asylum appeals and 60% of all other appeals'.[9] To achieve these targets they are expected to[10]:

1. 'Ensure each case is fully argued in court' by delivering 'a persuasive and cohesive argument'.
2. 'Pursue all relevant and appropriate aspects of the appellant's case or claim.'
3. 'In court, robustly defend the decision under appeal but be mindful that you must disclose evidence and material that is relevant to the facts at issue, irrespective of which party to the appeal this assists, in order to achieve a just determination of the case. You must not knowingly mislead the Immigration Judge or permit the Immigration Judge to be misled.'
4. 'Test the evidence …'.
5. 'You should ensure that cases are dealt with as efficiently and quickly as possible and oppose unmeritorious adjournment requests.'

Once we step back from official representations about HOPOs and examine them at work it is possible to discern significant discrepancies between the way their role is publicly defined and how they perform their work. One important observation is that unlike barristers/advocates, IJs and bailiffs, HOPOs are *not* 'officers of the court' who have an obligation to promote justice and the effective operation of the judicial system. Indeed HOPOs are *not* bound by a professional code of conduct which means that regardless of what is stated in Home Office professional standards guidelines, they are not legally required to assist the court to achieve a fair decision. Observation makes it clear that most HOPOs steadfastly see their job as 'defending' the initial Home Office decision regardless of whether that decision was fair. In this regard it is important to note that between 2007 and 2009 Home Office caseworkers refused at least 80% of all initial asylum applications they considered; however between 25 and 33% of all initial decisions were overturned on appeal in the Tribunal. Their task of defending the SSHD is ensured by the imposition of management targets on HOPOs and because, according to my informants, in 2001 the Home Office withdrew the right of HOPOs to concede a case. Today if a HOPO is allocated to defend a poorly argued decision they will 'redraft' a refusal letter or they may only make a brief final submission in court.

---

[9]Source: Home Office FOI request by S. Medley (dated 8th April 2013) Req. FOI 26714.
[10]Source: 'Presenting Officers Professional Standards' provided in FOI request 26714, dated 8th April 2013.

Litigating Appeals

Individuals who have applied to the Home Office for asylum but whose initial application was refused by the Home Office have a right of appeal to the AIT against that decision. The AIT presides over an adversarial legal arena which brings together parties with very different interests in the outcome of an appeal (Campbell 2017). The Tribunal is formally independent from the Home Office; nevertheless the decisions of IJs are increasingly constrained by the SSHD's rules and regulations which, as with HOPOs, limit their discretion in deciding claims. During an appeal Immigration Judges (IJ) use Tribunal Procedural Rules and Practice Directions to control proceedings and process appeals in a speedy and efficient manner. In the asylum appeals I followed all applicants were represented by legal counsel. More recently, however, it is clear that on average twenty-one percent of applicants were unrepresented in the period 2011–2012 (Burridge and Gill 2017: 30). When applicants are not legally represented this allows greater scope for HOPOs to influence the outcome of the appeal, i.e. more appeals are dismissed.

HOPOs 'resist' an appeal by defending the original decision of a Home Office case owner (who does not appear in court). Normally asylum appellants attend appeals. At the start of the hearing the IJ determines the order in which appeals will be heard and, together with legal representatives and the HOPO, s/he sets a nominal time limit for each appeal within which the parties are expected to conclude their arguments. Finally ushers and administrative staff assist the Tribunal to conduct its business.

Case 1. First Tier Asylum Appeal of HZ

The appellant was a 60-year-old national of Eritrea who was given leave to enter the UK as the spouse of a British citizen in May 2005. In 2007 he applied for 'Indefinite Leave to Remain' and was refused. Before his appeal was heard he applied for asylum in September 2007 'because of his political opinion'. The SSHD refused his appeal and issued removal directions to Eritrea. The Home Office 'Refusal Letter' (RFRL) argued that the appellant was an 'insufficiently prominent' member of a political opposition party and 'would not be of interest to the authorities' if he were returned to Eritrea.

His appeal was heard in early 2008 at a London Tribunal and concerned a *sur place* claim for asylum. As defined in the UNHCR Handbook (1992): 'A person who was not a refugee when he left his country, but who becomes a refugee at a later date, is called a refugee 'sur place' (paragraph 94). Expressed slightly differently, UNHCR notes that 'a person becomes a refugee 'sur place' due to circumstances arising in his country of origin during his absence' (paragraph 95). Two case 'bundles' were submitted to the Tribunal prior to the hearing which contained all the evidence and country reports which both parties relied upon to argue the claim. The Home Office bundle included a screening interview and 'Statement of Evidence Form' (SEF) with AK and the Home Office RFRL. The appellant's bundle contained his counsel's skeleton argument, a new witness statement by the appellant, extensive photographs, witness statements from his solicitor and his witness, a copy of a membership card indicating membership in an opposition political party and a copy of the party's political programme, two expert reports and eight objective reports addressing the political situation in Eritrea.

The IJ took an unusually active role in the proceedings. As the appellant was called to give evidence, the IJ echoed the statement of HZ's counsel that 'the issues are quite narrow' by stating:

> Very narrow! He made his claim when he did; there was no need to claim [earlier] because he was on family reunion. In terms of credibility, his case is to show his political activities to date pre-date his application [for asylum]. There it is, fairly narrow. The case of *Danian*[11] supports the appellant. It doesn't actually matter what his reasons were, this cannot be challenged. Is that about it?

The appellant's representative led him through his witness statements and asked him whether his 'activities were a ploy to claim asylum? Can you comment on this?' The appellant replied: 'I believe the Home Office is wrong. These are my beliefs and principles.'

The HOPO undertook an extensive cross-examination that questioned the appellant's knowledge of and engagement with Eritrean opposition politics. Fifteen minutes into the cross examination the IJ interrupted the HOPO to clarify a point of law regarding Immigration Rule 395C which

---

[11] The reference is to a case heard by the Court of Appeal, *Danian [1999] INLR 533*, which reaffirmed that a person who had a well-founded fear of persecution on Convention grounds could not be denied the protection of the Convention on the grounds that their activities after arriving in the UK gave rise to a fear of persecution even if they had been carried out in bad-faith. While the appellant's activities would need to be carefully scrutinised, if their action did give rise to the possibility of serious risk on return then they would be entitled to asylum.

allowed him discretion to decide the case,[12] an issue which the Home Office Refusal Letter had failed to raise. When the HOPO confirmed that the issue had not been raised, the IJ stated: 'Yes, it's wrong. Frankly this is a strong asylum case. I am reluctant that it should be kicked into touch'. At this point, cross examination resumed and addressed the nature of his activities in the UK, his membership in an opposition political group, his fear of being returned to Eritrea, and his Art. 8 claim under the European Convention on Human Rights regarding his right to a family and private life.

When cross examination concluded the IJ again stepped in by stating that 'There is nothing to re-examine is there?'. He asked a few questions of the appellant: 'Your sons are here. That's a strong link for you. But if suddenly there is an uprising in Eritrea you would go back to help rebuild?'. The appellant answered: 'Yes'.

The witnesses were then called to give evidence regarding the appellant and his involvement in opposition politics in the UK and the likelihood that the authorities were aware of his activities. When this concluded and it was time for the HOPO to cross-examine the witnesses, the IJ stated: 'Is there anything left?' The HOPO asked one question regarding how often the witnesses had seen the appellant distributing political material on public occasions.

As the HOPO began her final submissions, which relied upon the Refusal Letter and which did not take issue with the appellant's political activities in the UK, she was constantly interrupted by the IJ who commented that even though the appellant was likely to be subject to a 'low level' risk on return, nevertheless 'He probably would attract attention [...] From everything we read about Eritrea, it is a matter of concern.' The IJ also commented on 'the vast amount of high quality evidence' before him, including photographic evidence, and he stated that 'The case comes down to the objective evidence; nothing has gotten better in the past four years.'

Agreeing with the HOPO that Home Office COIS reports failed to provide information about the political organisation which the appellant had allegedly joined in the UK, nevertheless he concluded that the expert evidence on the political party was undisputable. The IJ then rhetorically stated: 'What tops it?' To which the appellant's representative said: 'His immigration history'.

---

[12]See: 'Goodbye Paragraph 395C?' at: https://www.freemovement.org.uk/goodbye-paragraph-395c/ accessed 1 July 2012.

The IJ stated: 'Yes. When the Home Office see this [i.e. an asylum claim made after entering the UK which alleges involvement in political activities] they are suspicious. But this is a different type of case. I am privileged to hear it.' The IJ then stated: 'I allow the asylum appeal and the human rights appeal'.

Comment: This appeal hinged on the failure of the Home Office to properly consider the application as a *sur place* asylum claim (because the appellant had entered the UK lawfully under a grant of family reunion) rather than as an unfounded claim as defined by Sec. 8 of the *Asylum and Immigration (Treatment of Claimants, etc) Act 2004*. Furthermore, the IJ invoked *IR 395C* to prevent the Home Office from withdrawing its original decision in order to reconsider the claim. IR 395C allowed the IJ to overturn the Home Office decision and grant the appeal. The appeal is unusual for a number of reasons. First very few *sur place* claims are made. Second most IJ's do not intervene quite so ` in hearings nor do they overrule HOPO arguments. Finally, it is extremely rare for an IJ to announce the decision at the end of the appeal (normally they 'reserve their decision', write it up afterwards and send it to the applicant and the Home Office within ten to fourteen days of the hearing).

Case 2. Second Stage Reconsideration Appeal of AK

When the Tribunal refuses an appeal against the initial decision of the Secretary of State, the applicant may have a right to appeal against the decision if the IJ made an error of law in deciding the appeal. In such cases the applicant's representative makes an application to the Upper Tribunal setting out why the decision should not be allowed to stand and asking the Tribunal for a reconsideration of the initial appeal.

In October 2006 the first tier of the Tribunal convened to hear an appeal by AK, a 35-year-old asylum applicant from Eritrea. The IJ dismissed AK's appeal.[13] The applicant's legal representative filed an application for reconsideration to the Upper Tribunal where, upon looking at the papers summarising the case, a Senior IJ (hereafter, SIJ) concluded

---

[13]I attended the reconsideration appeal and took my own notes of the proceedings. In addition I have the entire case file and an interview with the barrister who represented AK.

5 The World of Home Office Presenting Officers 101

that 'the IJ was procedurally unfair in finding that the appellant was no longer working for the Defence Forces until he left Eritrea without giving him the opportunity to deal with that point, when that evidence was accepted in the RFRL', i.e. Home Office Refusal Letter. That decision led to a 'First Stage Reconsideration' where an SIJ concluded that there was 'a material error of law' in the initial determination. The SIJ identified 13 issues in the initial decision that were linked to an 'evidential lacunae' for the period 1999 to 2005 in the appellant's account. A further error of law concerned the need to find 'the true circumstances in which he left Eritrea' (the reference was to *MA (Draft evaders—illegal departures—risk) Eritrea CG [2007] UKAIT 00059*)[14] which focused on the issue of 'illegal exit' from Eritrea and whether individuals who had left Eritrea without obtaining an official exit visa and a passport were at risk for a Convention reason if they were 'returned', i.e. deported as failed asylum seekers, to Eritrea.

The reconsideration appeal was heard in May 2008 by a Designated Immigration Judge (DIJ). The Home Office bundle included the Screening and Statement of Evidence Interviews, the RFRL and a copy of the first determination of the claim. The appellant's bundle contained the decision by the SIJ setting out the errors in law of the first determination, copies of all the original submissions made by the appellant, correspondence between the appellant's legal representative and the Home Office and a new witness statement by the appellant. This statement provided further evidence about: his military service; secondment to the Office of the President and his work there; his political activities and his departure from Eritrea. The bundle also contained two expert reports. Just before the appeal began, counsel for the appellant said to the HOPO 'I don't have the Home Office COI report on Eritrea. I don't need one unless you are relying on it. You didn't serve it at the directions hearing and I won't have time to read it.' At this point the HOPO handed her the COI report which he did rely upon.

The reconsideration appeal began with the Senior HOPO reaffirming the reasons set out in the original RFRL and rejecting the appellant's account that he had still been in government service when he left Eritrea. The applicant's representative, an experienced barrister, relied on *DK (Serbia) [2006] EWCA Civ 1747*[15] to argue that 'it was not logical

---

[14] See: https://tribunalsdecisions.service.gov.uk/utiac/37868 accessed 15 June 2011.
[15] See: https://court-appeal.vlex.co.uk/vid/ors-52569444 accessed 15 June 2011.

that he [the appellant] could be permitted to adduce evidence as to the nature of his work during that time but at the same time be prevented from trying to establish that he worked in the Presidential office'. In short, 'the question of where A was working cannot be said to be unaffected by the IJ's error as to what A was doing between 1999 and 2005.' This point was the key focus of the hearing although it was one strand of AK's evidence.

After some initial sparring between the HOPO and counsel for AK, the latter asked the appellant to confirm his written evidence but failed to take him through the details regarding how he left Eritrea. The DIJ immediately stepped in to ask about an untranslated document in the appellant's bundle which was said to confirm that the appellant had completed national service. He asked the court translator to translate the document which appeared to confirm that it was 'a certificate of work participation' issued by the Ministry of Defence to AK confirming his record of military service between 1996 and 1998 and which was intended to help him to 'get a part-time job'. The HOPO cross examined AK about his employment and his residence. The DIJ intervened to question AK about his computer training, but AK was not able to provide precise answers. The HOPO resumed his cross examination of AK and asked why the certificate had not been submitted to the first asylum hearing (he said that his mother had recently sent it to him). The HOPO also reiterated that AK had completed national service and he sought to clarify the nature of the computer files which had been submitted as part of AKs evidence (i.e. that he was a computer technician who had been assigned to work at Sawa military camp and that later he had been transferred to work at the office of the President of Eritrea).

The DIJ intervened on numerous occasions to ask about: the applicant's family; his job in the military and his computer training; the documents he was now submitting; conscription; the work he reportedly carried out as a computer expert; demobilisation cards; the photo's AK submitted showing him in a military uniform; and about whether his mother was detained by the authorities after he left the country. The DIJ also questioned AK's witness—who confirmed that 'no one is allowed to ask for release or demobilisation'—about his legal status in the UK. It emerged that neither AK's counsel nor the Home Office (who had been given a copy of his papers) had told the witness to bring verification of his legal status. The IJ asked the witness a number of questions about his knowledge of AK and was told that they had met at Sawa Camp in 1999 when both men were stationed there as conscripts and that AK had transferred to the President's Office in 2001.

At this point both parties made their final submissions to the DIJ. The principle submissions made by the Senior HOPO were:

1. He adopted the reasons set out in the RFRL.
2. AK was conscripted in 1994 in the 'first round' of conscription in Eritrea.
3. AK worked at Sawa military camp and at the President's Office from where 'he will never be released'.
4. AK was permitted to look for part-time work.
5. AK received demobilisation papers from the military.
6. AK doesn't fall within the draft evaders categories [as set out in *MA 'Draft evaders—illegal departures—risk) Eritrea CG [2007] UKAIT 00059*] nor is he a military deserter.
7. AK's appeal should be refused.

His counsel began her summing up by noting that 'the first issue is that the IJ's credibility findings are mixed; there are no challenges to his two years as a conscript or that he worked on IT at Sawa camp. The IJ didn't accept that he was involved in opposition politics while he worked at the Office of the President.' In addition, counsel noted that:

1. The expert reports confirmed that after initial military training there is no demobilisation for men until the age of 50. The majority of conscripts continue to perform National Service, not military service.
2. There has been no challenge that AK left the country illegally.
3. It has not be suggested that AK obtained an exit visa.
4. There has been no challenge to his witness, he is a refugee and he has status in the UK.
5. AK has attended political demonstrations against the Eritrean government in the UK and has submitted photographic evidence of this.
6. Regarding the gaps in AKs initial evidence for the period 1999 to 2005, if he was in military service in 1999 then, subject to injury, he would still be in military service. Finally
7. 'I accept that there are mixed credibility findings, you asked about other issues but these are not before you as we are limited by the Directions.'

Eight days after the appeal the Tribunal promulgated the DIJ's decision which strongly reflected his reading of the latest Home Office COI report on Eritrea. The DIJ's findings begin with a very clear statement: 'I come to the conclusion that the appellant has told so many lies that it is difficult to know what can be believed and what has been concocted for the claim' (paragraph 82). In the following 37 paragraphs of the decision the DIJ takes exception to every element of AK's claim and finds reason to doubt his credibility on every issue, including evidence that was not open for him to address. This comprehensive rejection of AK's evidence on the grounds that it lacked credibility allowed her to cite case law—*AH (Failed asylum seekers—involuntary returns) Eritrea CG [2006] UKAIT 00078*[16]—to refuse the appeal because AK had been found to lack credibility. In subsequent paragraphs she found that AK might have left the country on a scholarship, that his 'post-arrival' political activities were not put forward during the hearing, that the certificates of his educational training were not the originals (and could not be accepted) and that any *sur place* activities were 'opportunistic'.[17] As if her decision wasn't already clear, the DIJ concluded by stating that: 'I consider that the appellant has fabricated his account of his experiences in Eritrea and [I] do not accept that he left there for the reasons claimed or in the circumstances claimed. I am not satisfied that he has a well-founded fear ...' (paragraph 128).

Comment: This reconsideration appeal arose out of an error of law by the IJ who decided the first-tier appeal without carefully considering all of the appellant's evidence. When an appeal is set out for reconsideration, it is normal for the SIJ who reviewed the application for reconsideration to define the key error(s) in law which need to be revisited and to 'preserve' other findings of fact from being overturned by the Tribunal during the second appeal. It should be clear that the HOPO and counsel for AK created the space for the DIJ to take a very direct role in the appeal. The HOPO was not well prepared for the appeal and at several points failed to interrogate key elements of the evidence and the appellant's witness, which provided an opening for the DIJ to ask her own questions and take control of the proceedings. Similarly, counsel for AK seemed blasé if not ill-prepared. First, she failed to translate a key document supporting the appellant's case. Second, she did not take the court through the objective evidence on

---

[16] See: https://tribunalsdecisions.service.gov.uk/utiac/37945. The conclusion in this country guidance case which the DIJ seized upon was that 'Neither involuntary returnees nor failed asylum seekers are as such at real risk on return to Eritrea'.

[17] Contrast her reading of Danion with that of the IJ in Case 1 and see Footnote 9.

Eritrea. Third, she simply asked the appellant and his witness to confirm their written statements without exploring their evidence. The DIJ immediately stepped in to ask her own questions which included finding that the witness had not brought any documents to court to affirm his legal status in the UK. Overall, however, what is remarkable about the appeal and the decision is the extent to which the DIJ intervened during the appeal and the fact that she took exception with every element of AKs evidence in refusing his appeal. Indeed she even found a form of words and reasoning which allowed her to address and overturn findings of fact preserved by the SIJ who ordered that the appeal be reconsidered. Counsel for the appellant filed an appeal against this decision to the Second Tier of the Tribunal which was refused by an SIJ in July 2008 (the SIJ stated: 'I am not satisfied that it is arguable that the judge went beyond the issues identified for reconsideration'). An 'Application on the Papers' to the Court of Appeal was immediately made and initially granted but, one day before the appeal was scheduled, it was withdrawn by a Lord Justice because, on reading the papers, he decided that 'the expert report did not resolve questions for negative case law'. AK's claim was comprehensively found to lack credibility (see Sorgoni, this volume, for a critical discussion of this concept in the Italian context) and he was now subject to arrest and deportation.[18]

The Views of Immigration Judges About HOPOs

For good reasons IJs generally do not comment about the Home Office because they have to work with HOPOs and because their decisions may be challenged by the SSHD who may file an application to reconsider/re-hear their decisions (in the period 2006 and 2009 between 32 and 46% of applications for reconsideration made by the SSHD were granted; Campbell 2017: Chapter 6).

IJs' views about HOPOs are clearly influenced by the fact that their work is scrutinised by Home Office officials. Nevertheless, it is noteworthy that HOPOs are held in low regard by many IJs largely because of their lack of

---

[18]In the spring of 2017 I received an email from AK requesting my assistance to write an expert report for a fresh application for asylum which was to be heard by the Tribunal in September 2017. During the past 9 years he had been supported by an Eritrean family in London. His fresh application admitted that he had fabricated certain elements of his claim but he was adamant that he had never been demobilised from the military and that he left Eritrea illegally without obtaining an exit visa (the objective COI material supports this claim today as it did in 2008).

legal training. For instance one IJ told me that HOPOs always attack the credibility of appellants, even if that is not an issue. This occurs because HOPOs rely entirely on the initial Home Office Refusal Letter, because they ask 'irrelevant questions' and because they focus on minor discrepancies in an appellant's account without looking at the core issues or without examining the evidence in the round. The same IJ described HOPO's as 'xenophobic' in the sense of being biased because

> they want to win [...] if they can. I think they're fair, but they can be pedantic [...] they go into too many discrepancies which are not entirely reasonable, you know, sometimes empty submissions [...] which don't hold any weight. They just want to be heard [...] On the other hand, sometimes you get a good sensible one who knows that the case is watertight from the appellant's point of view, and who will simply say: 'Well I make no submissions'.

Another IJ noted that because HOPOs are not well paid and spend relatively little time preparing an appeal, their performance in court varies immensely ranging from a small number of 'fascist-like presenting officers who seem to get a great deal of glee from putting people on the spot' to the majority who 'appear to have a sort of workman mentality—it's a job, its going to get done to the best of my ability'. There were also the occasional HOPOs who, in addition to attacking an applicant's credibility were unable to put their argument in a succinct form by asking appellants straightforward questions. When this occurs the IJ will stop the HOPO and ask him to rephrase his question by breaking it down into as simple a question as possible (this is a particular problem if interpreters are being used). If that request fails, then IJs will rephrase the question and ask it themselves.

A third IJ told me that he believed that the training of HOPOs had improved in recent years and that the standard of their work was higher. He noted that if there was poor legal representation from either the HOPO or counsel for the appellant, he would 'decide the case on the evidence before me' without worrying about whether either party might seek to appeal his decision. Informally IJs were said to be scathing about the quality of representation by HOPOs *and* legal counsel, though neither type of representative appears to be reprimanded for poor professional conduct.[19]

---

[19]For instance I was told that Designated Immigration Judge's seldom 'carpeted' IJs for poor judicial decisions during their annual appraisal. It is not clear whether poor quality work by a HOPO attracts any sanction.

Conclusion

The adversarial nature of asylum and immigration appeals in the UK results in a tense, and sometimes fractious relationship between the judiciary, the Home Office and the legal profession. While the legal process is supposed to provide equal access to justice, the cases discussed in this chapter strongly suggest that persistent inequality prevails. This occurs because asylum and immigration law is complex and, given cuts to legal aid and the imposition of increased charges for filing claims, asylum applicants and individuals held in detention face insurmountable difficulties when they are unable to afford a lawyer (without whose assistance their appeal will almost certainly fail; Campbell 2014, 2015).

Elsewhere I have argued that in the last decade the balance of power has decisively shifted in favour of the Home Office due to its ability to draft legislation, create secondary legislation and new immigration rules—as illustrated in this paper by changing Paragraph 395C—and its ability to fund extensive litigation against asylum claims which compels asylum applicants and their lawyers to acquiesce with the particular interpretation or rubric of 'law' that the Home Office wishes to enforce (Campbell 2017).

This situation reinforces not only a wariness about the relation between the courts and the Home Office, but also a certain skepticism about the system that is reflected in the views and opinions held by judges, lawyers and government officials. For this reason it is unsurprising that HOPOs hold strong views about the importance of their work, about judges (who are variously seen as 'allowers', 'tough IJs' and 'dismissers'), about lawyers (seen as either 'top class QCs', 'bottom-feeders' or 'rogues') and country experts and appellants (who are viewed with extreme scepticism). In court each type of actor expresses a strong sense of identity and solidarity as a member of a profession, be it as a member of the judiciary, a member of the legal profession or as HOPOs from the same POU. The world of the HOPO is an insular one because of the adversarial way in which appeals are heard and decided; because of the limited nature of their 'legal' training; and because they are tasked with defending the SSHD regardless of the evidence before them. In this context legal challenges against decisions by the Secretary of State are viewed as a potential threat to the security of the country which needs to be fought against; appeals which overturn Home Office decisions are experienced as personal defeats. If HOPOs possess an elusive quality, it is because they often have to defend poorly considered decisions by other Home Office officials in a context where, despite the constraints placed on judges and lawyers by the power of the SSHD, judicial decisions often go against them.

References

Burridge, A., & Gill, N. (2017). Conveyor-Belt Justice: Precarity, Access to Justice, and Uneven Geographies of Legal Aid in UK Asylum Appeals. *Antipode, 49*(1), 23–42.

Campbell, J. (2014). *Nationalism, Law and Statelessness: Grand Illusions in the Horn of Africa*. Oxford: Routledge.

Campbell, J. (2015). Expert Evidence in British Asylum Courts: The Judicial Assessment of Evidence on Ethnic Discrimination and Statelessness in Ethiopia. In I. Berger, T. Hepner, B. Lawrance, J. Tague, & M. Terretta (Eds.), *Law, Expertise, and Protean Ideas About African Migrants* (pp. 102–120). Columbus: Ohio State University Press.

Campbell, J. (2017). *Bureaucracy, Law and Dystopia in the United Kingdom's Asylum System*. Oxford: Routledge.

Gill, N. (2016). *Nothing Personal? Geographies of Governing and Activism in the British Asylum System*. Oxford: Wiley-Blackwell.

UNHCR. (1992). *Handbook on Procedures and Criteria for Determining Refugee Status Under the 1951 Convention and the 1967 Protocol Relating to the Status of Refugees*. HCR/IP/4/Eng/Rev. 1. Reedited 1992. Geneva. Available at: http://www.unhcr.org/4d93528a9.pdf.

Open Access This chapter is distributed under the terms of the Creative Commons Attribution 4.0 International License (http://creativecommons.org/licenses/by/4.0/), which permits use, duplication, adaptation, distribution and reproduction in any medium or format, as long as you give appropriate credit to the original author(s) and the source, a link is provided to the Creative Commons license and any changes made are indicated.

The images or other third party material in this chapter are included in the work's Creative Commons license, unless indicated otherwise in the credit line; if such material is not included in the work's Creative Commons license and the respective action is not permitted by statutory regulation, users will need to obtain permission from the license holder to duplicate, adapt or reproduce the material.

6

Asylum Procedures in Greece: The Case of Unaccompanied Asylum Seeking Minors

Chrisa Giannopoulou and Nick Gill

Introduction

According to Human Rights Watch (2016), the violations of children's rights in Greece during 2015 and 2016 included, among others, arbitrary detention. Under international law, binding European directives, and national law, detention of unaccompanied asylum seeking children should be used 'only as a measure of last resort, in exceptional circumstances, and for the shortest appropriate period' (ibid.: 1). Human Rights Watch found that children often faced degrading conditions in police station cells and in Coast Guard facilities, and unsanitary conditions in pre-removal detention centres. In some cases, children said they were made to live and sleep in overcrowded, filthy, bug- and vermin-infested cells, sometimes without mattresses, and were deprived of appropriate sanitation, hygiene, and privacy. The national response capacity is very limited as there are only a small

---

At the time of the writing, the first author was working as a Legal Advisor for the NGO the Hellenic League for Human Rights in Skaramagas Refugee Camp, Attica Region, Athens. The fieldwork reported in this chapter was conducted solely by Chrisa Giannopoulou (hereafter 'Chrisa' in the text). Currently, she is a Post Doctoral Reserarcher at the Department of Geography, University of Aegean, Lesvos, Greece.

C. Giannopoulou (✉)
University of Macedonia, Athens, Greece

N. Gill
University of Exeter, Exeter, UK
e-mail: n.m.gill@exeter.ac.uk

© The Author(s) 2019
N. Gill and A. Good (eds.), *Asylum Determination in Europe*,
Palgrave Socio-Legal Studies, https://doi.org/10.1007/978-3-319-94749-5_6

number of available places in shelters. In many cases unaccompanied minors are therefore put in protective custody (i.e. detention) until a place in a shelter is available.

The same report found that children detained in police custody are not provided with critical care and services. Under international standards, unaccompanied asylum seeking children should be able to receive medical treatment, psychological counselling, and legal aid, and be interviewed in a language they understand in order to identify and address any specific needs, including those deriving from gender-based violence or trafficking. In Greece, such children are often unable to receive counselling, information about the reasons for and duration of their detention, and legal aid. Although the provision of interpreters at asylum interviews with children is by no means a guarantee of effective communication (Keselman et al. 2008) the lack of interpreters is a significant practical barrier to providing care and information (for a discussion of the role and importance of interpreters, see Rycroft 2005; Gibb and Good 2014). Human Rights Watch interviewed 35 children who were in police custody in Greece in mid 2016 and none of them said they had been given an opportunity to speak to the police with the help of an interpreter.

Furthermore, all unaccompanied asylum seeking children should have a legal guardian appointed to defend their best interests and help safeguard against risks like trafficking. None of the children interviewed by Human Rights Watch while in police custody had met their legal guardian, nor were they even aware they had one. Unaccompanied children in detention have a right to recreation and to education as well, but Human Rights Watch (2016: 3) found 'no evidence that the unaccompanied children in police stations had access to educational opportunities or recreational activities'.

This raises the question of how these human rights failings have been allowed to come about. Although a lack of leadership and resources have certainly had an impact (indeed, the lack of resources for the protection of refugees in Greece has been a challenge for decades, see Black 1994), in this chapter we argue that these factors are only part of the explanation. It is entirely possible for formal legal rules to exist, but for 'informal social control' (Woodman 1998: 45) to impede and inhibit the operation of these laws. In the case of child migrants in Greece, these informal social forms of control include categorisations and associations that find expression in two phenomena: the discourse that is used to refer to migrants, which has shifted in Greece from one that is based on refugees to one that is based upon 'clandestine' migration, and the perceptions of Greek migrant children through the lenses of vulnerability and responsibility, which squeeze out opportunities to recognise their agency. The contingency of protection on these phenomena exemplifies both the plurality of the Greek migration legal system (see Gill and Good, introduction to this volume), and the challenges that this plurality presents to asylum seeking children.

The first part of the chapter sets out the history of human rights failings in the refugee context in Greece and the second section reflects upon the role of discourse surrounding refugees as a way of explaining why these failings persist. Drawing on two and a half years of participant ethnography in a Greek reception centre for children in Konitsa Town, Prefecture of Ioannina, Greece and in the Skaramagas Refugee camp in Attica Region, Athens, the third section then identifies three basic stereotypes that shape the perceptions of asylum seeking children among host communities in Greece. First, in contrast to the recommendations of contemporary scholarship about childhood (e.g. James et al. 1998) childhood is viewed as a linear, universal process implying that all children have the same needs. Second, separated children are seen as dependent burdens with no knowledge of their own 'best interests'. And third, like their adult counterparts, they are seen as 'undeserving migrants' that should be viewed with suspicion. Taken together, these findings demonstrate that the discourses and perceptions surrounding refugee children in Greece have had a decisive influence over their experiences of legal systems.

Chrisa took an anthropological and participatory approach to the fieldwork (Hardman 1973). When conducting her research with unaccompanied minors she tried to approach them as active participants in the construction and determination of their experiences, other people's lives and the societies in which they live (O'Kane 2008). In doing so she followed the advice of Christensen and James (2008: 3) who argue that we 'should not take the age-based adult/child distinction for granted' (ibid.: 3) and advocate 'that the particular methods chosen for a piece of research should be appropriate for the people involved in the study, for its social and cultural context and for the kinds of research questions that are being posed' (ibid.: 3). Accordingly, she always tried to address her participants as if they were adults, since they had managed to do something she had not—namely, they had irregularly crossed borders and walked many miles to get away from their country. For the purposes of the research she followed the methodology of semi-structured interviews, questionnaires and open discussions. In order to protect their anonymity, the research participants chose their own pseudonyms and at times we have created fictional composite characters (discussed below in more detail) to convey the experiences of interviewees without revealing their identities.

Greece's Record on Refugee Protection

If the historical experience of refugees in Greece were a reliable indicator then we might expect Greece to be strongly committed to refugee protection. After the end of World War One and the signing of the Lausanne Treaty in January 1923, the Greek state received around one and a half million refugees from Asia Minor and Pontus as a result of the population exchange with Turkey at that time.[1] The newcomers were resettled mostly in rural areas, in an attempt by Eleytherios Venizelos (the then-Prime Minister of Greece) to rebuild and fortify the rural territories, which had suffered severe damage due to the successive wars in which Greece participated from the beginning of the twentieth century.

As Voutira (2003: 66) argues, the term 'refugee', when referring to the 1923 refugees, is usually associated with positive connotations due to the collective perception of the 'successful' integration and publicly acknowledged contribution of Asia Minor refugees into twentieth-century Greek economic, social and cultural development, especially in these rural areas. Accordingly, throughout the post-1989 arrivals of Soviet Greeks from Pontus, the newcomers preferred the term 'refugee', rather than 'repatriee' or 'returnee'.

What is more, if the international community's assumptions about Greek refugee protection before 2007 were at all well-founded, then we might also expect Greece to be a model of refugee protection. For some time Greece was vaunted as a location in which the Geneva Convention, that sets the criteria for the recognition of refugee status and envisages universally applicable criteria for their protection, was reliably observed. According to the provisions of the Dublin II Regulation in 2003,[2] Greece was a place to which individuals could be safely returned if they had prematurely entered another European country during the examination period of their asylum applications. In other words, the international community has historically considered Greece an (extremely convenient) safe host country on the fringes of

---

[1] The full text of the Lausanne Treaty is available at: http://www.hri.org/docs/lausanne/ [Accessed 17 July 2017]. The full text of the Convention Concerning the Exchange of Greek and Turkish Populations is available at: http://www.hri.org/docs/straits/exchange.html [Accessed 17 July 2017].

[2] Council Regulation (EC) 343/2003 establishing the criteria and mechanisms for determining the member state responsible for examining an asylum application lodged in one of the member states by a third-country national; see http://eur-lex.europa.eu/LexUriServ/LexUriServ.do?uri=OJ:L:2003:050:0001:0010:EN:PDF [Accessed 17 July 2017].

Europe as conveyed by its status as a *first asylum country* under article 1A of the Geneva Convention (Goodwin-Gill 1996).

In contrast to these assumptions about refugee rights in Greece, however, serious concerns about the provisions for refugees on the ground have been voiced for well over a decade. Skordas and Sitaropoulos (2004) for example argued that the deficiencies of the Greek refugee system included its archaism, the lack of efficient remedies and the inadequate social protection of refugees and asylum seekers. In October 2007, as a result of these and similar concerns, an extensive investigation into violations of the human rights of refugees at the various entry points into the country was carried out by the German non-governmental organisation 'PRO ASYL', with the participation of Greek organisations, and caused consternation due to the revelations that it produced (PRO ASYL 2007). The report cited evidence of the intentional refoulement of refugees at sea by the Greek coast guard by circling boats in order to cause waves that forced them to return, the deliberate damaging of refugee dinghies so that they could return to Turkey but not travel as far as Greece, the systematic abuse of newly arrived refugees, and the use of inhumane, degrading and illegal detention, as well as illegal deportation orders.

Following PRO ASYL's revelations various EU countries such as the UK, Germany, and Norway stopped referring asylum seekers to Greece (as the first country of entry according to the Dublin II procedure) while investigations into Greece's provision for refugees were carried out (see Craig and Zwaan, this volume, for a discussion of the principle of mutual trust between states subject to the Dublin regulations, as well as its modification under the Dublin III legislation). These investigations, and scrutiny from the international community more generally, prompted various attempted improvements to the Greek system of provisions. In November 2010, for example, Asylum Appeals Committees were introduced.[3] These were three-member quasi-judicial bodies, consisting of a civil servant as Chairman, a member nominated by the United Nations High Commissioner for Refugees (UNHCR) and a member selected by the Ministry of Interior from a list drawn up by the National Commission on Human Rights (EEDA), an independent advisory body to the state. Their mandate was to examine the appeals on asylum applications submitted before the 6 June 2013 and rejected at the first instance by the Ministry

---

[3]Precedential Decree 114/2010 in conformity with Council Directive 2005/85/EC on minimum standards of procedures in Member States for granting and withdrawing refugee status.

of Public Order (i.e. Greek Police officials). Furthermore, since November 2011 the Greek Police were no longer responsible for examining asylum applications.[4] Rather, an autonomous service within the Ministry of Citizen Protection now held this responsibility.[5]

Nevertheless, although these legislative changes aimed for a fairer and more independent system, the practical autonomy of the new asylum system and the quality of the procedures should still be queried. For example, during 2016 the Asylum Appeals Committees that were created in 2010 were temporarily entrusted with examining appeals of asylum seekers who had entered the country from 20 March 2016 onwards—that is, the date from which the joint EU-Turkey statement was implemented. These were asylum requests deemed inadmissible at first instance examination based on recommendations of the European Asylum Support Office (EASO) representatives. In 390 out of 393 cases the Asylum Appeals Committees overruled the negative decisions of the first instance, after ruling Turkey a 'non-safe country'. Roughly two months later however, by virtue of an amendment approved by parliament on the 16 June 2016, the Asylum Appeals Committees ceased to be responsible for these cases, the examination of which was assigned to new committees with a different composition. This change in legislation has been widely criticised by human rights organisations. Refugee rights lawyers believe this was a cynical political intervention by the government in order to protect and promote a policy related to the implementation of the EU-Turkey statement, since the previous Asylum Appeals Committees did not comply with the political goal of sending Syrians back to Turkey. The National Committee for Human Rights and the Secretary General for Human Rights expressed concern and opposition to the Ministry's initiative at the time. In a public letter denouncing the amendment, 18 former Committee members, appointed by EEDA and UNHCR, warned that 'managing legal issues by use of political priorities raises many questions about the future of the asylum system in Greece, the protection of human rights and the rule of law' (see ECRE 2016; PRO ASYL 2016).

---

[4]Law 3907/2011 on the establishment of an Asylum Service and a First Reception Service (transposition into Greek legislation from Council Directive 2008/115/EC on common standards and procedures in Member States for returning illegally staying third country nationals and other provisions).

[5]For an overview of the Greek Asylum Legal Framework, main legislative acts and regulations relevant to asylum procedures, reception conditions and detention before and after the EU-Turkey Common Declaration on the 18 March 2016, see various reports from the Asylum Information Database, available at: http://www.asylumineurope.org/reports/country/Greece/overview-legal-framework [Accessed 20 July 2017].

From Refugees to Clandestines

It is difficult to isolate a single root cause of the inadequate approach to refugee protection in Greece but economic factors must be seriously considered. The economic downturn that began in Greece in 2009 following the world financial crisis of 2007–2008, and culminated in Greece becoming the first developed country to miss an International Monetary Fund loan repayment in 2015, has been accompanied by significant economic hardship across the country. This is evident in widespread job and income losses, as well as increasing levels of inequality. Through their analysis of the inequitable effects of austerity policies Matsaganis and Leventi demonstrate that 'almost one in ten people in 2012 were found to be not just in relative, but in extreme poverty in the sense of being unable to purchase the basic necessities consistent with dignified living' (2014: 220).

In turn, 'the economic crisis has brought a massive realignment of the Greek electorate away from mainstream parties, giving rise to anti-system and anti-immigrant sentiments' (Ellinas 2013: 543). Symptomatic of this realignment is the rise of Golden Dawn, a far-right nationalist Greek political party, whose vote share in national elections increased from 0.29% in 2009 to 6.97% in May 2012 and 9.39% in 2014, with its popularity among young voters almost double this (Ellinas 2013, 2015).

Contemporary refugees in Greece are often viewed in negative and hostile terms. They are seen to represent a burden on the host country, and a particular source of discontent arises when refugees are perceived to have a better life than some of the Greeks themselves. While it is to the credit of the Greek news media that they apparently do not associate refugees with terrorists to the extent that the British press do (Fotopoulos and Kaimaklioti 2016), the perception that refugees enjoy better treatment by the state than Greek homeless people is a key source of political and social tension. Indeed, the incidence of racist attacks rose during the height of the refugee crisis in 2015, with 273 incidents of racist violence recorded during that year (Racist Violence Recording Network 2015). This violence coincided with more attacks on human rights activists and 'alarming' (ibid.: 3) rates of involvement of law enforcement officials in incidents of racist violence.

The well-being of the asylum seekers and refugees in Greece is challenged further by the replacement of the term 'refugee' with the term '*lathrometanastis*' (clandestine) in public discourse, mainly carried out by the media. This altered lexicon marks a distinction between the 1923 refugees who are strongly connected to the notion of national identity, and contemporary refugees. Although at the beginning of their settlement the 1923 refugees were in many cases treated as foreigners and described as Turk-originating, nowadays they are widely perceived as Greeks who survived a tragedy, and therefore of the same ethnicity as the host population. Contemporary refugees however, are viewed as foreigners, since their national identity is other than Greek.

The use of the term clandestine therefore deprives contemporary refugees of a semantic link to the positively-viewed refugees of the previous century. In Greek society, no distinction is made between foreigners and strangers: all of them are considered clandestine. The lack of distinction (according to the collective perception of Greek society) between migrants and refugees derives from the fact that they are all 'non-Greeks'. The reasons for their migration are not considered important enough to classify them as refugees. The 1922 refugees fought and fled from a national enemy, Turkey; although contemporary refugees have fled their enemies too, these enemies are not Greece's national enemies. Therefore, the identity label of 'refugee' seems to be reserved for migrants with a suitable national origin and a suitable enemy.

Such a blunt and essentialising distinction between Greeks and non-Greeks serves various purposes (see Young 1986). It references a mythological historical national purity, it 'denies difference' (ibid.: 1) by clumping together disparate identities, and it distances, or others, 'outsiders' in semantic and psychological terms. In turn, this distancing has physical effects. When entering Greece from the islands 'clandestines' are usually arrested and transferred to *hotspots*, with inferior living conditions (see Painter et al 2017; Pallister-Wilkins 2018; Taziolli and Garelli 2018). These are usually placed on the borders of Greece, far away from the capital and even further from the centre of Europe. The choice of these spaces is not random. It serves the policy of non-visibility: tactically employing distance and remoteness as ways to perform and inscribe the categorical differences that are being imposed (Mountz 2013; Gill 2016). In these ways the discourse surrounding 'clandestine' migration has spatial and legal manifestations. Migration law in Greece, then, must be viewed as co-produced: the product not only of formal rules and categories but also of social and linguistic norms. Discourses pluralise legal processes by constituting a set of informal norms that interact and compete with formal rules.

The Perception of Unaccompanied Minors in the Humanitarian Context

We now turn to the ways in which perceptions of children held by Greek officials have similar effects. Literature has highlighted how important it is to pay attention to whether refugee children are unaccompanied and/or separated from their parents in particular. Berman (2001) reviewed several studies that emerged on children and conflict following the Second World War and found that the importance of the family and community was a common theme throughout. It was shown that the separation of children from their parents was often more distressing than the bombs themselves (Berman 2001: 245). Garmezy (1983) also found that how children responded to living under the circumstances of war was greatly mediated by the significant adults in their lives.

The mid twentieth century witnessed an increased interest in protecting the rights of children and refugees. Several international conventions and agreements govern the treatment of asylum-seeking children.[6] Most notable among these instruments are the 1951 UN Refugee Convention, the 1967 Protocol Relating to the Status of Refugees, and the 1989 UN Convention on the Rights of the Child (CRC). These instruments, however, follow one dominant cultural conception of childhood. They imagine children as having the same needs, regardless of their social, political, historical and economic context. While recognising that accompanied asylum seeking children face their own difficulties (Ottosson et al. 2017) it is usually unaccompanied asylum-seeking children who are thought of as most needy and whose 'remarkable coping capacities' (Hopkins and Hill 2010: 407) are often overlooked and even impeded by systems of support.

As expressed in some legal narratives, the notion of children as non-agential, passive and as simple recipients of care has been critiqued from various perspectives. Chase (2010) for example, argues that producing children as subjects with little or no agency can provoke an unfortunate backlash: children withhold vital information during the processing of their claim as an attempt to regain or reclaim agency over their lives. Crawley (2010) is also critical of the passive view of children that is entrenched in the legal discourse around refugees and unaccompanied asylum-seeking children, pointing to how a particular conceptualisation of childhood to be found in the legal approach, 'undermines the ability of children to fully articulate their experiences and to secure access to the protection to which they are entitled' (ibid.: 162). In other words, conceiving of children as passive and non-agential can be experienced by the children themselves as a lack of trust and respect.

---

[6]According to the UNHCR (1997: 1) unaccompanied minors are persons who are under the age of 18 and "who are separated from both parents and are not being cared for by an adult who, by law or custom, is responsible to do so".

We now briefly set out the field sites in more detail, and then explore three ways in which perceptions of children held by officials impact upon young people's experiences of the legal processes that they go through.

The Field Sites

One of the field sites of the research was the reception centre in a small town in northwestern Greece. The space had been used since 1947, when Queen Frideriki established one of the so called Paidoupoleis—institutions that hosted children from the civil war stricken areas of Greece. In 1973 this Paidoupoli turned into an orphanage for Greek children. In the early 1990s it began hosting children from poor Albanian families as well. In 2008, following the need to create reception centres for separated asylum-seeking children, the Konitsa institution housed the first refugee children from Afghanistan and various African states. Chrisa visited this reception centre for the first time in 2009 and then spent a year visiting it on a daily basis while conducting field research for her Ph.D. thesis.

When she started visiting the reception centre, there were around 70 children residing there, belonging to three categories: orphan children from Greek families; children from Albanian families; and asylum-seeking children. Greek children were allowed to enroll in the Greek education system, or if they preferred they would attend the technical classes within the centre. The Albanian children were also allowed to attend the technical classes. The asylum-seeking children were not allowed to attend either a Greek school or the technical classes. The only provision for them was a daily two-hour class in Greek inside the centre. During discussions with them, they would often complain about life in the reception centre, how left aside and totally dependent on the decisions of the personnel they felt.

Another field site of the research is the Skaramagkas camp which started operating in April 2016, when a large number of asylum seekers who had been residing in the port of Piraeus in self-organised accommodation with tents were moved there by the Ministry of Migration. The space belongs to the Hellenic Navy and the site management is the responsibility of the Ministry of Migration.[7] The Hellenic Navy used to provide the food via a

---

[7]From June 2017 till February 2018 the camp remained without site management, a fact that raised serious protection issues for all the population and in particular unaccompanied minors. As the official registration in the site was the responsibility of the site management, many people who came to Skaramagkas during that period could not get registered as residents in the camp, a fact that excluded

catering contractor, and the Greek police are responsible for the safety of the camp. Beginning in June 2017, the NGO CARITAS (through UNHCR) provided cash cards with which the inhabitants could buy food.[8] At the time of writing (mid 2017) there are almost 3000 people residing in the camp, all of them living in containers. The majority of the population is Syrian, followed by a minority of Iraqi Yezidis and Afghans. There are around 20 unaccompanied minors in the camp. Skaramagkas camp has a Safe Zone for unaccompanied minors and a Child Friendly Space (CFS) which functions under the supervision of a Child Protection actor.[9] In her work as a legal advisor Chrisa has come across various cases that reflect unaccompanied minors' experiences of asylum procedures in Greece.

Since it was not possible to collect consent to use the interviewees' direct testimony during Chrisa's work as a legal advisor we employ a variety of measures. First, we do not quote from these interviewees at all. Second, we follow the methodology of composing fictions as a means of protecting the identity of the people Chrisa spoke to from this site (Gough 2008: 338–340). That is, we present fictional accounts concerning fictional characters. These accounts are analogous to the accounts that Chrisa heard but do not correspond to single, real individuals. They are intended to be realistic, but not real. They are broadly based on the experience of a number of individuals, but are fictionalised in terms of content, sequence as well as the correspondence between events and the narratives that we ascribe to the characters we discuss. In this way we are able to convey the frustrations of the people Chrisa spoke to without compromising their privacy. While 'in much everyday speech fiction is equated with falsehood' (ibid.: 339) this approach recognizes the narrative force of fiction as a means of conveying certain forms of truth. If the assumption is made that academic research is chiefly concerned with documenting facts without distorting them, then it is reasonable to suppose that there is no place for fiction in academic work. But academic work, especially ethnographic work that seeks to convey

---

them from the cash card program. Unaccompanied minors arriving at that time became invisible to the national response system as the actor responsible for registering them with EKKA (The National Centre for Social Solidarity, which is the institution responsible for placing them into shelters) was absent.

[8]In the months that followed the cash cards were provided directly by UNHCR.

[9]Safe Zones and CFS can be found in many camps both in the mainland and the islands of Greece. However, the Safe Zones have limited places and often cannot accommodate all the unaccompanied minors of the camp.

meaning and feelings, is concerned with more than the brute transmission of facts. As such, 'storying' (Piper and Sikes 2010: 568) can be an indispensable strategy towards the fulfilment of academic objectives and 'an important strategy for protecting vulnerable participants' (ibid.: 573). In what follows then, the characters Ali, Jamal, Jafar and Fatima are fictional.

In terms of languages used, in the case of Konitsa Reception Centre Chrisa used the Arabic and Farsi interpreters who worked in the centre. She spoke directly with African minors in English. In the case of Skaramagkas she used the Farsi, Sorani and Arabic interpreters working for an NGO operating in the site.

Childhood as Linear and Universal

The first perception of children that becomes evident in the two sites is the view of childhood as a linear and universal process that is highly dependent upon chronological age. This view has been lambasted by the new social studies of childhood, which emphasise that 'the child [should be] conceived of as a person [and...] a social actor [...] in its own right. It does not have to be approached from an assumed shortfall of competence, reason or significance' (James et al. 1998: 207). Anthropologists in particular have played a decisive role in critiquing the 'universalist account of childhood' (LeVine 2007: 250) that emerged in the last century from childhood cognitive development theory and developmental psychology.

One of the most revealing narratives in the case of the Konitsa reception centre came from the personnel themselves. According to one of them:

> They are kids, they don't know what is best for them. We treat them as our own kids. I wouldn't, for example, allow my child to visit friends that I don't know, or have a sleepover at someone else's house at that age. That is why we don't allow them to visit their friends in Ioannina [a nearby town]. They are under our responsibility.

In this view of childhood there is often the underlying assumption that children (taken to be people under 18 years of age) require protection, that they may not be capable of defining their 'best interests', and that they are less able to cope with violence and forced migration than their adult counterparts.

This view of childhood often backfires though, as "Ali's" case illustrates. Ali is a 16-year-old unaccompanied minor from Iraq who arrived in Greece with three of his older, adult male relatives in early 2015. Ali spent much of his early teenage years fighting for survival alongside his older relatives, and is a capable and agential individual. When they arrived in Chios Island, for example, they stayed on the streets for some days and then boarded a ship to Piraeus Port before travelling independently to Thessaloniki. There they followed a group of people who were heading towards Eidomeni (a village by the Greek—Macedonian Border).[10] They stayed there for a number of months but got separated when the border closed.

Ali's older relatives made it to Sweden but Ali was first detained for a few days and then sent to a shelter for unaccompanied minors in Thessaloniki after Eidomeni was evacuated. In this way measures that were framed as 'protective' became a source of aggravation for Ali, reminiscent of Fassin's (2005: 362) 'compassionate repression'. Because he was under 18 years old he was entered into a slower and more cumbersome administrative process, setting in motion a tension between his agential capabilities and the passive and immobile child that he was expected to be. He left the shelter there after a few days and returned to Piraeus Port where around 1500 migrants and refugees had set up an informal settlement in two of the port's docks. In Spring 2016 he was sent to Skaramagkas camp along with the majority of the people who had found shelter in Piraeus Port.

Later that year Ali was arrested and detained in Igoumenitsa Port, western Greece, while he was trying to board a ship to Italy. On his release Ali told the lawyer that he would not register again with a shelter and that he wanted to return to Skaramagkas camp. In other words he was once again refusing the 'help' that was provided for children. He also refused any referral to Child Protection officials who provide psychosocial support.

Eventually he reached France and has plans to leave for Sweden to join his older relatives. Throughout his time in Greece he insisted that he did not want to live in a shelter because he felt that he was treated as a child rather than as an adult. He did not want to be referred to Child Protection officials because they would not understand that he was capable of living on his own. Ali had lost his patience and did not trust the asylum procedures in Greece due to the huge delays in registering with the asylum service and the family reunification process. He never revealed his plans about leaving Greece irregularly to any of the adults involved in his 'protection', out of fear that they would call the public prosecutor to force him into a shelter. For

---

[10]Eidomeni is the place where, in the summer of 2015, refugees and migrants gathered to cross the border to Macedonia and continue their journey towards the North of Europe. Many made it through until February 2016, when Macedonia closed the borders. For detailed information concerning the situation at the Greek—Macedonian borders at the time see Amnesty International (2015).

him, all Child Protection officials did nothing to help his case and did not understand his anguish at being left behind by his older relatives. All he saw was a complicated bureaucratic system that was unsympathetic towards him, and adults who do nothing to help. In other words, Ali felt that he had to actively resist the model of childhood that was being imposed upon him by officials, who could not see past his numeric age. From his perspective their interventions were simply slowing his progress towards reunification with his family. Attempts to 'help' backfired in the sense that they not only caused additional frustration but also contributed to Ali's separation from his family and led him to take further risks in pursuit of reunification with them.

Ali's experience was not unusual. "Jamal", another 16-year-old from Iraq in the Skaramagkas camp, tried to leave Greece in the summer of 2016 and was arrested by the Greek Police. He had been trying for two months. He had arrived with his uncle but the Asylum Service did not allow his uncle to be registered as Jamal's legal guardian because of the lack of documentation proving that Jamal was really his uncle's nephew. As a result his uncle's immediate family were relocated to France, but Jamal could not follow.

Separated Children as Dependent Burdens

A second perception about asylum seeking children is that they are dependent, and therefore burdensome to either their guardians or to the state. According to Zetter (1999: 74) this dependency discourse is a powerful tool used to restrict and contain refugees. Refugees tend to be viewed as:

> a burden of dependency on the community. The concept of sanctuary coupled with the loss of familiar economic and social support systems and individual autonomy combine to construct a powerful image of dependency and the need for assistance.

The dependency discourse goes hand-in-hand with a humanitarian discourse. Malkki (1996) argues that the 'burdensome' representation of refugees—manifested in the work of refugee agencies, government and non-government organisations as well as media—has serious consequences for their lives. While she recognises that these representations help to raise funds and resources, they also silence their subjects.

> [R]efugees suffer from a peculiar kind of speechlessness in the face of the national and international organisations under whose object of care and

control they are. Their accounts are disqualified almost a priori, while the languages of refugee relief, policy science, and 'development' claim the production of authoritative narratives about refugees. (Malkki 1996: 386)

In the case of the refugee children Chrisa spoke to in Konista, the perception of children as dependent was at odds with their evident ability and desire to work, but at times was a self-fulfilling perception because it prohibited this very activity. Farzin from Iran, for example, explained that it was precisely the lack of opportunity to work that kept him trapped in the reception centre for children. 'I have walked for over a month to reach Greece. I can take care of myself', he explained,

> If I had had some money I would have left this place a long time ago. It is so boring and it offers us nothing. I am not afraid to go to Germany alone. Some friends of mine made it, why not me? With the proper amount of money, a smuggler can take you anywhere. That is why I have to find a job immediately.

Mohamad from Senegal concurred. 'We have requested that they allow us to work in the fields here in Konitsa, but they don't permit it,' he complained. 'But we need the money so we can get around by ourselves. Plus, what should we do all day? There is nothing here for us. We only sleep, eat and play football. They either treat us like very small children or they ignore us altogether.

The dependence discourse also acts to deny under 18s the opportunity to take part in supposedly 'adult' activities, which often reflects a western, conservative view of childhood. One under-18 Afghan refugee who spent time at the Konitsa reception centre explained that, 'They don't even allow us to help in the kitchen or suggest what we want to eat. We never chose our clothes, we get whatever people give us'. Another refugee, "Jafar", a 17-year-old from Afghanistan, travelled to Greece with his sister. She managed to reach the Netherlands and apply for asylum there but he was unable to follow. He wanted to stay in the Skaramagas camp, even though he conceded that it is more dangerous than a shelter for children like the one at Konitsa. Despite the fact that he has had his money and mobile phone stolen in the camp, and that he really hates the food there, he values the fact that he can smoke and go out at night, while in Konitsa he is treated like a little child. Jafar tried to leave Greece twice on his own and succeeded the second time.

One of the most concerning consequences of the dependency discourse is its ability to undermine the trust of refugees in systems of protection, which has been recognised as an 'essential component' (Hynes 2009: 97) of their effectiveness. "Fatima", a 14-year-old from Syria, arrived in Greece in 2016 with her adult brother and his family. They all applied for relocation but like Jamal, her brother could not be considered her legal guardian due to the lack of relevant documentation. Her brother, who lived in the Skaramagkas camp, was accepted by Germany via the relocation procedure. Thinking that Fatima faced the prospect of living in a shelter for unaccompanied minors in Greece, she and her brother made the decision for her to attempt to go back to Turkey on her own—a dangerous and illegal route—to try to reconnect with other members of her family there.

Fatima's attempt to return to Turkey was unsuccessful: she was caught and arrested in the Evros region. She was detained for almost ten days before she was sent to a shelter for children in Athens. Her experience raises the questions of who she was fleeing from, and who she was trapped by.

Separated Children as Undeserving

Another aspect of the rhetoric concerning asylum seeker children is that of the undeserving migrant who manipulates the social care system of the hosting country.[11] According to Watters (2008: 47): '"Asylum seekers" [has become] a term in everyday discussion inextricably linked to imagery of cunning and manipulative foreigners securing generous material rewards from a hopelessly gullible government'. This perception was strongly in evidence among the staff at Konitsa. 'They are not really refugees' one of them told Chrisa,

> They falsify their personal data to present themselves as refugees and take advantage of the protection our state gives them. Some of them are not even children. They are clandestine. I wonder, how could their parents ever let them travel so far away from home? Why don't they work, instead of sending their children to a foreign country to make money? I would never ask that of my son.

In her ethnography of a British detention centre, Alexandra Hall (2012) identifies the tendency among staff to assume that illegality is a matter of

---

[11]This is currently the case with unaccompanied minors from Pakistan, Bangladesh and African countries. Due to the perception of the Asylum Service that the citizens from these countries fall under the category of the migrant rather than the refugee, their asylum claims are usually rejected. The minors are thus put in a "limbo" situation with regards to their residence status, since they cannot be deported as long as they are minor, nor enjoy a rights holders' position.

individual choice. In turn, this illegality, for the staff, is 'because of their morally compromised and weak character rather than desperation and necessity' (ibid.: 102). This produces a perception of undeservingness, according to which certain supposedly nefarious individuals choose to take from, but not to contribute towards, their host society. In this discourse, migrants are viewed as attempting to 'escape work or fraudulently claim benefits, or to work illegally and escape paying taxes' (ibid.: 103). The telltale signs of such inauthenticity, as far as the staff at Hall's detention centre were concerned, included everything from complaining about conditions and displaying too much emotion to food refusal.

Under conditions of such skepticism, moral condemnation on the basis of undeservingness is common, and is keenly felt by the residents of Konitsa. 'The personnel do not like us' Mohamed from Senegal surmised. 'They never have time for us, they don't even have an interpreter in French. There is only one television with Greek channels. We have asked them many times to arrange it so we can watch some French channels as well, but nothing'. Rizula from Afghanistan agrees, explaining that:

> The personnel don't treat us well. They are much more giving towards the Albanians and the Greeks. They don't allow us to go to the Greek school and they don't allow us to attend the classes inside the centre either. When we tell them that we are bored here in Konitsa they never listen. There is nothing here but a small town and mountains.

These frustrations are exacerbated by not only insensitive media reporting, but also a feeling among the residents that the staff assent to such insensitivity. 'When we started visiting the local football pitch, the local newspaper wrote an article claiming that we suffer from infectious diseases,' Rizula told Chrisa. What made the situation worse was the distinct lack of support that the refugee children received from the staff at Konitsa. 'The personnel never supported us.' Rizula recalled, displaying her own moral indignation at their inactivity.

Conclusion

This chapter has demonstrated how 'nonlegal forms of normative ordering' (Merry 1988: 870) such as those that inhere in national discourses and perceptions, and that are held by legal subjects themselves, can interrupt and recast formal legal structures. While international law sets out a series of ways in which refugee protection is supposed to operate, the Greek case illustrates the importance of plural influences, beyond formal law itself, in the determination of legal experiences and outcomes. These include the influences of language, cultural history, economic conditions and assumptions about childhood. In other words, the case of refugee law is one example of how 'other forms of regulation outside law constitute law' (ibid.: 874).

In various ways, these influences do not auger well for refugee rights in Greece. The association of refugees with the discourse of clandestine migration has coincided with a marked increase in poverty, inequality and anti-immigration sentiment in the country. Although the lack of resources and its position as a first safe country of asylum under the Dublin regulations should not be overlooked in explaining the lacklustre approach to refugee rights in Greece (see Fili and Xythali 2017), the close 'relations between the legal discourse and other social discourses' (Teubner 1991: 1446) that scholars of legal pluralism identify is also a factor. The clandestine discourse has the effect of homogenising and othering the refugee population, which paves the way for the sort of exclusionary and illegal practices that PRO ASYL and Human Rights Watch have condemned in the country.

Nevertheless, as scholars of legal pluralism have argued, these interruptions can also 'sometimes be desirable' (Berman 2006: 1155) when they result in 'alternative ideas' (ibid.: 1155). The majority of the minors that participated in the research faced great difficulties in understanding the reasoning behind the asylum procedures in Greece and Europe and posed very particular questions: "why can't I go where I want", "why can't I chose how to live" and "why don't states ask me what I want"? To be sure, these difficulties often result in negative outcomes: distrust of authorities for example, risk-taking and reliance on dangerous social networks. By questioning these things and signaling their discontent, however, asylum seeking children are also insisting on a different conceptualisation of childhood. For example, most of them refused to identify themselves as just 'vulnerable' as they felt it deprived them of the right to claim their maturity. They would accept their legal classification as vulnerable only if it would speed up the legal procedures that concerned them. These sorts of extra-legal interruptions of the logic of international refugee law could be productive if they cause legal practitioners to reevaluate the categories, assumptions and values that this body of law associates with being under 18 years of age.

References

Amnesty International. (2015). *Europe's Borderlands: Violations Against Refugees and Migrants in Macedonia, Serbia and Hungary*. Available at: https://www.amnesty-usa.org/files/ser-mac_migration_report_final.compressed.pdf. Accessed 17 July 2017.

Berman, H. (2001). Children and War: Current Understandings and Future Directions. *Public Health Nursing, 18*(4), 243–252.

Berman, P. (2006). Global Legal Pluralism. *Southern California Law Review, 18*(24), 1–55.

Black, R. (1994). Livelihoods Under Stress: A Case Study of Refugee Vulnerability in Greece. *Journal of Refugee Studies, 7*(4), 360–377.

Chase, E. (2010). Agency and Silence: Young People Seeking Asylum Alone in the UK. *British Journal of Social Work, 40*(7), 2050–2068.

Christensen, P., & James, A. (Eds.). (2008). *Research with Children: Perspectives and Practices* (2nd Ed.). London and New York: Routledge.

Crawley, H. (2010). 'No One Gives You a Chance to Say What You Are Thinking': Finding Space for Children's Agency in the UK Asylum System. *Area, 42*(2), 162–169.

European Council for Refugees and Exiles (ECRE). (2016). *Greece Amends Its Asylum Law After Multiple Appeals Board Decisions Overturn the Presumption of Turkey as a Safe Third Country*. Available at: http://www.ecre.org/greece-amends-its-asylum-law-after-multiple-appeals-board-decisions-overturn-the-presumption-of-turkey-as-a-safe-third-country/. Accessed 20 July 2017.

Ellinas, A. (2013). The Rise of Golden Dawn: The New Face of the Far Right in Greece. *South European Society and Politics, 18*(4), 543–565.

Ellinas, A. (2015). Neo-Nazism in an Established Democracy: The Persistence of Golden Dawn in Greece. *South European Society and Politics, 20*(1), 1–20.

Fassin, D. (2005). Compassion and Repression: The Moral Economy of Immigration Policies in France. *Cultural Anthropology, 20*(3), 362–387.

Fili, A., & Xythali, V. (2017). Unaccompanied Minors in Greece: Who Can 'Save' Them? *Border Criminologies*. Available at: https://www.law.ox.ac.uk/research-subject-groups/centre-criminology/centreborder-criminologies/blog/2017/02/unaccompanied. Accessed 20 July 2017.

Fotopoulos, S., & Kaimaklioti, M. (2016). Media Discourse on the Refugee Crisis: On What Have the Greek, German and British Press Focused? *European View, 15*(2), 265–279.

Garmezy, N. (Ed.). (1983). *Stressors of Childhood*. Minneapolis: McGraw-Hill.

Gibb, R., & Good, A. (2014). Interpretation, Translation and Intercultural Communication in Refugee Status Determination Procedures in the UK and France. *Language and Intercultural Communication, 13*(3), 385–399.

Gill, N. (2016). *Nothing Personal? Geographies of Governing and Activism in the British Asylum System*. Oxford: Wiley-Blackwell.

Goodwin-Gill, G. (1996). *The Refugee in International Law*. Oxford: Oxford University Press.

Gough, N. (2008). Fictional Writing. In L. Given (Ed.), *The Sage Encyclopedia of Qualitative Research*. Los Angeles, London, New Delhi and Singapore: Sage.

Hall, A. (2012). *Border Watch: Cultures of Immigration, Detention and Control*. London: Pluto Press.

Hardman, C. (1973). Can There Be an Anthropology of Children? *Journal of the Anthropological Society of Oxford, 4*(2), 85–99.

Hopkins, P., & Hill, M. (2010). The Needs and Strengths of Unaccompanied Asylum-Seeking Children and Young People in Scotland. *Child and Family Social Work, 15*(4), 399–408.

Human Rights Watch. (2016). *"Why Are You Keeping Me Here" Unaccompanied Children Detained in Greece*. New York: Human Rights Watch. Available at: https://www.hrw.org/sites/default/files/report_pdf/greece0916_web.pdf. Accessed 17 July 2017.

Hynes, P. (2009). Contemporary Compulsory Dispersal and the Absence of Space for the Restoration of Trust. *Journal of Refugee Studies, 22*(1), 97–121.

James, A., Jenks, C., & Prout, A. (1998). *Theorizing Childhood*. Williston, VT: Teachers College Press.

Keselman, O., Cederborg, A., Lamb, M., & Dahlström, Ö. (2008). Mediated Communication with Minors in Asylum-Seeking Hearings. *Journal of Refugee Studies, 21*(1), 103–116.

LeVine, R. (2007). Ethnographic Studies of Childhood: A Historical Overview. *American Anthropologist, 109*(2), 247–260.

Malkki, L. (1996). Speechless Emissaries: Refugees, Humanitarianism, and Dehistoricization. *Cultural Anthropology, 11*(3), 377–404.

Matsaganis, M., & Leventi, C. (2014). Poverty and Inequality During the Great Recession in Greece. *Political Studies Review, 12*(2), 209–223.

Merry, S. (1988). Legal Pluralism. *Law and Society Review, 22*(5), 869–896.

Mountz, A. (2013). Mapping Remote Detention: Dis/Location Through Isolation. In J. Loyd, M. Mitchelson, & A. Burridge (Eds.), *Beyond Walls and Cages: Prisons, Borders, and Global Crisis*. Athens and London: The University of Georgia Press.

O'Kane, C. (2008). The Development of Participatory Techniques: Facilitating Children's Views About Decisions Which Affect Them. In P. Christensen & A. James (Eds.), *Research with Children: Perspectives and Practices* (2nd ed.). London and New York: Routledge.

Ottosson, L., Eastmond, M., & Cederborg, A. (2017). Assertions and Aspirations: Agency Among Accompanied Asylum-Seeking Children in Sweden. *Children's Geographies, 15*(4), 426–438.

Painter, J., Papada, E., Papoutsi, A., & Vradis, A. (2017). Hotspot Politics-Or, When the EU State Gets Real. *Political Geography, 60,* 259–260.

Pallister-Wilkins, P. (2018). Hotspots and the Geographies of Humanitarianism. *Environment and Planning D: Society and Space*. Online First.

Piper, H., & Sikes, P. (2010). All Teachers Are Vulnerable but Especially Gay Teachers: Using Composite Fictions to Protect Research Participants in Pupil–Teacher Sex-Related Research. *Qualitative Inquiry, 16*(7), 566–574.

PRO ASYL. (2007). *The Truth May Be Bitter But It Must Be Told: The Situation of Refugees in the Aegean and the Practices of the Greek Coast Quard*. Available at: https://www.proasyl.de/wp-content/uploads/2007/10/Griechenlandbericht_Engl.pdf. Accessed 19 July 2017.

PRO ASYL. (2016). *Greek Government in Court for Introducing Unconstitutional Second Instance Asylum Committee*s. Available at: https://www.proasyl.de/en/news/greek-government-in-court-for-overruling-independent-second-instance-asylum-committees/. Accessed 20 July 2017.

Racist Violence Recording Network. (2015). *Annual Report*. Available at: http://rvrn.org/wp-content/uploads/2016/04/Report_2015eng.pdf. Accessed 20 July 2017.

Rycroft, R. (2005). Communicative Barriers in the Asylum Account. In P. Shah (Ed.), *The Challenge of Asylum to Legal Systems*. London: Cavendish.

Skordas, A., & Sitaropoulos, N. (2004). Why Greece Is Not a Safe Host Country for Refugees. *International Journal for Refugee Law, 16*(1), 25–52.

Teubner, G. (1991). The Two Faces of Janus: Rethinking Legal Pluralism. *Cardozo Law Review, 13*, 1443–1462.

Tazzioli, M., & Garelli, G. (2018). Containment Beyond Detention: The Hotspot System and Disrupted Migration Movements Across Europe. *Environment and Planning D: Society and Space*. Early view.

United Nations High Commissioner for Refugees. (1997). *Guidelines on Policies and Procedures in Dealing with Unaccompanied Children Seeking Asylum*. Available at: http://www.unhcr.org/3d4f91cf4.pdf. Accessed 2 Aug 2017.

Voutira, E. (2003). Refugees: Whose Term Is It Anyway? Emic and Etic Constructions of 'Refugees' in Modern Greek. In J. van Selm, K. Kamanga, J. Morrison, A. Nadig, S. Špoljar- Vržina, & L. van Willigen (Eds.), *The Refugee Convention at Fifty: A View from Forced Migration Studies*. Lanham, MD: Lexington Books.

Watters, C. (2008). *Refugee Children: Towards the Next Horizon*. New York: Routledge.

Woodman, G. (1998). Ideological Combat and Social Observation: Recent Debate About Legal Pluralism. *The Journal of Legal Pluralism and Unofficial Law, 30*(42), 21–59.

Young, I. (1986). The Ideal of Community and the Politics of Difference. *Social Theory and Practice, 12*(1), 1–26.

Zetter, R. (1999). International Perspectives on Refugee Assistance. In A. Ager (Ed.), *Refugees: Perspectives on the Experiences of Forced Migration*. New York: Cassell.

Open Access This chapter is distributed under the terms of the Creative Commons Attribution 4.0 International License (http://creativecommons.org/licenses/by/4.0/), which permits use, duplication, adaptation, distribution and reproduction in any medium or format, as long as you give appropriate credit to the original author(s) and the source, a link is provided to the Creative Commons license and any changes made are indicated.

The images or other third party material in this chapter are included in the work's Creative Commons license, unless indicated otherwise in the credit line; if such material is not included in the work's Creative Commons license and the respective action is not permitted by statutory regulation, users will need to obtain permission from the license holder to duplicate, adapt or reproduce the material.

Part II

Communication

7

Why Handling Power Responsibly Matters: The Active Interpreter Through the Sociological Lens

Julia Dahlvik

Introduction

Current developments throughout the world and in specific regions have made asylum one of the key topics of today. Although Europe only hosts a small percentage of the millions of people who had to flee from their homes,[1] asylum seekers and reception conditions have been in the focus of European mass media and societal debates. As this book perfectly illustrates, social researchers too have started to explore many different aspects of this complex phenomenon. The administration of asylum claims is one of these crucial topics that has become a separate field of investigation. Embedded in the context of the legal procedure, this contribution sets out to highlight the fundamental role interpreters play in enabling communication between asylum claimants and representatives of the state. Most asylum hearings, often the key moment in an asylum procedure, could not take place without the work of an interpreter.

---

[1]No European country was among the top ten receiving countries; the list was led by Turkey with around two and a half million refugees, Pakistan with around one and a half million and Lebanon with over one million.

J. Dahlvik (✉)
University of Applied Sciences FH Campus Wien, Vienna, Austria
e-mail: julia.dahlvik@fh-campuswien.ac.at

I adopt a sociological perspective to first explore the relationship between public official and interpreter in asylum interviews. The basic assumption, based on existing literature, is that the relation is more complex than a simple contractee-contractor relation and, as a part of that, interpreters are often in a more powerful position than officials would want them to be. Meanwhile, it seems to be common understanding in the literature that interpreters are active agents rather than passive transmitters of utterances from one language into another (Rycroft 2005; Angelelli 2014). This ethnography hints at the complexity and contours of the power imbalance in asylum interviews. As a consequence, I argue that both researchers and practitioners need to focus more on professionalism and ethics in community interpreting, especially in the context of international protection. While it is no doubt vital to not only talk about interpreters, but also hear their opinion (as well as that of claimants), in this contribution I will focus on the perspective of decision-making officials.[2]

Since the turn of the century at the latest, there has been increasing sociological interest in translation and interpreting. The development of a sociology of translation, often a conceptual and theoretical endeavour, is based on works such as those of Pierre Bourdieu, Bruno Latour, Bernard Lahire, Anthony Giddens (Tipton 2008 in the context of asylum) and Niklas Luhmann, as the anthology edited by the Austria-based researchers Wolf and Fukari (2007) shows. One of the issues, which has nevertheless received too little attention to this date concerns professionalism and professional ethics. Among the few works are those by Wadensjö (1999, 2007) and Grbić (2010), who address the topic of professionalism in interpreting, or by Rudvin (2007), who focuses particularly on professionalism and ethics in community interpreting. Both the sociological perspective and the issues of professionalism and professional ethics are at least briefly mentioned in two recent introductory publications in the field of translation and interpreting studies (TIS) (Pöchhacker 2016; Munday 2016). This chapter aims to contribute to this area of research by exploring the relevance of professionalism and professional ethics in the context of asylum administration.

Since the asylum procedure takes place in a legal context, the perspective of legal interpreting and its particular challenges also provides valuable insights. Key works (Morris 1995; Colin and Morris 1996; Berk-Seligson

---

[2]Due to the institutional perspective of this study, interviews with non-institutional actors were not included. Quotes from interviews with interpreters originate from earlier research (Dahlvik 2009a, b).

2002) have identified a number of issues relevant to interpreting in this specific field, such as the controversial neutrality of the interpreter, which is connected to an inherent role ambiguity, or questions of power. In relation to professionalism and ethics, power in the interaction represents a key issue in this contribution, which connects to research on interpreter-provider collaboration and conflicts of control in the interpreter-mediated interaction (Hsieh 2010 in the medical context).

Interpreting in the field of asylum has increasingly become an object of research (Inghilleri 2007; Maryns 2013; Lee 2014), including a focus on the role of interpreters in this specific context (Barsky 1996; Rycroft 2005; Gibb and Good 2014; Good 2007). In the Austrian context, a number of studies have been carried out, investigating, for example, conflicting role expectations (Pöllabauer 2007), the interpreter's key role in co-producing the interview transcript (Pöchhacker and Kolb 2009), or mutual understanding and intercultural misunderstanding (Rienzner 2011). While such research is often undertaken from the perspectives of TIS, communication or linguistic studies, researchers are increasingly taking into account sociological aspects. Nevertheless, I argue that more in-depth empirical sociological research is necessary to investigate the interpreter-mediated asylum interview, a complex communication situation characterised by an important power imbalance, and its connection to interpreters' professionalism and ethics.

This chapter adds to existing research by providing new insights from an institutional perspective. First, it explores public officials' perception of interpreters and cooperation with them. Second, this contribution sheds new empirical light on interpreters' active role and room for manoeuvre in doing interpreting in the asylum hearing as well as its conditions and consequences. Building on this, the implications of the analysis for the practice of interpreting in asylum hearings with regard to professionalism are discussed.

The findings discussed in this contribution are based on an institutional ethnography (Smith 2006) case study of a branch of the former Austrian Federal Asylum Office[3] (FAO). Through a short-term internship at this institution I was able to investigate processes that are otherwise not accessible to the public. The larger study, which focused more generally on the social practices and processes at the FAO, was based on the 'crystallisation' (Richardson 2000) of semi-structured interviews with decision-making officials, participant observation of asylum hearings and office life, as well as analysis of records and other internal documents. For this study, I observed

---

[3]Since the 1 January 2014, 'Federal Office for Immigration and Asylum'.

six asylum hearings, which usually lasted several hours; all but one of them took place with an interpreter. In addition to conversations during field research, I carried out 14 semi-structured in-depth interviews with different actors, among them decision-makers at different levels of the Asylum Office (frontline workers as well as supervisors), staff of one of the Initial Reception Centres as well as a judge of the (former) Asylum Court. The analysed artefacts include internal documents, such as work instructions or training programmes, as well as three individual records of former asylum claimants. Data was generated mainly between 2010 and 2012. The analysis of observations, interviews and internal documents first focused on thematic coding (Strauss and Corbin 1990) and subsequently followed the approach of interpretive social research as outlined by Froschauer and Lueger (2009).

In the following, I provide a brief overview of the Austrian asylum system and illustrate how interpreters are typically involved in the procedure. In the second section I explore officials' perspectives on working together with interpreters, including the process of commissioning interpreters, quality considerations regarding the rendered services and officials' use of interpreters' 'expert' knowledge. This is followed by an analysis of interpreters' active interventions in the interaction which discusses them from the perspective of professionalism in interpreting. These interventions include managing the communication situation, taking over control of the situation, and undermining the official's authority as the leader of the hearing. I conclude by highlighting the importance of professionalism and professional ethics in dealing with power relations in such situations of what I call 'proxy communication', especially in the delicate context of international protection.

The Asylum Procedure in Austria and the Interpreter-Mediated Interview

An asylum application can be lodged with the police. The asylum claimant is then registered and brought to one of the Federal Care Facilities throughout Austria where she lives (at least) for the duration of the admission procedure. In the admission procedure, the Federal Office for Immigration and Asylum (FOIA) assesses whether Austria or another EU member state is responsible for the procedure. If Austria is not responsible, the country through which the claimant entered the EU first is responsible for the procedure (according to the Dublin Regulation). A claimant can lodge a complaint against the decision with the Federal Administrative Court, which will either confirm the decision of the FOIA or judge that Austria is responsible. If no complaint is lodged or the Court does not decide differently within several days, the claimant is transferred to the responsible EU country and can be taken into pre-deportation detention before that. If Austria is responsible, the asylum claimant is assigned an accommodation in a regional facility in Austria. The Länder are then responsible for the basic care. After admission, the FOIA assesses in the substantive procedure whether the asylum claimant is entitled to international protection. If the person is granted asylum and is thereby a recognised refugee, she can stay in Austria and has almost the same rights as an Austrian. However, if there are no flight reasons according to the Geneva Refugee Convention (GRC), but the claimant will be in danger in her country of origin, she receives subsidiary protection. If neither flight reasons nor danger in the country of origin exist, the person may still be able to remain in Austria. Reasons can be that the person has been in Austria for many years already, is well integrated or has family members in Austria. The asylum claim is rejected if no flight reasons according to the GRC are found and the claimant does not have to fear a severe violation of human rights in the country of origin. The claimant can lodge a complaint with the Federal Administrative Court, and subsequently a complaint against the Court's decision with the Constitutional or Higher Administrative Court. If no complaint is lodged with the Federal Administrative Court or the negative decision is confirmed, the claimant has to leave Austria. If she does not do that voluntarily she can be deported to her country of origin. A complaint or revision with the Constitutional or Higher Administrative Court is possible but these options are non-suspensive, meaning that a deportation will not necessarily be postponed until they have been concluded.

Interpreters can be involved at any stage of the procedure where face-to-face communication between asylum claimant and representatives of the authority is necessary, for example in the admission procedure, during legal counselling, or, if another interview is deemed necessary, in the complaints procedure at the Federal Administrative Court. This contribution focuses on the interview in the substantive procedure, which represents a cornerstone of the procedure. These interviews take place in caseworkers' offices, where claimant, official and interpreter are supposed to sit in a triangle. The official leads the interview and types the transcript at the same time. At the end of the interview, which follows a specific structure, the interpreter sight-translates the transcript back into the original language so that the asylum claimant has the possibility to make corrections before verifying the completeness and correctness of the transcript with her signature. The transcript is the key outcome of the interview and serves as a basis for future decisions. One of the interpreters explains why she likes to sit in a place where she sees the computer screen (a seating constellation which tends to ignore the prescribed triangle), 'Eventually, I'm liable for the transcript and the back translation. For many years I've been watching what the official is typing; it has become a habit.'

There are procedural rules on the involvement of interpreters as well as norms on the nature, extent and manner of interpretation, the exclusion (due to partiality) and liability of interpreters (Kadrić 2009) However, the concrete form of the interpreter's role and a delimitation of her duties are not legally defined (Maurer-Kober 2006). The Act on expert witnesses and court interpreters regulates the administration of oath and registration of court interpreters, but not their implementing power. At court, it is legally the judge's and not the interpreter's decision, what is interpreted and what is not. According to Kadrić (2009), however, interpreters are usually not prevented from acting independently. In addition, interpreters are often understood as experts and assistants and thus as advisors of the court (ibid.). The study findings suggest a similar situation at the authority. It is, however, important to note that in the administrative asylum procedure court-certification of interpreters is recommended but not legally required (Pöllabauer 2005). In addition, there are several languages for which no certified interpreters are available. Although it is possible to swear-in interpreters 'ad hoc' at court, Berk-Seligson (2002) points out that not even an oath sworn before court can guarantee sufficient qualification. Concerning the role of the interpreter in the Austrian asylum procedure, UNHCR Austria (2015) has recently edited a training handbook for interpreters in this context.

Discussion of Findings[4]

Officials' Perspectives on Working Together with Interpreters

This section explores how caseworkers perceive and relate to interpreters, who are not members of the government institution but externally commissioned. Decision-makers do not only have legal discretion; they also have room for manoeuvre in a broader sense, for example, regarding the choice of the interpreter. While officially they should commission different interpreters, as an official explains, the reasons for this rule are not quite clear; it might be regarded as a measure against coalition-building. According to

---

[4]Parts of this chapter are based on an earlier publication (Dahlvik 2018).

the official, however, the rule is rarely implemented since 'that's just difficult [...] because if you work well together with one [interpreter], are satisfied with him, he knows how you work, I have the feeling he's neutral, why should I then appoint another one?'. Considering her good and bad experiences with different interpreters, it makes more sense for her to re-appoint an interpreter with whom she already works well together. Commissioning interpreters is one of the areas where officials' individual approaches and strategies in dealing with asylum claims are visible.

A key issue regarding the cooperation between caseworkers and interpreters that emerged from the data is the quality of interpreters' work, which relates to issues of professionalism. Since court-approved interpreters exist only for a limited number of languages, for other languages uncertified interpreters need to be commissioned who may still have a university degree or other interpreting training. In addition, officials point out that whilst for some languages there is a larger pool of interpreters to choose from, for less common languages it is often difficult to find an 'appropriate' interpreter. To facilitate the commissioning process, there is thus an internal list of uncertified interpreters in addition to the official, publicly available list of certified interpreters. Again, this illustrates the coexistence and complementarity of formal and informal norms in the institution and is an example of legal pluralism (see Gill and Good, this volume).

Quality of Work as an Aspect of Professionalism

Some officials point out that the lack of competences of untrained interpreters can lead to specific problems in the interpreting situation affecting the other participants. A caseworker explains that some interpreters are not more than 'stopgap solutions which you don't [commission] anymore'. She adds, however, that sometimes there are no viable alternatives to commissioning problematic interpreters, 'for some countries [that is, languages] there are no good interpreters, but you still have to recourse to them time and again'.[5] Untrained interpreters are stopgap solutions esecially if they do not speak German properly. Officials are aware of this highly problematic situation, 'because you don't know, does he translate it correctly? Or when writing the transcript: you have to turn the sentence around three times and then you can be sure that it's not as the asylum claimant said it', a

---

[5]The quote also highlights the problem that countries of origin tend to be equated with one specific language, indicating a certain (deliberate) ignorance of the complexity of reality such as language varieties (Angermeyer 2013; Maryns 2017).

caseworker explains. This translation of 'her [the interpreter's] German into my German', as another official puts it, can obviously have profound consequences. The official, Gabi, remembers a 'catastrophic' interview 'with a desperate asylum claimant, all in tears, and an interpreter in quotation marks who doesn't speak German, who can't express herself'. It is needless to say that commissioning unqualified interpreters in these crucial communication situations, decisive for the granting of international protection, can have dreadful consequences. The communication between two parties who do not understand each other is necessarily bound to fail when the interpreter does not possess the required language and interpreting skills.

The cooperation between official and interpreter is also connected to the relation between interpreter and asylum claimant. Officials often mention that some interpreters may be biased which is regarded as problematic since it deviates from the idea of the neutral interpreter.[6] A potential bias, however, only seems to be a problem when it is oriented towards the claimant. In contrast, caseworkers typically tolerate or even appreciated it when interpreters act as their assistants in the inteview. In particular when 'former asylum claimants', as recognised refugees, are commissioned for interpreting—which is sometimes the case if no certified interpreters are available for a certain language—'you don't know on which side they are', a caseworker highlights. Officials point out that interpreters sometimes also take sides against the claimant, which is often related to ethnic group conflicts (see also Scheffer 2001). In other cases, however, when asylum claimants and interpreters share experience, for instance, from the same country of origin, officials argue that claimants hope to get support from interpreters; this, they say, is reinforced when the latter have also gone through the procedure as claimants before. Interpreters are thus potentially also in the position to do advocacy. As Inghilleri (2003: 259) points out, 'the decision to serve as conduit or advocate may result from interpreters' qualifications, experiences or cultural understandings of the applicants or what is at stake for the applicants in the proceedings'. But even if officials find biased interpreters problematic, there are often no alternative choices.

---

[6]While the position of intepreters as neutral language transmitters can still be found in some of the literature, this role definition has been challenged for some time now in TIS (Gile 2009).

The Interpreter as a Resource and Cooperation as a Game of Power

The idea that interpreters should be neutral seems to conflict with the fact that they sometimes take—or are brought into—the role of being officials' work colleagues. Since the official is the one who commissions the interpreter—the claimant generally does not have a say in this decision (except regarding gender)—it is in her interest to find a person she is able to work with. As mentioned above, the official, Gabi, finds it natural to re-commission an interpreter if they 'work well together'. The official describes her relation to an interpreter in the ideal case as a good team, that is, two persons who are well attuned to each other and know each other's expectations. If an official is satisfied with an interpreter's work she will thus commission her again instead of looking for another person (the same is true for commissioned experts). Continuous good cooperation may, however, provoke the appearance *vis-à-vis* an asylum claimant that official and interpreter work together in an alliance—and this might not only be an appearance. Consequently, the question of the interpreter's neutrality or bias arises again, since the interpreter might be seen as or even start to act like a member of the institution, especially if she is not professionally trained. This might be the case, for instance, when the interpreter starts questioning the claimant without the official having asked a question.

The observation that officials and interpreters cooperate—to a smaller or larger extent—suggests that interpreters do more than 'just' translate, as previous studies have also shown (Angelelli 2004; Llewellyn-Jones and Lee 2014). While one of the caseworkers first holds that interpreters 'are there to translate and do nothing else', he then admits that this does not correspond to reality by adding that 'for countries [of origin] where [he is] not really sure' he will also consult the interpreter for expertise. The official explains that he sometimes uses the interpreter's knowledge in order to verify the information provided by the claimant (see also Kadrić 2009). Although officials cannot know how up-to-date or valid an interpreter's knowledge is, this kind of information can feed into decisions on asylum claims. The fact that interpreters often also possess expert knowledge additionally makes them a valuable resource and partner for cooperation. In the asylum procedure, in order to decide upon an application, officials mostly depend on information from 'outside' the institution (such as independent expert opinions), and interpreters represent one such source.[7] Many interpreters who grew up or spent a long time in the country in question are hence regarded as knowledgeable concerning the local circumstances. 'Because some things you don't think of as an official because you're not from that cultural area [...]; sometimes there have been really good ideas or hints, which I'd never have thought of. I just think in a Western way and how it is here', the official Sabine explains. Due to their specific backgrounds interpreters can sometimes provide officials not only with additional knowledge but also with new perspectives, pointing out differences to life in Europe, as illustrated in the passage from an observed interview.

Official: Street names? House numbers? Do they exist there?
Interpreter: They don't exist.

Although officials depend on the interpreter for communicating with the asylum claimant, they are eager to manipulate the power balance to their benefit by trying to keep control of the situation. Officials can decide whether to ask an interpreter for advice but they also have the power to decide how to proceed with the information provided. Even if the official has recourse to the interpreter's knowledge, Veronika highlights that 'the decision is eventually mine'. On the other hand, the interpreter has the power to decide which information to give the official and which to withhold. An official remembers an interview situation where the claimants' children started to cry and the interpreter told him afterwards that the mother had told the children to cry. Hence, in some aspects the interpreter is always one step ahead, which puts her in a powerful position in relation to the official. This will become even more obvious in the following analysis of situations in interpreted asylum hearings.

Active Interventions in the Interaction

In line with existing research, the findings show that interpreters do not 'only' translate what other interaction participants say but often act in a proactive way. According to Wadensjö (1999), the interpreter's active participation is 'part and parcel of all interpreting'. The author thus also regards coordination as one of the interpreter's tasks, this includes both 'implicitly

---

[7] An official explained that some interpreters are even commissioned as experts to produce reports on specific topics.

co-ordinating or gatekeeping contributions' and 'explicitly co-ordinating contributions' (ibid.). Similarly, Turner and Brown (2001) argue that managing and negotiating the communication situation is one of the interpreter's responsibilities. In her analysis of court interpreters' behaviour, Berk-Seligson (2002) identifies different kinds of active intervention such as interrupting, explaining, silencing and 'controlling the flow of testimony'. Similar actions could also be observed in the present study; in this section they are analysed in the light of professional behaviour.

The statement of one of the trained interpreters highlights their room for manoeuvre regarding active interventions in the interaction as well as the unequal power balance among the actors:

> If something seems contradictory to me [...] then I ask [the claimant] what he means. Although that's also bad; actually the official should do that. When I think, 'that's impossible,' for instance, when [the claimant] mentions three different birth dates, then I make a comment to the official. Otherwise he might think that my translation is wrong [...]. Sometimes, I have to ask a spontaneous question of understanding [to the claimant]; then I explain that [to the official ...]. Often when there are longer passages ... it can be difficult to bring the translation to an end because the official says, 'we know that already' [...] Then I have little chance to complete the interpretation. But I rarely tell the asylum seeker that I haven't interpreted everything. That's a bad situation.

The quote illustrates different ways the interpreter can manage the communication situation, and that, in this case, they tend to be to the disadvantage of the asylum claimant. The interpreter feels that she has to justify her—seemingly inappropriate—behaviour in front of the official, but not vis-à-vis the claimant. At the same time, she knows and acknowledges that her action does not correspond with professional ethics, mentioning twice that the situation is 'bad.' She seems to find herself in a dilemma since she knows what would officially be the right thing to do but feels the urge to act differently. Professionalism and professional ethics immediately come into play and it seems difficult for the interpreter to make them compatible with the pressures of a real-life interpreting situation.

In a similar vein, the following scenes from observed asylum hearings show how the interpreter actively structures the interaction and thus—at least for a moment—takes control of the situation. In these situations, often a conversation between interpreter and official takes place while the claimant is left out of the conversation or talked about in the third person. I will discuss three key aspects: first, situations in which the interpreter's aim is to manage and clarify the communication situation; second, situations in which the interpreter tries to take over control of the communication situation; and third, situations in which it is questionable whether the interpreter takes her job seriously. While the first section includes situations where the interpreter demonstrates professional behaviour, the other two sections highlight problematic situations, where the interpreter acts in an unprofessional way. The analysis suggests that the interpreter's problem awareness and reflexivity about her own role and action—that is professional ethics—represent key issues that need to be tackled.

Professional Attitudes: Managing the Communication Situation

In some situations, the interpreter feels that she needs to clarify the communication situation because something is unclear, misunderstood or simply wrong. In one situation, for instance, the interpreter feels the urge to untangle the communication and prevent any misunderstanding. In the following example from an observed hearing, the interpreter is unable to follow the asylum claimant and keeps asking the claimant for clarification. This is what happens next:

> *Interpreter to claimant*: I don't know the story, so tell me the way that I understand it.
> *Interpreter to official*: I can only translate something when I understand him; otherwise you'll be confused too.
> *Official*: Please just translate anyway.
> *Interpreter*: Okay, I'll tell you what he says, but it won't make any sense.
> (interview 3)

Since the interpreter does not understand what the claimant is trying to say he asks him to explain it in a way that he will be able to understand what he means. In the same moment, the interpreter explains to the official why he just made an intervention and what the content of this intervention was in order to justify his unexpected behaviour. Aiming at preventing a misunderstanding, the interpreter takes the initiative to ask the claimant for clarification. The official, however, does not approve of this intervention and asks him to translate what the asylum claimant says without any further clarifications. He obviously does not want to lose control of the situation and wants to be able to judge the claimant's assertion himself without being patronised by the interpreter. The interpreter accepts the official's attempt to re-establish the formal power relation but warns him that the translation will not make much sense. In order to save his face, he thereby makes sure that the official knows that it is not his translation which is confusing but the claimant's assertion. The fact that he warns the official that misunderstandings might arise can also be interpreted as a measure to ensure his professionalism.

The following passage illustrates a situation in which the interpreter reacts to an odd, unexpected situation. While the interpreter is retranslating the interview transcript the claimant normally has the possibility to announce mistakes in the transcript, for example, when she said something different in the interview than what now appears in the transcript. In the current context, however, the claimant seems to fall asleep while the interpreter is back-translating the transcript:

> *Interpreter to official*: She [the claimant] is sleeping. Do you want me to continue to read?
> *The official does not react to his question.*
> *Interpreter to claimant*: Do you hear?
> *Claimant*: Yes.
>
> (interview 2)

Since the claimant's eyes are closed, the interpreter regards her service as unnecessary and asks the official whether she wants her to continue with the retranslation although the claimant seems not to be listening. But the official does not react; presumably because she does not listen and does not expect to be addressed in this moment. Since the official does not seem to care whether the claimant pays attention to the translation in order to verify the transcript's correctness, the interpreter takes the initiative and asks the claimant herself whether she is listening. When the claimant affirms that she is listening to the interpreter, the situation is clear and the interpreter continues with the back-translation.

Unprofessional Attitudes: Over-Cooperating with the Official

While sometimes interpreters need to manage a communication situation in order to establish clarity and prevent misunderstandings, in other observed interview situations the interpreter behaves like an assistant official; this is a well-known phenomenon (Donk 2016[1994]; Scheffer 2001; Pöllabauer 2005). The following scenes are examples of situations in which the interpreter seizes the power of definition concerning the course of the interview:

The claimant says something.

Interpreter to official: That's completely off-topic. (o.i. 6)

***

The claimant tells something.

Interpreter to official: She now continues to talk about her sisters. Do you want to…?
Official: How does it relate to the departure?

(interview 7, same interpreter)

In these two situations the interpreter does not translate what the claimant says but instead makes a comment to the official. Due to his experience regarding asylum hearings the interpreter claims to know what is relevant for the procedure and what is not. Instead of leaving the judgement to the official the interpreter judges himself that what the claimant says is not relevant. The interpreter does not translate the claimant's statement but presents his own conclusion, namely that the statement is off-topic. Only then, after his comment, he leaves it open to the official to decide whether she wants to hear the translation or not. In the second situation, the interpreter provides a summary instead of a translation, again taking over control of the communication. Before directly translating what the claimant says, he asks the official if she wants to know what the claimant is saying. The official, instead of listening to the translation, asks another question. The same is true for the following scene, where the interpreter again provides a summary instead of a translation:

Interpreter to official: He's now talking about the flight reason.
Official: No, I just want to know what's with the house.

[…]

Interpreter to official: Now he's repeating himself.

(interview 4)

The interpreter makes a comment to the official, assuming that what the claimant said is not what the official wanted to know. Instead of translating what the claimant said, the interpreter anticipates the official's reaction because he knows what he is expecting. The official confirms the interpreter's premonition by dismissing the translation and repeating the intention of his previous question. Also in the second observed instance the interpreter does not translate but provides a summary to the official. The interpreter refuses to translate what the claimant said because he has already translated it before since the claimant is allegedly repeating herself. Another scene focuses on a situation where the interpreter comments on the claimant's assertion and his in/credibility. During the interview the asylum claimant shows a big wound on the arm, explaining that a man bit her:

Official: Why do you think he [the perpetrator] bit you?
Claimant (Interpreter): Because I cried and maybe people heard it.
Interpreter to official: If someone bites me I'll cry even more.
(interview 1)

At this point the interpreter does not only translate the claimant's statement but subsequently adds his own opinion on this statement, instead of leaving the judgement to the official. The interpreter calls the claimant's credibility into question, assuming that what she said is not true. In addition, his judgement originates from a comparison with his own potential behaviour, thus measuring the claimant's assertion by his personal standards. In this case the interpreter does not provide specific expert knowledge to the official as discussed before but a personal opinion. Even if the official decides to ignore the interpreter's comment such interfering behaviour does not convey professionalism and strongly questions his alleged neutrality.

Unprofessional Attitudes: Not Taking the Job and the Asylum Claimant Seriously

The third aspect to discuss in the context of interpreters' practices relates to their general attitude and behaviour in doing their job, which can be understood as key elements of professionalism. For instance, an interpreter who demands that the claimant be interviewed without her children because she cannot concentrate otherwise (o.i. 7) shows that there are certain preconditions for her to be able to work properly. In contrast, there are interpreters who seem not to take their job seriously by not acting adequately for the context of an asylum interview. In the following scene, for example, the interpreter behaves in a disrespectful way towards the asylum claimant:

The interpreter is leaning backwards with stretched legs. The claimant keeps leaning forward when the interpreter translates what the official says.

During the interview the interpreter's mobile phone rings; he picks it up.

The official excuses the interpreter in front of the claimants.

Interpreter: It was only concerning my car.
Official: Can we continue?

The interpreter agrees by humming ('mhm').

[…]

Official: How far is it to the Indian border?
Interpreter: Not so far.
Official: Ask the asylum claimant please!

[…]

Official: Where are you living? Basic care, right, a guesthouse.
Interpreter: He says, he's living completely privately now.
Official: I'll check what's registered in the computer.

The interpreter does not interpret the official's comment.

Official to interpreter: Would you be so kind to tell it to him? (o.i. 5)

On the one hand, the interpreter shows disinterest through his body language, leaning backwards with stretched legs. In order to understand the interpreter, the asylum claimant seemingly has to lean forward as he does so every time the interpreter translates what the official says. On the other hand, the interpreter also behaves impolitely und disrespectfully when he picks up his mobile phone and starts talking during the interview. Without hesitation and without a comment to the asylum claimant or the official he interrupts the interview. Instead, the official, who seems to be embarrassed by the interpreter's behaviour, excuses the interpreter in front of the claimant. The official, however, does not sanction the interpreter's behaviour, for instance, by reprimanding him and reminding him of the official setting. After the interpreter finished his call and explained that it was nothing important, the official asks him whether they can now carry on with the interview.[8] In the course of the interview, the interpreter continues to disregard the claimant by not translating certain statements. At one point, he seems to believe that the official addresses him with a question, which is actually aimed at the claimant. Since the interpreter answers the question in

---

[8]The official is generally rather reluctant to criticise the interpreter's unprofessional behaviour in this interview, possibly to save the interpreter's face in front of me, the observer. Another explanation for why the interpreter is so powerful here could be that there are few alternative interpreters available for the required language, or other unknown dependencies.

lieu of asking the claimant, the official requests the interpreter to translate his question for the claimant. At a later point, this situation is repeated since the interpreter does not find it necessary to translate the official's comment for the claimant, but the official does, prompting the interpreter to translate his comment. The interpreter obviously did not deem it necessary to inform the asylum claimant of the official's intention. If the official were not so persistent in this communication situation (maybe due to my presence), the claimant would not have a serious chance to participate in this interaction. In sum, this interview is far away from a fair communication situation with equal participants.

Conclusion: Learning to Handle Power Responsibly

The empirical data discussed in this chapter illustrate that interpreters do more than 'just translate': while in some cases they provide the official with 'expert' knowledge, in other situations they influence or manipulate the communication between asylum claimants and officials. This influence can be in favour of the official or the interpreter themselves; but interpreters sometimes also actively try to help the claimant (Gill et al. 2016). The analysis reveals that instead of being neutral mediators, interpreters influence the interaction and thus the development of the further asylum procedure; if interpreters act unprofessionally, this can be to the detriment of a fair procedure. Professional action can be drawing the officials' attention to important issues, such as real and potential misunderstandings or mistakes in the transcript, or explaining their own behaviour to the official in order to prevent misunderstandings. In contrast, problematic and unprofessional behaviour can be summarising instead of translating, making judgements in lieu of the official or commenting on a claimant's account's credibility. Interpreters' work attitude, which is sometimes expressed through disrespectful, disinterested or lazy behaviour, such as deciding on the relevance of a statement by not translating it or not even listening to claimants' assertions, can have important consequences. In sum, this ethnography highlighted the dynamics of power in a situation of distinct power asymmetry. While interpreters' actions and decisions are influenced by different (social, professional, institutional) norms, they dispose of significant room for manoeuvre in the social interaction of asylum hearings, which calls for responsible agency and handling of power (see also Gibbels and Schmitz 2015).

Professionalism and professional ethics influence how interpreters perform their role and thus also how they handle power. This in turn affects their relation to officials and asylum claimants. Professionalism and professional ethics promote consciousness and reflexivity of the interpreter's own role. A professional role performance does not imply passive neutrality, it means conscious and reflexive—that is professional—active intervention. Although many authors have already insisted on the impossibility of the interpreter's neutrality (Rycroft 2005), the question continues to be discussed: Do neutrality and professionalism presuppose or complement or exclude each other? Gill et al. (2016) point out that 'interpreters who do not carry out the role of neutral facilitators of communication may not only confuse appellants as to their capabilities, but also lose their professional credibility in the eyes of other actors'. It is, however, still unclear what this neutrality is. I would argue that the same could happen if they try to provide a 'verbatim' translation—a requirement that seems to be a widespread legal fiction (Good 2011)—or do not take sides when it would be ethically necessary. In my view, a complete translation that contains all details is more important and can be more useful than a verbatim translation, which the official might not understand. Professional ethics should help to make the right decisions in order to reach a complete translation. For example, as mentioned in the first section, is it more professional to stick to the rule of sitting in a triangle or to make sure that the official produces a correct transcript? Ideally, a situation should be created where both are possible.

With this contribution I reiterate that neutrality is not generally desirable—setting aside the question whether it is principally possible or not—by bringing forth two points. First, neutrality is sometimes understood in the sense of impartiality; the question of taking sides is primarily a political one. Here, professional ethics should provide orientation for interpreters. If an asylum claimant is treated unfairly, it can be unethical not to take sides. Second, if neutrality means being someone else's (passive) mouthpiece—usually in the sense of verbatim translation—such action can be unprofessional and unethical. Professionalism and professional ethics may require the right intervention at the right time: Sometimes it would simply be unprofessional or unethical for an interpreter not to intervene.[9]

In sum, the importance of 'well qualified, experienced and professionally ethical interpreters provided with appropriate working conditions' (Gill

---

[9]Rycroft (2005), for example, discusses the frustrations an interpreter may face due to the limitations placed on her behavior. If she knows that a misunderstanding may be occurring but is officially prevented from clarifying this because of the rules of conduct she is required to observe, this in my view, is not the right understanding of professional and ethical action.

et al. 2016) cannot be stressed enough. A professional approach to dealing with power, which is related to professional ethics, is necessary in order to prevent situations such as in the examples discussed above. While the issue of professionalism is also pressing in other domains of community interpreting such as communication between physicians and patients, the asylum procedure puts claimants in a particularly vulnerable situation. As basic human rights are at play, it is essential that interpreters can deal with their power in a competent and responsible way. Although it was not possible to systematically collect data on the education or qualifications of the interpreters who interpreted in the observed hearings, the analysis clearly reveals elements of unprofessional behaviour. The findings discussed in this chapter suggest that it is highly problematic to employ interpreters without professional training in asylum hearings.

It is likely that such behaviour is connected to the lack of professional training and might be preventable otherwise. In Austria, the introduction of a voluntary qualification measure for interpreting in the asylum procedure (QUADA) provided by adult education centres in cooperation with UNHCR, introduced in 2015, is a first important step in the right direction.[10] The curriculum includes, among others, classes on the basics of interpreting as well as its techniques and ethical principles. As the importance of professionalism in interpreting, which includes knowledge of the techniques and ethics of interpreting, cannot be underestimated, especially in the delicate context of asylum applications, I would argue that such training should be compulsory and paid for by the state who is legally responsible for providing a fair hearing. Asylum claimants have a right to a professional interpretation.

The often observed fact that power plays such a crucial role in the interpreted asylum hearing calls for more attention by scholars and practitioners, especially with regard to professionalism and professional ethics.

References

Angelelli, C. V. (2004). *Revisiting the Interpreter's Role: A Study of Conference, Court, and Medical Interpreters in Canada, Mexico, and the United States*. Amsterdam and Philadelhpia: John Benjamins.

Angelelli, C. V. (2014). *The Sociological Turn in Translation and Interpreting Studies*. Amsterdam and Philadelhpia: John Benjamins.

---

[10]The whole course (12 modules) costs €1650, with the possibility to apply for funding. German skills at B2 level of the EU reference framework are a precondition for participation. Available at: http://www.vhs.or.at/594 [Accessed 1 July 2017].

Angermeyer, P. S. (2013). Multilingual Speakers and Language Choice in the Legal Sphere. *Applied Linguistics Review, 4,* 105–126.
Barsky, R. F. (1996). The Interpreter as Intercultural Agent in Convention Refugee Hearings. *The Translator, 2*(1), 45–63. https://doi.org/10.1080/13556509.1996.10798963.
Berk-Seligson, S. (2002). *The Bilingual Courtroom: Court Interpreters in the Judicial Process.* Chicago and London: University of Chicago Press.
Colin, J., & Morris, R. (1996). *Interpreters and the Legal Process* (1st ed.). Winchester: Waterside Press.
Dahlvik, J. (2009a). *Annäherung an die potentielle Gestaltungsmacht einer Dolmetscherin: eine soziologische Analyse von Interaktionen im Rahmen von gedolmetschten Einvernahmen und Verhandlungen am österreichischen Bundesasylamt und Asylgerichtshof.* Master thesis.
Dahlvik, J. (2009b). *Interaktion beim Dolmetschen im Asylverfahren: eine Analyse nach dem Modell von Becker-Beck.* Master thesis.
Dahlvik, J. (2016). Asylanträge verwalten und entscheiden: der soziologische Blick auf Verborgenes: Eine Forschungsnotiz. *Österreichische Zeitschrift für Soziologie, 41,* 191–205.
Dahlvik, J. (2018). *Inside Asylum Bureaucracy: Organizing Refugee Status Determination in Austria.* Springer. https://doi.org/10.1007/978-3-319-63306-0.
Donk, U. (2016[1994]). Der Dolmetscher als Hilfspolizist – Zwischenergebnis einer Feldstudie. *Zeitschrift Für Rechtssoziologie, 15*(1), 37–57. https://doi.org/10.1515/zfrs-1994-0104.
Froschauer, U., & Lueger, M. (2009). *Interpretative Sozialforschung: der Prozess.* Vienna: Facultas WUV.
Gibb, R., & Good, A. (2014). Interpretation, Translation and Intercultural Communication in Refugee Status Determination Procedures in the UK and France. *Language and Intercultural Communication, 14,* 385–399.
Gibbels, E., & Schmitz, J. (2015). Investigating Interventionist Interpreting via Mikhail Bakhtin. *Acta Universitatis Carolinae Philologica, 3,* 61–72.
Gile, D. (2009). *Basic Concepts and Models for Interpreter and Translator Training.* Amsterdam and Philadelhpia: John Benjamins.
Gill, N., Rotter, R., Burridge, A., et al. (2016). Linguistic Incomprehension in British Asylum Appeal Hearings. *Anthropology Today, 32,* 18–21.
Good, A. (2007). *Anthropology and Expertise in the Asylum Courts.* Abingdon: Routledge-Cavendish.
Good, A. (2011). Tales of Suffering: Asylum Narratives in the Refugee Status Determination Process. *West Coast Line, 68,* 80–89.
Grbić, N. (2010). "Boundary Work" as a Concept for Studying Professionalization Processes in the Interpreting Field. *Translation and Interpreting Studies, 5,* 109–123.
Hsieh, E. (2010). Provider–Interpreter Collaboration in Bilingual Health Care: Competitions of Control Over Interpreter-Mediated Interactions. *Patient Education and Counseling, 78,* 154–159.

Inghilleri, M. (2003). Habitus, Field and Discourse: Interpreting as a Socially Situated Activity. *Target, 15,* 243–268.
Inghilleri, M. (2007). National Sovereignty Versus Universal Rights: Interpreting Justice in a Global Context. *Social Semiotics, 17,* 195–212.
Kadrić, M. (2009). *Dolmetschen Bei Gericht: Erwartungen—Anforderungen—Kompetenzen* (3rd ed.). Wien: Facultas.
Lee, J. A. (2014). Pressing Need for the Reform of Interpreting Service in Asylum Settings: A Case Study of Asylum Appeal Hearings in South Korea. *Journal of Refugee Studies, 27,* 62–81.
Llewellyn-Jones, P., & Lee, R. G. (2014). *Redefining the Role of the Community Interpreter: The Concept of Role-Space.* Lincoln: SLI Press.
Maryns, K. (2013). Disclosure and (Re)Performance of Gender-Based Evidence in an Interpreter-Mediated Asylum Interview. *Journal of Sociolinguistics, 17,* 661–686.
Maryns, K. (2017). The Use of English as Ad Hoc Institutional Standard in the Belgian Asylum Interview. *Applied Linguistics, 38*(5), 737–758.
Maurer-Kober, B. (2006). Die Rolle von DolmetscherInnen aus juristischer Perspektive. In Österreichisches Bundesministerium für Inneres et al. (Eds.), *Handbuch Dolmetschen im Asylverfahren* (pp. 28–30). Vienna.
Morris, R. (1995). The Moral Dilemmas of Court Interpreting. *The Translator, 1*(1), 25–46. https://doi.org/10.1080/13556509.1995.10798948.
Munday, J. (2016). *Introducing Translation Studies: Theories and Applications.* Oxon and New York: Routledge.
Pöchhacker, F. (2016). *Introducing Interpreting Studies.* Oxon and New York: Routledge.
Pöchhacker, F., & Kolb, W. (2009). Interpreting for the Record: A Case Study of Asylum Review Hearings. In S. Hale, U. Ozolins, & L. Stern (Eds.), *The Critical Link 5: Quality in Interpreting – a Shared Responsibility* (pp. 119–134). Amsterdam and Philadelphia: John Benjamins.
Pöllabauer, S. (2005). *"I don't understand your English, Miss": Dolmetschen bei Asylanhörungen.* Tübingen: Gunter Narr Verlag.
Pöllabauer, S. (2007). Interpreting in Asylum Hearings. Issues of Saving Face. In C. Wadensjö, B. E. Dimitrova, & A.-L. Nilsson (Eds.), *The Critical Link 4: Professionalisation of Interpreting in the Community: Selected Papers from the 4th International Conference on Interpreting in Legal, Health and Social Service Settings, Stockholm, Sweden, 20–23 May 2004* (pp. 39–52). Amsterdam and Philadelphia: John Benjamins.
Richardson, L. (2000). Writing: A Method of Inquiry. In N. K. Denzin & Y. S. Lincoln (Eds.), *Handbook of Qualitative Research* (pp. 923–948). Thousand Oaks, California: Sage.
Rienzner, M. (2011). *Interkulturelle Kommunikation im Asylverfahren.* Frankfurt am Main, Vienna: Lang.
Rudvin, M. (2007). Professionalism and Ethics in Community Interpreting: The Impact of Individualist Versus Collective Group Identity. *Interpreting, 9*(1), 47–69. https://doi.org/10.1075/intp.9.1.04rud.

Rycroft R. (2005). Communicative Barriers in the Asylum Account. In P. Shah (Ed.), *The Challenge of Asylum to Legal Systems* (pp. 223–244). London: Routledge-Cavendish.

Scheffer, T. (2001). *Asylgewährung: eine ethnographische Analyse des deutschen Asylverfahrens.* Lucius & Lucius DE.

Smith, D. E. (2006). *Institutional Ethnography as Practice.* Rowman & Littlefield Publishers.

Strauss, A. L., & Corbin, J. (1990). *Basics of Qualitative Research: Grounded Theory Procedures and Techniques.* London: Sage.

Tipton, R. (2008). Reflexivity and the Social Construction of Identity in Interpreter-Mediated Asylum Interviews. *The Translator, 14,* 1–19.

Turner, G., & Brown, R. (2001). Interaction and the Role of the Interpreter in Court. In F. J. Harrington & G. H. Turner (Eds.), *Interpreting Interpreting: Studies and Reflections on Sign Language Interpreting* (pp. 152–167). Coleford, UK: Douglas McLean.

UNHCR Österreich. (2015). *Trainingshandbuch für DolmetscherInnen im Asylverfahren,* UNCHR. Global Trends. Forced Displacement in 2015. Available at: http://www.unhcr.org/576408cd7.

Wadensjö, C. (1999). *Interpreting as Interaction.* London: Pearson Education ESL.

Wadensjö, C. (2007). Foreword: Interpreting professions, professionalisation and professionalism. In C. Wadensjö, B. E. Dimitrova, & A.-L. Nilsson (Eds.), *The Critical Link 4: Professionalisation of Interpreting in the Community: Selected Papers from the 4th International Conference on Interpreting in Legal, Health and Social Service Settings, Stockholm, Sweden, 20–23 May 2004* (pp. 1–8). Amsterdam and Philadelphia: John Benjamins.

Wolf, M., & Fukari, A. (2007). *Constructing a Sociology of Translation.* Amsterdam and Philadelphia: John Benjamins.

Open Access This chapter is distributed under the terms of the Creative Commons Attribution 4.0 International License (http://creativecommons.org/licenses/by/4.0/), which permits use, duplication, adaptation, distribution and reproduction in any medium or format, as long as you give appropriate credit to the original author(s) and the source, a link is provided to the Creative Commons license and any changes made are indicated.

The images or other third party material in this chapter are included in the work's Creative Commons license, unless indicated otherwise in the credit line; if such material is not included in the work's Creative Commons license and the respective action is not permitted by statutory regulation, users will need to obtain permission from the license holder to duplicate, adapt or reproduce the material.

8

Communicative Practices and Contexts of Interaction in the Refugee Status Determination Process in France

Robert Gibb

Introduction

25 years ago, Michael Burawoy stated in the introduction to a collection of ethnographic studies conducted in the San Francisco Bay Area that the book's aim was 'to unchain ethnography from its confinement as a quaint technique at the margins of social science' (Burawoy 1991: 3). Since then, ethnographic research has moved to occupy if not centre-stage then at least a prominent place in many academic disciplines and fields of inquiry (Davies 2008: ix). Contemporary research on asylum determination in Europe, as Nick Gill and Anthony Good note in their introductory chapter to the present volume, frequently adopts an ethnographic approach. This is certainly the case for research on asylum processes in France, where an ethnographic perspective has recently been brought to bear on, among other subjects, reception centres for asylum applicants (Kobelinsky 2010), refugee-support organisations (d'Halluin-Mabillot 2012), decision-making at the French National Court of Asylum (Kobelinsky 2014, and this volume) and the role of interpreters (Gibb and Good 2014).

Against this background, I draw in the present chapter on material from an ethnographic study of the asylum process in France in order to explore the following questions: What can ethnographic research contribute to

R. Gibb (✉)
University of Glasgow, Glasgow, UK
e-mail: robert.gibb@glasgow.ac.uk

© The Author(s) 2019
N. Gill and A. Good (eds.), *Asylum Determination in Europe*,
Palgrave Socio-Legal Studies, https://doi.org/10.1007/978-3-319-94749-5_8

knowledge and understanding of the kinds of communication that take place at successive stages of the refugee status determination process in France? What light can it throw, more specifically, on the relationship between forms of communicative practice and the different contexts or spaces in which interaction between those involved occurs? Finally, what are some of the difficulties associated with adopting an ethnographic approach to investigate asylum processes and how can researchers attempt to address these?

In a classic ethnographic study of an English Crown Court, Paul Rock (1993: 6–7) emphasised that space and time were key factors influencing the behaviour and experiences of prosecution witnesses. Similarly, a central concern of this chapter will be to explore how communication and interaction between different participants in the French asylum process are shaped in part by specific features of the built environment in which they take place. After providing a brief overview of the refugee status determination process in France (as it operated in 2008–2009, when I carried out most of my research), I will examine in turn forms of communication in 'admissibility interviews', asylum interviews and appeals hearings, and offices and corridors. In so doing, my aim is to show that one of the advantages of adopting an ethnographic approach when conducting research on administrative and legal asylum determination procedures is that it throws light on the wide range of different types of communication and interaction that occur within them. Determining the specific impact of each of these on the decision-making process is not a straightforward matter, but I will suggest that describing and analysing them can deepen our understanding of the different contexts in which those involved in the asylum process communicate and interact with each other. The chapter is based on ethnographic research I completed in the Paris region between 2007 and 2009 as part of a comparative study of asylum procedures in the UK and France conducted in collaboration with Anthony Good.

Ethnography, Communicative Practice and Contexts of Interaction

The perspective on refugee status determination procedures in France adopted in this chapter is informed by particular understandings of ethnography, communication and interaction, and it is necessary to make these explicit at the outset. This is especially important for the term 'ethnography', since it is used in a wide variety of ways in contemporary scholarship, sometimes as little more than 'a legitimising label' (Davies 2008: ix) for work that departs significantly from how ethnographic research has traditionally been conceived within disciplines such as social anthropology and sociology. In this chapter, I follow Paul Willis and Mats Trondman in viewing ethnography as:

> a family of methods involving direct and sustained social contact with agents, and of richly writing up the encounter, respecting, recording, representing at least partly *in its own terms*, the irreducibility of human experience. Ethnography is the disciplined and deliberate witness-cum-recording of human events. (Willis and Trondman 2000: 5, italics in original)

This definition draws attention to two specific points that I discuss further in later sections. The first is that ethnographic research involves using a number of different methods; in other words, ethnography is not 'a method' or a synonym for 'participant observation', even if it is often presented in this way (e.g. Flood 2005: 33, 43 and 46). The second is that ethnography refers not only to a set of research techniques but also to the 'eventual written product', one that characteristically attempts to provide a detailed description and fine-grained analysis of the activities studied (Davies 2008: 4–5). Each of these two dimensions of ethnography poses its own challenges. For if, as John Flood (2005: 34) has suggested, 'the core of ethnography is to be alert and attentive to everything around you not just particular segments of theoretical reality', how can this be achieved in practice through specific research methods, and be adequately reflected in the subsequent written account? I return to this question in each of the three sections of the chapter where I introduce material from my fieldwork in France.

The present chapter and the others in this section of the book are centrally concerned with the issue of communication during the asylum determination process, and communication, like ethnography, is a term that can be used in different ways. In what follows the focus is on *communicative practices*, based on a view of communication as 'situated action' and of meaning as 'an active process of here-and-now projection and inferencing, ranging across all kinds of percept, sign, and knowledge' (Blommaert and Rampton 2016: 27). This approach is informed by a number of important advances in the study of communication within linguistic anthropology and social/cultural theory, which, in my view, point to specific ways of developing ethnographic research on communicative practices in the asylum process. Drawing on Jan Blommaert and Ben Rampton's (2016: 26–33) useful review of linguistic-anthropological and other research on communication, I would like therefore to highlight here four key ideas that have guided the analysis presented later in the chapter. The first is that meaning is not communicated solely through language, but is instead 'multimodal': 'People apprehend meaning in gestures, postures, faces, bodies, movements, physical arrangements and the material environment, and in different combinations these constitute contexts shaping the way in which utterances are produced and understood' (2016: 27). The second is that 'non-shared knowledge' and 'inequalities in communicative resources' can be 'systematically patterned in relations of power' (2016: 28–29, italics omitted). The third is what Blommaert and Rampton refer to as 'metapragmatic reflexivity', that is, the ways in which people reflect on their own and others' communicative practices (2016: 31–32). The final insight relates to the value of 'a multi-sited description of communications beyond, before and after specific events', through attending to processes of entextualisation, transposition and recontextualisation (2016: 32–33). These four ideas underpin the analysis of communicative practices in the French asylum process presented later in the chapter.

As has just been noted, communicative practices are influenced in part by the contexts in which they take place. In this chapter, I am interested, specifically, in exploring how different 'contexts of interaction' affect communication between those involved in refugee status determination procedures in France. The focus then is on social interaction, understood as 'that which uniquely transpires in social situations, that is, environments in which two or more individuals are physically in one another's response presence' (Goffman 1983: 2). At successive stages of the asylum process different sets of individuals interact, and I examine how the number of people present and the roles they play shape the nature of the communicative practices that occur and also how those concerned experience them. However, I also use the phrase "contexts of interaction" to refer to the different physical settings or locations in which individuals interact. Most obviously, these include the booths where asylum interviews are conducted and the courtrooms where appeals against negative decisions are heard, but I also examine the importance of communicative practices in two other kinds of space: staff offices and corridors. In so doing, my aim is to provide the kind of multi-sited description of forms of communication referred to above, one that is able to trace connections between what happens in different settings as opposed to viewing each in isolation from the others. The phrase "contexts of interaction" is also intended, finally, to direct attention to the possible impact of features of the built environment—for example, the size and layout of rooms—on communicative practices in the asylum process.

This chapter is based on ethnographic research conducted in the Paris region between 2007 and 2009. It focused on the working practices of state officials, judges, interpreters, lawyers and members of refugee-support organisations (rather than on the experiences of asylum applicants themselves), and involved observation and semi-structured interviews (in French) in three different fieldsites, as well as documentary research. Firstly, I observed asylum interviews conducted by case-workers from the French Office for the Protection of Refugees and Stateless People (*Office français de protection des réfugiés et apatrides*/OFPRA), and I also interviewed case-workers (*officiers de protection*), heads of unit and interpreters who worked at the OFPRA. Secondly, I interviewed judges, *rapporteurs* and heads of unit at the French National Court of Asylum (*Cour nationale du droit d'asile*/CNDA), where I also attended asylum appeal hearings; in addition, I observed preparatory meetings between barristers (*avocats*) and their clients. Thirdly, I carried out participant observation research in a drop-in centre for asylum applicants run by a refugee-support organisation. The chapter presents and analyses material from the first two of these fieldsites. After providing an overview of the asylum process in France as this existed during the central period of my fieldwork (2008–2009), I focus in turn on communicative practices in the following contexts: 'admissibility interviews' at the border; asylum interviews and appeal hearings; and staff offices and corridors. In each case, I preface my discussion by briefly considering the methodological issues that arose when researching the particular 'context of interaction' in question.

Determining Refugee Status in France

In France, the authority responsible for taking the first decision on an asylum application is the French Office for the Protection of Refugees and Stateless People (OFPRA). Created in 1952, the OFPRA is a public institution with legal personality and financial and administrative autonomy (CESEDA 2009: L.721-1). Its head office is located in Fontenay-sous-Bois, which is 11-kilometres to the east of Paris. Appeals against negative decisions by the OFPRA are examined by an administrative court, the French National Court of Asylum (CNDA) (CESEDA 2009: L.731-1), which is also situated near Paris, in the town Montreuil. In 2008, when most of the fieldwork on which this chapter is based was conducted, the OFPRA registered 42,999 applications for asylum (OFPRA 2009: 10), and the CNDA 21,636 appeals (CNDA 2009: 7). The following overview of key elements of the asylum procedure in France, as this operated during the main period of the research (2008–2009), focuses on 'admissibility interviews' and asylum interviews conducted by OFPRA case-workers, and on asylum appeal hearings at the CNDA.

In 2008, 5100 people arriving in France at an airport or port applied for admission to French territory on asylum grounds (OFPRA 2009: 26). There is a specific procedure under French law in relation to asylum applications lodged at the border. If the person does not possess a valid travel document permitting them to enter French territory, they can be held in a 'waiting zone (*zone d'attente*)' while their admission request is examined. At the time of my research, a case-worker from the OFPRA's Asylum at the Border Division was responsible for conducting what I will refer to here as an 'admissibility interview' with the applicant, in order to determine whether or not their application was 'manifestly unfounded' (CESEDA 2009: L.221-1).[1] In the case of applicants held in the waiting zone at Roissy Charles-de-Gaulle airport outside Paris, OFPRA case-workers conducted these interviews face to face in offices provided by the Interior Ministry inside the zone, with the assistance of an interpreter (where necessary) via a telephone.[2] After the interview, the OFPRA case-worker formulated an opinion (*avis*) on the application, which, subject to approval by the Head of the Division, was then communicated to the Interior Ministry. If the application was not considered manifestly unfounded, the person would be allowed to enter French territory in order to lodge an asylum application with the OFPRA in the same way as an in-country applicant (see below).

At the time of the research, a person on French territory seeking asylum had first to apply for temporary leave to remain at the Préfecture of their place of residence. At the Préfecture they would be given a copy of the asylum application form, which had to be returned to the OFPRA within three weeks (OFPRA 2011: 89). After being received by the OFPRA, an asylum application was assigned to a case-worker, a state employee recruited

---

[1]While the research was taking place, a non-governmental organisation published a report, based on an analysis of 96 decisions, in which it argued that there was evidence of a 'drift (*dérive*)' in this type of interview towards a more in-depth examination of, for example, the credibility of the applicant's account, making it in practice similar to an asylum interview (Anafé 2008).

[2]At the time of the research, admissibility interviews with applicants held in other waiting zones (for example, at Orly airport or in French ports) were conducted by telephone rather than face to face. Since then, however, these interviews have increasingly been carried out using video-conferencing software (see OFPRA 2015: 18; Palluel 2016: paragraph 19).

through competitive examination to either a permanent or a temporary post, and who belonged to a specific branch of the civil service (*fonction publique*). In most cases, the case-worker would subsequently interview the applicant, usually at the OFPRA's head office outside Paris. Interviews there were held in small booths, roughly four to five square metres in size, the top half of which was made of clear glass (Cimade 2010: 23; OFPRA 2011: 103–104). The case-worker and applicant would sit facing each other across a table, with the interpreter (where one was present)[3] usually sitting at the side of the table, at right angles to the other two. Since 2005, each booth has also been equipped with a computer, which case-workers would use to transcribe their questions and the applicant's answers for the 'report (*compte-rendu*)' of the interview. Asylum interviews varied considerably in length, but usually lasted between an hour and an hour and a half. They tended to be divided into two parts: in the first, the caseworker sought to establish the applicant's identity and to collect other basic personal information; in the second, the focus was on the applicant's narrative and reasons for applying for asylum. After the interview, the caseworker would forward a proposal to accept or reject the application to the head of their section (or division), the person responsible for signing the final decision. The applicant would then be sent a letter informing them of the outcome of their application.

As noted above, appeals against the OFPRA's decisions are examined by the National Court of Asylum (CNDA). Appellants are entitled to be assisted by a barrister (*conseil*) and an interpreter at their appeal before the CNDA. Before the hearing, a CNDA *rapporteur* prepares a written report on the appeal, concluding with an opinion (*avis*), based on the current state of the case-file, as to whether it should be accepted or rejected. In 2008–2009, most appeals at the CNDA were heard by panels of three judges. The chair (*président*) of each panel was a magistrate drawn from the administrative, financial or civil branches of the judiciary. The other two members of the panel were usually not magistrates and were commonly referred to as the 'HCR assessor (*assesseur HCR*)' and 'Administration assessor (*assesseur de l'Administration*)' respectively. The former, who had to be a French national, was nominated by the United Nations High-Commissioner for Refugees with the assent of the vice-president of the Council of State, while the Administration assessor was nominated by one of the Ministers represented on OFPRA's Governing Board. At the time of the research, both types of

---

[3]In 2009, 76% of OFPRA interviews were conducted with the assistance of an interpreter, compared to 46% in 2003 (OFPRA 2011: 106).

assessor, like the vast majority of magistrates, sat at the CNDA on a part-time basis (CESEDA 2009: L722-1).

Appeal hearings are held in large rooms at the Court, where the panel of judges sit behind a long table with their backs to the window. The chair of the panel is in the middle, flanked on either side by the 'Administration assessor' and 'HCR assessor' (to the chair's right and left respectively). Two other tables are placed at right angles to each side of the main table, forming an upside-down 'U' shape. The *rapporteur* sits behind the table on the side nearest the 'HCR assessor', while the clerk is seated at the opposite table, on the side nearest the 'Administration assessor'. The appellant sits in the middle of another table, facing the panel of judges (and therefore with his or her back to the rest of the room). If a barrister and/or an interpreter are present, they sit at the same table, to the appellant's right and left respectively. CNDA hearings are public (although the chair can order a closed session), and there are rows of seats just inside the door, where family members and friends, as well as appellants, barristers and interpreters waiting for their case to be called, can all sit.

In 2008, a panel of judges at the CNDA could hear up to 13 different appeals in any one morning or afternoon session. How long the hearing of an individual case lasts varies, depending on its complexity and a number of other factors. However, the Cimade (*Comité inter-mouvements auprès des evacués*), a French association that provides legal advice and other support to asylum seekers and refugees, observed 203 cases at the CNDA over a three-month period in 2009 and found that the average time taken to hear an individual appeal—including the report, which the *rapporteur* would read out at the start, and the barrister's statement—was 33 minutes (Cimade 2010: 47). At the end of the session, the room is cleared and the three judges discuss all the appeals that have just come before them, deciding in each case whether to annul the OFPRA's original decision (and therefore grant refugee status or subsidiary protection) or to reject the appellant's appeal against this decision. A letter is subsequently sent to the appellant, informing them of the outcome of their appeal.

This overview of successive stages in the refugee status determination procedure in France, as these existed at the time of the research,[4] has introduced

---

[4]Current asylum procedures in France differ in several important respects from those described here, particularly in relation to OFPRA interviews. Following new legislation that came into force on the 1st November 2015, a barrister (*avocat*) or a representative of an authorised human rights organisation can now be present with an asylum applicant at their OFPRA interview. The applicant can also ask to receive a copy of the 'transcription' of the interview produced by the OFPRA case-worker before a decision is made on their application (although in the case of applications examined under the 'fast-track'

three of the 'contexts of interaction' that form the focus of the remaining sections of this chapter. I begin by examining forms of communicative practice in 'admissibility interviews' between asylum applicants and OFPRA case-workers inside the waiting zone at Roissy Charles-de-Gaulle airport. I then describe and compare issues of communication in OFPRA interviews and CNDA appeal hearings, highlighting, among other points, how the physical setting in which they take place can affect the experience of those involved. Finally, I turn to consider two further places—staff offices and corridors—that the research showed were also contexts in which important kinds of communication occur during the asylum process.

Admissibility Interviews at the Border

Towards the end of my research in France, the Head of OFPRA's Asylum at the Border Division kindly arranged for me to visit the 'waiting zone' at Roissy Charles-de-Gaulle airport outside Paris and observe a series of admissibility interviews between case-workers and asylum applicants there. In this section, I focus on one of the interviews, and discuss the problems of communication that arose during it, and the implications for those involved. Before doing so, however, it is important to draw attention to the practical difficulties social scientists face in such situations, where tape recording is impossible and an official transcript either does not exist or is not available, with respect to the production of a full and accurate account of the proceedings. As Anthony Good (2007: 42–46) has explained, even with 'much frantic scribbling', the researcher is unlikely to be able to note down everything that is said 'verbatim', and so must decide what to record (and not to record) and, crucially, whether in later writing to paraphrase the exchanges or to present them as 'dialogue'. In his anthropological study of the role of expert evidence in the UK asylum courts, Good opted to use direct quotations, but nevertheless emphasised that the 'dialogues' he reproduced were 'not verbatim transcripts, although every effort has been made to make them accurate and intelligible, while not falsifying or misrepresenting the sense of what was said' (2007: 46). I adopt a similar approach, in this section of the

---

procedure, it may be provided together with notification of the decision). In addition, a sound recording (*enregistrement sonore*) of the interview is made, and the applicant can subsequently obtain access to this if their claim is rejected. For further information on the current procedures, see CESEDA (2017), OFPRA (2015) and Palluel (2016).

chapter and the next, regarding the presentation of translated extracts from the hand-written notes I took in French when observing admissibility interviews, asylum interviews and appeal hearings in France.

When the assistance of an interpreter is required for an admissibility interview conducted by an OFPRA case-worker with an asylum applicant at the border, this is usually provided by telephone. One of the interviews I observed in the waiting zone at Roissy Charles-de-Gaulle airport involved telephone interpreting, a service for which the OFPRA had signed a contract with a company. In the interview room, the case-worker and applicant sat opposite each other at a table, on top of which there was a conferencing phone unit incorporating a loud speaker and a microphone. When the applicant was brought to the interview room, the case-worker invited him to sit down at the table, and, after establishing that the man spoke neither French nor English, phoned the number of the interpreting services provider and was connected to an operator.

(2.30 pm)

> *Case-worker*: (*Introduces himself and explains why he is ringing.*) Do you have an interpreter available in (name of language) for an asylum application by a man from (name of country X)? Just one case (*dossier*).
> *Operator*: (*There is a pause while she checks.*) In (language) of (country X), there is no-one available at the moment. However, there is an interpreter available in (same name of language) from (country Y). Do you want to try?
> *Case-worker*: OK. We'll see how it goes.
> (*After a few minutes, during which time the music of the company's telephone hold system is relayed through the loud speaker, the case-worker is connected to the interpreter. After establishing that the interpreter has worked with the OFPRA before, the case-worker asks him to explain the procedure to the applicant. The interpreter then exchanges some words with the applicant, before addressing the case-worker again in French.*)
> *Interpreter (to C-W)*: He says to me that he doesn't understand me.
> *Case-worker*: He doesn't want to continue with you?
> *Interpreter*: No.
> *Case-worker*: Okay. Thank you.
> (*The case-worker hangs up and then phones the operator again.*)

(2.39 pm)

> *Case-worker*: We tried using an interpreter in (language) of (country Y) for an asylum application, but my applicant says that he doesn't understand. Can you try to find me another interpreter, in (language) of (country X).
> *Operator*: Okay, I'll try.

(For the next six minutes, the case-worker and applicant wait. The latter looks tired and anxious, and sits with his arms crossed. Then the operator's voice comes through the loud speaker again.)
Operator: I'm sorry, but I haven't been able to find an interpreter in (language) of (country X). Do you want me to keep trying?
Case-worker: Yes, please.
(After waiting a further nine minutes, the case-worker calls the operator again.)
Case-worker: I was just phoning to see how things were coming along.
Operator: I'm still trying, but I'm not certain I'll be able to find an interpreter.
Case-worker: Shall we give up then? What shall we do?
Operator: I'll keep trying.

(2.58 pm)

Operator: I've found an interpreter! Please wait a few moments.
Case-worker: In (language) of (country X)?
Operator: I hope so.
Case-worker (to RG): I hope so too!

(3.08 pm)

(The second interpreter comes on the line, and soon the case-worker starts to interview the applicant, asking him in turn to confirm his name, age and other personal details. This proves to be quite time-consuming, due to the fluctuating quality of the telephone line. Several times the case-worker has either to repeat his own question for the interpreter or ask the latter to repeat what he has just said, and the applicant sits hunched over the conferencing phone unit with his ear close to the loud speaker in an effort to hear the interpreter better.)

(3.32 pm)

(Suddenly, the telephone connection with the interpreter breaks. The case-worker phones the operator.)

Case-worker: I have been cut off with my interpreter.
Operator: I'll try to reconnect you.
(After a further eight minutes of the holding system music, the operator comes on the line again.)
Operator: I've been unable to re-connect you with the interpreter, but I've found another interpreter in (language) of (country X).
Case-worker: Okay. Let's go then.
(The case-worker is connected to the third interpreter, a woman, and resumes the interview with the applicant. There are no further 'technical problems' and the interview ends at 4.23 pm.)

This example highlights some of the potential barriers to achieving effective communication in the asylum process. These include the challenge of obtaining an interpreter in the appropriate language (as Dahlvik, this volume, attests), especially at very short notice, and the problem of relying on telecommunications devices such as telephones to provide interpreting services.[5] There is also, of course, the wider issue of the likely impact of the context of interaction itself on the communicative practices of those involved, in particular the asylum applicant. As a French non-governmental organisation has pointed out, the fact that the admissibility interviews are conducted inside the waiting zone, which is a place of detention, means that the applicant may not necessarily perceive the OFPRA case-worker to be 'neutral and independent of the border police' (Anafé 2008: 10, my translation). This could result in a reluctance on the part of the applicant to communicate fully to the case-worker the reasons for their application to be admitted to French territory.

The opportunity to observe the admissibility interview discussed above provided me with an insight, finally, not only into some of the communication problems that can arise in such contexts but also into the immediate implications of these for both the applicant and the case-worker. At the end of the interview, which had lasted almost two hours, with several false starts and delays, and the involvement of three different interpreters, the applicant must have felt exhausted. The interview must have been tiring and frustrating for the case-worker too, and he now found himself, as he explained to me once the applicant had left the interview room, in the situation of having just over half an hour to prepare decisions on several applications before he was due to finish work for the day. 'I don't know how I'm going to manage it', he said to me. An hour and a half later, when the Head of the Asylum at the Border Division and I left the waiting zone, the case-worker was still there drafting his decisions.

Asylum Interviews and Appeal Hearings

Two of the most important contexts where the issue of communication arises during the refugee status determination process are asylum interviews and appeal hearings. Many different kinds of communicative practice can

---

[5]In the other two admissibility interviews I observed before the one discussed here, no interpreter was used, as the case-workers conducted them directly in Arabic and French respectively.

occur during these events, and the aim of the present section is to explore some of these. I consider in turn OFPRA asylum interviews and appeal hearings at the CNDA, before briefly comparing the two contexts. The discussion focuses on how features of the built environment affected the communicative practices and interactions that took place in the interview booths and hearing rooms. As noted earlier, adopting an ethnographic approach involves an attempt 'to be alert and attentive to everything around you' (Flood 2005: 34), and this led me, when observing asylum interviews and appeal hearings in France, to notice how different the physical settings were in which they were conducted, and then, in subsequent interviews with key participants, to want to investigate the implications of this further.

At the time of the research, each interview booth at OFPRA's main office was equipped with a desktop computer, which the case-worker was expected to use to record their own questions and the applicant's answers as the interview proceeded. The fact that the entextualisation of the interview was carried out in this particular way—that is, in situ and by the case-worker responsible for conducting it—had a bearing on the nature of the interaction and on the communication of meaning. As one case-worker told me, the sound of the computer keyboard tended to resonate in the small booth, and this could make it difficult to hear what the applicant or interpreter was saying: 'There's the noise of the keyboard. You hear click click click click click click click click, and sometimes you can't hear anything else.' A more serious issue identified by participants, however, was the potential impact of the presence of the computer on the multimodal communication of meaning. As one interpreter commented:

> There are things that you [i.e. the interpreter] can feel (*ressentir*) by body movements or gestures, and which the case-worker will not necessarily see. Here too we shouldn't delude ourselves: the case-worker is in the process of examining the application, and they are asked to pay attention to this sort of detail, but at the same time they have to write, since *everything* must be recorded in minute detail. We [i.e. interpreters] are sitting facing the applicant. We *see* their body movements, we *see* everything that happens, we're aware if they hesitate or are in distress.

Many of the case-workers I interviewed also recognised that their having to transcribe the interview at the same time as conduct it could hinder effective communication with the asylum applicant. Two of them expressed the point as follows:

> We are so busy all the time typing the interviews – we have our eyes glued to the screen – that the relationship (*échange*) with the applicant can be difficult to establish. We don't look the applicant in the eye during the whole interview. Thus it's very difficult to establish contact.
>
> The drawback of the computer is that we look at the applicant less. As a result, you are in your bubble, and it's happened to me that suddenly I've heard the applicant cry and I've said to myself, 'Damn (*mince*), what's happened?' I didn't see it coming in fact.

What the above extracts highlight is how the adoption of a specific procedure for the entextualisation of an asylum interview, involving in this case a modification of the physical environment through the addition of a desktop computer to be used by the case-worker, affects the process of communication.

Appeal hearings at the CNDA take place in much larger rooms than the booths used for asylum interviews at the OFPRA, involve more people and are held in public. Here too, though, communicative practices can be shaped by aspects of the physical setting. In several hearings I attended, for example, I observed at a certain point that the CNDA *rapporteur* passed a note to the HCR assessor sitting to their right. Later, during an interview, a *rapporteur* explained to me what was happening on these occasions:

> There are certain presidents who ask the *rapporteur* at the end if they have a question to ask. It's quite rare. It's a personal choice [...]. But it is possible for us to intervene. We have little, informal practices (*petites pratiques*) with the HCR assessors, because it's the assessor who is seated nearest to us. So, sometimes there's a question that hasn't yet been raised, and which, for us, is really decisive. We write a little note, we ask the assessor if they would mind asking the question. But otherwise we do not normally intervene at all.

In other words, the seating arrangements facilitated informal interaction and communication between the CNDA *rapporteur* and HCR assessor during the actual proceedings. I did not observe such occurrences very often and their significance should not be over-stated, but they are the kind of 'detail' that ethnographic research can highlight, thereby contributing to a broader and deeper understanding of different forms of communicative practice in the asylum process.

Before concluding this section, I consider briefly interpreters' experiences of working in these two settings: OFPRA interview booths and CNDA hearing rooms. In France, the provision of interpreters in the asylum process has been organised since 2003 through a system of competitive tendering (*marchés publics*), covering both the OFPRA and the CNDA. Most of the interpreters I interviewed for the research had interpreted at the two institutions, and they were therefore in a position to compare them as 'contexts of interaction'. They could hold contrasting views, as the following extracts from interviews with two different interpreters show:

> The environment [at the OFPRA] is exhausting in fact. The booths are very small, the lighting plays a part too, the noise of the computer: all that contributes to (*joue sur*) the tension. It's similar (*proche*) to a police interrogation; at least, you could say that the conditions are similar to that. Therefore, I think that it's a lot more exhausting than in the [hearing] room.
>
> Here [at the OFPRA] we are in a different setting. We are a bit as if we were *en famille*, in inverted commas. We are in a small booth [...]. We are closer, both to the applicant and the case-worker. So, we are a bit more relaxed, in the way of working [...]. Whereas at the Commission [the CNDA], the hearings are public. We have to deal with everything that surrounds us: the noise from the corridors, people who are speaking [in the rows of seats] behind, crying babies, the panel of judges, the *rapporteurs*, and the lawyer. There's a certain number of actors who intervene and you have to put everything together [...]. Several people consider that it's easier to work at the OFPRA, because we are in a more relaxed setting.

What these comments highlight is the fact that individuals do not necessarily experience in the same way how characteristics of a particular setting influence the nature of the interaction and communication processes taking place within it. This may seem an obvious or even banal point, but I would argue that it is differences such as these that an ethnographic perspective can reveal, thereby contributing to a more detailed description and nuanced analysis of the asylum process.

Offices and Corridors

Significant forms of communication and interaction between participants in the refugee status determination process occur not only in asylum interviews and appeal hearings (although these are clearly crucial events) but also in other contexts. In this final section, I explore some of what happened, during the time of my fieldwork, in two much less prominent settings: the offices of OFPRA case-workers and CNDA *rapporteurs*, and the corridors[6] and waiting areas of the CNDA building. While I had access to the latter, I did not carry out observational research actually in staff offices. However, case-workers and *rapporteurs* talked to me about their offices when I interviewed them. This illustrates how an ethnographic approach, involving the combined use of several different research methods, has the potential to generate a multi-sited description of forms of communication, the importance of which has been emphasised by Blommaert and Rampton (as mentioned above).

Many of the OFPRA case-workers and CNDA *rapporteurs* I interviewed explained to me that they were based (or had been based) in 'open plan (*open space*)' offices with other colleagues having the same responsibilities, and that this facilitated communication between them. For example, one case-worker told me that she discussed her files, in an anonymised way, and exchanged useful information she had found on the countries of origin of applicants, with a small group of other case-workers. She added:

> What plays a role too is even the material structure itself. Obviously I talk with the people with whom I share my office. We are in a big office; there are four of us. It's true that we discuss the files, and I know that in our office if there's one of us who's working on a file and is asking herself a question about it, she interrupts the other three, asks them her question, and they reflect on it. We all do that, in fact.

Other case-workers and *rapporteurs* also emphasised the importance of open plan or shared offices (as well as corridors and staff canteens) for the 'socialisation' of newly appointed staff, 'collective work' and the informal 'pooling (*mutualisation*)' of knowledge, experience and information. This highlights that while case-workers and rapporteurs ultimately are individually responsible for examining particular asylum applications and preparing reports on specific appeals, respectively, it would be a mistake to view them as working in isolation throughout the whole process. Both before and after their involvement in asylum interviews or appeal hearings, they are engaged in forms of communicative practice with colleagues, in offices and other spaces, and these help to shape their work.

The final 'contexts of interaction' I wish to consider (albeit very briefly) in this chapter are the corridors and waiting areas of the CNDA. I went to the

---

[6]Social scientists working in other areas have suggested recently that greater attention should be paid to corridors (see, notably, Armstrong 2015). It would be interesting to investigate more thoroughly their role(s) as sites of interaction and communication in the asylum process.

Court on a regular basis over a period of nine months in order to observe appeal hearings, and I was struck by the amount of communication and interaction between participants that occurred outside the actual hearing rooms. In the waiting areas, for examples, secretaries would check that appellants, interpreters and barristers were present for particular hearings, and appellants sitting there would sometimes start talking to each other. Conversations involving judges, and sometimes also *rapporteurs*, interpreters and lawyers, would also take place in the corridors on the way to and from the coffee-machine during breaks between hearings, while barristers and their clients might have brief exchanges on their way to and/or from the hearing rooms.

The significance of corridors emerged particularly clearly in the interviews I conducted with interpreters who worked at the CNDA. Several interpreters explained to me, for example, that there was a tendency for appellants to try to make contact with them there, or for barristers to request their assistance ('Can you give me five minutes' help to explain two or three things to the appellant?'). In order to maintain their neutrality, they would therefore try to avoid putting themselves in that position. As one interpreter commented: 'We are obliged not to move about too much in the corridors and so on. We stay in the hearing room [while waiting to interpret in a particular case], but even there, they come looking for us!' Another interpreter contrasted the open, public nature of the CNDA hearings with the more closed environment of the OFPRA asylum interviews. In the latter, he remarked, the interpreter was already in the booth when the applicant entered after being called from the waiting area by the case-worker, and this contributed to creating a more formal atmosphere from the start.

In this section I have identified a number of different types of communication that occurred in staff offices, and in corridors and other spaces, during the asylum process in France at the time of my research. Each merits a much more detailed examination than I have been able to provide here. However, I have included them in this chapter in order to illustrate the point that an ethnographic approach to studying the asylum process can—and, I would argue, should—throw light not only on asylum interviews and appeal hearings, but also on what happens in other relevant (but less central) contexts.

Conclusion

This chapter brings an ethnographic perspective to bear on the issue of communication at different stages of the refugee status determination process in France. One of the advantages of adopting an ethnographic approach, not only to this specific question but also to the study of the asylum process more generally, lies in both the depth and the breadth of understanding it offers of the activities concerned. On the one hand, it can provide a richly detailed, contextualised account of a particular phenomenon; on the other, it holds out the possibility of tracing connections between apparently unrelated or distant phenomena. In this chapter, for example, I have sought to document forms of communicative practice in a range of 'contexts of interaction' involving participants in the French asylum process, and at the same time to show some of the links that exist between what happens in these different settings. This has led me, in a similar way to Rock (1993) in his ethnographic study of an English Crown Court, to explore ways in which space—and notably aspects of the built environment—can affect interactions between participants in legal (and administrative) processes and how these are experienced by those involved. In order to do this, it was necessary to use two main research methods: observation played an important part, but so did semi-structured interviews, generating valuable insights into forms of communicative practice I was not able to observe directly as well as into participants' reflections on their own and other people's situated actions. As I argue at the start of this chapter, ethnography is most appropriately viewed not as 'a' method or just another word for participant observation, but instead as a combination of research techniques and a distinct kind of written account.

Assessing the precise impact on the asylum determination process of the different communicative practices analysed in this chapter is not always a straightforward matter. In some cases, the nature of the effect is relatively clear and direct, as illustrated by the problems that having to rely on telephone interpreting caused for the OFPRA case-worker and asylum applicant in the admissibility interview described above. It is much more difficult, however, to evaluate the part played by conversations in staff offices and corridors, for example, on decision-making about specific asylum applications or appeals. This would require a much more detailed examination of the different factors that can influence the decision-making process, an exercise undertaken by the contributors to the final section of this collection but outwith the scope of the present chapter. Nevertheless, ethnographic research on different forms of communicative practice has, as I have aimed to show here, an important contribution to make to broadening and deepening knowledge and understanding of the complexity of refugee status determination processes, not only in France and other European countries, but elsewhere in the world too.

Acknowledgements I wish to thank François Bernard (former president, CNDA) and Jean-François Cordet (former director general, OFPRA) for granting me permission to conduct interviews with staff at their respective institutions; to Vera

Zederman (director, Legal Information Centre, CNDA), and Pascal Baudouin and Myriam Djegham (Research and Communication Service, OFPRA) for arranging interviews with staff; and to the individual members of staff who agreed to be interviewed. In addition, I am grateful to Anthony Good, Nick Gill, and Véronique Péchoux (Head of Mission, Asylum at the Borders, OFPRA) for their very helpful comments on an earlier version of this chapter. *Funding*: The research was supported by the Arts and Humanities Research Council (grant number AH/E50874X/1) under its Diasporas, Migration and Identities Programme.

References

Anafé (Association nationale d'Assistance aux Frontières pour les Étrangers/National Association for Assistance to Foreigners at the Borders). (2008). *Réfugiés en zone d'attente: Rapport sur les dérives de l'examen de l'asile à la frontière*. Paris: Anafé. Available at: http://www.anafe.org/IMG/pdf/anafe-rapport-asile-10-09-08.pdf. Accessed 6 Jan 2017.

Armstrong, S. (2015). The Cell and the Corridor: Imprisonment as Waiting, and Waiting as Mobile. *Time and Society* (Early Online Publication). Available at: http://journals.sagepub.com/doi/abs/10.1177/0961463X15587835. Accessed 19 Dec 2016.

Blommaert, J., & Rampton, B. (2016). Language and Superdiversity. In K. Arnaut, et al. (Eds.), *Language and Superdiversity*. New York and London: Routledge.

Burawoy, M. (1991). Introduction. In M. Burawoy, et al. (Eds.), *Ethnography Unbound: Power and Resistance in the Modern Metropolis*. Berkeley and Los Angeles: University of California Press.

CESEDA (Code de l'entrée et du séjour des étrangers et du droit d'asile/Code of Entry and Residence of Foreigners and of the Right to Asylum). (2009). Paris: LexisNexis.

CESEDA. (2017). Available at: https://www.legifrance.gouv.fr/. Accessed 6 Jan 2017.

Cimade. (2010). *Voyage au centre de l'asile: Enquête sur la procédure de détermination d'asile*. Available at: http://www.lacimade.org/publication/voyage-au-centre-de-lasile/. Accessed 6 Jan 2017.

CNDA (Cour nationale du droit d'asile/French National Court of Asylum). (2009). *Rapport annuel 2008*. Montreuil: CNDA. Available at: http://www.cnda.fr/content/download/5113/15469/version/1/file/cndarapportannuel2008.pdf. Accessed 6 Jan 2017.

Davies, C. A. (2008). *Reflexive Ethnography: A Guide to Researching Selves and Others* (2nd ed.). London and New York: Routledge.

d'Halluin-Mabillot, E. (2012). *Les épreuves de l'asile: Associations et réfugiés face aux politiques du soupçon*. Paris: Éditions de l'École des hautes études en sciences sociales.

Flood, J. (2005). Socio-legal Ethnography. In R. Banakar & M. Travers (Eds.), *Theory and Method in Socio-legal Research*. Oxford and Portland, Oregon: Hart Publishing.

Gibb, R., & Good, A. (2014). Interpretation, Translation and Intercultural Communication in Refugee Status Determination Procedures in the UK and France. *Language and Intercultural Communication, 14*(3), 385–399.

Goffman, E. (1983). The Interaction Order (American Sociological Association, 1982 Presidential Address). *American Sociological Review, 48*(1), 1–17.

Good, A. (2007). *Anthropology and Expertise in the Asylum Courts*. London: Routledge/Clarendon.

Kobelinsky, C. (2010). *L'accueil des demandeurs d'asile: Une ethnographie de l'attente*. Paris: Éditions du Cygne.

Kobelinsky, C. (2014). A Matter of Value: Exploring What Underlies Adjudication in the French Court of Asylum. *Migration Letters, 11*(1), 101–108.

OFPRA (Office français de protection des réfugiés et apatrides/French Office for the Protection of Refugees and Stateless People). (2009). *Rapport d'activité 2008*. Fontenay-sous-Bois: OFPRA. Available at: https://ofpra.gouv.fr/sites/default/files/atoms/files/rapport_dactivite_2008.pdf. Accessed 6 Jan 2017.

OFPRA. (2011). *Au coeur de l'Ofpra: Demandeurs d'asile et réfugiés en France*. Paris: La documentation française.

OFPRA. (2015). *Guide des procedures à l'Ofpra*. Fontenay-sous-Bois: OFPRA. Available at: https://ofpra.gouv.fr/sites/default/files/atoms/files/guide_de_procedure-ext_web_10-11-2015_vd.pdf. Accessed 14 Apr 2017.

Palluel, C. (2016). Le nouveau régime de la demande d'asile en rétention administrative: des garanties en trompe-l'œil. *La Revue des droits de l'homme* (Online), 10. Available at: https://revdh.revues.org/2470. Accessed 10 Apr 2017.

Rock, P. (1993). *The Social World of an English Crown Court: Witness and Professionals in Crown Court Centre at Wood Green*. Oxford: Clarendon.

Willis, P., & Trondman, M. (2000). Manifesto for Ethnography. *Ethnography, 1*(1), 5–16.

Open Access This chapter is distributed under the terms of the Creative Commons Attribution 4.0 International License (http://creativecommons.org/licenses/by/4.0/), which permits use, duplication, adaptation, distribution and reproduction in any medium or format, as long as you give appropriate credit to the original author(s) and the source, a link is provided to the Creative Commons license and any changes made are indicated.

The images or other third party material in this chapter are included in the work's Creative Commons license, unless indicated otherwise in the credit line; if such material is not included in the work's Creative Commons license and the respective action is not permitted by statutory regulation, users will need to obtain permission from the license holder to duplicate, adapt or reproduce the material.

9

Narrating Asylum in Camp and at Court

Matilde Skov Danstrøm and Zachary Whyte

Introduction

Seeking asylum is in fundamental ways a narrative undertaking. After all, the ability to construct a convincing, coherent, and consistent narrative is crucial to a successful asylum claim (Bohmer and Shuman 2008; Eastmond 2007; Good 2007). In Denmark, the Head of the Danish Refugee Appeals Board (RAB) Secretariat, has estimated that 9 out of 10 cases before the RAB are determined on the basis of credibility (*P1* 2014). Credibility, in turn, is often determined on the basis of judgments of narrative consistency (are there discrepancies, or 'divergences' as they are termed in the Danish context, in the narrative?) and authorship (does the narrative seem self-experienced?). This raises particular questions as to how narratives are constructed and assessed in the Danish asylum system—and indeed to what extent these two processes are separable. For asylum seekers, this narrative task is made more difficult by the opacity of the asylum system to them. Most cannot easily make sense of the bases for judgment of their asylum motives and this uncertainty fundamentally structures their experiences

---

M. S. Danstrøm (✉)
University of Copenhagen, Copenhagen, Denmark

Z. Whyte
AMIS, University of Copenhagen, Copenhagen, Denmark
e-mail: whyte@hum.ku.dk

© The Author(s) 2019
N. Gill and A. Good (eds.), *Asylum Determination in Europe*,
Palgrave Socio-Legal Studies, https://doi.org/10.1007/978-3-319-94749-5_9

of the system. The lawyers provided for them after an initial rejection are meant to help with this by re-presenting their claims before the RAB. The mediating role the lawyers play sheds light on both the narrative logics of the asylum determination system and the everyday narratives of asylum seekers waiting in asylum centres.

Drawing on ethnographic fieldwork in Denmark, this chapter investigates the ways in which asylum seekers and asylum lawyers present and re-present asylum narratives across two contrasting, yet interlinked, contexts: Danish asylum centres (termed 'camp' by the asylum seekers) and the RAB ('court' to asylum seekers). Among asylum seekers at Danish asylum centres, narratives of asylum almost never include the substance of asylum seekers' legal claims (their asylum motives). Details are guarded, not least from other asylum seekers. The asylum process itself, on the other hand, is a recurring topic, where interpreters, caseworkers and the general attitude of the Danish asylum system are regularly discussed. By contrast, asylum narratives presented at the RAB are meant to focus exclusively on content and performance (which is so crucial to asylum claims, as Kobelinsky, this volume, attests), at least insofar as they relate to the specifics of the asylum seekers' claim as mediated by their asylum lawyers. While context thus strongly shapes the kinds of asylum narratives that are presented and shared, this chapter suggests that themes of uncertainty, credibility and authorship are central both in the Danish asylum process and for the ways in which it is understood by the actors invested in it.

A terminological note is in order from the outset. While we write broadly of 'asylum narratives' as any of a range of narratives associated with the asylum system, we distinguish between two modes of narrating asylum in the two contexts of court and camp, which we might conceive of as stories *for* and stories *of* asylum. The first is what lawyers and adjudicators call the 'asylum motive,' that is the narratives processed by the Danish asylum authorities, which form the basis for their decisions on the application. The second is what we term 'asylum talk' which covers the narratives asylum seekers tell each other about the system they are caught up in. These two kinds of narratives are of course quite distinct: They have separate structures, turn-taking conventions, and consequences. They are part of different kinds of narrative exchanges and subject to different sorts of judgments. However, they do also connect and influence each other, if unevenly. The stories asylum seekers tell each other about the asylum system may influence the ways in which they tell their stories in the court setting. Conversely, it is often experiences with the asylum determination system that shape the kinds of stories told in the camps.

The uneven power relations between the two contexts can be seen in the bearing they have on each other. The judgment of the credibility of the asylum motive at court has profound consequences for the future lives of asylum seekers, while the narratives about asylum in circulation at the camp have little or no effect on the bureaucratic system of judgment. This is illustrated neatly by the fact that while court is a frequent topic of conversation at the camps, life in the camps is largely considered irrelevant at court. This disconnection is in itself important for how asylum seekers view the asylum system. It shapes the kinds of conversations they have about the system, and may thereby also shape the ways in which asylum seekers experience and participate in court proceedings.

A Narrative Approach

Asylum motives are often the main evidence on which asylum decisions are made (Kjær 2001; Bohmer and Shuman 2010), and narrative approaches naturally have some history in the study of forced migration, particularly when conceived methodologically e.g. as the collection of life stories (Krulfeld and MacDonald 1998; McKinley 1997; Omidian 1994). Narrative approaches to the asylum process have usefully examined issues of credibility (Good 2007), emotion (Kobelinsky 2015), resistance (Smith 2015, 2016) and mistrust (Daniel and Knudsen 1995; Bohmer and Shuman 2008; see also Kobelinsky, this volume). Marita Eastmond (2007), building on Edward Bruner (1986), has scrutinised narrative as a field of knowledge production, which 'provides a site to examine the meanings, which actors ascribe to experience' (2007: 260). Experience, Eastmond argues, gives 'rise and form' to the narratives, but is also 'organised and given meaning' when it is narrated (2007: 249). Eastmond points out that what is remembered and expressed by a narrator is situated in the specific encounter between the narrator and the audience, marked by the power relations between them. What is expressed is affected both by accounts of the past and present, but also by thoughts and dreams of the future (ibid.).

Our approach here differs somewhat in that our primary focus is not so much to understand the experiences of asylum seekers before they came to Denmark, but rather to better understand the Danish asylum system itself. In this chapter, we ask what sorts of narrative conventions structure Danish asylum practice, how are they practised, and how do asylum seekers make sense of these structures?

Following a brief description of the Danish legal context, we consider the trajectory the asylum motive takes before it reaches the RAB. Our task is not to look at the content of the asylum seekers' life stories as such (Kälin 1986; Blommaert 2001; Ghorashi 2008), but rather to look at the production of the asylum motive as a narrative tool to analyse the systems of judgement. Indeed, we argue that the asylum determination system profoundly shapes the asylum motives, while at the same time ascribing authorship of them solely to the asylum seeker.

We then turn to the narrative work asylum seekers engage in at the camps, as they struggle to make sense of the Danish asylum bureaucracy. Refugee narratives are often judged based on how they conform to standards of 'good' narration (Vogl 2013), but these standards are more visible to asylum lawyers than asylum seekers. Struggling to make sense of these narrative models and to find avenues for action to help guide their cases in a favourable direction, asylum seekers draw on their own experiences and those of others, conveyed through narrative, as they discuss systemic logics, individual caseworkers, and possibilities for action.

Finally, the Refugee Appeals Board serves as a site of narrative judgment, in which various actors work to present and re-represent the asylum motive, ascribed to the asylum seeker. Judgments often turn on the presence of 'divergences' and on whether asylum motives are deemed 'self-experienced.' Here the performance of the asylum motive can play a crucial role in the determination. However, this performance at court takes place as frustration has built among asylum seekers in the camps, and lawyers are particularly alert to the importance of managing the affective presentations of asylum seekers. In this sense, the trajectory of the asylum motive is influenced by the trajectory of what we might call asylum seekers' 'asylum careers', and asylum motives and asylum talk intermingle.

Methods

This chapter draws on ongoing ethnographic engagement with the Danish asylum context from the two authors. Danstrøm conducted five months of fieldwork in 2012 with Danish asylum lawyers, which included participant observation at the RAB and with asylum lawyers, as well as interviews with lawyers, judges, NGOs, and Immigration Service officials. She was the first researcher to be granted access to the closed RAB hearings, which came about in large part through her participant observation with the asylum lawyers. Whyte originally conducted a year's fieldwork among asylum seekers at a Danish asylum centre in 2001–2002, which included participant observation and formal and informal interviews with asylum seekers, Red Cross staff, and Immigration Service caseworkers. Since then, he has continued his engagement with the field, conducting several shorter research projects with asylum seekers and refugees in Denmark. This chapter thus draws both on the authors' original findings and later ethnographic work in various contexts. By juxtaposing these ongoing engagements, we aim to examine the 'linkages' (Colson 2007) that shape the interactions across the two narrative contexts of camp and court. We have anonymised all our informants and cases and use pseudonyms throughout.

Legal Context and Background

The criteria to achieve refugee status in Denmark are formalised in the Danish Aliens Act (DAA 2016). The Danish system of course draws on the 1951 UN Refugee Convention, and can grant full Convention status under 'Section 7.1' of the Aliens Act. However, a number of subsidiary forms of protection have been added. Thus 'Section 7.2' refers to Article 3 in the European Convention on Human Rights (EC 1950), granting a separate status to a wider group of refugees, while a new 'Section 7.3' was implemented in 2015 to grant temporary protection for one year (to be assessed by the authorities annually). The latter was aimed at the Syrians entering Denmark at the time. These subsidiary forms of status do not all give access to the same range of rights, e.g. to family reunification or welfare services, as Convention status does.

The Danish Immigration Service (DIS), under the Ministry of Integration, processes asylum applications in the first instance in Denmark. Initially, the case will be assessed according to the Dublin regulation, which among other things entails that asylum applications can only be processed in one EU country. DIS can further dismiss cases as 'manifestly unfounded' if they are considered without substance or prospects according to section 53b. These cases cannot be appealed, but will instead be assessed by an NGO, the Danish Refugee Council, which may refer the case back to the so-called 'normal procedure'.

In the last few years, first instance recognition rates have been exceptionally high. In 2016, 72% of asylum claims were granted one of the three forms of protection status. However, just five years earlier, in 2011 average recognition rates were only 33%. This change is in large part due to the relatively large number of Syrians and Eritreans, who claimed asylum in the last few years.

In the normal procedure, a rejection is automatically appealed to a quasi-judicial body, the RAB. Established in 1983, the aim was to have independent adjudicators settle the practice on asylum in Denmark, rather than the previous ad hoc administrative system (Christensen et al. 2006: 464ff.). It is a uniquely Danish construction. In most other European countries asylum rejections can be appealed and processed in (specialised) courts with open hearings. By contrast, RAB hearings take place behind closed doors and with the involvement of both judges and others. It consists of a number of smaller boards, which comprised five members in 2014: a judge from the regular court system, who functions as a chairman; two judicial representatives from the Ministry of Integration and the Ministry of Foreign Affairs respectively; a lawyer from The Danish Bar and Law Society; and lastly a member appointed by the Danish Refugee Council (DRC). The Ministry of Integration is thus represented both by the DIS, presenting the reasons for their first instance rejection, and by a representative sitting on the Board to which that decision is appealed.

However, the number of board members and the institutions they represent have changed several times from seven to three to five members, following shifting political priorities of successive governments. In particular, the members appointed by DRC have been subject to political discussion—and a new amendment to the Aliens Act effective from 1st January 2017 once again removes the DRC members (as well as the Ministry of Foreign Affairs to keep an uneven number). These changes speak directly to the heavily politicised nature of the Danish asylum system.

Another important aspect of the Danish system is that appeals to the RAB are final. The substance of the cases cannot be appealed beyond the RAB (Section 56, 8 in the Danish Aliens Act (DAA 2016)). The only exceptions are on the basis of complaints concerning procedural irregularities. However, even cases brought on procedural grounds have generally been referred back to the RAB with the conclusion that the complaint was in fact linked to the substance of the case (see note 1008 to Section 56, 8, DAA 2016). Further, cases cannot be taken before the Ombudsman, who can only initiate cases concerning asylum himself (Section 58, DAA 2016). Nevertheless, there are some other options used by asylum seekers and their lawyers. In theory, there is a possibility of getting temporary humanitarian protection upon a separate application (section 9b paragraph 1), though this possibility has been undermined in recent years, and was only granted in 76 cases in 2012 (DIS 2013). Further, asylum seekers can apply for a 'reopening' of their case. However, this requires that 'new substantial information' has come to light in the case. Lastly, if all national options have been exhausted, the case could be taken to the UN Committee or the European Court of Human Rights. However, since asylum seekers do not receive legal aid from the Danish state beyond the RAB and this appeal is not suspensive, this is rarely exercised.

The Trajectory of the Asylum Motive

The asylum motive—what we have called the story for asylum—is not a fixed narrative. Rather, it is ambiguously perpetuated and re-shaped through a number of versions before it reaches the RAB. Jan Blommaert calls this process 'discourse circulation' (2001: 438), stressing the trajectory (cf. Maryns 2006) of the narrative going from oral to written, passing different interlocutors or co-narrators even, including interpreters, along the way. Spotti and Gibb (this volume) explore this process, which they refer to as 'entextualisation', while Dahlvik (this volume) discusses the influence interpreters can have over narratives.

To illustrate these points, it is worth sketching out this trajectory before the motive comes before the RAB. In doing so, one further point must be kept in mind: The asylum motives that come before the RAB are a particular subset of the asylum motives, since they by definition have been rejected in the first instance. While this may speak to the particularities of the case and the credibility of the asylum seeker, we argue that the trajectory itself also shapes the asylum motive, as it is presented and represented through the determination system.

An asylum case in Denmark starts with an initial registration of the claimant by the police, who record their identity and travel route. After the registration, the asylum seeker will be asked to fill out an asylum application form in their native language, if possible. If this is done, it will be translated and serve as the basis for the case throughout the process. A short 'motive and information interview' is then conducted through an interpreter, after which a DIS caseworker summarises the case.

The next version, the asylum interview, is sometimes enacted up to a year after arrival depending on the current caseload. This is carried out by a DIS caseworker (and an interpreter), who questions the asylum seeker in more detail. The caseworker produces a written summary of this interview, which forms the basis for the first instance judgment by the caseworker. This text, in other words, combines summary with judgment. For rejected cases that end up before the RAB, the summaries are often explicitly skeptical of the asylum motive. In one example, the caseworker wrote: 'When asked if the applicant does not agree that it seems implausible to be able to see the three men accurately from a 50 meters distance […]'. Or: 'It seems odd that they would give the applicant a bible only two to three months after they met the first time […]'. Also phrases like, 'it seems striking' or 'it seems noticeable' are commonly used, as are terms such as 'implausible' and even 'weird' or 'strange'. The language then is often one of disbelief or suspicion tied to particular narrative conventions (Good 2007; Vogl 2013). The representatives from the DIS explained that this line of questioning was meant to help the asylum seeker by giving them a chance to explain what seemed unlikely to the representative. 'It's to be fair to them', as one put it. The lawyers, however, felt that it confused their clients, and some lawyers expressed the concern that this was intended to 'test' the asylum seekers on the motives and provoke the so-called 'divergences' that could undermine the asylum seekers' credibility. As Hanne, an asylum lawyer, put it in frustration with a particular summary, 'In other judicial proceedings, an interrogator would stop the suspects if they were saying things to harm their case before a lawyer was present. But in the DIS it's as if the opposite is the case'. In any case, as we will discuss in the following section, this explicit mistrust is experienced keenly by the asylum seekers themselves.

If a case is rejected in the first instance, it is automatically appealed, and a lawyer is appointed, who receives the existing case files, as do the adjudicators. The lawyer usually has a meeting lasting from two to six hours with the client to go through the case again. On this basis, the lawyer writes a submission to the RAB, summarising the asylum motive yet again, but in a manner designed to support a positive judgment.

Two of the key elements forming the basis for asylum decisions are whether the asylum motive contains 'divergences' and whether it seems 'self-experienced'. These terms tie in closely to concerns with consistency and credibility. As a RAB chairman put it: 'If the asylum seekers' explanations show some significant discrepancies of one kind or another […], then you can get the suspicion that this in fact is a fabricated asylum motive.'

Susan Coutin has shown in Salvadoran and Guatemalan asylum cases in the US that the smallest 'plot hole' in the narrative can lead to a rejection (2001: 84). The lawyers' job is therefore to sort out the versions from the first instance and frame yet another, in the form of the submission, to address these 'plot holes'. As the lawyer Martin complained, 'We are never invited in until afterwards, right? […] and if there are the least of divergences between the summary of the [asylum] interview and some report from the police […] then we are sold. You are out. That is definitely wrong […]'.

This focus on divergences can play out in ways that highlight both issues of interpretation and authorship. An Afghani asylum seeker's interview with DIS was too long to finish in one day, so his interview was split in two sessions with one month between them. In the first summary, it was stated among other details that he had 'a conflict with his relatives'. In the second interview, it was stated that he had 'a conflict with his cousins' and was 'scolded by the local community'. However, the terms 'relatives' and 'cousins' were seen as diverging by the DIS caseworker. At his meeting with his lawyer, the client explained that he used the term 'scolding' [*skæid ud*], in a sense more severe than the Danish translation could capture, meaning something like 'personal threats'. The case was rejected in the RAB as well. In this case, it seems the adjudicators read the translation and the written summaries as if they were the exact words of the asylum seeker. The words were considered his own, though the asylum seeker did not recognise their use or the meaning of the Danish term '*skæld ud*'—to which he was ascribed authorship.

The perception of divergences in the asylum motive alongside a number of other elements (see below) may lead adjudicators to suggest that the asylum motive is not 'self-experienced'. Indeed, one of the common rejection phrases used is that 'the RAB does not find that the explanations seem self-experienced'. This speaks directly to questions of authorship, suggesting that the asylum seeker is not the proper author of the asylum motive. The bureaucratic and legal practice is quite clear: the asylum motive belongs to the asylum seeker alone and judgments of the asylum motive will determine whether the asylum seeker is granted protection status or not. However, the authorship of the asylum motive is rather more vexed than the asylum system presumes and accepts. Indeed, lawyers complained that the common issues of poor translations in the system, in which interpreters might change aspects of the narrative (see Dahlvik, this volume), carried little weight before the RAB. However, as we have seen, even beyond issues of translation, the asylum motive is co-produced by a range of other actors and is repeatedly represented and summarised in a way that may render it unrecognisable to the asylum seekers themselves. As Bruner has shown, narratives emerge in collaboration between speaker and audience (Bruner 1986). Indeed, the multiple narrative contexts and audiences may risk facilitating the narrative 'divergences' that shape decisions on credibility. Thus the procedure disempowers asylum seekers in putting forward the asylum motive on their own terms (cf. Giordano 2008: 590; Good 2007: 23). While the asylum motive thus risks fragmentation across its trajectory, the different versions are held together by the ascription of authorship to the asylum seeker.

In practice, then, asylum motives are continually produced in the asylum system through particular narrative contexts, audiences, and modes of questioning, meaning that they reflect not only the experiences the asylum seekers present as a basis for their asylum claim but also the asylum determination system itself. While the experiences narrated are of course not about the asylum system, the manner in which they are presented, the questions asked to elicit them, and especially the ways in which individual experiences are joined to form a narrative—the asylum motive—are structured by the asylum system. The key point here is that there is no 'original' asylum narrative that may be elicited in or twisted by the asylum process. The asylum motive is a narrative that only makes sense within the asylum determination process.

Before discussing how the assessment takes place before the RAB we look at how the tales of the asylum system, asylum talks, circulate in the asylum centres and how this circulation is somewhat separated from the legal context.

The Circulation of Asylum Talk at the Camp

While waiting for their cases to be processed, asylum seekers in Denmark are housed in asylum centres—'camps' to the asylum seekers. These are located around the country, often some distance from urban centres. DIS is responsible for the accommodation and care of asylum seekers, but they subcontract this work to other organisations. Currently, the Red Cross operates about a third of Danish asylum centres, while municipalities run the remaining two-thirds. Unlike other countries, no private contractors run asylum centres in Denmark, though many are involved in catering, maintaining buildings, and security tasks.

Life at the camps is marked by the tight living conditions and the uncertainty of the asylum process. Asylum seekers often live four or more to a room with little or no privacy and very limited funds (called 'pocket money', paid out bi-weekly). They are restricted from working and pursuing education, while they wait. Their lack of money and the generally remote locations of the camps make mobility very difficult, so many asylum seekers simply sit and wait for the months or years it takes for their cases to be processed. The asylum system requires asylum seekers to participate in 'internships' [*praktik*] and other activities with the explicit goal of avoiding inactivity. However, these tasks often relate to cleaning, operation, and services at the asylum centre itself. They largely fail to counter the impression of stasis and wasting one's time prevalent among asylum seekers. In practice, the life of asylum seekers involved a great deal of sitting around, drinking tea, smoking cigarettes, playing pool, and watching tv, while waiting for news of their asylum case. This said, the common category, asylum seeker, tends to obscure the diversity of asylum seekers. Experiences of waiting (cf. Rotter 2016; Griffiths 2014) and of the asylum system more generally are fundamentally informed by the diversities of gender, age, class, health, ethnicity and so on.

At the same time, the asylum period is one of profound uncertainty for all asylum seekers. They wait while fundamental decisions about their future are made elsewhere in bureaucratic systems that are often opaque to them. This uncertain waiting takes its toll. As has been well established in the literature, extensive waiting times in the asylum period carry serious mental health consequences (Filges et al. 2016). However, they also impinge on social life at the asylum centres. Asylum seekers are unsure of the role the asylum centre operators have, and what their connection is to other asylum authorities, like the Immigration Service. This shapes their interactions with staff, who they worry may cause them problems but also hope may help their cases. They are also unsure of other asylum seekers, whose motives they may mistrust and who they are concerned may react unpredictably, because of the mental strains many are under. While social life among asylum seekers at the camps was thus at times strained, it nevertheless was an important part of most asylum seekers' daily lives. Most found friends, even if these were fleeting acquaintances, given the suddenness with which asylum seekers could move or be moved.

Asylum seekers seldom discussed their cases at the camps, and this was so for a number of reasons. First, the narratives presented to asylum authorities were often of a very personal and at times shameful nature. They might include experiences of humiliation, abuse, and even sexual assault. These were not stories to share with virtual strangers—nor indeed necessarily stories to share even with close family. Second, the experience of profound mistrust from asylum authorities and the fact that the narratives making up their cases were so to speak already in process made it a pragmatic point to keep quiet and wait for a decision. Third, many asylum seekers did not trust each other. There were everywhere stories about spies and enemies, also among compatriots and co-ethnics, who might use personal knowledge against the narrator and not least family in the home country. Fourth, some stories were embellished or outright constructed. Some asylum seekers presented narratives, which they had been told by smugglers or other people they trusted in this matter, were likely to gain them 'positive' decisions.

Or they embellished stories in manners they thought or had been told were strategic. This did not necessarily indicate that they did not have a valid asylum claim, but it did certainly make this minority less likely to discuss these narratives in public (cf. Beneduce 2015).

For all their reticence about their individual cases, asylum seekers routinely discussed the asylum system itself. They talked about named caseworkers, but also the vulnerability of the system to random factors. As one asylum seeker nervously joked, 'Sometimes I think what if the person sitting with my case had a bad day. Maybe their dog was run over and they come to the office and then look at my application. How will they decide? Maybe on that day, everyone gets negative'. Similarly, we have heard versions of a story about two brothers seeking asylum from the same village for the same reasons, but where one got positive and the other negative, repeated across more than a decade. Further, there was an oft-expressed worry that asylum authorities were not able to distinguish truth from falsehood. Asylum seekers spoke of how 'people with real problems', who did not have the time and opportunity to go about finding corroborating evidence for their claims before they fled, were at a disadvantage to 'cheaters' because asylum authorities could not tell who was who. In other words, there was a widespread concern that the asylum system did not properly 'see' them (Whyte 2011; Kobelinsky, this volume).

And they spoke in detail about the problem of incompetent—or even malicious—interpreters. Stories abounded of interpreters who did not speak the language properly, who made unprofessional comments, or who simply seemed not to like the asylum seeker in question. This is part of a larger problem of interpretation in asylum hearings (Gibb and Good 2014; Pöllabauer 2004; Dahlvik, this volume), but also a specific problem in Denmark where a troubling number of court interpreters have been shown not to be up to their jobs (Christensen and Martinsen 2012; Graversen et al. 2015).

These kinds of conversations were a basic part of camp sociality: ways of interacting with other asylum seekers, who one did not know, in uncertain circumstances. One key aspect of this form of sociality at the camp was that the asylum seekers with most experience of the asylum system naturally were the ones who had waited the longest. But these were also a particular subset of asylum seekers, whose cases for one reason or another were dragging on. Asylum seekers were of course well aware of this, and people with a greater expectation of receiving asylum, often based on their country of origin, generally took these stories with a pinch of salt.

But asylum talk can also be seen as an attempt to better understand the uncertainties of the asylum system, in much the same way as asylum seekers' discussions of the role and meaning of documents in Denmark (Whyte 2015). Many of these narratives were not necessarily coherent (Hyvärinen et al. 2010), but spoke in fragmented form to particular understandings of and attempts at understanding the asylum system. Unlike the required structuring of their asylum motives, concerns about consistency were not paramount, nor were the sources of these stories probed.

Walking back to the camp with Nazir, a young Afghan man, he started talking again about his waiting time:

> I wait and wait and nothing happens here. I have been waiting 11 months now and still no interview, no letter, nothing. My friend told me that I should go to Norway, present all my papers there. They will send me back here, of course, but then they will have to give me a decision. What do you think?

This sort of plan was not uncommon and spoke to a common conception of having been forgotten. Reminding the asylum authorities of one's existence in one way or another might then reactivate the processing of one's case. But it was also considered dangerous, as it could cause annoyance and possibly delay matters further. Nazir was not convinced that it was a wise move. 'I talked to a man called Sader, some of the other Afghanis told me about him. He knows about these things, he has some kind of organisation to help Afghanis. He told me not to do it. He said it would make my case more complicated. But still [...]'.

Though not many asylum seekers necessarily carried out plans like these, they still returned to them time and again. This kind of asylum talk can be seen as a way of trying to find ways forward in an opaque system. Like attempts at procuring documents to strengthen one's case (Whyte 2015), Nazir's 'But still [...]' speaks to his desire to reclaim a sense of agency, to do something to advance his life. Unlike some others, Nazir recognised that this plan was not necessarily well-judged. But in any case it also had a significant social element. Connecting with and seeking advice from other people, also created and maintained certain forms of sociality prevalent at the camp. In that sense, asylum talk was both text and context for everyday life in the camps.

Discussions of the asylum system were often accompanied by sudden outbursts of anger and bitterness. 'I hear that in England they give passports even to their dogs. Their dogs! But here I cannot get positive. I get nothing. Negative. This is Europe: we think it is a democratic place, but for them us black-haired people are less than their dogs,' as a young Palestinian man said bitterly. Or as Abu Minna explained sitting in the kitchen at camp, his voice rising as he spoke about his interview with the Immigration Service, 'How can they tell me I am lying! They do not know my situation. I was in prison! The police beat me! Now this woman [the caseworker] talks to me as if I am a liar. I was so angry!'. His coffee cup quivered on the way to his lips. 'First they put us in this prison,' he waved his hand around the camp kitchen. 'Wait wait wait, every day. Every day, nothing. Then they treat us like liars. I get so angry!'

These attempts at understanding the asylum system went hand in hand with the emotional outbursts. And they were of course brought with them to the RAB, to which we now turn.

Asylum Narratives at the RAB

Having described the trajectory of the asylum motive and contrasted them with the asylum talk of the camp, we turn now to the RAB as a specific site of narrative judgment in which competing versions of asylum motives are presented, represented and performed.

In so doing, it is worthwhile establishing the 'stage' on which these performances take place. The RAB is made up of two waiting rooms for the asylum seekers, where lawyers have pre-meetings with their clients; one police room, where the lawyers and interpreters sit: one room for the lawyers (which is mainly used for discussing determinations with clients after the hearings); and one room for DIS representatives. In addition, there are rooms for the actual hearings.

The chairman always initiates the hearing by stating the rights and duties to the asylum seeker and explaining the process of the hearing. But a number of versions of the asylum motive co-exist and compete there. All of the written versions of the asylum motive across its trajectory are present in the paperwork. It is worth noting that the various interviews are not normally recorded (until recently asylum seekers were not allowed to record their own interviews), therefore it is not possible to go back and listen to the initial story to clarify any misunderstandings. The RAB is dependent on the written versions before them. On top of this, an oral version of the narrative is performed, when the lawyer interviews the client (through an interpreter) before the adjudicators, who also ask questions to illuminate the case. A representative from the DIS is also present to defend their rejection, though the vigour with which they do so varies significantly. While some only state, 'DIS recommends an affirmation of the rejection', others interview the asylum seeker again. These proceedings are taken down as minutes by a legal secretary. When all parties have had a chance to ask questions, the lawyer adds a new version in the form of the closing statement. This generally has the form of a competing reading of the various versions of the asylum motive, designed to explain possible discrepancies and to give the impression of consistency.

On the basis of this process and the various competing presentations of the asylum motive, the RAB renders its judgment. In so doing, it produces a final edition of the motive, which comes in two different written versions. The adjudicators in the RAB vote immediately after the hearing and draw up the final determination to the applicant. Besides the outcome of the case, it also consists of a summarised asylum motive as written by the legal secretary. This version can be found online as part of the 'RAB practice' in short form containing the asylum motive together with the outcome. The practice is important to refer to in future cases for both lawyers and adjudicators (RAB 2014).

While the various competing versions of the asylum motive are all important, a key part of the proceedings comes from the performance of the asylum seekers themselves. As a chairman explained: 'They [asylum seekers] can look alike when they are on paper, but the credibility impression can be very different [during the hearing in the RAB]'. This is a performance that their lawyers work hard to manage to ensure that the asylum motive steers clear of 'divergences' and appears 'self-experienced'. This is illustrated in an interview with Mette, talking about the meeting between the lawyer and the client:

'The meeting is about making [the clients] understand what it takes to get [the adjudicators] to believe their story. I explain how a story affects others. If you just sit and answer yes and no and if there are divergences, then you don't seem credible. You have to explain it down to the detail. You have to mention things that you only can say if you have experienced them yourself. For example 'and then he did this and then I thought that was strange…'. Or 'this officer wore these clothes, there were five stars on the shoulder…'. If he can make small descriptions of how it all adds up somehow. And then try to make them understand. It is also important that you can feel that it affects them to sit there and tell the story that you can feel that this is something they have experienced. It can be hard to make them understand. They also have a different cultural background for how to tell a story'.

For Mette, then, a successful presentation did not just involve telling the story coherently and avoiding divergences, but also had to be told in particular ways, involving the cultural repertoires of the narrator and the audience (Eastmond 2007: 249). Mette tried to make her clients understand that the judges had to 'feel' that the applicant was actually there through the performance of the narrative. This embodiment of the narrative was not something that all asylum seekers practised in a way that was appreciated by the adjudicators, as indicated by the quote. What Mette was implying was that representation is also about instructing the asylum seekers in the importance of presenting the asylum motive in an appropriate way. That is, using the body to convince the RAB, during the actual hearing, that it is in fact 'self-experienced'.

One of the problems facing lawyers in this endeavour is the built-up frustration, fear, and anger of the asylum seekers. Hanne was representing a couple from Iran with a young daughter. The mother was crying in the asylum seekers' waiting room, as Hanne was in the midst of the pre-meeting with her client. She turned to the mother: 'You really ought to stop crying. It doesn't pay off to cry in front of the Board; you don't win anything by doing that'. Here it becomes clear that the anger and frustration that is so evident in the camp—in the asylum talk—cannot be exposed in the RAB. It is to be separated from the legal procedure and assessment of the asylum motive even though, for the asylum seekers, these contexts are inseparable. In other words, while it was important for asylum seekers to convey feelings about their past in an appropriate way, it was equally important to keep their feelings about their present hidden away.

Before the Board, the husband explained that the police in Iran had held him back, and that their home had been searched several times. Hanne interrogated him about the incidents in his home: 'What happened exactly when the police came to your house? How many officers were there? (Client/interpreter): 'There were many; maybe four. They held me like this' [the client gets up, takes his arms together on the back to show that he was handcuffed. He bends down, indicating that they pushed his head towards the floor]. 'They searched my house for flyers; everything was torn into pieces. That happened several times'.'

After the hearing, Hanne seemed satisfied: 'They really explained themselves well; you really felt like you were present. That is really good'. After a short waiting time we were called back into the hearing room. The adjudicators stressed that the explanation seemed 'self-experienced' and was thus 'accepted'. The couple was granted asylum. Both the lawyer and adjudicators thus emphasised the performance of the narrative as a decisive factor.

For asylum seekers, this experience was often demeaning. Many experienced the court setting in highly moral terms as a space in which they were mistrusted and even accused of dishonesty. As one young Afghani man said, as he returned to the RAB waiting rooms, shaking with anger, 'They didn't believe me! That man [from the Immigration Service] spoke lies about my father! He said I was lying!'. His older brother, whose case was being heard with him, looked slightly stunned himself, cheeks flushed, but put his hand on his brother's shoulder. 'Wait, just wait'. 'I wanted to punch him. How can he sit and lie like that? And the lawyer! He said nothing!'.

Conclusion

As will be evident from this description, camps and courts provide two radically different narrative contexts for asylum seekers. They are connected by the asylum seekers themselves of course, but also by the negotiations of legal and moral judgements that frame the two contexts. While the RAB sees itself as making legal judgements on specific cases, it seems clear that they also take account of a range of extra-legal factors from credibility to performance. For asylum seekers, these factors tend to loom large and often formed grist for the mill of their asylum talk.

At court, asylum seekers' asylum motives are significantly formed in interaction with powerful interlocutors and re-presented by their lawyers. While asylum seekers remain responsible for these narratives, in the sense that they are the ones who bear the consequences of the RAB's decision on them, the motives are also significantly beyond asylum seekers' control. Asylum motives are attributed to asylum seekers but are not necessarily fully theirs in an experiential sense. Indeed, as we have argued, the performative requirements put on them may tend to leave little space for their own sense of presence at the court. They tend not to feel heard or understood throughout the asylum determination system. However, the right kind of performance, the embodiment of the narrative, can in some cases overrule a narrative that was previously in the procedure considered not credible—when it affirms the 'self-experience' of the incidents expressed. By contrast, in the camp, asylum seekers are all too frustratingly present. They feel they are wasting their time there, waiting for their cases to move forward. But they do not generally discuss their asylum motives at the camp, instead engaging in what we have called 'asylum talk' through which they attempt to make sense of the seemingly opaque asylum process they are in together.

References

Beneduce, R. (2015). The Moral Economy of Lying: Subjectcraft, Narrative Capital, and Uncertainty in the Politics of Asylum. *Medical Anthropology, 34*(6), 551–571.

Blommaert, J. (2001). Investigating Narrative: African Asylum Seekers' Stories in Belgium. *Discourse and Society, 12,* 413–449.

Bohmer, C., & Shuman, A. (2008). *Rejecting Refugees: Political Asylum in the 21st Century.* London and New York: Routledge.

Bohmer, C., & Shuman, A. (2010). Narrating Atrocity: Uses of Evidence in the Political Asylum Process (DIIS Working Paper, 25). DIIS.

Bruner, E. M. (1986). Experience and Its Expressions. In V. W. Turner & E. M. Bruner (Eds.), *The Anthropology of Experience* (pp. 3–33). Chicago: University of Illinois Press.

Christensen L. B. et al. (2006). Udlændingeret. 3. udgave, 1. oplag. København: Jurist- og Økonomiforbundets Forlag.

Christensen, T. P., & Martinsen, B. (2012). *Retstolkens rolle—En spørgeskemaundersøgelse blandt danske domstolsjurister om deres forventninger til og oplevelser med retstolke.* Research Report, Aarhus University, Business and Social Sciences, Department of Business Communications.

Colson, E. (2007). Linkages Methodology: No Man is an Island. *Journal of Refugee Studies, 20*(2), 320.

Coutin, S. B. (2001). The Oppressed, the Suspect, and the Citizen: Subjectivity in Competing Accounts of Political Violence. *Law and Social Inquiry, 26*(1), 63–94.

Daniel, E. V., & Knudsen, J. C. (1995). *Mistrusting Refugees.* Berkeley: University of California Press.

DAA, *The Danish Aliens Act.* (2016). Available at: https://www.retsinformation.dk/Forms/R0710.aspx?id=180093. Accessed 7 Dec 2016.

DIS. (2013). Tal og Fakta. Udlændingestyrelsen. Nyidanmark. Available at: http://www.nyidanmark.dk/NR/rdonlyres/2934917B-F967-4EDF-BEDF-753D190BA6C2/0/tal_og_fakta_2012.pdf. Accessed 3 Jan 2014.

Eastmond, M. (2007). Stories as Lived Experience: Narratives in Forced Migration Research. *Journal of Refugee Studies, 20*(2), 248–264.

Filges, T., Montgomery, E., & Kastrup, M. (2016). The Impact of Detention on the Health of Asylum Seekers: A Systematic Review. *Research on Social Work Practice* (pp. 1–17).

Ghorashi, H. (2008). Giving Silence a Chance: The Importance of Life Stories for Research on Refugees. *Journal of Refugee Studies, 21*(1), 117–132.

Giordano, C. (2008). Practices of Translation and the Making of Migrant Subjectivities in Contemporary Italy. *American Ethnologist, 35*(4), 588–606.

Gibb, R., & Good, A. (2014). Interpretation, Translation and Intercultural Communication in Refugee Status Determination Procedures in the UK and France. *Language and Intercultural Communication, 14*(3), 385–399.

Good, A. (2007). *Anthropology and Expertise in the Asylum Courts.* New York: Routledge-Cavendish.

Graversen, C., Jacobsen, B., & Nørgaard A-J. (2015). *Tolkning i den offentlige sektor. Den aktuelle tolkesituation. Afrapportering af spørgeskemaundersøgelse blandt tolkebrugere i den offentlige sektor.* Copenhagen: Translatørforeningen.

Griffiths, M. (2014). Out of Time: The Temporal Uncertainties of Refused Asylum Seekers and Immigration Detainees. *Journal of Ethnic and Migration Studies, 40*(12), 1991–2009.

Hyvärinen, M., Hydén, L.-C., Saarenheimo, M., & Tamboukou, M. (Eds.). (2010). *Beyond Narrative Coherence*. Amsterdam: John Benjamins.

Kjær, K. U. (2001). Bevissituationen i Asylsager. *Karnov Group Denmark* (pp. 1–5).

Kälin, W. (1986). Troubled Communication: Cross-Cultural Misunderstandings in the Asylum-Hearing. *International Migration Review, 2*(2), 230–241.

Kobelinsky, C. (2015). Emotions as Evidence. An Ethnographic Exploration of Hearings in the French Asylum Courts. In D. Berti, A. Good, & G. Tarabout (Eds.), *Of Doubt and Proof: Ritual and Legal Practices of Judgement*. London: Ashgate.

Krulfeld, R. M., & MacDonald, J. L. (1998). *Power, Ethics, and Human Rights: Anthropological Studies of Refugee Research and Action*. Oxford: Rowman and Littlefield.

Maryns, Katrijn. (2006). *The Asylum Speaker: Language in the Belgian Asylum Procedure*. Manchester: St. Jerome.

McKinley, M. (1997). Life Stories, Disclosure and the Law. *PoLAR, 20,* 70–82.

Omidian, P. A. (1994). Life Out of Context: Recording Afghan Refugees' Stories. In L. A. Camino & R. M. Krulfeld (Eds.), *Reconstructing Lives, Recapturing Meaning: Refugee Identity, Gender, and Culture Change*. Amsterdam: Gordon and Breach.

P1, Hvad der skete siden? (2014). [Documentary], P1 Dokumentar, See: http://www.dr.dk/radio/ondemand/p1/p1-dokumentar-94#!/. Accessed 5 Jan 2014.

Pöllabauer, S. (2004). Interpreting in Asylum Hearings: Issues of Role, Responsibility and Power. *Interpreting, 6*(2), 143–180.

RAB. (2014). *Flygtningenævnets praksis*. Available at: http://fln.dk/da-dk/Praksis. Accessed 23 Mar 2014.

Rotter, R. (2016). Waiting in the Asylum Determination Process: Just An Empty Interlude? *Time and Society, 25*(1), 80–101.

Smith, K. (2015). Stories Told By, For, and About Women Refugees: Engendering Resistance. *ACME: An International E-Journal for Critical Geographies 14*(2), 461–469.

Smith, K. (2016). Telling Stories of Resistance and Ruination: Women Seeking Asylum. *Journal of Resistance Studies, 4*(2), 33–64.

Vogl, A. (2013). Telling Stories from Start to Finish: Exploring the Demand for Narrative in Refugee Testimony. *Griffith Law Review, 22*(1), 63–86.

Whyte, Z. (2011). Enter the Myopticon: Uncertain Surveillance in the Danish Asylum System. *Anthropology Today, 27*(3), 18–21.

Whyte, Z. (2015). In Doubt: Documents as Fetishes in the Danish Asylum System. In B. Berti, A. Good, & G. Tarabout (Eds.), *Of Doubt and Proof: Ritual and Legal Practices of Judgement* (pp. 141–162). Farnham: Ashgate.

Open Access This chapter is distributed under the terms of the Creative Commons Attribution 4.0 International License (http://creativecommons.org/licenses/by/4.0/), which permits use, duplication, adaptation, distribution and reproduction in any medium or format, as long as you give appropriate credit to the original author(s) and the source, a link is provided to the Creative Commons license and any changes made are indicated.

The images or other third party material in this chapter are included in the work's Creative Commons license, unless indicated otherwise in the credit line; if such material is not included in the work's Creative Commons license and the respective action is not permitted by statutory regulation, users will need to obtain permission from the license holder to duplicate, adapt or reproduce the material.

10

Interactions and Identities in UK Asylum Appeals: Lawyers and Law in a Quasi-Legal Setting

Jessica Hambly

Introduction

Asylum appeals in the UK have been characterised as problematic, chaotic and inconsistent by academics, practitioners, governmental and non-governmental organisations (Amnesty International, Still Human Still Here 2013; Asylum Aid 2011; Bail for Immigration Detainees 2006; Baillot et al. 2012; Feder 2010; Gill et al. 2015, 2016, Good 2007; Independent Asylum Commission 2008; Jubany 2011; Thomas 2011). A common focus amongst critiques is the heavy reliance on judicial discretion in the credibility assessment process, which creates space for substantial variances in terms of how appeals are decided. However, previous socio-legal research on adjudication in other contexts highlights the significance of interactions and relationships between judges, representatives and other courtroom actors (Conley and O'Barr 1990; Cowan and Hitchings 2007; Eisenstein and Jacob 1977; Fielding 2011; Kritzer 2007; Leverick and Duff 2002; Mack and Roach Anleu 2010). Asylum appeals represent a unique site of symbolic struggle, where law functions as one resource among many. This chapter explores how interactions and identities shape the asylum appeals process. It does so by focusing on the experiences and work of asylum lawyers, exploring differences in professional backgrounds, personal relationships and organisational

---

J. Hambly (✉)
University of Exeter, Exeter, UK
e-mail: J.Hambly@exeter.ac.uk

© The Author(s) 2019
N. Gill and A. Good (eds.), *Asylum Determination in Europe*,
Palgrave Socio-Legal Studies, https://doi.org/10.1007/978-3-319-94749-5_10

dynamics. Success in asylum appeals depends on mastering the rules of the tribunal game. This requires an appreciation of what matters alongside 'the law', and understanding how to act, engage, and mobilise resources effectively. This chapter argues that by looking at the role of interactions and identities, we gain a sense of the numerous legal and non-legal rules of engagement in asylum appeals. Concordant with Gill and Good's reflections in the Introduction to this volume, the present chapter demonstrates the multiple legal pluralities of the asylum process. This offers a new perspective on how legal values of fairness and justice in refugee determination procedures are so often subsumed by political, administrative and economic concerns to control migration.

Adjudication is a complex social process of communication and competition between actors, organisations, and institutions (Bourdieu 1987; Hawkins 2002; Moorhead and Cowan 2007). Asylum appeals, like other adjudicatory processes, are not a simple application of law to a set of facts. Law operates through relationships, networks, routines and symbols (Bourdieu 1987), and 'incorporates countless, varied and often ambiguous rules [...] operating with different purposes and with vastly different material and symbolic resources' (Ewick and Silbey 1998: 17). The construction of legal decisions is dependent on the personalities, preconceptions and dispositions of actors involved, but is also linked to wider social, political, economic and historical contexts (Hawkins 2003; Lipsky 1969).

Asylum representatives are said to work 'in the space between law and administration' (James and Killick 2012: 430). By centering the voices of asylum advocates and observing them in action at the tribunal, this chapter constructs a picture of how law functions in asylum appeals as one social force among the multiple, often conflicting, duties, goals, values, and internal logics at play in the appeals system. The quasi-legal nature of asylum appeals manifests in relationships and communication between actors situated in multiple, intersecting social fields. In this sense, asylum appeals can be conceptualised as 'semi-autonomous social fields' (Moore 1973). Such a methodological approach calls for the study of law, rules and official behavior in terms of their social context and 'connection(s) between the internal workings of an observable social field and its points of articulation with a larger setting' (Moore 1973: 742). While legal rules and procedures play a significant part in setting the rules of the game, those wishing to play (and do well) are also subject to extra-legal forces. The significance of 'semi-autonomy' of the social field lies in the way norms, decisions and practices are generated both within the field, and through interactions and vulnerabilities vis-a-vis the wider social matrix (ibid.: 720).

This chapter unpicks the dilemma whereby asylum appeals are anticipated by lawyers, and indeed appellants, to be determined within a system of 'legal rational norms', whereas what they frequently encounter is the 'highly politicised' system of immigration control (Appelqvist 2000: 87). Key to analysis here is an exploration of the significance of personal and professional identities and relationships. Emphasis shifts away from individual immigration judges, instead zooming out to the wider tribunal workgroup and the role of *non-lawyers* and *non-law* in the asylum appeals process.

The UK Asylum System

Asylum decision-making in the UK is a hybrid process; both administrative and judicial bodies deal with claims for refugee status. Protection claims are initially made to the Home Office, either on arrival to the UK at the port of entry, or, more often, at a later date in Croydon (South London). The applicant first undergoes a screening interview by an Immigration Officer (Home Office civil servant), covering basic information about their background and reasons for claiming asylum. At this stage, the individual risks being detained if their case is seen as straightforward—for example, if the Home Office wishes to invoke Dublin procedures, meaning the individual's application will be processed by the first EU Member State where fingerprints were taken or an asylum application was made.[1] Alternatively, the applicant will be assigned a caseowner and given a longer, more detailed substantive interview. A legal representative may be sought at any stage, but legal aid funding is not available until the substantive interview. Even then, many asylum applicants are unable to access legal representation owing to time constraints and lack of available service providers. Based on the evidence given in interviews and any additional evidence submitted, the Home Office makes a decision on eligibility for refugee status or for a subsidiary form of protection on human rights or humanitarian grounds.

Positive decisions result in a grant of refugee status and leave to remain for five years.[2] However, most claims are not successful; approximately 65%

---

[1]The Detained Fast Track (DFT) procedure is currently suspended following a series of legal challenges. In January 2017 a High Court ruling confirmed the fast-track procedure in operation between 2005 and 2014 was unlawful.

[2]Until recently, this status would be upgraded to 'settlement' or 'indefinite leave to remain' on application after five years. Now, after the initial five years, a person with refugee status will need to undergo a 'safe return review' procedure to assess whether circumstances have changed such that they are no longer in need of protection.

of initial decisions are refusals. Of these, around three quarters go on to appeal to the First Tier Tribunal (Immigration and Asylum Chamber). It is at this stage, when seeking to appeal an initial refusal, that many will look to lawyers to guide them through the more legal stage of the process. Indeed, a common reason for negative initial decisions going unchallenged is lack of access to quality legal advice, due to scarcity of legal service provision and changes to legal aid funding (Burridge and Gill 2017).

The Immigration Tribunal was originally conceived as an administrative body staffed by lay personnel. Over time, the tribunal has become increasingly judicialised (Rawlings 2005; Thomas 2003a, b). It is now run by Her Majesty's Courts and Tribunals Service and presided over by legally qualified judges appointed by the Judicial Appointments Commission. At the time of fieldwork (2012–2014) there were 19 hearing centres spread across the UK. On average, around one quarter of appeals at that time resulted in the Home Office's initial refusal being overturned. However, research has shown sizeable discrepancies in terms of success rates across different tribunals (Gill et al. 2015).

Appeals against First Tier decisions may be taken to a superior level—the Upper Tribunal—with permission from the First Tier. If the First Tier Tribunal refuses, the appellant may apply to the Upper Tier to have that decision overturned. A small number of cases may progress outside the Tribunal system to the Court of Appeal (Court of Session in Scotland) and Supreme Court where 'important points of principle or practice' or 'other compelling reasons' are at stake (*R (Cart) and ors v. Upper Tribunal and ors [2011] UKSC 28*).

The asylum process has been characterised as a system caught between administration and adjudication (Thomas 2011). While civil servants at the Home Office deal with initial claims, the appeal stage marks a shift into a more legal arena. Yet actors at this level continue to be a mix of legal and non-legal professionals; even though judges are now required to have a legal background, representatives are not exclusively drawn from the legal profession. A lawyer may represent the Home Office, but most often it is a Home Office Presenting Officer (HOPO) who does the job of arguing against a protection claim (see Campbell, this volume). On the appellant's side, where a representative is present they may be regulated by one of four different professional bodies.[3] Not all asylum representatives are 'lawyers', understood in the narrow sense as solicitors and barristers. The four professional bodies that

---

[3] A number of asylum appellants appear unrepresented in hearings, with the proportion of unrepresented varying significantly between tribunal locations (for detailed discussion of this see Burridge and Gill 2017).

regulate asylum representation are the Solicitors Regulation Authority (SRA); Bar Standards Board (BSB); Office of the Immigration Services Commissioner (OISC); and the Chartered Institute of Legal Executives (CILEx). A person accredited by any of these four regulatory bodies may represent appellants in appeals to the tribunal. This arrangement invites a complex mix of personal, organisational and institutional pressures into asylum appeals, and contributes to the unique character of this adjudicatory setting (Thomas 2011: 48).

Methodology: Studying Lawyers in Asylum Appeals

The focus of the present work is on the perspectives and work of asylum lawyers at the tribunal. The advocacy stage of the process is often undertaken by barristers, having been instructed by solicitors or advisers.

Fieldwork consisted of in-depth, semi-structured interviews with 15 asylum advocates (11 barristers, two solicitors and two solicitors who had trained as barristers) and 25 days of observations at two different hearing centres. The interview sample size was small, and not intended to be representative, although did include a number of well-known asylum lawyers, seen as significant players in the field. Participants were recruited via a range of methods: websites (blogs and chambers), social media (twitter), personal contacts in asylum and refugee networks, and invitations to participate handed out at tribunals. While some advocates were clearly identifiable as 'cause lawyers'—doing legal work as a way to fight (what they saw as) an unjust immigration regime, others were motivated by intellectual interest, career progression or had just landed on asylum work by chance. Thus, while not representative, interview data gave rich insights into the experiences and work of a small cross-section of asylum advocates.

The tribunals were selected for several reasons. First, the advocates interviewed appeared relatively frequently at one or both of the centres. And, second, the sites had contrasting characteristics in terms of size (fewer than ten courtrooms/over 20 courtrooms), location (out of town/town centre), and appeal success rates (low end of the scale/high end of the scale). Ethical issues including consent, anonymity, risk to participants, and impact on the asylum field were given detailed consideration. For interviews, signed consent forms were used and names, workplaces, and identifying features were anonymised. Asylum hearings are generally open to the public. However, given the rarity of observers, and the close and intense nature of many asylum hearings, it was felt appropriate to speak to the tribunal staff in advance of hearings. In any case, advocates and judges often wanted to know who was present prior to hearings commencing. Where any objection was made owing to the nature of the appeal or vulnerability of the appellant, the hearing was not observed. Detailed notes were taken during hearings, but names, locations and any identifiable features of the case were left out. In terms of impact on the asylum field, the commitment to anonymity reflected a concern to reflect accurately the interview and observational data, without risking relations between advocates, clients and judges.

Lawyers occupy a distinct vantage point owing to their movement between different tribunals and interactions with different communities of practice. Their perspectives—how they experience their roles, the day-to-day practicalities, constraints, and pressures faced—give significant insights into variations in practices of judges, representatives and hearing centres. Rock's (1993) seminal ethnographic study of a Crown Court characterised the courthouse social world in terms of a network of concentric circles, with judges at the centre—the 'most august, sacred and protected' circle—and, at the outer reaches, civilians—those who pass through in large volumes without spending much time. Between these layers are degrees of insider status. Proximity to the inner circles depends on frequency with which actors meet 'in conditions of intimacy and interdependence', and the extent to which actors are 'sentimentally' and 'practically' embedded within the organisation (Rock 1993: 185–192). Trials under the adversarial system, argues Rock, are staged conflicts between actors playing out defined roles, where insider and outsider status can be key in terms of shaping role performance. In asylum appeals, Rock's social circles are tested by a disrupted adversarial model, whereby insider status is garnered not only by regular interactions at a particular location, but also depends on professional background and status (Gibb, this volume, as discusses the significance of space and layout to legal processes in the context of the French asylum determination system).

Previous studies from the UK, US and Canada have demonstrated the critical role played by lawyers in asylum proceedings (Bail for Immigration Detainees and Asylum Aid 2005; James and Killick 2012; Rehaag 2011; Schoenholtz and Bernstein 2008; Schoenholtz and Jacobs 2002; Thomas 2011). It has been argued that it is up to lawyers to bridge the divide between the 'fearful chaos of the refugee experience and the logical and unrealistic expectations of law and government' (Showler 2006: 210). To succeed in an asylum appeal, individuals must convince the judge of a credible account of persecution, relating to one of the Convention categories (see Sorgoni, this volume, for a critical discussion of the concept of credibility).

However, many asylum stories are complex, fractured accounts that do not fit into the technical requirements of refugee law. Individual experiences of persecution require shaping into a legal claim for protection. Lawyers often conceptualise their role as translators, turning people's stories or problems into the language of the law:

> I tell all my clients - our role is to act like an interpreter. Instead of interpreting their words from their national language into English, I translate their words into what we call the law.

But this act of translation into 'the law' is a complex process of communication and interaction. Lawyers' framing devices—their structures of knowledge, experience and meaning used when making decisions (Hawkins 2002: 52)—are built on past interactions and relationships, not only with individuals, but also with their institutional and organisational contexts (Morison and Leith 1992). It has been argued:

> [T]he process whereby barristers creatively construct legal information is shaped by the nature of the information available, time limitations, a consideration of how the information will be viewed by the judge/court, policy questions, their own experience of the courtroom and trials, and practical demands of the situation, rather than general caselaw principles. (Roach Anleu 2010: 93)

Although judges determine the final outcome of the asylum appeal, lawyers may also be seen as decision-makers in their own right; the process of building and presenting an asylum appeal involves numerous judgments by lawyers about what information is significant, and how others will receive it. In this sense, lawyering is a contextual and collegial endeavour. Looking at what guides divorce lawyers in their day to day work, Mather et al. (2001) identify three traditional perspectives. The first sees lawyers guided by their law school socialisation and formal professional codes ('the professional'). The second view looks to economic incentives and material conditions of work driving lawyers ('the workplace'). Third, lawyers are seen as motivated by their individual identities, values and characteristics ('the personal'). To these three outlooks, Mather et al. add a fourth—'professionalism in practice'. This amalgamates the three traditional approaches into an enhanced model of how lawyers understand and make decisions at work. Legal practice is constituted through professional, personal and practical action. Moreover, they argue referencing Lave and Wenger's (1991) key concept, lawyers act within 'communities of practice'—loosely-defined, overlapping groups built around particular courts, law firms (or chambers) and specialisms.

Through their communities of practice, lawyers are motivated to act according to 'common expectations and standards' (Mather et al. 2001: 6). But, as shown below, lawyers in the asylum field find themselves working within multiple fractured and intersecting communities, where aims and expectations vary according to differences in personal and professional identities. From the lawyers' perspective, a fundamental concern when it comes to the problematic nature of asylum appeals is the intrusion of political and administrative personnel and values into what (they say) ought to be an adversarial system built on juridical values. The battle between governmental rationality and legal authority in asylum appeals has received in-depth analysis by Thomas (2011). In his comprehensive review of asylum tribunal architecture, Thomas argues that:

> the influence the immigration bureaucracy exerts on both the design and operation of the appeals process (means that) the structural relationship between the tribunal and the Home Office reinforces the sense that while the legal model plays an essential role in the decision process, it is a supporting role nonetheless. (2011: 55–58)

The view that asylum appeals should operate predominantly under an administrative, or bureaucratic, decision-making model where efficiency and value for money are prioritised over juridical values such as independence and procedural fairness is resisted by asylum lawyers, as will be seen below, and by the judiciary, as expounded by the outgoing President of the Immigration and Asylum Chamber of the Upper Tribunal in 2016:

> We are not a statistically driven conveyor belt. Rather we, the Judges of this Chamber, are serious professionals, constantly alert to the judicial oath of office and the privilege of serving the community in the best possible ways.[4]

Asylum lawyers find themselves, and more importantly their clients, caught at the centre of this conflict between law, politics and administration. Asylum appeals represent a unique adjudicatory setting, where individual identities, professional actors and social worlds collide. The work and experiences of asylum advocates provide insight into the problematic nature of asylum appeals, where the significance of law, in the narrow sense, is put into doubt. To

---

[4]Justice Bernard McCloskey's section on the Immigration and Asylum Chamber in the Senior President of Tribunals' Annual Report 2016 at p. 38. Available at https://www.judiciary.uk/wp-content/uploads/2016/02/The-Senior-President-of-Tribunals-Annual-Report-2016-final-1.pdf. Accessed 18 September 2018.

understand how legal rules function in asylum appeals requires looking at the broader 'operative rules of the game' (Moore 1973: 243). Exploring the social context of asylum tribunal adjudication, we can observe the role of organisational pressures, relationships, status, and expertise in conditioning the appeals process.

Lawyering in a Hostile Environment

> 'It's one rule for the state and another rule for my clients'.

Asylum is a challenging area of legal practice. One immigration barrister describes this area of work as 'the hardest and most bitterly fought, most controversial, most convoluted, perhaps most poorly funded and sure most tilted battleground between the individual and the state' (Yeo 2012).

Asylum applicants face an ever-thickening web of practical challenges such as access to legal advice, criminal sanctions, and restrictions on access to healthcare, housing and other social services. Historically, UK attitudes to seeking asylum have been bound up in political, media and social paranoia surrounding 'benefit tourism', 'bogus' asylum seekers and 'clamping down on abusive claims' (Clayton 2010: 15). In 2012, the creation of a 'hostile environment' for irregular migration became official government policy. Hostile environment measures in the Immigration Acts of 2014 and 2016 included greater barriers to healthcare, housing, bank accounts, and a reduction in appeal rights against deportation. However, the ripple effect of the hostile environment is felt beyond these schemes. Asylum decision-making is frequently described as operating within a 'culture of disbelief' (Anderson et al. 2014; Griffiths 2012; Jubany 2011; Souter 2011; Schneider, this volume) and in an atmosphere of 'lawlessness' (Juss 1993; Shah 2005). In the tribunal, advocates felt the impact of broader social currents:

> I've had comments from judges that say things like 'times are hard', you know, 'we can't afford to let this person become a burden on the taxpayer'. Or things like 'if we open the door to this one, when's it going to end?'. So there are definitely political judgments.
>
> It's so political. So political. And you feel a lot of the time as though it's not about the law at all. It's about what the front page of tomorrow's Mail or tomorrow's Express is gonna look like. And that is very difficult.
>
> I think it's such a political thing. And we talk about, you know, this Judge has got the Daily Mail tattooed on their inner eyelids. You know, they come in with all those anti-immigrant headlines very fresh in their minds, and seem to come in with a view that everybody's lying, everybody's here for the benefits, everybody's here for the NHS […].

Lawyers felt their role as *legal* representatives was undermined by decisions based on politics of exclusion and denial, rather than legal rules and principles. This was felt more acutely in some hearing centres than others, suggesting that decision-making practices were linked to the wider tribunal community, not only individual judges.

> I think there are certain cultures that grow around hearing centres. And they're not really applying the law; they're applying the kind of culture that is in that particular place.

Advocates expressed preferences for certain tribunals based on multiple, interlinked characteristics. These include the general feel of the tribunal—'unpleasant', 'polite', 'bleak', 'less adversarial', 'a little bit more liberal', and more specific reasons relating to differences in decision-making practices, relationships with judges and personnel, and the practicalities of hearing centre locations. Significantly, these perceptions of differences between tribunal cultures were further linked to quality of justice; where an appeal was listed for hearing was seen as a 'massively important factor' in terms of how an appeal would run.

Going deeper into these preferences, and drawing on observational data from two tribunals, the remainder of this chapter explores differences in appeal processes by looking at the significance of lawyers' communities of practice, and ways of building, and benefiting from, insider status at the tribunal. First, insider status was gained through establishing ongoing personal relationships between actors working together frequently. This was seen as advantageous in respect of improving advocates' ability to litigate, but undermined by even closer relationships between HOPOs and judges. However, a different kind of insider status was felt through professional lawyer networks, which were seen as inaccessible to 'non-lawyer' HOPOs. The intersections of professional communities of practice with those based on locality, and the blurred lines around insider status created by these relationships, directs us to consider further the atypical nature of adversarial adjudication in asylum appeals.

'If They Like You, It Helps': Personal Relationships and the Significance of Being Local

Alongside formal law and legal training, advocates' work is shaped by routines, repetition, development of informal knowledge and status as insider or outsider in the everyday workgroup (Kritzer 1990, 1998; Morison and Leith 1992: 77–78). By looking at 'beliefs and practices shared by personnel, such as judges, solicitors and clerks, working in a particular court' (Leverick and Duff 2002: 43), previous court culture studies highlight how shared practices, expectations and informal norms develop among participants who work together regularly and condition adjudicatory processes (Eisenstein and Jacob 1977; Mather et al. 2001).

In asylum appeals, local networks were seen as significant in shaping advocates' interactions with tribunal staff and judges. Regular attendance at a hearing centre was advantageous where it facilitated building relationships of trust and personal rapport. Advocates found that being known by judges and Home Office representatives could afford additional reliability and legitimacy to their case. There was a suggestion that advocates who lived and worked in the same area as tribunal staff and judges were afforded 'a little bit of favour'. As one advocate remarked:

> I mean, I know them [so] I think it probably does [help] a bit. Does it help the eventual decision? I hope it does. Does it help my day-to-day work? Yes. I mean, they probably accept things from me. They know I'm not going to, you know, pull the wool over their eyes.

Of the two tribunals studied here, one had a relatively small body of staff and judges, and advocates appearing regularly there felt they knew most members of the workgroup. At this location, local ties between regular participants were signified by the use of forenames or 'mate' (more often between men). Also at this location, small talk and friendly chat between local advocates, tribunal staff and Home Office personnel was common. Some advocates spoke of having close relationships with judges and others outside the tribunal workplace, often going to the same social and sporting events. Some advocates had links with the local Home Office Unit, who they would phone in advance of a hearing to clarify issues. This, they said, led to more effective and fairer hearings, because both sides were more attuned to what the other would be arguing.

To the contrary, advocates based far away from the smaller hearing centre, or who attended infrequently, found this a difficult place to represent appeals. One advocate spoke of the significance of regional accents in terms of marking out advocates as locals or outsiders, which, he said, impacted on interactions with tribunal staff. In his experience, advocates with non-local accents had experienced harsh treatment, for example having their appeals dismissed despite calling ahead to say they were late. At the smaller tribunal there was a clearer group of Rock's *habitués* (1993: 192–194)—advocates who were not part of the inner most circle, but who were known by tribunal staff, HOPOs and judges. The differences between insiders and outsiders were more marked at the smaller tribunal than the larger tribunal.

While the advantage of relationships at the smaller tribunal was linked to familiarity and trust, at the larger tribunal, with the pool of judges, staff, Home Office representatives and advocates much larger, workgroups were more fluid and relationships of familiarity harder to foster. However, knowing the judges and Home Office representatives was still seen as advantageous owing to greater predictability; advocates were better able to understand and anticipate how appeals would run.

Advocates with knowledge of particular judges said this often gave them an immediate indication of which way a hearing would go:

> Generally, the more you go to the tribunals, and the more you get to know judges (…), when you know on the day who you've got as a judge, it tends to be a fairly good indicator of how your prospects will end up.

Advocates do not know the identity of the judge until arrival at the tribunal. Each morning, hearing room schedules are displayed on the wall of the common space, with the name of the Judge, the Home Office representative, appellants' representatives and the hearing type (asylum appeal, immigration appeal, or visa appeal, for example). A day's list generally comprises two or three appeals, depending on factors such as anticipated level of complexity and number of witnesses to be cross-examined. All hearings are listed for 10 a.m. At this time, usual practice is for the Judge to invite all parties into the hearing room to establish who everyone is, discuss any issues and set an order for the day's proceedings. By this point, many advocates said they already had a good idea of the outcome of their hearing, based on prior knowledge of judges as 'refusers', 'dismissers', or conversely, judges who were seen as particularly accepting of asylum claims. For instance, before one hearing, the appellant's advocate remarked to the Home Office representative 'I mean, look, we're before Judge M-. He's not gonna dismiss it, let's be honest!' That said, whereas some judges were viewed as serial refusers or allowers, others were seen as notoriously unpredictable:

> When you find out who the judge is, that's gonna give you an indication as to how long you're gonna be there, if your case is 50:50 – which way it's gonna go, et cetera. And then you get some judges that just make it the most unpredictable event in the world, 'cos it's massively inconsistent […].

These were seen as the most difficult judges to appear before. Advocates preferred predictability, even where this meant knowing there was a strong chance they would lose the appeal, because even in this scenario they were better able to plan their strategy and more alert to the possibilities of onward appeals. Advocates spoke of methods for collating information on different judges—lists, spreadsheets and keeping files with judges' previous determinations. Where an advocate had no prior experience with a particular judge, they might text or email around on the morning of the hearing to gauge others' experiences. In this way, the decision-making environment is conditioned by repetitive interactions between judges and representatives, not only through personal interactions but also via reputation.

Predictability was significant not only in terms of having an idea of which way the hearing would go, but also when it came to how advocates managed the appeal. Whilst the core substance of the asylum claim would remain the same, advocates adapted their performance in recognition of judicial preferences. Advocates developed a sense of how best to handle different judges, for example where judges were seen as more active or interrogatory, advocates might anticipate this, and warn their clients to be patient and tolerant of interruptions. Some judges were known to require more in terms of advocates setting out the law, whereas other judges considered themselves the experts and, as one lawyer said, 'they don't want a lecture in refugee law.' By building up experience and knowledge of other actors, advocates developed a sense of how to 'read (one's) court'. As a senior judge said to one lawyer—'well, I'm sure you know, Mr C, what you can say to some judges and what you can't say to others.'

Appellant lawyers come and go with their clients, whereas judges and Home Office representatives sit through the day's hearings together. Even where advocates felt they benefited from pre-existing workgroup relationships, their opposition—the Home Office—benefited even more so.

> Sometimes you can know a judge has a certain tendency or whatever you can use to your advantage or at least mitigate it if you know it's going to be a problem. But the Home Office spend far more time there than we do, so they get to know their idiosyncrasies in even more detail than we do […].
>
> The judges and HOPOs certainly seem very friendly together […] and they probably trust one another because they work together quite frequently.

HOPOs were seen as much closer to the inner circle of the tribunal. This was reinforced by the provision of permanent, private office space for the Home Office on tribunal sites, and the fact that HOPOs and judges were seen as moving in shared spaces inaccessible to lawyers. Segregated zones varied between hearing centres, but included lifts, stairways, corridors and meeting spaces. The layout and circulation routes of hearing centres facilitated interactions between some, while preventing interactions between others. Lawyers' access was restricted to the same as their clients: waiting rooms, public corridors and a few private consultation rooms or booths available on a first come, first served basis. That Judges and HOPOs were seen as interacting in spaces behind closed doors fuelled perceptions of the Home Office as a favoured litigant, better able to benefit from personal relationships than lawyers who, although they might be regulars, are less embedded within hearing centre communities.

Knowing each other is seen as advantageous insofar as a level of trust, personal rapport and reliability is built between actors at tribunals. Insider status is built through regular interactions and the development of social capital. However, while personal ties are perceived to play a role in shaping the course of appeals, lawyers highlight another significant form of insider status, linked to professional, rather than geographical, communities of practice.

'We Recognise Our Own': Professional Relationships and the Significance of Being a Lawyer

> When you're in the tribunal there's more of a concentration on knowing that your opponent is not a lawyer [...]. As a lawyer, there's a certain approach to the law you have in relation to looking at a case, the analysis and how you present a case.

A defining element of asylum tribunal adjudication is the presence of 'non-lawyers' as representatives of the Home Office. Barristers may appear on behalf of the Home Office as part of a scheme initiated to plug a gap that left many appeals unrepresented on the Home Office side, but most appeals are done by HOPOs (see Campbell, this volume). Some have a legal background, but may not have progressed through the vocational stage of training to become a qualified barrister or solicitor. For lawyers, this made a marked difference to the way hearings were run, notably with respect to: a mismatch in professional duties; divergent organisational pressures; conflicting aims in adjudication; and imbalanced skills and work techniques.

> As an officer of the court I've got duties to the court [...] it's about providing a fair hearing for the client's case.

Barristers have an overriding 'duty to the court in the administration of justice'. This is found in the Bar Code of Conduct, and includes specific obligations to: not knowingly or recklessly mislead or attempt to mislead the court; take reasonable steps to avoid wasting the court's time; and ensure one's ability to act independently is not compromised. The barrister's duty to his or her client is subject to this primary duty to the court.

> [The Home Office] don't have the duty to the court in the same way as we do. I mean, they're not lawyers. They're civil servants and they're there to do a job.

The key aim of the HOPO is to 'ensure appeals go through the system efficiently' (HOPO Training Pack: 108). HOPOs' professional standards emphasise maintaining 'a high degree of professionalism and (behaving) consistently in line with Home Office values', delivering 'robust' defence of the decision, and quick and efficient case disposal. This contrasts with the legal advocate's duty to ensure the administration of justice. HOPOs are precluded from knowingly misleading the Judge, or advancing arguments not in accordance with the law. However, conflicting professional values led advocates to view HOPOs as 'institutionalised' into Home Office culture, where the aim was always refusal rather than ensuring a fair hearing.

Lawyers were frustrated by what was seen as an undermining of core legal principles and failure to facilitate proper functioning of an adversarial process. They contrasted Home Office culture ('it's just statistics, statistics, statistics') with legal culture, in which primacy was given to rule of law and justice. HOPOs were seen by lawyers to discard legal rules as unimportant, just 'niceties of a fair hearing'.

> It's very frustrating, I suppose, because it's not two-sided. There's things we have to do, you know. We can't tell the judge things about the law that we know aren't true. Whereas the Home Office have been instructed by their superiors to make submissions which the Home Office knows are unlawful […]. It just doesn't seem fair.

Such feelings were perpetuated by evidence of the target culture at the Home Office, where the stated aim was to control 'win rates' (Home Affairs Select Committee 2012: 25), with incentives such as gift vouchers, cash bonuses and extra holidays offered to HOPOs for meeting targets (see also Campbell, this volume).

The asylum chamber is characterised by legal actors as 'a place where facts are meant to be established in a collaborative process which is not hostile and not meant to re-traumatise the person'. Collaboration and cooperation were seen as possible where the Home Office was represented by a barrister.

> My face lights up when I realise I've got counsel on the other side because you can have a sensible conversation. And they don't seem to have this mentality that they need to always have their Home Office hat on, even when we're having counsel to counsel discussions.

Appeals with a HOPO, on the other hand, were generally more confrontational and hostile—'I am for the Secretary of State; you are for the appellant. I see no need for cooperation.'

A further distinction lies in the nature of the 'client' on either side. Part of a lawyer's duty to their client is to try and reach agreement on some things—'So you go in there, before the judge, and say "look, can we agree on any of this?"' In asylum appeals, however, the lawyer–client relationship is not reflected on both sides.

> I take instructions from my client. I advise my client. My client tells me what to do. Who instructs the HOPO? Unfortunately that's why it's difficult. Because, you know, if they had a client and you had a client and both your clients were in the room, you could say to them, 'Look, you talk to your client, I'll talk to my client, and we'll see what we can do'. But their client isn't a client. Their client's this monster; it's the Secretary of State for the Home Department.

The breakdown in the idealised adversarial model espoused by the advocate here reflects the presence of different institutional actors at the tribunal, with alternative, and often incompatible, modes of practice. Home Office materials also demonstrate this opposition in relation to ethos and language:

> Whilst it is unavoidable that technical issues will have to be addressed, there is no necessity to use some of the language that the judiciary or legal professionals may use. For instance, if you are presenting an immigration case, the decision you are supporting is not your 'instructions' – it is a decision made in another business area in line with the law, the Immigration Rules and UK Border Agency policy that you are advancing in support of the strategic aims of the Agency. (HOPO Training Pack: 105)

Advocates often produce a skeleton argument prior to the hearing, outlining the main issues, evidence and any calls for further instructions on either side. The skeleton argument is passed to the judge and opposition on the morning of the hearing, or a couple of days before. In addition to this, advocates often liked to get a sense of who they were up against—'to try and test the water…' so they might have an idea what to expect during cross-examination, or be able to streamline the issues for the hearing.

> The good thing about being an advocate is that the advocacy doesn't start at the time of the hearing. The advocacy starts well before the hearing, because even before the hearing commences, you go in and you see your opponent

Pre-hearing exchanges ranged from informal conversations about weekend activities, sport and mutual acquaintances, to more formal discussions of the legal issues. However, this practice was not seen as useful in all circumstances, where a particular HOPO was seen as 'unpleasant', 'confrontational', or 'frankly quite irritating', or because HOPOs lacked discretion to concede or narrow many points.

A further divergence in work techniques arises in the main body of the asylum hearing—the cross-examination. Lawyers had a strong preference for being against a similarly qualified opposition, not because it made their case any easier (on the contrary, it was often seen to make things harder), but because this gave greater predictability and integrity to proceedings. As one advocate said of the junior barristers instructed by the Home Office:

> They knew how to cross-examine; they knew how to focus on the issues. So although on the one hand they were more effective as representatives, at the same time, because they were doing things in a fairer way, it was a much better hearing and the outcomes were often fairer.

Home Office barristers were seen as more polite, focused, adept at getting to the point and skillful at putting forward the case for the opposition. Cross-examination by HOPOs, on the other hand, was described as hostile, insensitive, and 'just interminable, useless, repeating the same points again and again […]'.

> One thing you'll get from counsel is that they're bound by the Bar Code of Conduct, and they know how to cross-examine. So, that's a double-edged sword. If your client is telling the truth, um, that can often work in your favour. Because […] they won't ask irrelevant questions, and they won't just dig… whereas HOPOs will do that. On the other hand, with counsel it's, you know, when you're trained, you'll ask a question, get the answer you'd want and then back off. One of the things you learn in bar school, in pupillage, is:

don't ask a question you don't know the answer to. Don't. And know when not to ask a question too many.

Fairness, as argued by the previous advocate, was also a question of predictability (knowing what your opponent was going to do) and respect for customary legal practice and training. Advocates' preference for strong representation on the opposing side was built on an idealised view of the asylum hearing as a legal exchange between two, similarly qualified, opposing factions. The adversarial system is designed 'not as an inquiry into the final truth of a matter, but as a struggle [...] between two competing, partial and incomplete cases' (Rock 1993: 31). Such a model presumes a level of equality on both sides in terms of legal skill and knowledge. A fair and effective hearing was seen as one in which the issues were properly focused and probed without resort to hostile or insensitive questioning techniques. Advocates had confidence that cross-examination would be 'proper' where they encountered a similarly trained (and regulated) opposition, even though this was more likely to highlight gaps in evidence that they would rather not have revealed. Thus, the threat identified by advocates here is to the 'ceremonial, disciplined, and staged' (Rock 1993: 27) nature of adversarial hearings. Winning appeals for clients was important. But of comparable importance was adherence to professional codes and display of good legal practice.

Advocates felt subject to double standards, with Judges' 'huge tolerance' of 'systematic flouting' of the rules and 'egregious errors' made by HOPOs reinforcing a view of the Home Office as a favoured party (Yeo 2012). This was particularly infuriating given the significant difference between the Home Office and legal aid lawyers in terms of funding and resources. The following exchange took place between an asylum barrister and judge when the Home Office appeared at the tribunal unprepared, without an evidence bundle, and requested an adjournment:

Barrister: As a matter of law, we don't need the Home Office bundle. It is down to maladministration of the Home Office. Why should [the witnesses] have given up their day of paid work for nothing? It is in the interests of justice to go ahead.

Judge: And therefore your proposal would be to go ahead part-heard?

Barrister: It seems exceptionally troubling. My client was ready for his previous appeal last year. The Home Office pulls the rug from beneath his feet and withdrew their decision. As a matter of law, all we have to prove is that my client is not returnable. Why should he have to wait a few more months just because the Home Office can't get its act together?

Judge: I've heard what you have said. The Home Office's actions are entirely unsatisfactory. I'm sure [the HOPO] will convey the dissatisfaction of the court to the Home Office.

The barrister, despite his insistence that 'as a matter of law' the hearing could proceed, failed to persuade the Judge that day. Reluctance on the part of Judges to do anything more than note dissatisfaction or annoyance was felt by other advocates, citing routine failures of the Home Office to comply with directions from the tribunal, resulting in increased time, cost and inconvenience to their clients and witnesses. But the force of law, in these instances, was rendered impotent.

Advocates' legal arguments and expertise are often not enough to secure victory in asylum appeals—not because the opposition is more skilled—but because the value of legal expertise is diminished in the asylum tribunal setting. Advocates *wanted* it to matter that they were better litigators, and were often quick to identify the 'non-lawyer' as an intruder in the adversarial process. Indeed, it has been argued, '(l)awyers appear to be the only occupational group to have coined a new word—nonlawyer—to divide the world between insiders and outsiders' (Mather et al. 2001: 42). But asylum appeals do not take place in an ordinary adversarial environment. Mastering the rules of the legal game—being a *legal* insider—is not enough.

Conclusion

> The practical content of the law which emerges in the judgment is the product of a symbolic struggle between professionals possessing unequal technical skills and social influence. (Bourdieu 1987: 827)

This chapter has argued that what matters in asylum appeals is not only law, in the narrow sense of rules and procedures, but a range of interacting, and often conflicting social currents. Looking at sites of friction and struggles between conflicting institutional ideologies and organisational goals can give greater insight into an area of social life (Bourdieu and Wacquant 1992; Madson and Dezalay 2002). Furthermore, the operation of law and legal rules can be better understood by studying them in their social context and in relation to other 'non-legal' forces (Moore 1973). The tribunal occupies a site of organisational complexity, between law, politics and administration. The asymmetric nature of asylum appeals, with the inclusion of Home

Office personnel, protocols and values, sets it apart from other traditional adjudicatory settings, such as criminal courts, which might be conceptualised as operating within the boundaries of the legal field. At the asylum tribunal, we observe multiple 'intersecting, yet incompatible fields' (Anderson et al. 2014: 13) with alternate logics and stakes of play (Calhoun 2003: 277; Harker et al. 1990; Gill and Good, this volume).

The insights gathered here relate to the stakes of play in asylum appeals. Insider status is valued; knowing the other tribunal members is seen as significant in terms of improving chances of success. This kind of social capital is more readily accumulated and deployed by those closer to the inner circles of a particular hearing centre. The other type of insider status discussed here—being legally qualified and belonging to professional lawyer circles—attracts a different kind of value. It can enhance reputation and standing within lawyer circles. The process of becoming a lawyer gives lawyers a set of rules governing language and conduct in litigation. A common understanding of rules, roles and what is acceptable conduct gives lawyers confidence; it makes the legal game more predictable and, through this, contributes to reassuring them that the game is played fairly.

However, asylum appeals at the tribunal are permeated by numerous codes, protocols, assumptions and forms of communication as a result of the history and development of the tribunal as both an overseer of administrative action and an instrument of immigration control. The divide between lawyers and non-lawyers in asylum appeals represents a struggle between actors, identities, organisations, and institutions. Advocates are open to some forms of 'extra-legal givings'—for example the benefits gained by developing relationships through interactions with judges or the opposition (particularly where this works in their favour). Yet the legitimacy of other extra-legal environmental forces is heavily resisted.

Despite tribunal reforms that affirm commitments to upholding traditional legal values and procedural guarantees, advocates experienced a system driven by scepticism of the outsider, administrative pressures to curb immigration, bureaucratic efficiency initiatives and swingeing resource cuts. This limits the effectiveness of good quality legal representation in appeals and goes some way in explaining why success rates remain at a relatively static 25% for appellants, despite significant advances in opening up Convention categories. For legal advocates, the game is about achieving fair and just consideration of protection claims according to the rules, procedures and practices of law. However, the force of law in asylum appeals is contained by other, more powerful, social forces.

References

Amnesty International, Still Human Still Here. (2013). *A Question of Credibility: Why So Many Initial Asylum Decisions Are Overturned on Appeal in the UK*. Amnesty International.

Anderson, J., Hollaus, J., Lindsay, A., & Williamson, C. (2014). *The Culture of Disbelief: An Ethnographic Approach to Understanding an Under-Theorised Concept in the UK Asylum System* (Refugee Studies Working Paper Series, 102). Oxford: University of Oxford.

Appelqvist, M. (2000). Refugee Law and Cause Lawyering: A Swedish Study of the Legal Profession. *International Journal of Refugee Law, 12*, 71–89.

Asylum Aid. (2011). *Unsustainable: The Quality of Initial Decision-Making in Women's Asylum Claims*.

Bail for Immigration Detainees. (2006). *Working Against the Clock: Inadequacy and Injustice in the Asylum System*.

Bail for Immigration Detainees and Asylum Aid. (2005). *Justice Denied—Asylum and Immigration Legal Aid—A System in Crisis*.

Baillot, H., Cowan, S., & Munro, V. (2012). "Hearing the Right Gaps": Enabling and Responding to Disclosures of Sexual Violence Within the UK Asylum Process. *Social and Legal Studies, 21*, 269–296.

Bourdieu, P. (1987). The Force of Law: Toward a Sociology of the Juridical Field. *Hastings Law Journal, 38*, 814–853.

Bourdieu, P., & Wacquant, L. J. D. (1992). *An Invitation to Reflexive Sociology*. Cambridge: Polity.

Burridge, A., & Gill, N. (2017). Conveyor-Belt Justice: Precarity, Access to Justice, and Uneven Geographies of Legal Aid in UK Asylum Appeals. *Antipode, 49*, 23–42.

Calhoun, C. (2003). Pierre Bourdieu. In *The Blackwell Companion to Major Contemporary Social Theorists* (pp. 274–309). Oxford: Blackwell.

Clayton, G. (2010). *Immigration and Asylum Law*. Oxford: Oxford University Press.

Conley, J. M., & O'Barr, W. M. (1990). *Rules Versus Relationships: The Ethnography of Legal Discourse*. Chicago and London: University of Chicago Press.

Cowan, D., & Hitchings, E. (2007). 'Pretty Boring Stuff': District Judges and Housing Possession Proceedings. *Social and Legal Studies, 16*(3), 363–382.

Eisenstein, J., & Jacob, H. (1977). *Felony Justice: An Organizational Analysis of Criminal Courts*. Boston: Little, Brown.

Ewick, P., & Silbey, S. S. (1998). *The Common Place of Law: Stories from Everyday Life*. Chicago: University of Chicago Press.

Feder, B. (2010). A Credible Judge of Character? A Psycho-Legal Analysis of Credibility Assessments for Asylum Applicants with a History of Sexual Violence. *Journal of Immigration Asylum and Nationality Law, 24*, 295–323.

Fielding, N. (2011). Judges and Their Work. *Social and Legal Studies, 20*, 97–115.

Gill, N., Rotter, R., Burridge, A., Allsopp, J., & Griffiths, M. (2016). Linguistic Incomprehension in British Asylum Appeal Hearings. *Anthropology Today, 32,* 18–21.

Gill, N., Rotter, R., Burridge, A., Griffiths, M., & Allsopp, J. (2015). Inconsistency in Asylum Appeal Adjudication. *Forced Migration Review, 50,* 52–54.

Good, A. (2007). *Anthropology and Expertise in the Asylum Courts.* Oxon: Routledge-Cavendish.

Griffiths, M. (2012). "Vile Liars and Truth Distorters". Truth, Trust and the Asylum System. *Anthropology Today, 28,* 8–12.

Harker, R., Mahar, C., & Wilkes, C. (Eds.). (1990). *An Introduction to the Work of Pierre Bourdieu: The Practice of Theory.* Basingstoke: Macmillan.

Hawkins, K. (2003). Order, Rationality and Silence: Some Reflections On Criminal Justice Decision-Making. In *Exercising Discretion: Decision-Making in the Criminal Justice System and Beyond* (pp. 186–220). Cullompton: Willan Publishing.

Hawkins, K. (2002). *Law as Last Resort.* Oxford Socio-legal Studies. Oxford University Press.

Home Affairs Select Committee. (2012). Fifth Report: The Work of the UKBA (December 2011–March 2012) (p. 25). House of Commons. Available at: https://publications.parliament.uk/pa/cm201213/cmselect/cmhaff/71/71.pdf. Accessed 18 Sep 2018.

Independent Asylum Commission. (2008). Fit for Purpose Yet? *The Independent Asylum Commission's Interim Findings.*

James, D., & Killick, E. (2012). Empathy and Expertise: Case Workers and Immigration/Asylum Applicants in London. *Law and Social Inquiry, 37*(2), 430–455.

Jubany, O. (2011). Constructing Truths in a Culture of Disbelief: Understanding Asylum Screening from Within. *International Sociolology, 26,* 74–94.

Juss, S. S. (1993). *Immigration, Nationality and Citizenship.* London: Mansell.

Kritzer, H. (2007). Toward a Theorization of Craft. *Social and Legal Studies, 16,* 321–340.

Kritzer, H. M. (1998). *Legal Advocacy: Lawyers and Nonlawyers at Work.* Ann Arbor, MI: University of Michigan Press.

Kritzer, H. M. (1990). *The Justice Broker: Lawyers and Ordinary Litigation.* New York and Oxford: Oxford University Press.

Lave, J., & Wenger, E. (1991). *Situated Learning: Legitimate Peripheral Participation.* Cambridge: Cambridge University Press.

Leverick, F., & Duff, P. (2002). Court Culture and Adjournments in Criminal Cases: A Tale of Four Courts. *Criminal Law Review, 39,* 39–52.

Lipsky, M. (1969). *Toward a Theory of Street-Level Bureaucracy* (p. 48). Pap: Institute for Reasearch on Poverty.

Mack, K., & Roach Anleu, S. (2010). Trial Courts and Adjudication. In *The Oxford Handbook of Empirical Legal Research* (pp. 545–570). New York: Oxford University Press.

Madson, M. R., & Dezalay, Y. (2002). The Power of the Legal Field: Pierre Bourdieu and the Law. In *An Introduction to Law and Social Theory* (pp. 189–207). Oxford and Portland: Hart.

Mather, L. M., McEwen, C. A., & Maiman, R. J. (2001). *Divorce Lawyers at Work: Varieties of Professionalism in Practice.* Oxford: Oxford University Press.

Moore, S. F. (1973). Law and Social Change: The Semi-autonomous Social Field as an Appropriate Subject of Study. *Law Society Review, 7,* 719–746.

Moorhead, R., & Cowan, D. (2007). Judgecraft: An Introduction. *Social and Legal Studies, 16,* 315–320.

Morison, J., & Leith, P. (1992). *The Barrister's World—And the Nature of Law.* Milton Keynes: Open University Press.

Rawlings, R. (2005). Review, Revenge and Retreat. *Modern Law Review, 68,* 378–410.

Rehaag, S. (2011). The Role of Counsel in Canada's Refugee Determination System: An Empirical Assessment. *Osgoode Hall Law Journal, 49,* 71–116.

Roach Anleu, S. (2010). *Law and Social Change* (2nd ed.). London: Sage.

Rock, P. E. (1993). *The Social World of an English Crown Court: Witness and Professionals in the Crown Court Centre at Wood Green.* Oxford: Clarendon Press.

Schoenholtz, A., & Bernstein, H. (2008). Improving Immigration Adjudications Through Competent Counsel. *Georgetown University Law Center: Journal Legal Ethics, 21,* 55–60.

Schoenholtz, A., & Jacobs, J. (2002). The State of Asylum Representation: Ideas for Change. *Georgetown University Law Center: Immigration Law Journal, 16,* 739–772.

Shah, P. (Ed.). (2005). *The Challenge of Asylum to Legal Systems.* London and Portland: Routledge-Cavendish.

Showler, P. (2006). *Refugee Sandwich: Stories of Exile and Asylum.* Kingston, ON: McGill-Queen's University Press.

Souter, J. (2011). A Culture of Disbelief or Denial? Critiquing Refugee Status Determination in the United Kingdom. *Oxford Monitor of Forced Migration, 1*(1), 48–59.

Thomas, R. (2003a). The Impact of Judicial Review on Asylum. *Public Law,* 479–510.

Thomas, R. (2003b). Asylum Appeals Overhauled Again. *Public Law,* 260–271.

Thomas, R. (2011). *Administrative Justice and Asylum Appeals: A Study of Tribunal Adjudication.* Oxford: Hart.

Yeo, C. (2012). Open Season On Immigration Lawyers. *Free Movement.* Available at: https://www.freemovement.org.uk/open-season-on-immigration-lawyers/. Accessed 14 June 2014.

Open Access This chapter is distributed under the terms of the Creative Commons Attribution 4.0 International License (http://creativecommons.org/licenses/by/4.0/), which permits use, duplication, adaptation, distribution and reproduction in any medium or format, as long as you give appropriate credit to the original author(s) and the source, a link is provided to the Creative Commons license and any changes made are indicated.

The images or other third party material in this chapter are included in the work's Creative Commons license, unless indicated otherwise in the credit line; if such material is not included in the work's Creative Commons license and the respective action is not permitted by statutory regulation, users will need to obtain permission from the license holder to duplicate, adapt or reproduce the material.

Part III

Decision-Making

11

What Do We Talk About When We Talk About Credibility? Refugee Appeals in Italy

Barbara Sorgoni

Introduction

In this chapter I focus on a specific moment in the Italian procedure for granting international protection, the first level of appeal. In Italy, asylum seekers should apply for protection upon their arrival in the country, filling in a form (Modulo C/3) at a police headquarters. They are usually hosted in different types of centres while they wait for their hearing in front of a Territorial Commission (TC), the administrative board in charge of the first evaluation of asylum applications. If they get a negative decision, or a lesser protection than the one expected, they can appeal in front of one civil tribunal out of the 26 presently competent on asylum and, in case of a second negative or unsatisfactory decision, they have a right to a second-level appeal at a Court of Appeal. In particular, I use the much discussed 'credibility issue' as a lens through which to observe how this notion is conceived of and employed by appeal judges in two different sites. I also show how this approach can help us understand the nature of this 'quasi-legal category' (Sweeney 2009) as a flexible device which is, at the same time, a core issue in the refugee status determination

B. Sorgoni (✉)
Department of Culture, Politics and Society, University of Turin, Turin, Italy
e-mail: barbara.sorgoni@unito.it

procedure,[1] a sensitive category to handle with care,[2] and an almost-empty shell that can be used for various purposes, stretching out far beyond the tribunals themselves. Such purposes can only be grasped when shifting the gaze from the mechanics of civil law as enacted inside specific local sites, towards national and supra-national migratory policies rooted in an entangling culture of indifference (Gill 2016). In their introduction to this volume, Gill and Good argue that the current attempt to consolidate a "Common European Asylum System" coincides with an unprecedented pressure on that same system, due to a drastic increase in the number of asylum seekers mostly fleeing from the war in the Middle East. They conclude by stressing how the 'harmonisation' of the European asylum system is still far from sight (see also European Commission 2016).

Against this context, to take a closer look at the way in which the asylum appeal procedure actually works in Italy is quite important, for three reasons. Firstly, because Italy is in the spot-light of European and international bodies governing migrations, being along with Greece (Cabot 2014), both a strategic check-point to guard the external frontiers of Europe, and one of the main doors for migrants to enter Europe. Secondly, because of some specificities of its asylum system—with two degrees of appeal on the merits (plus the possibility to challenge the legality of the decision before the Supreme Court), and with appeals being heard by civil courts instead of administrative ones.[3] And finally, because it reveals an interestingly high degree of opacity, instability and variations of both decisional practices and underlying norms and assumptions, in a context which is as much vociferously discussed by the media as it is closed to the public and difficult to access for research purposes.

This chapter does not aim to be 'context-free', as in Bruno Latour's extremely engaging work on the making of law; on the contrary, and instead of trying 'to capture [...] *the essence of law*' (2010: x), I rather focus in detail on the civil tribunal of Bologna where I conducted research in 2013–2015, and relate it to that of Turin where I interviewed some magistrates in 2016. Despite Turin and Bologna being located some 300-kilometers apart, as the main towns of separate regions, the two were connected in relation to asylum: the Bologna TC was, at the time of my research, a subsection of the

---

[1] See Coffey (2003), Byrne (2007).
[2] As the many Manuals recently published under the CREDO project show: IARLJ (2013), UNHCR (2013), CREDO (2015).
[3] As I write, a highly contested reform is being discussed (D.L 13–17), whereby the procedure is reduced from three to two levels of decision: i.e. TC and first Tribunal appeal only.

Turin one.⁴ My empirical data are drawn from participant observation of a tribunal determination, interviews with magistrates and lawyers, and a collective analysis of over 200 appeal decisions. By choosing to remain close to the local level, making space for ethnographic details, I do not intend to give up the possibility of showing the complex relations that tie specific legal procedures to a global understanding and (attempts at) governing asylum rights. On the contrary, I try to show how local practices would otherwise remain rather obscure if not related to the national and supra-national ideological and political frames that, paraphrasing Antonio Gramsci, De Genova has recently called 'the "European" Question' (2016).⁵ Conversely, by focusing on specific sites at different times, we can see how the repeated use of the notion of "refugee crisis" in Europe, and the 'politics of austerity, acutely affecting southern European countries in particular, coupled with border enforcement strategies that preemptively illegalise mobile people seeking asylum' (Tazzioli and De Genova 2016: 5), strongly impact on local-level decisional procedures of recognition or rejection.

A Prequel

In June 2011, the lawyer I had contacted for my research on Refugee Status Determination Procedure (RSDP) managed to persuade a judge at the Civil Division of the Bologna tribunal to let me participate as observer in a case regarding a denied asylum seeker from Pakistan. I had already learned that the first instance appeal takes place at the Civil Division of one of the many tribunals in the country, where appeals are set up as a *camera di consiglio* (chamber of council) which—as in other legal processes where privacy protection is privileged over the public nature of the proceedings - is not open to the public and, in the case of asylum, has a monocratic composition. Thus a magistrate, the claimant, their representing lawyer and a linguistic interpreter are the only actors involved.⁶ I therefore considered myself lucky

---

⁴While in 2010 ten TCs were operating in Italy, their number has presently risen to some 45 TCs, each composed of 4 members from the institutions involved (Prefecture, Police, Local authority and UNHCR): extended interviews are carried out by only one member, while final decisions are taken collectively.

⁵Or the need to redefine 'what is Europe', when the Schengen area of free mobility, at the core of European integration itself, seems to have failed.

⁶Asylum appellants usually cannot afford a lawyer: it is up to them to find those willing to give 'free' legal aid (*patrocinio gratuito*), whereby their fee is actually met by the State at a lower rate. As for the interpreter, things differ from one tribunal to another; in Bologna, they had then recourse to resident migrants who consented to translate for free or for a minimal reimbursement.

to be allowed into a usually closed context, although I was not quite sure about what to expect. What I definitely did not anticipate, was how quickly it all would go.

On the morning of the hearing I met the lawyer at the tribunal, and she led me, the appellant and the interpreter to the judge's office: a small room simply furnished with a few shelves containing files and law books, a few chairs and a desk. On the walls and on the desk, some Catholic religious images and items were displayed. After introducing myself I was accommodated in a corner, while the appellant, his interpreter and his lawyer found seats at the desk, facing the judge. With both her posture and tone of voice, the judge made clear that she did not intend to waste any time, so while quickly flipping through the pages of the file she addressed the lawyer directly in Italian, questioning the nature of two new documents she found in the file. Since the interpreter had started to translate, the judge stopped him, explaining he should only translate when told to do so, and asked him first to confirm that he was the linguistic interpreter 'from Pakistani language'.

The lawyer explained to the judge that the two new documents were, respectively, a medical certificate from the hospital attesting to the injuries suffered by the appellant's relatives, and the police report following the assault on the appellant's relatives by a group of neighbours.[7] She then added:

> the scope of the appeal is to eliminate any doubt. The TC expressed doubts about this case in relation to a lack of documentation concerning medical certificates and police reports, which we now produce. But the TC did not provide clear reasons for the final denial: this fact alone is, for many judges, a reason to appeal.[8]

The judge finally told the interpreter to translate what the lawyer had affirmed, and to ask if the appellant wished to add anything. He replied with a plea; 'to the Italian government, that I may be allowed to remain in Italy at

---

[7] I knew from the lawyer's file that behind the assault was an attempt to grab the land of the appellant's patrilineage following the death of his father and brother; yet during the appeal there was no reference to those reasons, nor to documented land disputes in rural Pakistan, where the police are often unable or unwilling to offer protection to the party harmed, or complicit with the offenders, as Refworld Report attested. See: http://www.refworld.org/docid/5072ca722.html.

[8] The lawyer was referring to the fact that, in denying all three types of protection—refugee status, subsidiary protection, and humanitarian protection (a national protection granted under Legislative Decree 25 July 1998, no. 286, art. 5 c. 6)—the TC omitted to explain the reasons for each individual denial.

least until the situation in Pakistan is solved. I am the only one left to support my large family and if I go back my life is at risk.' It was at this point of a very short hearing that, in a few seconds, everything changed: from the tone of voice of the judge and the look in her eyes, to the colour of the lawyer's face. The judge quickly re-read her notes through, asking the interpreter to translate sentence by sentence for the appellant to agree and sign the minutes. It thus appeared she had annotated 'economic support'; when questioned by the lawyer on this point, she conceded: 'I may have added "economic" to the word "support" myself, but I do not really think this is a matter for interpretation, do you?'. She handed over the minutes for signature, and murmuring the ritual sentence—'I shall reserve my decision'[9]—she quickly dismissed us all. Being my first time, I did not immediately catch why the lawyer was literally trembling with fury, thinking this was due to the rapidity of the procedure and the absence of a real interview. But, as she explained when she burst out in front of her client, she already knew the outcome would be rejection because he had wrongly suggested material difficulties; 'and he shouldn't have! I had explained this very clearly in my office only half an hour before. He said he understood! He should not have ever mentioned economic reasons. He should have stuck to the truth!'.

What struck me then about what I had witnessed was the apparent ease with which a person who is endowed with the authority can decide in such a short time (about 20 minutes altogether) on issues relating to the life and death of another person. But over time, I came to realise that many more things characterised this particular type of legal encounter. For instance, it was possible to apprehend there how inaccurate the previous interview in front of the TC had been, where no motivation for rejection was offered, and a negative decision was based merely on 'scepticism' due to a lack of appropriate documentation.[10] It also revealed that no real second interview may take place even though the judge herself had convoked the appellant; that complex social and cultural realties are reduced to transparent facts that need no further investigation, rather than being recognised truly as 'matters of interpretation' (Gibb and Good 2013); and that additional documents could be totally neglected, despite the whole appeal revolving around them. Finally, it showed how—vis-à-vis a very poor knowledge of the appellant's country of origin (as signaled by the reference to a 'Pakistani language'), and

---

[9]With this closure sentence the judge defers the decision to a later moment.

[10]Notwithstanding the fact that in RSDP 'the duty to ascertain and evaluate all the relevant facts is shared between the applicant and the examiner' (UNHCR 1979): a principle confirmed in Italy by the Supreme Court (Cass. S.U. 17/11/2008, no. 27310).

no further enquiry into the nature of violence connected to land disputes—the decision could be based on one single 'wrong' word.

At the Tribunal

In 2013, two years after this experience, I was involved in the co-coordination of research to be carried out at the Bologna tribunal. The president of a newly born association to which I belong[11] obtained permission to conduct research on the files concerning asylum appeal determinations taken by that tribunal. During an introductory meeting, the president of the Civil Division—competent, among other issues, on asylum—explained how the system worked: the Division received and temporarily stored files about single appellants, containing all the documents assembled up to that stage.[12] Those documents were received only as print-outs, so they were extremely vulnerable: there was only one copy for each file, and if they *migrated* to the Court of Appeal, they might not come back or might be dismembered. All the files that did come back (and those which never migrated) should then be sent to the archive, located in a different building. But the files' careers didn't stop there. Once in the archive, the files underwent a new transformation, becoming nearly invisible: they still existed, but could not be easily retrieved. This happened (indeed, at that time, across the whole country) because asylum cases were not labelled under a single specific code but rather drowned in the vast sea of files from the Home Office which, as the president stressed, 'literally encompasses everything'. As the president went on with her explanation, another quite peculiar obstacle became clear: namely, that our admission to the archive for study purposes would be 'out of the question', since 'the archivist in charge doesn't tolerate any other presence there, besides herself and a few clerks'.[13]

---

[11]Founded in 2013, Asilo in Europa brings together experts on asylum issues from different countries, in order to create a network to share knowledge and praxis, and to offer comparative and updated information of different types across Europe.

[12]These comprised: the first request-form filled at a police headquarter (C3); the transcript of the TC's extended interview; its final decision; its notification to the claimant; any documentation provided by the claimant at the first hearing; the appeal motivation from the assisting lawyer; any documentation added at the appeal stage; transcript of the eventual appeal hearing; the judge's decision; its notification to the appellant.

[13]Meeting at the Bologna tribunal, 15th of March 2013. On archival relevance for anthropological studies and the materiality of paper documents also in asylum, see Basu and De Jong (2016), Cabot (2012), Hull (2012), Latour (2010), Sorgoni and Viazzo (2010), Stoler (2009).

In sum, if we add together the fact that asylum files exist only as one-copy print-outs, that they might migrate and get lost or damaged on the way, and that they were not catalogued as a homogeneous category, we easily understand the recent admission of Prefect Trovato at his hearing in front of a Parliamentary commission monitoring the influx of migrants. 'We possess total national data on the number of accepted or rejected appeal claims', he explained, adding that in order to get separated statistics on single judiciary bodies, 'we should go and look from tribunal to tribunal' (Parliamentary Hearing 2015: 13, my translation). This admission renders Asilo in Europa's research (2015) extremely valuable, being so far the only existing quali-quantitative study of first instance asylum appeals (in a specific tribunal) in Italy.

Over a period of about a year, members of the association studied and classified some 233 appeal files relating to decisions from 2011 to 2013. On the one hand this time span was compulsory, since only recent files were still temporarily stored inside the tribunal while waiting to be sent to the main archive. But on the other hand, the period proved strategic, giving us the additional possibility of verifying whether the unrest in Tunisia, the so called 'Arab spring', and the Libyan war in 2011–2012—which had resulted in a consistent increase in the number of migrants to Italy, and in ad hoc reception policies labelled ENA (North African Emergency)—significantly impacted on the decisions and, eventually, in what way. I come back to this latter issue below; here I want first to give some numerical data about asylum appeals in Bologna, as they emerged from our research.

To classify the files, we selected some relevant criteria: age, sex and country of origin of the appellant; length of the entire determination procedure; if appealing from an open centre or a CIE (Centre for Identification and Expulsion, i.e., administrative detention); if falling under the ENA label; the percentage of procedurally-based decisions vis-à-vis decisions on the merits; and the completeness of the file. About the latter point, it is important to note that out of 233 files, only 22 were complete in the sense defined earlier (see Footnote 12). Also, out of 233 files, 21 contained no trace of any decision while in 41 cases the decision was founded solely on procedural grounds, which left us with 171 files to analyse thoroughly. Out of 171 files, 110 (64%) ended with a rejection of the appeal, while in 61 cases (36%) the judge decided to allow the appeal: in these cases, only one person obtained refugee status, with 22 obtaining subsidiary protection, and 38 (over 62%) a one-year humanitarian protection.

Turning now to the so-called ENA, and in order to understand its impact on appeal decisions in Bologna, we need to switch momentarily from the determination procedure to the reception system, since what made that phenomenon a publicly recognised political *débâcle* was not only the substantial increase in the number of migrants (from less than 5000 in 2010, to over 62,000 in 2011), but also the Government decision to assign their reception to the Civil Protection Corps, usually in charge of natural disasters.[14] A new and temporary reception system was thus abruptly set in place with full power, running parallel to (and at times conflicting with) the already existing and tested one. To cut a long and disastrous story short,[15] it is important to know that the logic behind the reception of those migrants consisted mainly in separating Tunisians from 'Libyans', both in spatial and procedural terms. The former were initially given six-months leave and de facto allowed to cross the national border (mostly to France), and later forcibly repatriated according to the Italy-Tunisia Treaty hastily signed in March 2011; the latter were distributed across the country in new 'ENA centres' where they were to wait until their claim for protection was processed (which turned out to take about two years). This second group was almost entirely composed of sub-Saharan Africans who had been living and working—many already for years—in Libya when the war started, and who fled the country across the Mediterranean. Thus, many of those who applied in the first year received a denial, usually on the grounds that they could safely 'go back' to their respective 'real' countries of origin. In fact in 2011, over 76% of asylum applications (out of 37,350 total applications) concerned persons from Africa—mostly from Nigeria, Ghana, Mali (coming from Libya), and Tunisia. At the end of that year, 65% of Nigerians, 76% of Ghanaians and 82% of Malians respectively, were denied any type of protection (Ministero dell'Interno 2016b).

What the Italian Government had not anticipated was the clogging of both the TCs—which collapsed under the pressure of such high numbers—and the tribunals, which started to receive appeals from those denied. This further resulted in an unforeseen extension of the declared 'state of emergency', and consequently of the life (and costs) of the new and supposedly temporary ENA hosting centres. After almost two years, the Home Office issued a circular[16] suggesting the TCs granted humanitarian protection to all those known as

---

[14]For detailed descriptions and critical assessments of the ENA process see Marchetti (2012), Bracci (2012), Olivieri (2011) on local and national aspects respectively.

[15]During a public conference (Bologna, 12 April 2013) on the Civil Protection management, Prefect Compagnucci acknowledged that 'in the sacred chambers of power we soon realised this had been a mistake, yet we did not change it. This resulted in far too lengthy procedures at an enormous cost'.

[16]Home Office, Circular no. 400/C/2012, 31 October 2012, Overcoming North African Emergency.

'ENA asylum-seekers', a solution which eventually afforded the opportunity to put a political end to the emergency itself, and finally close the centres.

The present relevance of this story is that it also impacted directly on the tribunal's decisions. As shown above, before the 2012 government disposition, TCs all over Italy tended to deny any protection to sub-Saharan Africans fleeing the war in Libya, on the ground that they could go back to their 'country of origin'; many of them appealed against the denial. A founding principle of democracy, the separation of powers is particularly relevant in human rights issues, and a fundamental principle according to EU law.[17] As Sicakkan (2008: 218) proved in his research on asylum systems in 17 European countries, 'institutional decision-making frames where central authorities act as the first instance and legal courts as appeal instance' are associated with procedures which are fairer with regard to applicants' rights. Thus, in the ENA situation, the fact that the decisions' outcome at first (state) instance switched from flat denial to humanitarian protection after the 2012 ministerial circular, may come as no surprise.[18] But in a 'separate system', appeal courts are then expected to decide in relation to individual cases independently from the administrative instance's previous decision. Indeed, the main purpose of a tribunal system is to allow individuals to appeal to an independent judicial body against a negative decision from the government. It should therefore be a surprise that, among the 37 appeal files that we analysed relating to men from Ghana fleeing from Libya, those seven who appealed before the 2012 government circular were all rejected, while 26 out of the 30 who appealed after the circular had the first negative decision turned into humanitarian protection.

This example seems to point to the fact that the separation of the administration and the judiciary, while existing in theory, may blur in the actual making of the law, especially under certain circumstances. In this specific event, we may reasonably think that such circumstances had mostly to do with the sudden and unexpectedly high increase in the number of asylum claimants in the space of a few months. While this is partly the case, in the last section I argue that there are more reasons of a diversified political and cultural nature behind all this. Or, to phrase it differently, the continual resort to notions such as "refugee crisis" or "migrants emergency" is productive of specific policies, whereby human rights, embedded in a unique

---

[17]Art. 47 Treaty of Nice.

[18]Indeed in 2012, when the Home Office inverted its policy, 80% of Nigerians and 89% of Ghanaians received Humanitarian Protection, while 78% of Malians got subsidiary protection (Ministero dell'Interno 2016b).

relationship between an individual claim and a specific hosting State, are instead managed as political issues of border control between States, mediated by EU and international agreements (Hansen and Stepputat 2005; Sorgoni 2011, see also Gill and Good's Introduction to this volume). The ENA situation also uncovers a mechanism based on collective decisions rather than on the careful evaluation of individual stories, which translates into similar stories resulting in divergent outcomes. For instance, in seven cases the judge accorded humanitarian protection on the ground that 'the appellant can be included among those addressed by the 30.10.2012 circular' (Asilo in Europa 2015: 12, my translation) independently from their personal story, while in 16 decisions the reason for allowing the appeal referred to 'a dignified affective and working life in Libya' which had been destroyed by war (ibid.). No mention was made about Ghana as a safe country of origin where the appellant could 'go back', or that the appellant had first left for 'mere personal and economic reasons', as stated instead in all the negative decisions issued before the 2012 circular. Again, rather than an example of arbitrary interpretation of human rights laws, this shows asylum as governed by more or less visible migratory politics of containment and control.

So, What Does Credibility Mean?

Credibility in refugee law has been a matter of concern at least since the first steps towards the formulation of a common asylum policy in the late nineties. UNHCR (1998) stressed the importance of oral testimony as evidence, especially when, as is often the case with asylum, claimants do not possess other types of material evidence attesting to their identity and their story of persecution. Given precisely this peculiarity of international protection law, an evaluation of the credibility of claimants' narratives has always been an issue (Coffey 2003). The subsequent Qualification Directive (2004/83/EC) consequently allows decision makers to evaluate the coherence and plausibility of the asylum seekers' oral testimony, and their general credibility, when other material evidence is unavailable[19] (see Craig and Zwaan, this volume, for an introduction to this Directive).

But the credibility issue in asylum hearings has become the object of intense scrutiny in recent times—as the CREDO project and its publications

---

[19]The Directive 2011/95/EU (transposed in Italy in January 2014) replaced the 2004 QD introducing no amendments on this point.

testify—with the specific aim of setting judicial criteria and standards. All these Manuals highlight how the effort is particularly needed in the face of 'the unique nature of decision-making in this arcane and highly specialised area of law' (IARLJ 2013: 11), where a core legal category in the *common* European procedure is also one which is 'understood differently across national asylum systems' (CREDO 2015), partly because the word itself is used with different meanings in each national language. In a somewhat circular logic, the effect (heterogeneity being the necessary outcome of the decision to employ a notion which is historical and contextual, relating as it does to philosophical and cultural understandings of concepts like truth, reality, and person) is turned into a cause (different national understandings of credibility introduce arbitrariness and dis-homogeneity in an otherwise common system), therefore the notion needs to be standardised. Recent attempts to define it more clearly, intend to try and reduce such ambiguities: 'What is needed therefore, in linguistic terms, is "contextual disambiguation" to ensure the concept of "credibility" is used correctly' (IARLJ 2013: 12). This, it is proposed, may be obtained by avoiding 'loose' definitions of the term ('the credibility of everything related to the claim'), concentrating rather on the 'claimant's past and present *factual* background' (ibid., my emphasis). The material facts in the claimant's story must be found internally and externally consistent (i.e., assessing discrepancies within the evidence presented by the claimant, or with evidence provided by experts or Country of Origin Information [COI] Reports). The decision-maker should take into consideration the totality of the findings of fact (and not found the decision on single or marginal ones); any type of evidence produced should be carefully weighted (including documentary evidence acquired by the decision-maker); and relevant COI should be obtained and evaluated.

It seems that the above attempt at disambiguation consists mainly in narrowing the meaning of the notion, while at the same time limiting its weight: credibility is therefore explicitly linked to the facts narrated rather than to the individual per se; and it should be measured in relation to both the totality of the facts, and also other types of evidence (both material and non-material). By stressing the need to reduce the relative weight of 'credibility' in RSDP, such recent efforts also indirectly signal the increased importance the notion had gained, vis-à-vis other types of evidence (Sorgoni, under review). The research at the Bologna tribunal confirmed the central role played by credibility: in 171 files, 76 (44%) were rejected because—among other things—either the applicant or the story were declared 'not credible' (and also 'not plausible', or 'inconsistent'); in 11 cases (14%) the lack of credibility figured as the only ground for rejection, often without any further explanation (Asilo in Europa 2015). In a national legal context in which the adherence to a common system was at the time still young (Cherubini 2015), the European directives only just transposed, and a COI system—which could counter-balance decisions based solely on the narrative's evaluation—virtually non-existent, the use of the credibility notion in those years was so pervasive that the category came to mean anything, and nothing.

Again, the case of a man from Pakistan of Shiite orientation living in a Sunni majority area can help illustrate this. The TC had already denied him the right to any protection on the ground that the *facts* narrated appeared 'poorly credible' because, after having been abducted and tortured by a group of Sunnis, he did not report to the police; his story was 'contradictory' since he had mentioned the need to support his family; and he himself appeared not credible because he was not able to state the consequences he would face if returned, having merely declared: '*I don't know* what could happen to me'.[20] Five months later, at the appeal, he produced a medical certificate attesting to the injuries suffered by his son during a similar assault, and the related report to the local police. While no mention of this documentation was made by the judge, he likewise found the appellant not credible, mainly because he presented no proof of his Shiite faith, nor any information 'about his sustenance while in Italy'.[21] When weighted against the suggestions put forward by the above Manuals, the application of the credibility notion in this decision is definitely very loose, based as it is on marginal or totally irrelevant facts, without the acquisition on the part of the judge of documentary evidence or COI, and with the dismissal of primary documents produced by the appellant.

But credibility can reach a 'ground zero' level, when it is reduced to an empty wrapper. This is the case of a young woman and single mother from Senegal who was denied international protection without having been interviewed: since she could not attend the first screening, the TC assumed she was not genuinely motivated. During the appeal hearing, she explained to the judge that she had obtained an official remittal of the first screening, but had missed its re-scheduling because they had changed the location. Despite the fact that no other question was raised, in the eyes of the judge the

---

[20]The TC interpreted the sentence literally, suggesting that if the applicant didn't even know what he risked, there was clearly no real danger in going back. It goes without saying that a non-literal translation could convey a totally different meaning, as in the semantic form of preterition.

[21]Notwithstanding the fact that the 'sustenance' issue has some relevance for economic migrations, but has none in relation to RSDP.

appellant's behaviour undermined her credibility since she failed to attend the interviews 'without adducing any justification' and she 'reported nothing in relation to her way of sustenance in Italy' so that 'in sum, *her whole story* appears inconsistent, vague, without any possible ascertainment'. The problem, in this case, lies in the fact that there was no story to evaluate, neither at the first hearing (which never took place), nor at the appeal stage where only irrelevant or inappropriate questions were asked.

A loose evaluation of credibility can also take other forms, as in the case of a young man from Iraq. His story was in principle sadly simple: it could have been easily classified as an 'instrumental later claim' to avoid deportation, from an 'illegal migrant' who had been working irregularly in Italy for over 9 years. When his irregular position was accidentally detected by the police, he was taken to a CIE with a repatriation order, and applied for asylum. He was interviewed by the TC a month later and, upon denial, he appealed: despite the hearing being scheduled only two months later, this was a non-suspensive appeal which never took place, since he had been deported. If the preceding story was a zero-level credibility instance—the non-credibility of the story grounded on an absent story—in this case we find an apparently unreasonable excess in the recourse to the credibility notion. In face of a lack of valid residence permits and a regular job, an asylum claim put forward to avoid deportation is considered, by definition, not genuine and leads to rejection. So why did the TC feel the need to refer to the (non)credibility of the story in order to justify its negative decision? Indeed, by merely evaluating the testimony's credibility, the TC should come to an opposite decision. For what is incoherent about an illiterate Iraqi Kurd raised by his mother in Syria until her premature death, who then worked in Libya before moving to Italy? And why is it implausible that he could not name current political parties, the outcome of the last elections, and a very famous museum, all in relation to a country he fled under the bombs, at the age of 6?

Beyond Credibility

The research I have presented shows a very loose and unmotivated, excessive recourse to the notion of credibility to ground negative determinations, so that to a certain extent a better knowledge and a more careful employment of the suggestions put forward by the many existing manuals on asylum determination, could have limited the sense of arbitrary unfairness one gets from reading those files.

Yet, I am not sure that, by switching from the credibility of the applicant to that of the application—the credibility of the person *vs* that of the account (CREDO 2015)—the (inherent) ambiguity of the notion vanishes. What appears in the CREDO manuals as a move towards maximising objectivity, in fact obscures other aspects that cannot be neglected. One is the decision-makers' own subjectivity, the processes at work in their minds in the specific setting of asylum hearings (Johnson 2013), as well as their 'personal theories of "truth" and "risk"', which those recent manuals acknowledge (suggesting they should be minimised, while leaving aside how and if this is altogether possible); another is the 'need to understand subtle cultural, gender, demeanour and linguistic issues' (IARLJ 2013: 19), a task that cannot be improvised and proves extremely difficult to address; and finally the inter-subjective nature of the claimants' narrative, produced with the active participation of many subjects beside the claimant him/herself, through an elaborate en-textualisation process (see Spotti, Gibb, this volume) which *ex post* attributes to asylum seekers, as 'their own words', what is in fact a stratified texture woven by many hands at various stages of a long procedure, in different institutional settings (see Danstrøm and Whyte, this volume).[22] Therefore, while a loose use of the notion could and should be avoided, I believe that a residual and irreducible trace of ambiguity will necessarily remain.

But my intention here is not to offer ad hoc solutions to make the existing asylum system fairer to those 'happy few' who land alive at the external frontiers of Europe, thus supporting the positivist illusion that finding yet more technicalities, or refining existing ones, will eventually render the screening of human beings 'objective'.[23] While acknowledging that legal processes are (necessarily?) intrinsically positivist, this recognition does not render the procedure 'objective': rejected claimants may not be 'objectively undeserving', but appear to be so after having been processed by a long, non-homogeneous and fragmented procedure. A procedure in which hidden cultural assumptions 'typically permeate the mind-set of lawyers' and judges (Grillo 2016; Ballard 2010), and which is embedded in (macro)political orientations. A fair recognition of the aspiration of a multitude to a digni-

---

[22]These aspects have long been addressed in anthropological critique of the asylum system; see among others: Blommaert (2001, 2009), Good (2007), Gibb and Good (2014), Jacquemet (2005), Maryns (2006), Cabot (2011) on Greece, Sbriccoli and Jacoviello (2011), Sorgoni (2013) on Italy.

[23]See Campbell (2013) on supposedly objective technicalities in UK; Fassin and Kobelinsky (2012) on deontological ethics of appeal judges in France. On a personal level, the general system presupposes a belief in the right to select between 'the drowned and the saved' (Levi 1986): a moral position I do not wish to embrace.

fied and safe life does not depend on correcting some faults in the asylum system, as if the system itself existed in a vacuum, independent and detached from those global migratory politics and rhetorics in which, on the contrary, it is radically embedded. Such politics and rhetorics magnify the commitment to homogeneous and objective determinations, while obfuscating how a few fair decisions are predicated upon the potentially extremely unfair rejection and exclusion of the majority, and their confinement in the global south, or in some new no man's land as the *hotspots* in Greece and Italy, where most migrants are summarily labelled as 'economic migrants', i.e. illegal migrants with no right to even begin to access the asylum procedure.[24]

In the same vein, the findings discussed here are not intended as a way to judge the judges: while we can acknowledge the many failings of the determination system as practiced at the tribunal in 2011 in Bologna,[25] it would be unfair and definitely myopic to stop there. Those faults had various causes: the absence of a proper COI system which could provide updated information on the socio-political situation of the area of origin; the workload of judges not specifically nor solely dedicated to asylum issues; their reduced number vis-à-vis that of appeals; their (often) poor preparation in international protection and EU law; and their poor familiarity with playing an active role and sharing the burden of the proof.[26] But we should look also beyond the tribunal's rooms, the imperfections of the system, or the credibility issue itself.

And if we look at asylum recognition rates in Italy from 2008 to 2015, we discover that denials peaked twice: in 2011 and 2015 (Anci et al. 2016: 103). The first is the period addressed with the former research in Bologna, the second coincides with my current research in Turin. There are significant differences between the two contexts: in Turin judges now share a database on determinations, classified by country and type, that allows them to compare similar cases to avoid divergent outcomes; they circulate information from reliable and updated COI websites; an interpreter is present and paid by the tribunal. They are also aware of the traps of the credibility notion especially for 'civil law judges, who are more familiar with documents than

---

[24]As a response to the "refugee crisis", the European Agenda on Migration adopted on 31st May 2015 (European Commission 2015) introduced new border points in Greece and Italy, denominated hotspots, where Europol, Easo and Frontex officials support national ones to ensure quicker identification and fingerprinting procedures. So far, this is probably the most disputed issue of the Agenda (Amnesty International 2016).
[25]Asilo in Europa Report (2015) offers some recommendations in that sense.
[26]A magistrate to the author, Turin, November 2016.

with life stories'.[27] Most of all, they are acutely critical about their insufficient numbers and 'the loneliness of the asylum judge', especially since asylum is but one among their many duties. And they relate to their insufficient number the fact that '*now* we don't interview [the appellants] any more'.[28]

In 2011, for the first time, the European myth of safe external borders crashed; again in 2015 all the securitisation measures adopted proved useless in face of the Syrian civil war. In both cases the EU, or single European states, reacted by signing 'treaties' with non-European states in order to block the migrants before they even reached its external borders, while the rhetoric of the 'refugee crises' became a media and political *leitmotiv* and the term 'crisis' itself self-explanatory (Roitman 2014; De Genova and Tazzioli 2016; Knight and Stewart 2016). At a national level, on both occasions governmental circulars pushed for either collective decisions (as with ENA in 2012), or cursory ones (as with the 19.6.2015 circular pretending each TC evaluate at least 16 claims per day[29]), justifying such extraordinary measures with reference to the sudden increase of migrants. And yet in 2015, 154,000 migrants entered Italy (while in 2014 there were 170,000), out of which 84,000 applied for asylum (as opposed to 60,000 in 2014). Rather than supporting the fabricated sense of invasion, the numbers expose a long lasting political choice and self-representation of Italy as a transit country, an accidental destination to be dealt with through *laisser-passer* formal and informal policies (Ciabarri 2016; Kersh and Mishtal 2016; Tuckett 2015, 2016) that periodically reiterate the 'migrants emergency' issue as a sudden and unexpected event that threatens national cultural and religious identity (Giordano 2014). This is a 'politics of scarcity' (Vacchiano 2011: 194) where the collapse of the system is not due to an excess of migrants, but to a deliberate adoption of ever-temporary measures, and a systematic avoidance of adopting serious policies of recognition, reception and inclusion. Such policies would include, among other things, a strengthening of the national asylum system, both in qualitative and quantitative terms. In the absence of this, the different responses at Bologna and Turin are but two sides of the same coin, and a fairer asylum system—albeit morally due—is but a band-aid solution fed by the same 'culture of denial' (Souter 2011), and the same self-fulfilling prophecy that 'they' are not here to stay. The day after the release of an official EC video on the effective sealing of borders,[30] a

---

[27]A magistrate to the author, Turin, December 2016.
[28]Ibid.
[29]Such circulars are not public but this one was mentioned in an official publication: (Ministero dell'Interno 2016a: 34).
[30]2016: the year the EU took robust action to control migration flows https://youtu.be/EYO0z2Tnr2A?list=PLXPWZG37uPbOH-i8kqpPoxGzLLDt9i1Sd [14 December 2016].

judge commented: 'why don't they simply say that we cannot afford to protect human rights, so that we just quit?'.

References

Amnesty International. (2016). *Hotspot Italia. Come le politiche dell'Unione Europea portano a violazioni dei diritti di rifugiati e migrant*. Available at: https://www.amnesty.it/rapporto-hotspot-italia/.

Anci, Caritas italiana, Cittalia, Fondazione Migrantes, SPRAR, UNHCR. (2016). *Rapporto sulla protezione internazionale in Italia 2016*. See: www.viedifuga.org.

Asilo in Europa. (2015). *Ricerca sui provvedimenti del Tribunale di Bologna in materia di protezione internazionale*. Available at: http://asiloineuropa.blogspot.com/2016/01/ricerca-sulle-decisioni-del-tribunale.html.

Ballard, R. (2010). *Applied Anthropology: A Viable Career Path in Contemporary Britain?* EASA Conference Workshop on Public Anthropology for a World in Crisis, Maynooth, Republic of Ireland, August 2010. Paper Available at: http://www.casas.org.uk/papers/pdfpapers/appliedanth.pdf.

Basu, P., & De Jong, F. (2016). Utopian Archives, Decolonial Affordances [Introduction to Special Issue]. *Social Anthropology/Anthropologie Sociale, 24*(1), 5–19.

Blommaert, J. (2001). Investigating Narrative Inequality: African Asylum Seekers' Stories in Belgium. *Discourse and Society, 12*(4), 413–449.

Blommaert, J. (2009). Language, Asylum, and the National Order. *Current Anthropology, 50*(4), 415–441.

Bracci, F. (Ed.). (2012). *Emergenza Nord Africa. I percorsi di accoglienza diffusa. Analisi e monitoraggio del sistema*. Pisa: Pisa University Press.

Byrne, R. (2007). Assessing Testimonial Evidence in Asylum Proceedings: Guiding Standards from the International Criminal Tribunals. *International Journal of Refugee Law, 19*, 609–638.

Cabot, H. (2011). Rendere un 'rifugiato' riconoscibile. Performance narrazione e intestualizzazione in una Ong ateniese. *Lares, 77*(1), 101–122.

Cabot, H. (2012). The Governance of Things: Documenting Limbo in the Greek Asylum Procedure. *PoLAR. Political and Legal Anthropology Review, 35*(1), 11–29.

Cabot, H. (2014). *On the Doorstep of Europe: Asylum and Citizenship in Greece*. Philadelphia: University of Pennsylvania Press.

Campbell, J. (2013). Language Analysis in the United Kingdom's Refugee Status Determination System: Seeing Through Policy Claims About 'Expert Knowledge'. *Ethnic and Racial Studies, 36*(4), 670–690.

Cherubini, F. (2015). *Asylum Law in the European Union*. London and New York: Routledge.

Ciabarri, L. (Ed.). (2016). *I rifugiati e l'Europa*. Milano: Raffaello Cortina.

Coffey, G. (2003). The Credibility of Credibility Evidence at the Refugee Review Tribunal. *International Journal of Refugee Law, 15*(3), 377–417.

CREDO. (2015). *Credibility Assessment in Asylum Procedures. Expert Roundtable.* Budapest, Hungary, 14–15 January 2015. Available at: http://helsinki.hu/wp-content/uploads/CREDO-training-manual-2nd-volume-online-final.pdf.
De Genova, N. (2016). The 'European' Question: Migration, Race, and Post-Coloniality in 'Europe'. In A. Amelina, K. Horvath, & B. Meeus (Eds.), *An Anthology of Migration and Social Transformation: European Perspectives* (pp. 343–356). New York: IMISCOE.
De Genova, N., & Tazzioli, M. (Eds.). (2016). *Europe/Crisis: New Keywords of 'the Crisis' in and of 'Europe'*. Zone Books online. http://nearfuturesonline.org/europecrisis-new-keywords-of-crisis-in-and-of-europe/.
European Commission. (2015*). A European Agenda on Migration*. Brussels 13 May 2015. See: http://ec.europa.eu/anti-trafficking/sites/antitrafficking/files/communication_on_the_european_agenda_on_migration_en.pdf.
European Commission. (2016). Press Release: *Commission Presents Options for Reforming the CEAS and Developing Safe and Legal Pathways to Europe.* Brussels, 6 April 2016. Available at: http://europa.eu/rapid/press-release_IP-16-1246_en.htm.
Fassin, D., & Kobelinsky, C. (2012). Comment on juge l'asile: l'institution comme agent moral. *Revue française de sociologie, 53*(4), 657–688.
Gibb, R., & Good, A. (2013). Do the Facts Speak for Themselves? Country of Origin Information in French and British Refugee Status Determination Procedures. *International Journal of Refugee Law, 25*(2), 291–322.
Gibb, R., & Good, A. (2014). Interpretation, Translation and Intercultural Communication in Refugee Status Determination Procedures in the UK and France. *Language and Intercultural Communication, 14*(3), 385–399.
Gill, N. (2016). *Nothing Personal? Geographies of Governing and Activism in the British Asylum System.* Oxford: Wiley-Blackwell.
Giordano, C. (2014). *Migrants in Translation. Caring and the Logics of Difference in Contemporary Italy.* Berkeley: University of California Press.
Good, A. (2007). *Anthropology and Expertise in the Asylum Courts*. Abingdon and New York: Routledge and Cavendish.
Grillo, R. (2016). Anthropologists Engaged with the Law (and Lawyers). *Antropologia Pubblica, 2*(2), 3–24. Available at: https://riviste-clueb.online/index.php/anpub/index.
Hansen, T. B., & Stepputat, F. (Eds.). (2005). *Sovereign Bodies. Citizens, Migrants and States in the Post-colonial World.* Princeton and Oxford: Princeton University Press.
Hull, M. (2012). Documents and Bureaucracy. *Annual Review of Anthropology, 41*, 251–267.
IARLJ. (2013). *Assessment of Credibility in Refugee and Subsidiary Protection Claims Under the EU Qualification Directive.* Available at: www.iarlj.org/general/images/stories/Credo/Credo_Paper_18Apr2013.pdf.
Jacquemet, M. (2005). The Registration Interview. Restricting Refugees' Narrative Performance. In A. de Fina & M. Baynham (Eds.), *Dislocations/Relocations. Narratives of Displacement* (pp. 197–220). Manchester and Northampton: St. Jerome Publishing.

Johnson, T. A. M. (2013). Reading the Stranger of Asylum Law: Legacies of Communication and Ethics. *Feminist Legal Studies, 21,* 119–139.

Kersch, A., & Mishtal, J. (2016). Asylum in Crisis: Migrant Policy, Entrapment and the Role of NGOs in Siracusa, Italy. *Refugee Survey Quarterly, 35,* 97–121.

Knight, D. M., & Stewart, C. (2016). Ethnographies of Austerity: Temporality, Crisis and Affect in Southern Europe. *History and Anthropology, 27*(1), 1–18.

Latour, B. (2010). *The Making of Law. An Ethnography of the Conseil d'Etat.* Cambridge and Malden: Polity Press.

Levi, P. (1986). *I sommersi e i salvati.* Torino: Einaudi.

Marchetti, C. (2012, December). *Framing Emergency. Italian Response to 2011 (Forced) Migrations from Tunisia and Libya.* Paper presented at the RSC 30th Anniversary Conference: Understanding Global Refugee Policy, Oxford, 6–7.

Maryns, K. (2006). *The Asylum Speaker. Language in the Belgian Asylum Procedure.* Manchester and Northampton: St. Jerome Publishing.

Ministero dell'Interno. (2016a). *Piano Accoglienza 2016. Tavolo di Coordinamento Nazionale.* Available at: http://www.vita.it/attachment/d601c9b0-b314-46ba-b708-d4341546c2d9/.

Ministero dell'Interno. (2016b). *Quaderno Statistico 1990–2015,* http://viedifuga.org/wp-content/uploads/2016/05/Quaderno_statistico_1990-2015_INTERNO_4_2016.pdf.

Olivieri, M. S. (2011). L'accoglienza frantumata sotto il peso dell'emergenza'. In Lunaria (Ed.), *Cronache di ordinario razzismo. Secondo libro bianco sul razzismo in Italia* (pp. 35–44). Roma: Edizioni dell'Asino.

Parliamentary Hearing. (2015). XVII Legislatura, *Comitato parlamentare di controllo sull'attuazione dell'Accordo di Schengen,* Seduta no. 31, http://documenti.camera.it/leg17/resoconti/commissioni/stenografici/html/30/indag/c30_flussi/2015/06/04/indice_stenografico.0031.html#stenograficoCommissione.tit00020.int00020.

Roitman, J. (2014). *Anti-Crisis.* Durham: Duke University Press.

Sbriccoli, T., & Jacoviello, S. (2011). The Case of S: Elaborating the 'Right' Narrative to Fit Normative/Political Expectations in Asylum Procedures in Italy. In L. Holden (Ed.), *Cultural Expertise and Litigation: Patterns, Conflicts, Narratives* (pp. 172–194). London: Routledge.

Sicakkan, H. G. (2008). Political Asylum and Sovereignty-Sharing in Europe. *Government and Opposition, 43*(2), 206–229.

Sorgoni, B. (2011). Pratiche ordinarie per presenze straordinarie. Accoglienza, controllo e soggettività nei centri per richiedenti asilo in Europa. *Lares, 77*(1), 15–33.

Sorgoni, B. (2013). Chiedere asilo. Racconti, traduzioni, trascrizioni. In B. Pinelli (Ed.), Migrazioni e Asilo Politico, *Antropologia, 13*(15), 131–151.

Sorgoni, B. (under review). The Location of Truth. Bodies and Voices in the Italian Asylum Procedure. *PoLAR: Political and Legal Anthropology Review.*

Sorgoni, B., & Viazzo, P. P. (2010). Documenti. In C. Pennacini (Ed.), *La ricerca sul campo in antropologia. Oggetti e metodi* (pp. 323–45). Roma: Carocci.

Souter, J. (2011). A Culture of Disbelief or Denial? Critiquing Refugee Status Determination in the United Kingdom. *Oxford Monitor of Forced Migration, 1*(1), 48–59.

Stoler, A. L. (2009). *Along the Archival Grain. Epistemic Anxieties and Colonial Common Sense*. Princeton and Oxford: Princeton University Press.

Sweeney, J. A. (2009). Credibility, Proof and Refugee Law. *International Journal of Refugee Law, 21*(4), 700–726.

Tazzioli, M., & De Genova, N. (2016). Europe/Crisis: Introducing New Keywords of 'the Crisis' In And of 'Europe'. In N. De Genova & M. Tazzioli (Eds.), *Europe/Crisis: New Keywords of 'the Crisis' In And of 'Europe'*. Zone Books online. http://nearfuturesonline.org/europecrisis-new-keywords-of-crisis-in-and-of-europe/.

Tuckett, A. (2015). Strategies of Navigation: Migrants' Everyday Encounters with Italian Immigration Bureaucracy. *The Cambridge Journal of Anthropology, 33*(1), 113–128.

Tuckett, A. (2016). Moving on: Italy as a Stepping Stone in Migrants' Imaginaries. *Focaal, 76,* 99–113.

UNHCR. (1979). *Handbook on Procedures and Criteria for Determining Refugee Status*. Geneva. Available at: www.unhcr.org.

UNHCR. (1998). *Note on Burden and Standard of Proof in Refugee Claims*. Geneva. Available at: http://www.unhcr.org/.

UNHCR. (2013). *Beyond Proof. Credibility Assessment in EU Asylum Systems*. Geneva. Available at: http://www.unhcr.org/.

Vacchiano, F. (2011). Discipline della scarsità e del sospetto: rifugiati e accoglienza nel regime di frontiera. *Lares, 77*(1), 181–198.

Open Access This chapter is distributed under the terms of the Creative Commons Attribution 4.0 International License (http://creativecommons.org/licenses/by/4.0/), which permits use, duplication, adaptation, distribution and reproduction in any medium or format, as long as you give appropriate credit to the original author(s) and the source, a link is provided to the Creative Commons license and any changes made are indicated.

The images or other third party material in this chapter are included in the work's Creative Commons license, unless indicated otherwise in the credit line; if such material is not included in the work's Creative Commons license and the respective action is not permitted by statutory regulation, users will need to obtain permission from the license holder to duplicate, adapt or reproduce the material.

12

Making the Right Decision: Justice in the Asylum Bureaucracy in Norway

Tone Maia Liodden

Introduction

Asylum decision-making inherently involves high stakes: when asylum seekers present their story to an immigration officer, they place their lives in the hands of another country's authorities. Making a wrong decision can, at worst, be fatal. The decisions are under constant debate in the media, as immigration authorities are criticised either for wrongly rejecting genuine refugees or for admitting bogus asylum seekers. The public debate is characterised by disagreement, strong emotions and conflicting ideas about justice. In this chapter, I explore what justice looks like from the point of view of some of the individuals who make these difficult decisions daily, namely caseworkers in the Norwegian Directorate of Immigration (UDI). What are the main challenges involved in making just decisions? What does 'justice' mean to the caseworkers who decide claims? And finally, how does the production of justice inside the institution relate to public expectations of refugee protection? The goal is to investigate some of the underlying normative

---

This chapter is based on the doctoral dissertation, 'The burdens of discretion. Managing uncertainty in the asylum bureaucracy' (Liodden 2017).

T. M. Liodden (✉)
The Work Research Institute, Oslo Metropolitan University, Oslo, Norway
e-mail: tone.liodden@oslomet.no

issues that are played out in the process of assessing asylum applications, and to consider the relationship between justice, discretion, and bureaucratic goals and values.

Refugee protection holds symbolic value to most democratic states, as refugee rights are based on liberal-universal notions of justice that are important to the identity of democracies (Boswell 2005). There is a deep tension between the wish of European states to adhere to their human rights commitments, while limiting migration as much as possible (Carling 2011). This tension means that asylum decision-makers have to handle two seemingly contradictory goals in their daily work. On the one hand, they have to ensure that bona fide refugees are accorded their rights through protection. On the other hand, they have to maintain control and restrict entry of those not considered eligible for refugee status. The main task of caseworkers is to make correct distinctions among applicants, or in other words, to accord justice to the right group of people.

The analysis in this chapter is based on 24 interviews with UDI caseworkers. The data collection process was guided by principles of institutional ethnography (Smith 2005), which is an inductive method of inquiry that takes the experiences of a particular group of people as a point of departure for exploring an institution. The focus of the inquiry is thus not on individuals, but on the institution (McCoy 2006). The experiences of the interviewees serve as a window to understanding institutional processes that shape the perception of justice in the asylum bureaucracy.

Uncertainty and Discretion in the Decision-Making Process

Under the Norwegian Immigration Act of 2008, paragraph 28, a foreign national should be recognised as a refugee if he or she 'has a well-founded fear of being persecuted for reasons of ethnicity, origin, skin colour, religion, nationality, membership of a particular social group or for reasons of political opinion',[1] or 'faces a real risk of being subjected to a death penalty, torture or other inhuman or degrading treatment or punishment upon return to his or her country of origin' (Ministry of Justice and Public Security

---

[1] The word 'race', which is used in the Refugee Convention of 1951, was replaced in the Norwegian law in 2011 by 'ethnicity', 'origin' and 'skin colour' (Stortinget 2011). Similar changes have been made in legislation on discrimination. The term 'race' remains controversial in the Norwegian setting, even thought it has a well-established meaning in the context of international law.

2010). If an applicant is not granted refugee status, he or she will automatically be considered for a permit on 'humanitarian grounds' (paragraph 38), which can be granted in some instances for example because of life threatening illness or other grave circumstances, or because the applicant has a particular connection to Norwegian society.

If the legal criteria in paragraph 28 are considered to be fulfilled, there is no room for discretion in the sense that the applicant *shall* be granted asylum. The discretionary space in asylum decisions is related to establishing the facts of the case and determining whether the criteria are, indeed, fulfilled. In order to do so, caseworkers have to interpret ambiguous terms such as 'persecution' and 'well-founded fear' and apply them to individual cases. Moreover, applicants often lack documentation that can corroborate their stories, which makes the assessment of credibility crucial to the outcome in many cases. This constitutes one of the most difficult and contagious points in asylum decisions, because issues frequently considered to be signs of non-credibility may equally be a consequence of, for example, communication challenges, cultural differences, anxiety, and symptoms of post-traumatic trauma and stress (see e.g. Rousseau et al. 2002; Gibb and Good 2014; Herlihy et al. 2012). Another difficulty is related to the use of country of origin information. Such information is often central to determining both risk of persecution upon return, and the 'external' credibility of the story—whether the applicant's description of events is in line with 'generally known facts' (UNHCR 2011: 39). Establishing these facts is often challenging, since the country reports that caseworkers rely upon frequently contain information that is ambiguous, uncertain, and can be interpreted in many ways (Liodden 2017: Chapter 7).

The many uncertainties in the decision-making process together make up a substantial space for discretion that decision-makers have to manage in order to reach a decision. Discretion is not only exercised at the end point of the process, when the law is applied, but throughout the entire decision-making process (Hawkins 1992b: 14). Moreover, it is largely a collective enterprise. Together, caseworkers have to answer a number of difficult questions, such as: At what point do acts of violence and discrimination constitute 'persecution'? What does it take for a claim to be credible enough? How should ambiguous information about the applicant's home country be interpreted? When should the benefit of the doubt be applied?[2]

---

[2]On the benefit of the doubt, see Good (2015).

Legal scholars conceive of discretion as a space where subjective forces enter and may threaten the rule of law—and thereby the justness of legal decisions. The legal profession has tended to see discretion as 'subjective justice; rules are formal justice' (Handler 1986: 169). From this perspective, discretion constitutes an unruly space outside of law. Arbitrary and subjective use of discretion is certainly problematic, but as Brodkin points out, discretion matters more 'not when it is random, but when it is structured by factors that influence informal behaviors to develop in systematic ways' (Brodkin 2012: 942). There are a number of 'extra-legal' factors—organisational, psychological, political and social—that limit and order the use of discretion (Hawkins 1992b; Lipsky 2010). I am interested mainly in those factors that shape discretion in systematic ways, paying particular attention to how interviewees described the development of what they referred to as 'practice' in asylum decisions, which I will elaborate on below.

Justice in Decision-Making

In the context of administrative-legal decision-making, justice has often been used to describe the substantial outcome or accuracy of a decision-making process, whereas fairness has been associated with the process itself. Conceptually, they have been brought together under the term *administrative justice,* which encompasses both outcome and process (Sainsbury 1992: 302). This framework provides a set of goals or values that are useful to understanding bureaucratic decision-making processes. In his analysis of the asylum system in the UK, Robert Thomas argues that there are four basic goals in legal-administrative institutions that are important to quality of decisions: accuracy, fairness, cost management and timeliness (Thomas 2011: 14). There is often a trade-off between these different values, 'as any effort to promote one value will often only be capable of being achieved by moderating the achievement of other values' (Thomas 2011: 15).

It is beyond the scope of this chapter to analyse all these goals and how they are balanced in the asylum bureaucracy. In addition to timeliness, I focus on two issues related to administrative justice that became points of interest during the analysis: the notion of accuracy, and fairness in the shape of impartiality and equal treatment.[3] Accuracy is related to the substantial

---

[3]Thomas (2011: 25) does not explicitly include equal treatment when he considers fairness of procedure, but he mentions it as an important goal in systems where many different decision-makers are involved.

decision. It refers to establishing the facts of a case in an accurate manner—which in asylum decisions usually means assessing the credibility of the applicant's story—and subsequently applying the correct rules or criteria to determine the outcome. Accuracy is often described as the primary demand of administrative justice, since 'no matter what other desirable attributes a decision-making process might embody, its decisions are unlikely to be acceptable if they are wrong' (Sainsbury 1992: 302). In the words of one caseworker: 'That should be the essence in what we do. That we make the right decisions'. Despite the importance of accuracy to just decision-making, it is often an issue that is very difficult to determine in asylum cases, where decisions often revolve more around the facts than the law, and where the assessment of evidence often involves substantial uncertainty (Thomas 2011: 13). A decision can be legally sound, but it is hard to know whether the facts are correctly assessed. For asylum decisions, there is 'no external, objective standard against which to assess their accuracy' (Thomas 2011: 70). Decision-makers rarely receive reliable feedback on their decisions; moreover, since asylum assessments are geared towards future risk, they are 'essentially an essay in hypothesis, an attempt to prophesy what might happen to the applicant in the future' (Goodwin-Gill and McAdam 2007: 54).

Equal treatment is not related directly to the substance of the decision, but to ensuring that one individual is not treated unjustly as compared to others, embodied in the notion that one should '[t]reat equal (like) cases equally (alike), and unequal (different) cases unequally (differently)' (Carr 1981: 211). The principle of equal treatment presumably ensures consistent decision-making, i.e. that the outcome of cases should be relatively similar, regardless of who the decision-maker is. While *consistent* decision-making does not ensure accuracy—it is entirely possible for decisions to be fully consistent, yet substantially wrong—*inconsistent* decision-making is often considered a symptom of inaccurate decisions: '[I]f a decision-making process produces disparate outcomes, then surely some of its decisions must also be substantively incorrect—either because genuine claims have been rejected and/or non-genuine claims accepted' (Thomas 2008: 490). Studies from other contexts indicate that consistent decision-making is a major difficulty in asylum assessments, as different decision-makers appear to reach different conclusions in similar claims (Ramji-Nogales et al. 2009; Rehaag 2012; Riedel and Schneider 2017). Inconsistent decision-making challenges the idea of refugees as a clear-cut category. As Whyte (2015: 156) writes:

> Refugee status is a right, conferred on appropriate persons, not something to be bartered for. This formal understanding of refugee determination is largely

fictional, as actual refugee determination procedures vary dramatically across space and time, resulting in much more uneven implementations of who are actually recognised as refugees than the rights-based ideal.

The idea of "the refugee" as an objective identity remains strong in the public debate about asylum and bolsters the perception of a just system where distinctions between refugees and non-refugees can be clearly made. In the following sections I will, however, suggest that who a refugee is to some extent may be settled among decision-makers who together develop a local yardstick of what a just decision looks like. The present study indicates that this was achieved in part through comparison of cases and a focus on equal treatment.

Equal Treatment: Creating Local Justice?

Some caseworkers considered the uncertainty involved in the decisions to be one of the most difficult aspects of the job: 'The uncertainty is the hardest part. That you sort of never get a final answer about whether what you've been doing for the past five years is right or wrong'. Similarly, one caseworker said that 'in our work, we never get a certain answer, we never know if what we do is right or wrong, if we make the wrong decision, nobody tells us, if we reject, we never hear about it again'. In a context of uncertainty, where many decisions were emotionally difficult, equal treatment was a form of justice over which caseworkers had a measure of control:

> *Researcher*: What do you think, our asylum politics are often referred to as strict, but fair. Do you think that's a good description of the situation?
> *Caseworker*: Yes. Our policies are definitely not among the most liberal, if you compare with other countries. So in that way you could say that it's strict. If it's fair depends a bit on the point of view. We try to be fair in what we do, in the sense that we have a principle of equal treatment, but if it's fair that we do not admit families with children who are in a difficult position […]. I mean, that's an impossible question to answer.

This caseworker's view of fairness is here primarily connected to equal treatment—whether the decisions are fair more broadly is an issue that she is reluctant to go into. In addition to equal treatment, impartiality was a value caseworkers emphasised when they spoke about making correct decisions. Like several other interviewees, the decision-maker above referred to the fact that her role was to implement law and policy, which also entailed making decisions she did not necessarily agree with. Making the right decision seemed to many caseworkers to be closely related to their identity as neutral bureaucrats who followed the rules in an impartial manner, thus echoing classical ideas connected to the *ethos of bureaucracy* (Weber 1978; Du Gay 2000). As in other studies of bureaucracy, caseworkers tended to emphasise the clear boundaries between policymaking and administration (see e.g. Eggebø 2013; Wettergren 2010), which meant that their personal opinion about the justness of the decision did not—and should not—affect their work.

The role of the law was ambiguous. On the one hand, caseworkers frequently referred to the law as a point of reference regarding whether or not they made the right decision. Drawing on the authority of law is probably particularly important in a field where decisions are emotionally and morally challenging, and their correctness is frequently under dispute. On the other hand, the legal framework often seemed to provide limited guidance in the actual decision-making process, apart from narrowing the scope of eligibility. Most caseworkers I spoke to were not educated in law and did not engage actively with the legal framework (see also Eule 2014: 54; Dahlvik 2014: 157). Moreover, as already mentioned, many decisions revolve around establishing facts rather than legal issues. In the words of one caseworker: 'There is nothing in the law that we can use in a decision'. She also points to equal treatment as a proxy for a just decision when accuracy is difficult to determine:

> We refer to the law. Every time someone asks us or criticises us: it's the parliament that has passed the law. But the law only says that those who deserve asylum should be granted asylum, those who do not deserve it, should not be granted asylum, that's what the law says […]. So then [it comes down to] our practice notes, how we've treated previous cases. In that way, it's equal treatment. But whether we are right – who knows?

The legal definition of the refugee narrows the scope of eligibility. You cannot, for example, be granted asylum on the basis of dire poverty or illness. Because there is such a large discretionary space, however, caseworkers had to find additional means to distinguish between eligible and non-eligible applicants.

Caseworkers did this by developing a common understanding of the assessment of cases, referred to as 'practice' in the quote above. Notes that describe current practice in the assessment of cases in the UDI constitute binding guidelines for caseworkers. They describe the most common reasons for seeking asylum for applicants from a particular country and how such cases normally are assessed, given interpretations of the law and country information (see e.g. UDI 2016).[4] Simply put, the legal 'practice' of a public institution is made up of similar decisions in a specific field, which serve as precedents in subsequent assessments. Practice is considered to be a formal source of law, below the legal framework and preparatory works in the legal hierarchy, that may guide the interpretation and application of general rules and legal provisions (Boe 2010: 145). The importance of practice for understanding the outcome of cases will depend on how much discretion there is. In situations where there is a large degree of discretion, such as in the field of asylum, there is potentially considerable scope, both for the political level and decision-makers at the street-level, for influencing the development of practice and thereby the outcome of many asylum cases.

Practice could not, however, be understood merely by reading the notes and the formal texts they were based on. It also appeared to involve a degree of tacit or experience-based knowledge that caseworkers shared, but which was difficult to put into words (see also Jubany 2011: 87). This tacit knowledge depended on knowledge of previous assessments, close communication with colleagues, and trust in their judgments. Caseworkers considered decision-making as a practical skill that had to be acquired through hands-on experience. Over time, they seemed to acquire a 'sense of outcome' (analogous to the intime conviction that Kobelinsky discusses, this volume) that—at least in part—appeared to be based on recognising patterns in the case that were similar to or departed from previous ones. In this context, too, equal treatment was a central principle in determining the correct outcome. By comparing cases and looking to the assessment of similar cases in the past, caseworkers established a common understanding of what a rejection or an acceptance looked like.

This understanding appeared to differ somewhat from one unit to another. Such differences became particularly visible when caseworkers from time to time moved from one unit to another, or helped out with the caseload in a different unit than the one they normally worked in. This quote illustrates the perception of such differences:

> *Caseworker*: Practice probably differs a bit for different countries. I know that on some countries, they have a totally different approach, it's sort of: 'This might have happened', and then they accept the case. There are cultural differences between the units.

---

[4]Author's translations from Norwegian.

Researcher: Yes, why do you think that is? It's perhaps difficult to say.
Caseworker: I don't know. But the culture in different units is really different. A uniform practice... No. It depends on which interviewer you meet and what caseworker you get.

This caseworker suggests that what is considered to be credible or not, differs between units. Some are stricter whereas others are more lenient. In a recent study of the asylum bureaucracy in Norway, the researchers similarly concluded that the 'threshold of what is considered to be credible, seems to differ in different units' (Bollingmo et al. 2014: 97).[5] They suggested that the variation could probably be explained by the different nature of the cases that units handle, but they also considered structural and cultural difference between the units to be important.

The development of differences may be a consequence of what Emerson has referred to as *case-set effects* (Emerson 1983). While most research on decision-making takes the individual case as the point of departure when considering outcomes, decision makers tend to 'respond to cases in relation to, or as part of, some larger, organisationally determined *whole*' (Emerson 1983: 425). Asylum decision-makers often encounter many similar claims. Making many similar decisions tends to produce shorthand ways of dealing with and classifying cases (Hawkins 1992a: 40). Comparison of similar cases within a caseload and with decisions in the past was an important tool in the assessment. For example, one caseworker said that she sometimes took a pile of cases with claims from the same country and categorised them. She tended to establish the clear rejections first. Once they had been established, it was easier to assess the rest. The advantage, she said, was that:

> You work faster, at least. It's more efficient. You treat like cases alike. You have a better chance to compare the cases and you establish a kind of, well, gut feeling where you see the outcome much faster.

This approach entails that the outcome of one individual case will depend in part on the nature of the other cases in the portfolio. For example, Emerson points to studies where criminal offenses are perceived as more or less serious depending on the other cases to which officers or legal administrators are accustomed. Similarly, the evaluation of risk in an individual case may be influenced by the comparison with cases where the risk is much more severe (see also Bailliet 2003: 183). The characteristics of other cases may

---

[5]Author's translations from Norwegian.

contribute to slightly shifting the thresholds of persecution or perceived risk among caseworkers in one unit compared to those in another unit, who are exposed to different kinds of case sets. The same is likely to be true of credibility assessments. Having assessed many cases with similar claims, caseworkers may establish an image of what a credible applicant looks like. When more, similar cases come along, they will probably have to live up to that standard—or an even higher standard—in order to be considered credible. If many cases follow the same pattern, it will take increasingly more for a case to appear convincing, because it will come across as generic and fabricated if it does not appear in a shape that underscores a personal or authentic dimension not encountered previously. At the extremities of the scale—very clear-cut rejections and very clear-cut acceptances—case load effects presumably have less impact. It seems likely, however, that cases in the grey zone in the middle of a scale, which could potentially 'land' on either side of the line, will be affected by the features of the cases at the extremities. The outcome in individual cases may therefore be substantially influenced by the caseload as a whole and the sequencing of cases.

A locally created yardstick of what the right decision looks like, based on comparison, produces consistency at a local level, but such consistency potentially co-exists with a great deal of variation across different units. Thus, due to the continuous influence of past decisions and the emphasis on equal treatment, discretion does perhaps not so much create subjective justice, but rather produces a kind of local, comparative justice (Feinberg 1974).

The Production of Cases

It is inherently difficult to find ways of assessing the quality and accuracy of decisions that involve a large degree of discretion, particularly when organisational goals are ambiguous or conflicting (Lipsky 2010: 49). Measuring productivity and timeliness can be monitored much more easily. From 1998, as part of a New Public Management trend in the Norwegian welfare state, the government began to introduce goal and result measures to increase the performance of the UDI (Christensen et al. 2006: 128). Unit leaders have to report regularly on the 'production' of cases, both to their leaders in the UDI and to the Ministry in charge. Making accurate decisions has to be balanced against the fact that the resources available for each decision are not unlimited, and against the need to produce timely decisions. Caseworkers are instructed to make decisions that are, according to the quality guidelines for decision-making, 'good enough', which means striking a balance between acceptable quality and efficiency (UDI 2010). Several caseworkers were concerned that the focus on production could potentially affect the quality of decision-making: 'They should really take seriously that this is a knowledge-based organisation. We don't produce tyres or tooth brushes. It's actually dangerous if we make mistakes'. Some caseworkers said they felt as though the pressure was increasing, while the resources and recognition they received from the organisation were diminishing. At the same time, the 'production' of cases is a tangible goal that caseworkers could strive for in a context where much else was uncertain. For example, this unit leader focuses on production goals when she is asked about uncertainty over the outcomes of decisions:

> *Researcher*: Would you say that the majority of cases from [country X] are quite easy to assess, that it's quite clear whether it's an acceptance or a rejection?
> *Caseworker*: Yes, it's become more difficult now since we no longer have the general prohibition of return, but I would say that in most cases it is possible to reach a decision within the set time limits. It's eight days after the interview. It's quite tough, but it's possible. The backlog that we've had in our unit has been a disruptive factor.

Instead of considering the content of the decision—and whether or not there is uncertainty—she emphasises the fact that more difficult cases challenge the ability to reach a decision within the set time frame. Focus is shifted from the content to the context of decision-making, where production is central. Another caseworker described the assessment of cases from a specific country as 'navigating in the dusk', because there was so much uncertainty about the outcome. Because there was very limited and unreliable country information and most cases were different from each other, it was difficult to establish a common practice that could guide the assessments and thus provide a sense of whether the outcome was right or not:

> It's difficult for two reasons: First of all, it's difficult to know whether you've reached the right decision. That's one thing, and the other thing—which for many of us is the most bothersome—is that these cases are very time consuming, and there is no one in this organisation who understands that. You're measured on production. And if you have a case that you can deal with in two hours, while I am on a case where the interview has stretched over several days, it takes three weeks to find out what to do—then there's no understanding of that. So workwise, that really sucks.

Because she navigates 'in the dusk', it is difficult to know whether she is making the right decision. But it is a reality that is difficult to change: there is no certain answer. This concern seems to become almost secondary to the pressing issue of production. Difficult cases that involve uncertainty about the outcome are time consuming. If she spends a lot of time on a case, this undermines her productivity. Hence, it is not the uncertainty around the accuracy of the decision that is the most difficult, but the fact that these kinds of decision increase work pressure. To some extent, production goals shift attention from the substance of decisions to the efficiency of the process. It can be seen as a classic example of goal displacement, where the need to process cases quickly becomes an end in itself (Lipsky 2010: 44).

Deferred Justice? The Role of the Immigration Appeals Board (UNE)

Appeals mechanisms are a means of increasing the likelihood of accurate decisions, thereby enhancing administrative justice (Sainsbury 1992: 319). If an asylum claim is rejected by the UDI, the decision can be appealed to the Immigration Appeals Board (UNE). Moreover, if the two institutions treat cases systematically differently, the UDI will usually align its practice with that of the UNE (UDI 2010). To individual caseworkers, one of the most important functions of the UNE appeared to be that it contributed to alleviating doubt and uncertainty about the accuracy of decisions. Interviewees found comfort in the fact that the UNE would correct potential mistakes, thus redressing potential injustices. This is in line with other studies that describe how decision-makers feel reassured by the fact that someone else will make a second assessment (Dahlvik 2014; Baillot et al. 2014: 533), deferring 'responsibility for the final outcome to another superior body or role-player' (Baillot et al. 2014: 535). In the words of one caseworker: 'There is the appeal. Sometimes I have to tell myself that: there is actually the possibility of appeal'. In Carlsen's (2011) study of the UDI, one interviewee points to the idea that the notion of 'deferred' justice may allow caseworkers to work more efficiently: 'We've termed it "risk control"—it means that our bosses accept that we make mistakes in case processing. The idea is that as long as we keep up a certain efficiency, potential mistakes will be corrected during the appeal' (case worker cited in Carlsen 2011: 82).[6]

---

[6]Author's translation from Norwegian.

In an interview, I spoke to a caseworker about a change in country information, which now corroborated many applicants' credibility instead of undermining it. When I asked her how she felt about the previous decisions—when asylum seekers perhaps had been wrongly rejected—she said that she took comfort in the fact that by the time these cases were processed in the UNE, they too would have updated their information and would correct the decisions:

> It's no fun to think about the cases that…we've probably rejected a few cases that according to this [new practice] would have been accepted. And then you have to think, okay, but those cases still have not been treated at the UNE, and the UNE will update their practice.

As a means to address the problem of the time lag between country information and development on the ground, the appeal plays an important role. It may, however, be problematic to rely too much on the appeal for an independent assessment in difficult cases. Bailliet (2003) found that some caseworkers tended to reject cases when they were unsure about how to resolve a complex issue, assuming that the applicant would appeal the case to the UNE. Caseworkers then expected the UNE to provide a signal to the UDI about how such cases should be solved. She comments: 'This tactic does not always prove successful in those cases in which the UNE Secretariat adopts the same language and argumentation utilised by the UDI with little variation' (Bailliet 2003: 169). In fact, a relatively limited number of decisions are changed upon appeal. In 2016, the UNE overruled 8% of UDI's asylum decisions; for 2015, the number was 16%.[7] When decisions are not overturned, this too serves as a form of feedback, suggesting that decisions are correct. According to the caseworker in the following quote, the UNE usually overrules UDI decisions because of changes in circumstances. With more than ten years of experience as a decision-maker, she could not recall a single case that had been overturned due to a different credibility assessment:

> *Researcher*: If they [UNE] change a decision in one of the cases you've assessed—what do you think then?
> *Caseworker*: That usually happens because a lot has changed during the appeal process. New information, that the applicant has become ill. It's

---

[7]See: https://www.une.no/statistikk/asylsaker/ [Accessed 24 July 2017].

usually in those cases—psychological illness, serious physical illness—that the UNE changes the decision. Or due to changes in the situation of the country of origin [...]

Researcher: So it's quite rare that they overturn your credibility assessments?
Caseworker: I don't think I've seen that.
Researcher: So it's quite similar [...]
Caseworker: I think they are stricter than us. I think so.

This lends support to the idea that credibility 'sticks'—once lack of credibility has been established, it can be difficult to rebut (see e.g. Coffey 2003). One reason for this may be that much of the indeterminacy has been dealt with before the case reaches the UNE. Many of the discretionary decisions that caseworkers make during the process of assessing asylum cases can be considered 'second order decisions' (Hawkins 1986). They are numerous, but often invisible by the end of the process. Second order decisions 'may not seem to be particularly significant, such as what information should be included as part of the raw material of a case, but they may have enormous implications for how subsequent primary decisions are made' (Hawkins 1986: 1166). By contrast, 'first order decisions' are the salient, visible decisions in the career of a legal case—such as the status as an accepted or rejected applicant. The numerous second order decisions that caseworkers in the first instance make about information processing and interpretation are not visible in the documents that the UNE receives, but they may nevertheless contribute to constructing the case in a particular manner. Perhaps more importantly, most UNE decisions are made on the basis of documents only; in 2016, applicants were given the opportunity to provide oral testimony in 4% of cases (UNE 2017: 18). As Sainsbury (1992: 304) points out, one of the most important ways of addressing the challenge of incomplete, contradictory or unclear evidence is to actively involve claimants in the information collection process. It is presumably much more difficult to justify changing a credibility assessment when the decision-maker at appeal has not heard the claimant giving evidence in person. While decision-makers in the UDI trusted the UNE to correct potential mistakes, it is possible that the limited number of oral hearings challenges the UNE's ability to make truly independent decisions. This, in turn, may affect the UNE's capacity to redress potential injustices.

The Media Debate: Criticism and the Production of Certainty

The public debate in the field of asylum is a source of critique that can lead to deliberation about the justness of current practices and the accuracy of decisions. In a field where it is difficult to know whether decisions are accurate or not, such critique can be considered one of the few sources of feedback. Interviewees varied in their perception of the media debate; some found it interesting and enjoyed working in a contested field while others considered it a source of stress. They had in common, however, that critique in the media rarely was seen as indicative of whether or not cases were assessed correctly. For one thing, there is no consensus in the public debate. Caseworkers are sometimes criticised for being too harsh—at other times, for being naïve and too lenient. Moreover, criticism was often considered misguided and based on emotions instead of knowledge of the rules. Knowing the process from the inside changed the perspective: It meant understanding the constraints under which the work was conducted, the criteria that must be fulfilled, and the details that could produce different outcomes in two seemingly similar cases. Only work peers were fully able to understand the wide range of considerations in the assessments.

Several caseworkers appeared to feel that it was important to shield themselves from the emotional climate in the media debate, which could threaten the impartiality required to assess cases in a just manner. They emphasised the importance of *non-responsiveness* to external pressures (Lindberg 2013: 217). If caseworkers were to become too affected by issues raised in the media, it could potentially conflict with their political and legal accountability as impartial implementers of law and policy. The media's tendency to focus on specific individuals could in itself be viewed as a potential source of injustice.[8] In this context, 'justness' was largely equivalent to treating like cases alike, and did not entail an evaluation of the decisions more substantially. The justness of the system more broadly was considered a political matter, since, in the words of one interviewee, 'we don't decide, we implement'. It followed that the target of critique should be the political level and not those in charge of policy implementation. Making an exception because of

---

[8]The most striking example that several caseworkers mentioned was the case of Maria Amelie, an exceptionally articulate, well integrated young woman whose asylum application had been rejected. The deportation of Amelie created public outrage and evoked broad sympathy across the political spectrum. Several caseworkers mentioned that with their knowledge of practice, they found the intense focus on Amelie to be highly unjust to other applicants.

media attention might be possible within the scope of the law, particularly in cases concerning permits on humanitarian grounds, where legal discretion is rather large.[9] According to established practice, however, such exceptions would violate the norm of equal treatment and therefore be highly unjust to other applicants who might have been rejected under much more dire circumstances.

The nature of the asylum assessments may serve as a potential buffer against criticism in itself. Modern bureaucracy has been criticised for the fact that the complexity of the system makes it difficult to establish a clear link between action on the part of any one individual and the outcome or consequences of their actions (see e.g. Bauman 1989). The consequence of a rejection in asylum cases may be particularly diffuse. For one thing, as noted, asylum assessments are directed toward future risk and are thereby hypothetical by nature. Moreover, the facts of many cases are unclear and under disbelief, rendering the consequences of a rejection even more elusive and difficult to imagine. Applicants whose stories are portrayed in the media and who have been rejected due to lack of credibility are by definition not trustworthy sources and the lack of reliable feedback means that decision-makers rarely find out if they make mistakes. The importance of establishing a link between a decision and its potential consequences may explain why several caseworkers appeared to feel that the greatest injustice was done in cases concerning humanitarian protection that were rejected. In these cases, there was usually no question about the accuracy of facts. The adverse consequences of return to the home country were often rather straightforward—clearly exposing the relationship between a negative decision and its consequences. Cases concerning health issues, in particular those involving children, spurred the greatest sense of injustice in some of the interviewees, to the point where some of them questioned the legitimacy of the legal categories (compare to Gianopoulou and Gill, this volume). For example, one caseworker considered some of these rejections to be 'unreasonable', 'horrible' and 'grossly unjust'.

In an interview, one caseworker said: 'We are very certain of ourselves. And I believe that's because we are never told that we make mistakes'. She added: 'I sit here and do this day after day, I am never told that there are mistakes, only that this is correct. Then you become more and more certain that what you are doing is right'. These statements may at first sight seem puzzling, considering the frequent debate about asylum decisions in

---

[9]Note, however, that decision-makers are subject to political instructions in cases concerning humanitarian protection. These instructions limit their scope of discretion, but there is nevertheless some leeway, depending on the country of origin and the nature of the claim.

the public sphere. The caseworker does not refer to lack of debate in general, however, but to the fact that the immigration authorities rarely admit to mistakes in public. There is a striking contrast between the uncertainty that goes into the assessment of asylum cases, and the certainty with which politicians and representatives of the institution talk about asylum decisions in public. The following quote from the former head of UNE, Terje Sjeggestad, serves as an illustration: 'Luckily, the UNE is not aware of a single documented example of the fact that we have returned someone to persecution' (Stavanger Aftenblad, 18 November, 2010). The remark may not be representative for the UNE's stance in general, but there are strong incentives for the asylum bureaucracy to present outward certainty. The complexity of refugee determination calls for the confidence to make decisions that may have fatal consequences if they are wrong (Luker 2013: 514). The display of outward certainty is presumably important to bolster the confidence and morale of decision-makers, as well as signaling justness to the public.

The need to maintain certainty about decisions can paradoxically be an impediment to attempts to monitor their accuracy. There are occasional public claims about asylum seekers who have been subjected to torture or death upon return, but there is no system for monitoring rejected applicants in Norway. In a written response to a request about monitoring after return, the Norwegian Ministry of Justice replied:

> The situation upon return has been assessed when a decision has been made to reject a case. The Norwegian immigration authorities consider that in each case, the assessment of protection and the rule of law should be at a standard that makes it unnecessary to monitor whether or not someone who has been returned will be subjected to persecution (Anundsen 2015).[10]

In this quote, dismissing the need for monitoring is equivalent to expressing confidence in the assessments and the rule of law. In an interesting parallel, the Netherlands attempted to monitor returnees to Iran at one point in the 1990s. According to a Dutch country advisor, the monitoring desisted in part because Iranian authorities disapproved, but also because monitoring could 'leave the impression that Dutch authorities did not trust their own assessments'.[11] Monitoring may signal uncertainty that contributes to undermining belief in a just system.

---

[10]Author's translation from Norwegian.

[11]E-mail from country advisor in Dutch country of origin information department, March 30th 2011 (Landinfo 2011: 2). Author's translation from Norwegian.

Discussion

The institution of asylum is a powerful tool of protection and a symbol of a nation's adherence to human rights; however, the institution also serves as a gatekeeper to the nation and is an effective tool of exclusion of those not considered eligible. For exclusion to be acceptable, it must be done on legitimate grounds. This becomes particularly urgent in a policy field where negative decisions often entail high human costs, such as deportation and detention. For example, the media regularly brings up deportations of families, focusing particularly on children. The communication of legality and certainty alleviates the moral discomfort connected to the consequences of asylum politics. The clear-cut distinction between genuine refugees and others who do not have eligible grounds for protection plays an important role for the public acceptance of asylum politics and the perception of such politics as 'strict, but just', which has been the slogan to varying degrees in Norway for the past several years.

The idea of the refugee as a clear-cut, objective identity is reflected in the language surrounding refugees. We speak of 'refugee recognition' as if it were an identity that is objectively present among certain individuals that simply needs to be uncovered. The status is 'declaratory', which means that someone 'does not become a refugee because of recognition, but is recognised because he is a refugee' (UNHCR 2011: pt. 28). Public expectations about justice appear to be based on this idea of clearly demarcated individuals, whose rights are being fulfilled according to the law. In many asylum cases, however, the question is not primarily about the law, but about facts. During the decision-making journey, a legal decision constitutes the final destination, but the law often does not provide much guidance on the way.

A more accurate description is perhaps that refugees are defined into being in the encounter with the host states, and more specifically, during the refugee determination procedure (see also Stevens et al. 2014; Zetter 1991). Decision-makers participate in the negotiation about the boundaries of the refugee category daily in their work. The many uncertainties that often characterise decision-making, combined with the specialised knowledge of decision-makers, open up a discretionary space that is difficult to control from above and is shielded from public view. Like other street-level bureaucrats, caseworkers not only implement policy, they also shape it in important ways. They try to answer many complex questions in a context where they are under time pressure, there is limited or ambiguous information, they receive scarce reliable feedback, and the decisions can be emotionally difficult. While decision-makers refer to the same legal framework, they develop local norms through the comparison of cases that serve as a yardstick for what the eligible refugee looks like. It is, however, difficult to know how this yardstick relates to external reality, particularly in case portfolios where credibility assessment is central to the outcome. Equal treatment, or 'following the same practice', can be considered to become a proxy for justice in a context where it is hard to evaluate the accuracy of decisions. Such consistency at a local level may, however, easily co-exist with inconsistencies on a broader level documented by research in other countries (see e.g. Ramji-Nogales et al. 2009; Rehaag 2012; Riedel and Schneider 2017). To some extent, then, justice becomes locally produced.

While decision-makers appear to become more confident in their decisions with experience, they do not necessarily make more accurate—or just—decisions over time, particularly when there is lack of reliable feedback. Considering the psychological cost of doubting previous decisions in asylum cases, where the stakes are exceptionally high, it is even possible that experience may increase self-confidence at the expense of self-scrutiny. An institution that is constantly under criticism is perhaps less likely to provide an environment that encourages deliberation about the justness of its decisions. It seems, however, to be of vital importance to open up such 'critical spaces' (Crépeau and Nakache 2008), if not in public, then at least internally. In a situation where there are no clear answers, engaging with the uncertainty and doubt that are inevitably there, may be the best way of improving the conditions of just decision-making.

References

Anundsen, A. (2015). *Skriftlig spørsmål fra Karin Andersen (SV) til justis- og beredskapsministeren.* Available at: https://www.stortinget.no/no/Saker-og-publikasjoner/Sporsmal/Skriftlige-sporsmal-og-svar/Skriftlig-sporsmal/?qid=61658. Accessed 6 Jan 2015.

Bailliet, C. (2003). *Study of the Grey Zone Between Asylum and Humanitarian Protection in Norwegian Law and Practice.* Available at: https://www.jus.uio.no/ior/personer/vit/ceciliab/dokumenter/KRD-rapport.pdf. Accessed 20 July 2017.

Baillot, H., Cowan, S., & Munro, V. E. (2014). Reason to Disbelieve: Evaluating the Rape Claims of Women Seeking Asylum in the UK. *International Journal of Law in Context, 10,* 105–139.

Bauman, Z. (1989). *Modernity and the Holocaust.* Cambridge: Polity Press.

Boe, E. (2010). *Grunnleggende juridisk metode - en introduksjon til rett og rettstenkning.* Oslo: Universitetsforlaget.

Bollingmo, G. C., Skilbrei, M.-L., & Wessel, E. (2014). *Troverdighetsvurderinger: Søkerens forklaring som bevis i saker om beskyttelse (asyl)*. Available at: https://www.udi.no/globalassets/global/forskning-fou_i/beskyttelse/troverdighetsvurderinger-sokerens-forklaring-som-bevis-i-saker-om-beskyttelse.pdf. Accessed 23 July 2017.

Boswell, C. (2005). *The Ethics of Refugee Policy*. Aldershot: Ashgate.

Brodkin, E. Z. (2012). Reflections on Street-Level Bureaucracy: Past, Present and Future. *Public Administration Review, 72*, 940–949.

Carling, J. (2011). The European Paradox of Unwanted Migration. In P. J. Burgess & S. Gutwirth (Eds.), *A Threat Against Europe? Security, Migration and Integration* (pp. 33–46). Brussels: Brussels University Press.

Carlsen, C. B. (2011). *Makt og motmakt i utlendingsforvaltningen. En studie av saksbehandlingskultur i UDI*. Master's thesis, University of Oslo, Oslo.

Carr, C. (1981). The Concept of Formal Justice. *Philosophical Studies, 39*, 211–226.

Christensen, T., Lægreid, P., & Ramslien, A. (2006). *Styring og autonomi: Organisasjonsformer i utlendingsforvaltningen*. Oslo: Scandinavian University Press.

Coffey, G. (2003). The Credibility of Credibility Evidence at the Refugee Review Tribunal. *International Journal of Refugee Law, 15*, 377–417.

Crépeau, F., & Nakache, D. (2008). Critical Spaces in the Canadian Refugee Determination System 1989–2002. *International Journal of Refugee Law, 20*, 50–122.

Dahlvik, J. (2014). *Administering Aslylum Applications*. Dissertation, Universität Wien, Vienna.

Du Gay, P. (2000). *In Praise of Bureaucracy. Weber—Organizations—Ethics*. London: Sage.

Eggebø, H. (2013). 'With a Heavy Heart': Ethics, Emotions and Rationality in Norwegian Immigration Administration. *Sociology, 47*, 301–317.

Emerson, R. M. (1983). Holistic Effects in Social Control Decision-Making. *Law and Society Review, 17*, 425–456.

Eule, T. G. (2014). *Inside Immigration Law*. Farnham: Ashgate.

Feinberg, J. (1974). Noncomparative Justice. *Philosophical Review, 83*, 297–338.

Gibb, R., & Good, A. (2014). Interpretation, Translation and Intercultural Communication in Refugee Status Determination Procedures in the UK and France. *Language and Intercultural Communication, 14*, 385–399.

Good, A. (2015). The Benefit of the Doubt in British Asylum Claims and International Cricket. In D. Berti, A. Good, & G. Tarabout (Eds.), *Of Doubt and Proof: Ritual and Legal Practices of Judgment*. Farnham: Ashgate.

Goodwin-Gill, G., & McAdam, J. (2007). *The Refugee in International Law*. Oxford: Oxford University Press.

Handler, J. F. (1986). *The Conditions of Discretion. Autonomy, Community, Bureaucracy*. New York: Russel Sage Foundation.

Hawkins, K. (1986). Discretion in Making Legal Decisions. On Legal Decision-Making. *Washington and Lee Law Review, 43*, 1161–1242.

Hawkins, K. (1992a). The Use of Legal Discretion: Perspectives from Law and Social Science. In K. Hawkins (Ed.), *The Uses of Discretion*. Oxford: Clarendon Press.

Hawkins, K. (Ed.). (1992b). *The Uses of Discretion*. Oxford: Clarendon Press.
Herlihy, J., Jobson, J., & Turner, S. (2012). Just Tell us What Happened to You: Autobiographical Memory and Seeking Asylum. *Applied Cognitive Psychology, 26,* 661–676.
Jubany, O. (2011). Constructing Truths in a Culture of Disbelief: Understanding Asylum Screening from Within. *International Sociology, 26,* 74–94.
Landinfo. (2011). *Iran: Returnerte asylsøkere.* Oslo: Landinfo.
Lindberg, S. I. (2013). Mapping Accountability: Core Concepts and Subtypes. *International Review of Administrative Science, 79,* 202–226.
Liodden, T. M. (2017). *The Burdens of Discretion. Managing Uncertainty in the Asylum Bureaucracy.* Ph.D., University of Oslo.
Lipsky, M. (2010). *Street Level Bureaucracy. Dilemmas of the Individual in Public Services.* New York: Russel Sage Foundation.
Luker, T. (2013). Decision Making Conditioned by Radical Uncertainty: Credibility Assessment at the Australian Refugee Review Tribunal. *International Journal of Refugee Law, 25,* 502–534.
McCoy, L. (2006). Keeping the Institution in View: Working with Interview Accounts of Everyday Experience. In D. Smith (Ed.), *Institutional Ethnography as Practice.* Oxford: Rowman and Littlefield.
Ministry of Justice and Public Security. (2010). *Act of 15 May 2008: On the Entry of Foreign Nationals into the Kingdom of Norway and Their Stay in the Realm (Immigration Act).* Available at: https://www.regjeringen.no/en/dokumenter/immigration-act/id585772/. Accessed 24 July 2017.
Ramji-Nogales, J., Schoenholtz, A. I., & Schrag, P. G. (Eds.). (2009). *Refugee Roulette. Disparities in Asylum Adjudication and Proposals for Reform.* New York: New York University Press.
Rehaag, S. (2012). Judicial Review of Refugee Determiniations: The Luck of the Draw? *Queen's Law Journal, 38,* 1–57.
Riedel, L., & Schneider, G. (2017). Dezentraler Asylvollzug diskriminiert: Anerkennungsquoten von Flüchtlingen im bundesdeutschen Vergleich, 2010–2015. *Politische Vierteljahresschrift, 58,* 23–50.
Rousseau, C., Crépeau, F., Foxen, P., & Houle, F. (2002). The Complexity of Determening Refugeehood: A Multidisciplinary Analysis of the Decision-Making Process of the Canadian Immigration and Refugee Board. *Journal of Refugee Studies, 15,* 43–70.
Sainsbury, R. (1992). Administrative Justice: Discretion and Procedure in Social Security Decision Making. In K. Hawkins (Ed.), *The Uses of Discretion.* Oxford: Clarendon Press.
Smith, D. E. (2005). *Institutional Ethnography. A Sociology for People.* New York: Altamira Press.
Stevens, D., Kneebone, S., & Baldassar, L. (2014). Law, Identity and Protection: Concluding Reflections. In S. Kneebone, D. Stevens, & L. Baldassar (Eds.), *Refugee Protection and the Rule of Law. Conflicting Identities.* London: Routledge.

Stortinget. (2011). *Lovvedtak 22 (2011–2012)*. Available at: https://www.stortinget.no/globalassets/pdf/lovvedtak/2011-2012/vedtak-201112-022.pdf. Accessed 2 Aug 2017.

Thomas, R. (2008). Consistency in Asylum Ajudication: Country Guidance and the Asylum Process in the United Kingdom. *International Journal of Refugee Law, 20,* 489–532.

Thomas, R. (2011). *Administrative Justice and Asylum Appeals: A Study of Tribunal Adjudication*. Oxford: Hart Publishing.

UDI. (2010). *Kvalitet i saksbehandlingen. RS 2010-109*. Available at: https://udiregelverk.no/no/rettskilder/udi-rundskriv/rs-2010-109/. Accessed 25 July 2017.

UDI. (2016). *Asylpraksis - Iran. PN 2016-002*. Available at: https://udiregelverk.no/no/rettskilder/udi-praksisnotater/iran-pn-2016-002/. Accessed 28 July 2017.

UNE. (2017). *Årsrapport 2016*. Oslo: Utlendingsnemnda.

UNHCR. (2011). *Handbook and Guidelines on Procedures and Criteria for Determining Refugee Status Under the 1951 Convention and the 1967 Protocol Relating to the Status of Refugees*. Available at: http://www.unhcr.org/3d58e13b4.pdf. Accessed 18 July 2017.

Weber, M. (1978). Bureaucracy. In G. Roth & C. Wittich (Eds.), *Economy and Society II*. Berkeley: University of California Press.

Wettergren, Å. (2010). Managing Unlawful Feelings: The Emotional Regime of the Swedish Migration Board. *International Journal of Work Organisation and Emotion, 3,* 400–419.

Whyte, Z. (2015). In Doubt: Documents as Fetisches in the Danish Asylum System. In D. Berti, A. Good, & G. Tarabout (Eds.), *Of Doubt and Proof: Ritual and Legal Practices of Judgment*. Farnham: Ashgate.

Zetter, R. (1991). Labelling Refugees: Forming and Transforming a Bureaucratic Identity. *Journal of Refugee Studies, 4,* 39–61.

Open Access This chapter is distributed under the terms of the Creative Commons Attribution 4.0 International License (http://creativecommons.org/licenses/by/4.0/), which permits use, duplication, adaptation, distribution and reproduction in any medium or format, as long as you give appropriate credit to the original author(s) and the source, a link is provided to the Creative Commons license and any changes made are indicated.

The images or other third party material in this chapter are included in the work's Creative Commons license, unless indicated otherwise in the credit line; if such material is not included in the work's Creative Commons license and the respective action is not permitted by statutory regulation, users will need to obtain permission from the license holder to duplicate, adapt or reproduce the material.

13

Taking the 'Just' Decision: Caseworkers and Their Communities of Interpretation in the Swiss Asylum Office

Laura Affolter, Jonathan Miaz and Ephraim Poertner

Introduction

'Political and ethical issues are [...] found at the heart of public debate on asylum, which oscillates between a preoccupation with the management of migratory flows and the principle of protection of victims of persecution' (Fassin and Kobelinsky 2012: 469). This leads to tensions and aporia with which decision-makers are confronted in their everyday work. Fassin and Kobelinsky (2012: 470) identify three such aporia. The first refers to the need to simultaneously enhance the 'greater good' of the institution, i.e. asylum protection, and, at the same time, to challenge asylum applications and put them in doubt. The second has to do with what they define as 'the core value' in decision-making, as it is perceived by decision-makers themselves: 'that of

L. Affolter (✉)
University of Bern, Bern, Switzerland
e-mail: laura.affolter@anthro.unibe.ch

J. Miaz
University of Lausanne, Lausanne, Switzerland

J. Miaz
University of Neuchatel, Neuchatel, Switzerland
e-mail: jonathan.miaz@unil.ch

E. Poertner
Department of Geography, University of Zurich, Zurich, Switzerland
e-mail: ephraim.poertner@geo.uzh.ch

the just decision' (ibid.). The term 'just', thereby, stands both for 'correctness'[1] and 'fairness'. The third relates to the sanctioning of (moral) sentiments and their simultaneous importance as a means for determining the veracity of asylum claims as well as for rendering the institution 'human'. Related to this view, but more on a micro-level, much of the existing literature on street-level bureaucracies has dealt with practical decision-making dilemmas, particularly the juggling between, on the one hand, 'compassion and flexibility' and, on the other hand, 'impartiality and rigid rule-following' (Lipsky 2010: 15–16; see also Maynard-Moody and Musheno 2003).

However, what became apparent in our fieldwork is that these 'dilemmas' or aporia were generally not formulated as such by the caseworkers[2] themselves. Fassin and Kobelinsky also underline this with regard to rapporteurs and magistrates in the French National Asylum Court (2012: 470). This, we argue, is not a coincidence. Hence, even if these different rationales of decision-making appear to stand in conflict, ways of resolving or at least reducing this tension are essential for caseworkers to do their job. In this chapter, we look at how this is done. Our aim is not to argue that these 'dilemmas' are never experienced as such by decision-makers. Sometimes they are. However, while this has been dealt with extensively in existing literature, not much attention has been paid to the fact that more often they are not. In this chapter, therefore, we deal with the 'non-experience' of dilemmas arising from what are from the 'outside' perceived as conflicting rationales of decision-making and the ways in which decision-makers deal with these rationales and make them fit. We argue that decision-makers' 'volitional allegiance' (Gill 2009: 215) with the asylum institution plays a crucial role thereby. This chapter develops an enquiry that illuminates how state officials themselves are governed (see also Gill 2016; Mountz 2010) through their involvement in particular groups within the office and the allegiances they develop towards them. Such an analysis involves talking to caseworkers about their 'desires', affiliations and their attempts to deal with the different exigencies of their work.

Just as Fassin and Kobelinsky (2012: 470) describe, for the caseworkers we spoke to decision-making is, ultimately, about taking 'correct' and 'fair' decisions. By drawing on their notion of the 'just decision' (encompassing both 'correctness' and 'fairness') we attempt to illuminate how asylum

---

[1] 'Correctness' of decisions is based on decision-makers' evaluations and not on that of applicants.
[2] By caseworkers we mean the people in the office who conduct interviews, collect evidence, write decisions and thus produce asylum cases.

decision-makers in the Swiss administration make sense of their work: how they invoke notions of correctness and fairness with regard to decision-making practices, but also the greater good of the asylum institution in providing protection for those deserving it, and moral sentiments such as sympathy and compassion towards applicants and their stories. In this chapter, we show that how decision-makers make sense of what they do is influenced by their affiliations to and allegiances with what we call 'communities of interpretation'.[3] We define 'communities of interpretation' as groups with which people identify. They have a 'shared repertoire' of knowledge and meanings (Wenger 2003) on how to interpret the law and (best) make sense of their work. These communities of interpretation evolve along the fissures between different asylum units and divisions, professional backgrounds, amount of working experience, and hierarchical positions. Different communities of these kinds coexist within the same office. They are crucial to the processes whereby notions of the 'just decision' develop and become shared amongst different subdivisions of the asylum office. Gill argues that state officials are not only 'compelled, disciplined or incentivised to act ["in accordance with state objectives"], but [are, furthermore,] ideationally conditioned to freely choose to conduct themselves' in such ways (Gill 2009: 219–220). We argue that these little communities of interpretation play an important role in this regard.

By placing the relationship between asylum caseworkers and (parts of) the office at centre stage in this article, we shed light on an issue that has received much less attention than, for instance, the relationship or encounter between asylum seekers and decision-makers (Jubany 2011; Gill 2009, 2016; Kobelinsky 2015; Maryns 2006; Probst 2011; Souter 2011), the social and legal conditions in which caseworkers apply the law (Miaz 2017), as well as the role of evidence in such encounters (Doornbos 2005; Good 2007; Gibb and Good 2013; Scheffer 2001). Thus, to understand why decision-makers do what they do, we argue that it is important to look at what decision-makers themselves claim that they 'do in the name of the state' (Gupta 1995: 376). It is here that their relationship with (part of) the office and their volitional allegiance to it become important.

After a short section on 'just decisions', where we explain how we analytically approach 'just' decision-making and describe our methods and data, we develop our argument in three main parts. The first two are organised

---

[3]We derive this term from Wenger's 'community of practice' (2003).

around the two dimensions of what caseworkers and their superiors considered to make their work 'just': 'correctness' and 'fairness'. In the first part we discuss meanings ascribed to correct decision-making. We show that what 'correct' comes to mean is shaped by institutional constraints related to legality, productivity and accountability. Furthermore, we argue that other actors such as superiors, peers and magistrates of the Federal Administrative Court as well as imagined figures such as 'the Swiss people' or 'the tax payers' play an important role in shaping what it means to take a 'correct' decision. In the second part we analyse how caseworkers negotiate 'fairness'. We argue that different considerations—legal, organisational, relational, and moral—play into these negotiations and orient the caseworkers' practices and decision-making. In this section we also show that caseworkers develop particular ideas about the rightful positioning in this landscape of different (and at times conflicting) considerations (see also Liodden and Schneider, both this volume). In the last part of the chapter we show how developing such ideas is influenced by the communities of interpretation that decision-makers affiliate themselves with, or are affiliated with, as well as by the allegiances with these communities that they develop.

Tracing the 'Just Decision'

Following Laroche (1995) we understand 'just decisions' as social representations. Rather than approaching decision-making as being about an individualised notion of 'choice', we focus on how caseworkers and their supervisors speak about 'just' decisions and decision-making and try to make sense (and/or convey a certain sense to us, the researchers) of their work and the competing normative orders they have to manoeuvre within their daily work. Thus, in this chapter, we trace decision-makers' practical reasoning (Barnett 2011: 247) of 'just' decision-making through their verbal accounts when explaining, justifying and distancing themselves from certain events, which we relate back to everyday practices of asylum decision-making that we have observed and participated in.

Since 'just' decision-making is not directly observable but only constructed in the verbalisation of practices and practical knowledge, the main bulk of data in this chapter is conversational in nature. The verbal accounts we draw on are, on the one hand, conversations between us and caseworkers of the Swiss State Secretariat for Migration SEM, including semi-structured and open-ended interviews with caseworkers as well as informal conversations with them; and, on the other hand, conversations between different caseworkers that we observed, for instance, during so-called consulting sessions between superiors and their employees or training sessions for new caseworkers.

As described in the introduction, what constitutes 'just' decision-making is contested within the institution. Such contestations render the differing ideas of just decision-making visible. However, other aspects of what 'just' decision-making means may be self-evident within the institution. It is precisely such 'normalities' that we must attempt to grasp as ethnographers (see Breidenstein et al. 2013: 36). Yet, Shore and Wright also warn against becoming 'inured' to these normalities and claim that it is important to 'maintain sufficient critical distance to be able to keep asking fundamental questions about how [officials] conceptualise their worlds and what this means for theoretical debates' (2011: 15). This was something that all three of us struggled with. During our fieldwork, we all became inured to certain 'normalities'.[4] Working together and sharing our thoughts and experiences has helped us to recognise our own 'normalities' and regain critical analytical distance. Our different disciplinary backgrounds—Ephraim Poertner is a human geographer, Jonathan Miaz a political scientist and Laura Affolter a social anthropologist—also proved enriching in this interpretative endeavour.

Asylum seekers must file their asylum application in one of the SEM reception centres, where they are submitted to the first steps of the procedure. The procedure comprises two asylum interviews. If the reception centre cannot decide on the asylum application within 90 days, the asylum seeker is allocated to a canton responsible for his or her accommodation and support. The procedure continues at the headquarters, where the file is further processed, usually by conducting the second interview, undertaking investigations and, ultimately, taking the decision.

We all did fieldwork in different units at the SEM headquarters and in one or two reception centres. Jonathan Miaz conducted his fieldwork between 2010 and 2012, Ephraim Poertner between 2012 and 2014 and Laura Affolter between 2013 and 2015.[5] Apart from our conversations with decision-makers, during our field-stays we also shadowed people in their daily work, went to coffee breaks and team meetings with them, sat in on

---

[4]However, maintaining and regaining distance is not difficult only because one becomes inured to one's interaction partners' normalities, but also because as researchers we become personally involved and develop relationships of trust with our interaction partners (see Van Maanen 1982).
[5]Whilst Poertner and Affolter mostly worked with German-speaking staff, Miaz predominantly dealt with French-speaking caseworkers.

asylum interviews, took part in the training sessions for new employees, etc. Thus, we all collected vast amounts of material by combining an approach of 'classical' in-depth ethnography of one particular site with multi-sited ethnography.[6] A lot of this material we shared with each other to write this chapter. We first pooled parts of our anonymised ethnographic material and then both jointly and separately categorised it.

What 'Correctness' Means

Decision-making in the SEM is, to a great extent, about taking 'correct' decisions. This can be seen in the following statement by a head of unit when describing her role as a superior:

> I have to make sure my people write decent [*ordentliche*] and correct decisions. And enough. And exactly in this order. You see, for me quality is more important than quantity.[7]

But what do she and others mean by correct decisions? And how is the correctness of decisions checked and measured? These are the questions we deal with in this section. Furthermore, we deal with the issue of quantity, which the superior also mentions.

A correct decision is often understood by decision-makers as one that one manages to get past the superior and—in case of an appeal—past the court. Thus, decisions that have been double-signed by the heads of units (even if the caseworkers know that their superiors do not always check their decisions very closely) and decisions that have been affirmed by the court are often quasi automatically perceived to be correct. When superiors check decisions, they pay particular attention to whether the decision is legally correct, whether it adheres to institutional practice and whether its argumentation is solid.

For a decision to be considered legally correct it must be consistent with the Swiss Asylum Act, the Federal Act on Foreign Nationals, the 1951 Refugee Convention and the rulings of the court. What 'according to institutional practice' means, on the other hand, is contested and keeps

---

[6]Miaz and Affolter also did fieldwork in the Federal Administrative Court. Furthermore, Miaz included legal advice offices in his research.

[7]Nora, head of unit, headquarters. To protect the anonymity of our interaction partners, all names are pseudonyms.

changing over time. Officially, institutional practice refers to the *Asyl- und Wegweisungspraxis* (practice of asylum and expulsion; APPAs), the institutional guidelines on how to decide asylum cases from specific countries or regions and with specific flight motives.[8] However, we argue that institutional practice encompasses more than is explicitly stated in these guidelines, namely the collective ways for taking specific decisions within different communities of interpretation in the office. This is illustrated by the following quote, in which a caseworker speaks about decision-making in the different reception centres and the headquarters:

Carmen: Sometimes we apply different measurements. And then it's kind of a legal inequality. For example, we [reception centre A] once had a lot of [people from country Y]. With 'country tests' and everything we tried to expose them and to show that they did not really come from [country Y]. So, we started rejecting their claims. At the same time in [reception centre B] they were doing interviews and just waving them through [quickly giving them positive decisions]. Just because the practice had not been coordinated. It got going after a while, but it always takes an outcry first that something is going wrong to get something going […].
Researcher: But don't you have the APPAs, which define what the common practice is?
Carmen: Yes, […] but some APPAs are just not up to date. Sometimes we have already moved a step further, but it's not in the APPA yet.
Researcher: So this means you are at liberty to create your own practice here?
Carmen: Yes, of course, but naturally in consultation with those responsible for that country at the headquarters. For example, the case of [people from country Y]; [the practice of giving more negative decisions] started here. We in the reception centres are usually the first ones to pick up new trends. It is here where you just notice them first.[9]

Several reception centre officials remarked that because they are physically so much closer to the asylum seekers (they are housed in the same building) and it is at the reception and procedure centres where the asylum seekers first arrive, they are better equipped to pick up new trends than the people at headquarters and can thereupon adapt their practice. But because they are

---

[8]The APPAs are created and kept up to date by the *Federführung*, the person(s) in charge of a particular country at the headquarters in Berne. APPAs exist for the most common countries of origin.
[9]Carmen, caseworker, reception centre.

not in charge of the APPAs and do not hold any *Federführungen*,[10] this can result in them taking decisions that seem appropriate to them and trying to get them past the Federal Administrative Tribunal. If they manage to do so, these decisions serve as a kind of confirmation of the 'practice' and may, therefore, lead to the establishment of a new institutional practice.[11] This shows how caseworkers 'shape and mediate polic[ies] while translating and implementing [them] into action' (Wedel et al. 2005: 34).

As mentioned at the beginning of this section, rulings by the Federal Administrative Court constitute a further means for measuring correctness. Hence, the units and divisions of the SEM keep records of how many of their employees' decisions are quashed and for what reasons. A distinction is made between quashings that could have been avoided and those that could not have been and are, therefore, not really perceived as mistakes. Avoidable quashings are those occurring because of so-called 'formal' mistakes SEM caseworkers had made, for instance, not granting the asylum seeker the proper right to be heard or not making all the necessary enquiries. In contrast, quashings on the basis of the court judging the credibility of asylum claims or the scope of the refugee definition differently than the SEM official did, are regarded as unavoidable. If individual caseworkers and/or units receive too many quashings, especially of the 'avoidable' kind, this is conceived of as bad decision-making. Not only do such quashings reflect badly on the quality of decision-making, they also cost time (and money) and, therefore, stand in the way of efficient decision-making.

Efficiency plays an important role in decision-making. Thus, decision-makers' work is not only checked in so-called qualitative terms, but also in quantitative ones. 'Somehow we are always confronted with this dilemma (*in diesem Clinch*) of not just having to demand qualitatively correct work from our people, but also that it 'yields a profit' (*es muss auch etwas rausschauen*)',[12] said Markus, a head of unit at the headquarters. With 'yielding a profit' he was referring to the institutional demand to produce so-called 'output'. This focus on numerical accountability is typical of contemporary (asylum) administrations (see Gill 2016: 39; Poertner 2017). Quantitative targets are set on a regular basis for the whole institution. There is a lot of (political) pressure to deal with asylum applications fast and reduce the

---

[10]In German, '*die Federführung haben*' means 'to have the lead'. Here it refers to the person or the group of people responsible for determining a country or thematic practice doctrine.

[11]Of course, this is not something that is only done by officials working in the reception centres but also those at the headquarters.

[12]Markus, head of unit, headquarters.

number of pending cases. Setting quantitative targets is a way of doing justice to these demands.[13] This political pressure for efficiency becomes apparent in the statement by the same superior, Markus, that 'we [the SEM (officials)] have a responsibility towards the Swiss people and the tax payers to not just take correct decisions but decisions of "the right quality"'. He then goes on to say: 'And I deliberately speak of "the right quality" and not of "optimal quality", because it could always be done better'.[14] With 'right quality' Markus implies that the efforts invested to make decisions qualitatively better has to be measured against the quantitative demands of the office: it is not only important for decisions to be correct and thorough, but the time and effort involved matter too. That Markus considers this to be a political demand becomes apparent through the reference he makes to 'the Swiss people' and 'the tax payers'. Markus appears to have internalised a certain sense of accountability towards these imagined, generalised and blurred figures. In caseworkers' and their superiors' discourses, these two figures are usually used to justify restrictive practices and the measures for a greater productivity.

The concept of 'the right quality' bridges quantitative and qualitative demands. Doing one's job well in the SEM means making an adequate effort. It requires 'practical knowledge' to be able to assess for each specific case what 'adequate' means. Overall, it means going into sufficient depth when dealing with a case, but not investing more time and resources than necessary. This can be seen in the example of Theodor, a caseworker, who said that his superior had instructed him to stop always looking for material evidence in order to argue for the non-credibility of asylum claims using the criterion 'contradiction to facts' (*Tatsachenwidrigkeit*). The superior considered this too time-consuming and had asked him to focus instead on framing his arguments along the lines of 'insufficient substance', which could be done on the basis of the asylum interview minutes alone. The example shows that out of all the possible legal ways to argue in a case the most economical ones are usually promoted.

---

[13]While many of the caseworkers who had been working at the SEM for more than 15 or 20 years told us that there had always been numerical measures, most of them felt the output pressure had increased over recent years.

[14]Markus, head of unit, headquarters.

Negotiating 'Fairness'

> *Corinna*: I limit myself to [applying institutional practice], because I have to. Even if sometimes it doesn't reflect my personal opinion. [But] sometimes we also have to think like a human being and not like a person who makes the law.[15]
>
> *Nora*: For me being 'fair' means that we use the same standards for evaluating each claim. This also means that if the applicant does not fulfil the eligibility criteria we don't 'bend the rules' [*drehen und biegen*] and write a positive decision, just because it's quicker. It means that when we reach the conclusion that the case must be rejected, we take the trouble to write a negative decision, even if this takes us three to four days, and if one had just said 'yes, it's coherent', it might only have taken half a day. That's what it means to be 'firm but fair' [*in der Härte gerecht*]. On the other hand, we try hard to do justice to each individual case, each individual problem. I can also sometimes 'turn a blind eye' [*fünf gerade sein lassen*] if my gut feeling tells me that I shouldn't be obstinate and that I should try to do justice to the individual case. [...] it means that we will look at the case more closely and that we do not hide behind formal arguments too readily.[16]

We start with these two quotes because they show similar patterns regarding what is perceived as fair decision-making. Both officials stress the importance of following rules (stemming from the law and institutional practice). This is often described as being 'firm' or 'strict', which are regarded as necessities and virtues. For Nora being firm means treating everyone equally, which she (and many others) believe is what asylum decision-making should be about. Both also seem to imply that not (strictly) following the rules should constitute an exception. Corinna describes these 'exceptional' moments as situations in which one thinks 'like a human being'. For Nora these exceptional moments arise when her gut feeling tells her to deal with a case more closely than usual. Both of them, therefore, imply that not only legal and organisational norms and constraints orient decision-makers' practices but also moral considerations, emotions and feelings.

However, in this section we go beyond this dialectical depiction by extending the story in two ways. First, we argue that dealing with this 'dilemma' (whether it is perceived as such by the caseworkers or not) is not ('just') about using one's room for manoeuvre to either 'be compassionate'

---

[15]Corinna, asylum caseworker, headquarters.
[16]Nora, head of unit, headquarters.

or 'follow the law', but about making these demands meet. Second, we argue that the tension between what we call 'doing justice to the individual' and 'doing justice to the system' is about more than just 'compassion' and 'impartial rule-following'. It is about finding one's position in a 'moral economy' (Fassin 2012: 441) fraught with pitfalls on various grounds: upholding legal and formal considerations without falling into the trap of becoming overly formalistic; seeing your room for manoeuvre in the right spots—whether in your fight against abuse or to provide protection to as many as possible; coping with being regularly lied to as well as being exposed to excruciating stories of suffering. No simple solution to these tensions exists, but caseworkers struggle in justifying their own position in this field of contradictory convictions on what 'just' decision-making ultimately means. We argue on the basis of this that decision-makers not only have an idea of what is 'just' in an individual case, but develop a representation about the 'rightful' positioning in this landscape of contested moral measures.

Decision-makers' volitional allegiance to (parts of) the office and the important role that 'protecting the system' plays in their work are crucial in this regard. Caseworkers often tend to refer to 'the system' and their affiliation to it when explaining why they have to be strict in their application of the law. In Switzerland, like other countries of the global North, discourses on 'abuses' and on 'bogus' refugees loom large (Zimmermann 2011). The work of asylum caseworkers is, thus, marked by suspicion concerning asylum seekers' motives for applying for asylum, which becomes particularly visible in credibility assessments. They argue that they have to refuse those asylum seekers who do not correspond to the legal definition of the refugee in order to protect the asylum institution from abuse, to preserve the credibility of the system and, finally, to continue to protect 'those who deserve protection', as this quote nicely shows:

> I think that saying 'no' to someone who's not a refugee in the sense of the UNHCR and of the Refugee Convention contributes to the protection of the asylum institution. One has to say 'no' to those who are not refugees in order to be able to say 'yes' to those who are.[17]

Fassin and Kobelinsky (2012: 465) relate these kinds of legitimation narratives back to the historical change in decision-making, when in the mid

---

[17]Johann, asylum caseworker, headquarters.

1980s most requests went from being granted to being rejected. They argue that the 'only morally acceptable means to solve this problem is to make a separation between valuing asylum while devaluing those who claim it'. Decision-makers

> not only believe that they do good work, in which they sincerely believe, but are also convinced that they do it even better when they are more scrupulous in their examination of claims and parsimonious in granting refugee status. (ibid.)

Decision-makers, therefore, tend to make use of explanations such as the one quoted above to explain how they do justice both to the system, and to the individual asylum seeker. Whilst some decision-makers told us that doing justice to the system and doing justice to the individual asylum seeker created a dilemma they had to deal with in their daily work, many seemed to agree with the idea that 'just' decision-making was about bringing doing justice to the individual asylum seeker into accordance with doing justice to the system. The quote above shows how this is done.

The meanings ascribed to fair decision-making so far pertain to legal equality. A further meaning often associated with fair decision-making is that of impartiality, as Nora's quote at the beginning of this section indicates. The ideal of fair decision-making is, therefore, commonly understood to be about finding one's middle ground, as this quote shows:

> We sometimes tease each other a bit. If one of us takes a rather strict decision: 'Oh, what a hardliner'. And if someone says that they had to turn a blind eye or take an 'in dubio pro [refugio]'[18] decision: 'What a wimp you've become'. I think it's important to find a middle ground somewhere. So, that you don't slide towards one extreme, you see?[19]

It is very common within the office to denounce other decision-makers, asylum units, divisions and even centres as being either 'softies' or 'hardliners'. Who is considered to be a 'softy' or a 'hardliner', and what that constitutes, vary. What some consider impartial decision-making, might already be regarded as the act of a 'softy' by others. In the following quote Jenny

---

[18] This means to give the applicants the 'benefit of the doubt'.
[19] Lucy, asylum caseworker, headquarters.

criticises 'leftists', who are often considered to be 'softies' for pursuing egoistic projects:

> And then there are those that one knows are totally left-wing and would like to save the world. And they think they've done something good [by 'just waving those people through' on the basis of family reunification], even though some of these 16 and 17-year old women disappeared and never officially arrived here. [...] That's very egoistic [...] and frowned upon, you see? Because it's 'professionally' [*fachlich*] just completely wrong and also legally. I mean, that's just so problematic.[20]

Jenny uses this example to show why for her doing what one feels to be 'personally right' fails to do justice to the individual. She, thus, gives a twist to the narrative of why rightful decision-making should be orientated towards what is professionally and legally right, which extracts the moral basis from narratives that justify decision-making focusing on individual suffering. Attitudes like Jenny's are, however, also criticised by decision-makers. They blame their co-workers (and/or themselves) for not being open enough towards asylum seekers and their individual circumstances and for having become 'cynical', 'overly formalistic' and what they sometimes call 'law machines'.

Both kinds of criticism seem to involve an inherent assumption that 'just' decision-making implies making personal convictions, feelings, ethics and notions of ethos fit. However, how this is to be achieved—whether it is about putting different notions of 'just' decision-making into a hierarchical order, what this order should be, and, thus, how different ideas of what makes decision-making 'just' should be weighted—or whether it is about merging personal and professional ideas of the 'just decision' and to what extent this is desirable—is a matter of contestation. This leads to tensions that decision-makers often experience and have to deal with in the course of their everyday work. How they deal with it, may, in turn, depend on caseworkers' different affiliations and allegiances, on the one hand, but also on the particular situation: the case they are dealing with and the person they are talking to.

---

[20]Jenny, head of unit, reception and procedure centre.

Communities of Interpretation

> I have to do what the office says, otherwise I will somehow betray the office and I don't want that either.[21]

The expression of 'betraying the office' in this quote suggests a close affiliation between the official and the office that, we suggest, cannot be taken for granted. It implies a struggle for the 'ideologically affected desires of state personnel' (Gill 2009: 215), their 'volitional allegiance' (ibid.) with the office (also standing for 'the system'). It is important, however, not to perceive the office solely as a unified whole. Rather, it appeared to us to be divided along complicated and evolving lines of affiliations and allegiances. These changing allegiances profoundly influence what 'just' decision-making means for caseworkers in particular situations. Thus, decision-makers align with what are imagined as 'just decisions' in the communities of interpretation they identify themselves with and are identified with, and distance themselves from other senses of 'just' decision-making.

These communities of interpretation evolve along the fissures between units, divisions, professions, experience, and hierarchy, and are crucial in order to grasp how notions of 'just' decision-making develop and become shared amongst different subdivisions of the office. However, we acknowledge that these fissures are not dividing lines: they are, to some extent, situational: not only are they complicated and evolving, but sometimes the fissures run right through individuals that feel torn between competing senses of 'just' decision-making. Also, there is arguably more mutual understanding between the various divisions than this rather antagonistic representation allows us to acknowledge. Officials in the office are affiliated to multiple 'communities' and may 'change sides'. In this part we show contestations between different communities of interpretation evolving around the role of expertise and experience for correct and fair decision-making as well as around the importance of a legal approach versus so-called intercultural sensitivity and of compassion.

Nearly all caseworkers we spoke to in the reception centres tended to identify themselves primarily with their centre rather than with the SEM as a whole. In our conversations with them they often mentioned why they thought the work they did was better—in the sense of being more correct and fairer—than that of decision-makers working at the headquarters.

---

[21] Corinna, asylum caseworker, headquarters.

The latter did the same. Decision-makers, both in the reception centres and at headquarters, considered it to be unfair that their decision-making sometimes differed. However, in order to overcome these differences they all expected the respective other to adapt to their way of doing things. Officials in the reception centres often highlighted that people at the headquarters in Bern were not as close to the claimants as they were. They used this closeness to the claimants to explain their own different, more 'reality-grounded' approach to decision-making. Officials in the headquarters, in turn, expressed reservations about practices in the reception centres that they considered to be 'shirt-sleeved' or 'rush rush' approaches, that suffered from a lack of either distance from the claimants or the necessary expertise. At stake here are different notions of 'expertise' that are considered necessary for correct and fair decision-making. Officials in the reception centres perceive their expertise to derive from their 'close contact' with asylum seekers and the vast number of conversations they have with them (since they conduct both the short and long asylum interviews, whilst the decision-makers in Bern only do the latter). Many decision-makers at the headquarters, on the other hand, consider their expertise to be greater and of more value, because they hold all the *Federführungen* and, therefore, have all the experts and their expertise 'in house'.

> *Daniel*: Those in the 'country teams' they're supposed to be the specialists. But then someone who's been working at the SEM for half a year or so tells you what to do. Well [...].
> *Researcher*: You mean that someone who's new takes on a *Federführung*?
> *Daniel*: Yes, exactly. [...] To give you a specific example; I once interviewed a woman from Somalia. She couldn't [tell me] anything. So I asked the *Federführung* in Bern how this works with Somali women, whether I could give her a removal order. And then someone [from the *Federführung*] wrote back to me and said: 'As a women she [belongs to] a vulnerable group'. As a woman you're not per se vulnerable. [...] I didn't do it. I gave her a removal order anyway. And I was backed up.[22]

Here we see a caseworker from a reception centre challenging the expertise and authority of a colleague at the headquarters. In this case, he simply does not follow her advice. Furthermore, the friction between newcomers or 'inexperienced' decision-makers and old-established officials becomes apparent in his statement.

---

[22]Daniel, asylum caseworker, reception centre.

Newcomers sometimes accuse old-established officials of having developed a 'cynical' attitude towards asylum applicants over the course of their career that they deem incompatible with rightful decision-making. Although they often express a certain understanding for developing cynicism and even sometimes state that nobody should do this job for too long, they are most impressed by old-established officials who have managed to maintain the ability to 'see the humans behind applications' and to make an effort to 'reset' after every interview, approaching 'every asylum applicant as if she or he were the first'. Old-established officials, in turn, are sometimes sceptical of approaches to decision-making that they consider put personal opinions and feelings above the values of the larger 'community of interpretation', the office. Instead, they feel that some of the newcomers pursue 'egoistic projects'. Hence, whilst experience is regarded by newcomers and old-established officials alike as essential for decision-making, experience is also believed to sometimes stand in the way of 'just' decision-making.

However, what 'seeing the human behind the application' means in practical terms is contested. What for some might fall within 'seeing the human, instead of a number', might already be regarded as 'egoistic' and 'unfair' by others as we showed in the previous section. These differences in decision-making are often related back to decision-makers' political opinions, and also—more often—to their units, divisions or centres being 'softer' or 'harder'.

Furthermore, in the office, different professional backgrounds of caseworkers and superiors are also mentioned as indicative of diverging perspectives on what correct and fair decision-making is. The main fault line seems to run between those with a legal background and those without, the latter usually having a social sciences or humanities background. As the asylum procedure involves writing legal orders, conducting interviews in complex intercultural settings (see Kälin 1986) and evaluating the credibility of asserted origin and persecution narratives, caseworkers often disagree on what 'just' decision-making means regarding these contrasting facets of their work. Thus, caseworkers quite often openly acknowledge taking a 'legalistic' approach or one that departs from it and express a clear preference for one way or the other. Of course, this is not only related to their professional background, but also to how they have been trained and socialised in the asylum office. Hence, whilst some superiors expressed a clear preference for employing new decision-makers who are legally versed and/or have a legal background, others prefer people who have travelled, 'who know how things work abroad – not just in Russia, America or France, but in Bangladesh or Uganda for example – [and] who can free themselves from a eurocentric perception'.²³ These different employment strategies and the fact that the superiors themselves employ their decision-makers, explain to some extent why the different asylum units become important communities of interpretation. Of course, this also has to do with the hierarchical structure; with the superiors checking their employees' decisions and deciding whether they are correct or not; and with decision-makers being trained on the job within the units.

A further fault line of affiliation and allegiance—one that is not specific to the asylum office but haunts most hierarchical bureaucratic organisations in some form or other—is that between the management and frontline staff or 'street-level bureaucrats' (see Lipsky 2010). While the former are concerned with broader strategic planning, organising the work of the latter and 'steering' the processes and outcomes of the whole, the latter are those typically meeting 'clients', processing cases and taking decisions in individual cases. A main tension in the office, as discussed above, arises between the management emphasising numbers and output and frontline staff who consider an (over-)emphasis on numbers problematic if not counterproductive to the complex work they do.

Vast differences seem to exist in the ways in which heads of divisions and units pass on the pressure to yield numbers to their subordinates: while some actively shield their staff from too rigid output target enforcement, others seem less able or willing to do so. And, as the following example highlights, they may themselves feel pressured or inclined to put the output first for career reasons or out of fear of losing their position:

> It appears quite markedly; we're only human. Now, for example: The head of division of the asylum procedure was only appointed ad interim and then they said: 'Well, maybe he will then be appointed but maybe it [the position] will also be advertised'. And then he got really stressed out and he had to produce as good numbers as possible. So, he sat down with all the head of units and then they said: 'What do we do now? We really have to increase the output, now that we've hired so many new people, now it has to rise'. [...] It's quite logical that these people are not efficient in the first three, four months and that the output rather decreases if the more experienced ones have to instruct the new people, if they come with questions, and they have to teach modules and so on. And this is logical, everybody knows that, actually in every operational management this is clear except, apparently, in the SEM, where one is afraid of the pressure, and of politics and such things, because these Swiss

---

²³Nadia, head of unit, headquarters.

Federal Councillors[24] probably need to show results soon, and therefore one has decided, well yes, we have to increase the output.[25]

This example nicely shows that even if output goals are frowned upon on the street-level, caseworkers try to make sense of the rationalities behind them. That does not mean, however, that they see them as 'necessary' and unavoidable as they feel the management sometimes implies. And, more importantly, it shows that they see them as a barrier that gets in the way of what they consider 'just' decision-making.

Conclusion

'Always remember: you are the office', new decision-makers are constantly reminded in the training sessions. Thus, the expectation is that they should think and behave like that and not like individuals. They are asked and instructed to follow the objectives of the office, which—with it being a state institution—we can also call 'state objectives'. The meanings ascribed to 'just' decision-making by caseworkers and superiors that we have discussed in this chapter seem to be very much in line with these objectives. Following Gill (2009: 219), we argue that 'states [...] command powers that are capable of engendering the *will* to act in accordance with state objectives, rather than simply generating the necessity or imperative to do so'. We argue that the need and wish to 'fit in' plays an important role in this regard. Above we described the widespread denunciation of other decision-makers as well as whole units, divisions and centres as being either 'hardliners' or 'softies'. Most decision-makers do not want to be denominated as either, especially if the denomination does not fit with that of the community or communities of interpretation they most identify with. When taking decisions, therefore, caseworkers not only try to anticipate their superior's take towards their decisions, but sometimes also worry about what their peers might think about them, as this quote shows:

> And then this case with 'in dubio pro [refugio]'. Sometimes you feel really bad [doing this]. Because [...] people speak about you behind your back: 'Oh, she chose the easy way out; just quickly taking a positive [decision]. But maybe

---

[24]The seven Swiss Federal Councillors are also ministers. One of them leads the Federal Department of Justice and Police, of which the SEM is a part.
[25]Benjamin, asylum caseworker, headquarters.

you really struggled with [the decision]. Because sometimes, even though the story is not at all convincing, but if you don't find any arguments – truly not and not just out of laziness – your only choice is to take a positive [decision]. Well, ok, maybe you could show the case to someone else first.[26]

This quote is typical in two ways. First, it shows the role one's co-workers—or rather the anticipation of what they might think—play in decision-making. In line with this, many newcomers told us that it was primarily through their 'coaches', 'godmothers' and 'godfathers'—who are co-workers from the same unit that train new employees to do the job—that they learnt how to 'think the right thoughts'. Second, it is not a coincidence that Helen refers to what her co-workers might think with regard to her taking a 'too lenient' decision rather than one that is 'too harsh'. While 'overly strict' and 'cynical' decision-making is also frequently criticised and regarded as bad decision-making, we have never heard it being called 'unprofessional', whereas 'lenient' and so-called 'naïve' decision-making is (see also Alpes and Spire 2014: 269; Fassin and D'Halluin 2005: 6006; Kelly 2012; Scheffer 2003: 456; Whyte 2011).

Being professional and fitting into their communities of interpretation are important for decision-makers. This can help explain decision-makers' volitional allegiance to the asylum office and its objectives and ultimately to 'the state' and its objectives. Through these communities of interpretation things become self-evident, like the need to protect the asylum system from being abused and to save protection for those 'who really deserve it'. At the same time, it seems to be self-evident within the office that decision-makers should always be able to endorse and stand by the decisions they take and the way they go about doing so.

References

Alpes, J., & Spire, A. (2014). Dealing with Law in Migration Control: The Powers of Street-Level Bureaucrats at French Consulates. *Social and Legal Studies, 23*(2), 261–274.

Barnett, C. (2011). Geography and Ethics: Justice Unbound. *Progress in Human Geography, 35*(2), 246–255.

Breidenstein, G., Hirschauer, S., Kalthoff, H., & Nieswand, B. (2013). *Ethnografie. Die Praxis der Feldforschung*. Stuttgart: UTB.

---

[26]Helen, asylum caseworker, headquarters.

Doornbos, N. (2005). On Being Heard in Asylum Cases; Evidentiary Assessment Through Asylum Interviews. In G. Noll (Ed.), *Proof, Evidentiary Assessment and Credibility in Asylum Procedures* (pp. 103–122). Leiden and Boston: Martinus Nijhoff.

Fassin, D. (2012). Moral Economy and Local Justice. *Revue française de sociologie, 53*(4), 651–656.

Fassin, D., & D'Halluin, E. (2005). The Truth from the Body: Medical Certificates as Ultimate Evidence for Asylum Seekers. *American Anthropologist, 107*(4), 597–608.

Fassin, D., & Kobelinsky, C. (2012). How Asylum Claims Are Adjudicated: The Institution as a Moral Agent. *Revue française de sociologie, 53*(4), 444–472.

Gibb, R., & Good, A. (2013). Do the Facts Speak for Themselves? Country of Origin Information in French and British Refugee Status Determination Procedures. *International Journal of Refugee Law, 25*(2), 291–322.

Gill, N. (2009). Presentational State Power: Temporal and Spatial Influences Over Asylum Sector Decisionmakers. *Transactions of the Institute of British Geographers, 34*, 215–233.

Gill, N. (2016). *Nothing Personal? Geographies of Governing and Activism in the British Asylum System*. Oxford: Wiley-Blackwell.

Good, A. (2007). *Anthropology and Expertise in the Asylum Courts*. London: Routledge-Cavendish.

Gupta, A. (1995). Blurred Boundaries: The Discourse of Corruption, the Culture of Politics, and the Imagined State. *American Ethnologist, 22*(2), 375–402.

Jubany, O. (2011). Constructing Truths in a Culture of Disbelief: Understanding Asylum Screening from Within. *International Sociology, 26*(1), 74–94.

Kälin, W. (1986). Troubled Communication: Cross-Cultural Misunderstandings in the Asylum-Hearing. *International Migration Review, 20*(2), 230–241.

Kelly, T. (2012). Sympathy and Suspicion: Torture, Asylum, and Humanity. *Journal of the Royal Anthropological Institute, 78*, 753–768.

Kobelinsky, C. (2015). In Search of Truth: How Asylum Applications Are Adjudicated. In D. Fassin (Ed.), *At the Heart of the State: The Moral World of Institutions* (pp. 67–92). London: Pluto Press.

Laroche, H. (1995). From Decision to Action in Organizations: Decision-Making as a Social Representation. *Organization Science, 6*(1), 62–75.

Lipsky, M. (2010). *Street-Level Bureaucracy, 30th Anniversary Edition: Dilemmas of the Individual in Public Service*. New York: Russel Sage Foundation.

Maryns, K. (2006). The Asylum Speaker: Language in the Belgian Asylum Procedure. *The International Journal of Speech, Language and the Law, 14*(2), 295–300.

Maynard-Moody, S., & Musheno, M. (2003). *Cops, Teachers, Conselors. Stories from the Front Lines of Public Service*. Ann Arbor: University of Michigan Press.

Miaz, J. (2017). From the Law to the Decision: The Social and Legal Conditions of Asylum Adjudication in Switzerland. *European Policy Analysis, 3*(2), 372–396.

Mountz, A. (2010). *Seeking Asylum. Human Smuggling and Bureaucracy at the Border*. Minneapolis: University of Minnesota Press.

Poertner, E. (2017). Governing Asylum Through Configurations of Productivity and Deterrence: Effects on the Spatiotemporal Trajectories of Cases in Switzerland. *Geoforum, 78*, 12–21.

Probst, J. (2011). Entre faits et fiction: l'instruction de la demande d'asile en Allemagne et en France. *Cultures and Conflits, 84*, 63–80.

Scheffer, T. (2001). *Asylgewährung: eine ethnographische Analyse des deutschen Asylverfahrens*. Stuttgart: Lucius and Lucius.

Scheffer, T. (2003). Kritik der Urteilskraft - Wie die Asylprüfung Unentscheidbares in Entscheidbares überführt. In J. Oltmer (Ed.), *Migration steuern und verwalten: Deutschland vom späten 19. Jahrhunder bis zur Gegenwart* (pp. 423–458). Göttingen: Vandenhoeck and Ruprecht.

Shore, C., & Wright, S. (2011). Conceptualising Policy: Technologies of Governance and the Politics of Visibility. In C. Shore, S. Wright, & D. Però (Eds.), *Policy Worlds. Anthropology and the Analysis of Contemporary Power* (pp. 1–25). New York, Oxford: Berghahn Book.

Souter, J. (2011). A Culture of Disbelief or Denial? Critiquing Refugee Status Determination in the United Kingdom. *Oxford Monitor of Forced Migration, 1*(1), 48–59.

Van Maanen, J. (1982). Fieldwork on the Beat. In J. Van Maanen, J. M. Dabbs, & R. R. Faulkner (Eds.), *Varieties of Qualitative Research* (pp. 103–151). Beverly Hills, London, and New Delhi: Sage.

Wedel, J. R., Shore, C., Feldman, G., & Lathrop, S. (2005). Toward an Anthropology of Public Policy. *Annals of the American Academy of Political and Social Science, 600*, 30–51.

Wenger, E. (2003). Communities of Practice and Social Learning Systems. In D. Nicolini, S. Gherardi, & D. Yanow (Eds.), *Knowing in Organizations: A Practice-Based Approach* (pp. 76–99). Armonk, NY: M.E. Sharp.

Whyte, Z. (2011). Enter the Myopticon. Uncertain Surveillance in the Danish Asylum System. *Anthropology Today, 27*(3), 18–21.

Zimmermann, S. E. (2011). Reconsidering the Problem of "Bogus" Refugees with "Socio-economic Motivations" for Seeking Asylum. *Mobilities, 6*, 335–352.

Open Access This chapter is distributed under the terms of the Creative Commons Attribution 4.0 International License (http://creativecommons.org/licenses/by/4.0/), which permits use, duplication, adaptation, distribution and reproduction in any medium or format, as long as you give appropriate credit to the original author(s) and the source, a link is provided to the Creative Commons license and any changes made are indicated.

The images or other third party material in this chapter are included in the work's Creative Commons license, unless indicated otherwise in the credit line; if such material is not included in the work's Creative Commons license and the respective action is not permitted by statutory regulation, users will need to obtain permission from the license holder to duplicate, adapt or reproduce the material.

14

Becoming a Decision-Maker, or: "Don't Turn Your Heart into a Den of Thieves and Murderers"

Stephanie Schneider

Introduction

As a particular kind of authorial work practice, asylum casework revolves around the central goal of producing sovereign decisions. But how are people taught to decide asylum cases on a routine basis? How are they expected to deal with the uncertainties, ambiguities, and the moral and ethical quandaries involved in carrying out this task? Based on observations of an introductory training course for decision-makers, the present paper will show how the induction of caseworkers in Germany centrally revolves around (a) the proper type and degree of emotional involvement and (b) the proper type and degree of individual autonomy and creativity in handling the 'stuff' of casework. It is argued that casework may usefully be understood as an ongoing process of boundary work (Gieryn 1983) in which the written decision functions as a boundary object (Star and Griesemer 1989; Star 2010) circulating among different groups of actors. During the training, references to emotions and materialities became linked in specific ways, depending on the phase of the procedure and the potential addressee. The analysis shows how seemingly mundane and routine aspects of asylum casework are deeply conflictual and emotionally charged.

S. Schneider (✉)
Department of Social Sciences, University of Siegen, Siegen, Germany
e-mail: schneider@soziologie.uni-siegen.de

Asylum decisions are acts of certification that produce categories of identity, status and belonging. Bureaucratic work rests on systems of classification and categorisation (Bowker and Star 1999), it continuously imposes, (re)produces and is itself bound by 'principles of vision and division' (Bourdieu 1994: 12–18) that present themselves as universal, disinterested and oriented towards the 'common good'. What constitutes a 'good' decision, however, was and is an object of constant struggles. To mention but a few: administrative asylum decision-making is characterised by goal conflicts such as 'offering protection' vs. 'preventing abuse of the asylum system'. In processing cases, staff members are expected to not only act legitimately but also efficiently—a point that is of particular importance in asylum systems with high caseloads. Furthermore, and this will be at the centre of the following discussion, a decision must both be as transparent as necessary and remain as opaque as possible. A minimum of transparency is required both for organisational steering efforts and for ensuring legal certainty. At the same time, not all considerations that impact on the decision-making-process (e.g., organisational quotas concerning the duration of asylum interviews, caseworkers' feelings and emotions) find their way into the end-product of casework. In the written decision, the work that is invested into juggling these potentially conflicting demands is naturalised, objectified, and hence rendered invisible (Bourdieu 1989: 21ff.).

A number of studies have investigated asylum authorities 'from within' and pointed to the significance of individual and collective routines in dealing with the uncertainties, ambiguities and dilemmas of asylum procedures (Affolter 2017; Dahlvik 2014a; Probst 2012; Scheffer 2001; Schittenhelm 2015; Wettergren and Wikström 2014). They have stressed the extent to which a "culture of disbelief" impacts on decision-making-practices within the authorities and shown that the categorisations that caseworkers use in their daily work are to a great extent determined by organisational subcultures rather than by law or politics (Jubany 2011; Good 2015; Whyte 2015; Wikström and Johansson 2013). The present chapter builds on and seeks to contribute to this body of research by asking how newly recruited staff are initiated into practices of interviewing and decision-making. For newcomers, the above-mentioned ambivalences are exacerbated by their lack of knowledge about organisational routines, expectations and rules. While I do not by any means suppose that training courses are in any simple way causally linked to actual refugee status determination practices, they are enlightening insofar as they constitute situations in which the taken-for-grantedness of organisational routines becomes an object of explication. During the training, particular aspects of casework were problematised, rendered explicit and in this sense made *public* (Schmidt and Volbers 2011) to both the participants of the training and the outside observer. By focusing on how relations to different actors, objects, and emotions are rendered relevant during the training, the asylum administration becomes analysable as part of an only ever *relatively* autonomous field (Moore 1972; Bourdieu 1998; Bourdieu and Wacquant 2013; see Gill and Good, this volume) and the processual and conflictual character of asylum casework come into view.

The chapter is structured as follows: after a section on fieldwork and methods, I provide a brief overview of the administrative setting at the time of fieldwork in 2013/2014 and point to major changes since then. Subsequently, I focus on the ways in which beginning caseworkers are inducted into asylum procedural practices and interviewing and decision-making in particular. In the concluding section, I return to the role of emotions and materialities in boundary work in the asylum administrative setting.

Fieldwork and Methods

Fieldwork was conducted within the German Federal Office for Migration and Refugees (Bundesamt für Migration und Flüchtlinge, BAMF) in 2013 and 2014.[1] As a participant observer, I took part in three different training courses for decision-makers. Semi-structured interviews were conducted with trainers, caseworkers and headquarter staff involved in training and quality measures. As a non-participant observer, I visited different branch offices for short periods of one to five days. In the course of fieldwork, a variety of documents pertaining to asylum casework (training material, handbooks, guidelines, country of origin information: etc.) was collected.

For data analysis, I use a multi-method design that combines mapping techniques developed for situational analysis (Clarke 2012) with the documentary method (Bohnsack 2010; Nohl 2012), a procedure based on a sociology of knowledge approach. These are employed to develop different and partial perspectives on the material (Mannheim 2013 [1936]: 237–280). Situational maps were used to 'lay out the major human, nonhuman,

---

[1]The data were collected in the context of a research project on transnational administrative cooperation between European asylum authorities entitled 'Europeanization of Asylum Administrative Practice?' (headed by Christian Lahusen and Karin Schittenhelm at the University of Siegen), and funded by the German Research Foundation (DFG) as part of the research group 'Horizontal Europeanization' (FOR1539).

discursive, and other elements in the research situation of concern and provoke analyses of relations among them' (Clarke 2003: 559). The reconstructive interpretations of select passages from interviews and field notes were geared towards a more detailed analysis of the frames of reference and patterns of perception, interpretation and evaluation of research participants by focusing on *how* they narrate, describe, argue and evaluate either during the interview or in the situations observed. For the purposes of this paper, I concentrate on field notes taken during a five-day introductory training course for asylum caseworkers. Since interviewing and decision-making form the core tasks of caseworkers, the two units that were devoted to these aspects were singled out for the following analysis. For presentation purposes, the original German vignettes were slightly shortened and translated into English by the author.

Before going into the training, the next section will offer a brief overview of asylum procedural practices in Germany at the time of fieldwork. Where applicable, I indicate and describe more recent changes.

The Asylum-Administrative Setting in Germany

The German Federal Office for Migration and Refugees (*Bundesamt für Migration and Flüchtlinge*: BAMF) is the central operative authority responsible for deciding upon asylum applications. It is subordinate to the Ministry of the Interior and exercises its functions via decentralised branch-offices across the country. While people seeking international protection may be registered by several state institutions, to initiate the formal asylum procedure and to become an applicant in the legal sense, the protection seeker must apply for asylum in person at a branch office of BAMF.[2] Unlike in some other European countries (e.g., Sweden, see Schneider and Wottrich 2017), BAMF is solely responsible for taking decisions on asylum requests whereas all issues related to residence, social security, health, work, and housing are dealt with by the local foreigners' authorities under the jurisdiction of the federal states. That is, caseworkers of the federal office will usually have very little information on the living conditions of the people whose cases they process. In addition, even the direct consequences of their decisions, i.e., either the granting of a residence permit or a deportation

---

[2]In exceptional cases, an application may be lodged in writing. In 2015, this was the case for a considerable number of applications from Syria, Iraq, and Eritrea (Deutscher Bundestag 2015).

order, will be administered and carried through by local authorities and/or the police.

After an all-time low of 19,164 initial applications in 2007, there has been a rapid increase in entry figures with 109,580 initial applications in 2013 and 441,899 in 2015 (Bundesamt für Migration und Flüchtlinge 2016: 13). Furthermore, the overall backlog of undecided cases has grown substantially, from 10,926 in 2007 and 95,743 in 2013 to 364,664 in 2015 (Bundesamt für Migration und Flüchtlinge 2016: 56; Thränhardt 2014).[3] Due to the very restricted recruitment of new asylum caseworkers from 1993 onwards (Kreienbrink 2013: 406) and with the massive recruitment wave of 2015 and 2016, there is now a considerable age gap between staff that have twenty and more years of professional experience within BAMF and newly hired staff (Schittenhelm and Schneider 2017). As of 1st January 2014, roughly 289 caseworkers were responsible for investigating and deciding on asylum and/or Dublin cases, i.e., cases in which the responsibility of a member state for processing an asylum claim has yet to be determined (Deutscher Bundestag 2014: 38). By 1st September 2016 this number had risen to 1687 (Deutscher Bundestag 2016: 7, 11), although a substantial portion only had time-limited employment contracts. Until recently, caseworkers were mainly recruited from institutions qualifying for entry into public administrative service (such as the Federal University of Applied Administrative Science) or from other federal authorities (e.g., the federal police, the armed forces, the federal pension fund or the customs authorities). Since 2015, entry requirements have been loosened so that anybody with a bachelor's degree may apply. The specific kind of knowledge relevant for asylum casework is largely acquired on the job and during internal training measures. The length and nature of the induction phase have changed considerably over the last couple of years. At the time of fieldwork, new staff members were usually trained on-the-job for a period of roughly three months (sometimes less) under the supervision of more experienced colleagues or mentors. In addition, they received training courses at the headquarters in Nuremberg that covered legal aspects, intercultural training, Country of Origin Information (COI), and more practical aspects of casework. Starting in 2015, qualification centres have been set up where newcomers undergo somewhat more systematic but very short initial training courses of four to eight weeks, depending on anticipated tasks.

---

[3]This backlog and the significant delays in stepping up the office's staff and resources when applications started to increase from 2012 onwards were a recurrent theme in conversations during fieldwork.

At the time of fieldwork, there was no explicit differentiation between the functions of conducting the substantive interview on the one hand and delivering decisions on the other. To the contrary, the unity of investigating and decision-making functions was something that the organisation aspired to in order to ensure adequate credibility judgements and to prevent a mass-processing of cases on the basis of the file alone. In practice, however, a considerable number of cases were decided by people who had not conducted the interview, especially in branch-offices with extreme case overload or in situations where certain countries of origin were prioritised. With the introduction of so-called arrival- and decision-centres in 2015, the separation of tasks into interviewing and decision-making has become even more common.

With the passing of the immigration act in 2005, BAMF was assigned greater responsibility for issues of quality assessment and assurance.[4] Since then, caseworkers are subject to the directives of their superiors (and, ultimately, the Ministry of the Interior) whereas before they were to decide independently and on the basis of the law only.[5] Unity of decision-making-practices is supposed to be guaranteed by internal guidelines and directives for particular case-constellations or countries of origin, including templates for writing decisions. That is, over the last couple of decades, the categorisations relevant for decision-making have become more explicit and more binding—in a sense, more bureaucratic. The reforms of 2015/2016 towards 'integrated refugee management' have further strengthened these tendencies since cases are now clustered into four main categories (countries of origin with a protection rate above 50%, countries of origin with a protection rate below 20%, 'complex profiles', Dublin-cases) before they even reach case-officers' desks. Unlike in many other European asylum authorities where decisions are evaluated and signed by senior officials, caseworkers sign the written decision with their own name on behalf of BAMF. Via forms containing a brief overview of the decision, these are cross-checked by superiors in local branch offices. Appeals against negative decisions have to be lodged at the administrative courts within seven or fourteen calendar

---

[4]Before, this had been the task of the Federal Commissioner for Asylum Matters who was responsible for safeguarding the public interest and establishing uniform decision-making-practices within the asylum authority and before the courts (Kreienbrink 2013: 400). In the vast majority of cases, he appealed positive decisions (Weber 1998: 65; Unabhängige Kommission 'Zuwanderung' 2001: 144).

[5]The former practice was aimed at insulating asylum decision-making from political interference (Unabhängige Kommission 'Zuwanderung' 2001: 143). However, caseworkers seemed to apply legal provisions in an overly restrictive manner, which eventually came into conflict with political expectations (especially in the context of European efforts at harmonisation).

days depending on the type of rejection. Appeals against simple rejections have suspensive effect whereas those against claims rejected as manifestly unfounded or inadmissible do not. Applications to restore substantive effect must be substantiated and forwarded to the courts within seven calendar days. Decisions of the administrative courts are usually final: only in exceptional cases is it possible to appeal to higher instances (the High and the Federal Administrative Courts) or to lodge a constitutional complaint at the Federal Constitutional Court.

Organised Detachment

Interviews and observations at branch-offices showed how the organisation of casework on the ground further contributed to spatial, temporal, and emotional distance between caseworkers and asylum applicants. At local branch offices, staffs of the middle administrative service were responsible for registering the asylum request. They had their offices on the ground floor of the administrative buildings, which was also where the reception areas and waiting rooms for asylum applicants were located. With the help of an interpreter, staff informed applicants about the procedure, conducted a short initial interview on identity, travel routes and family relations, and opened up the electronic file. In the 'ED-Room', applicants were fingerprinted, photographed, and their height measured. These procedures inevitably involved some form of bodily contact, especially when bodies did not conform to the requirements of the technical devices used, as is often the case with fingerprinting.[6] It was also here that the scanners, printers and photocopying machines that served to produce and reproduce all the data that would eventually find their way into the electronic file were to be found. In short, this was where the 'dirty work' was done. This area was usually separated from the other areas of the building by security doors which—unless you were in possession of a key card—could only be opened from the inside. At the end of this initial screening, applicants were handed their residence permit (*Aufenthaltsgestattung*) for the duration of the procedure and told they would be informed about their appointment for the substantive interview at a later stage.

The offices of the members of the higher administrative service who are the subject of this paper, i.e., the people who conduct interviews and make

---

[6]Apart from deliberate manipulation, fingers might be too old, too leathern from work, etc.

decisions, were located in the upper storeys of the building. Generally, it was much quieter and cleaner here and the pace of work seemed slower, at least to the outside observer. Applicants could only enter this area once they had been collected from the waiting-rooms downstairs and brought to their interviewing officer. All applicants were invited for eight o'clock in the morning, meaning that many had to wait long hours, often with no access to food and beverages since branch offices were often located in far out and inhospitable areas. Asylum case officers usually only met their 'clients' on this one occasion. The interviews took place in caseworkers' offices which—apart from smaller individual details—were quite similarly furnished with officers seated behind large desks fitted with computers, and applicant and interpreter at a smaller desk in front on which water, tissues, a few sheets of white paper and pens were placed. In most cases, I took my seat at the side or in a corner near the door, facing the caseworker. At none of the interviews I observed was a legal counsel present and caseworkers told me that in their daily work this was nothing unusual.[7] Routinely, the interview situation was thus restricted to an interaction between caseworker, interpreter, and applicant. While interviewees often emphasised that this setting helped to generate an atmosphere of trust, it also contributed to the opacity of the substantive interview (Schneider and Wottrich 2017).

While the interviews seemed highly ritualised regarding both their opening[8] and ending[9] sequences, differences in interviewing style became apparent with regard to the heart of the substantive interview. Here, applicants are asked to freely narrate their reasons for seeking protection and caseworkers are supposed to further enquire into the facts of the case and to give applicants the chance to clarify possible discrepancies or contradictions. Regarding the observed differences in interviewing techniques, our research has shown that there is a strong belief among German caseworkers that this is and should remain a matter of personality and individual style (Schneider and Wottrich 2017). Next to the ways in which questions are asked, the transformation of the spoken and translated word into the written protocol is a complex process with its own challenges and pitfalls (Dahlvik 2014b;

---

[7]Unlike in some other European countries, e.g., Sweden, free legal counsel is not provided for during first-instance procedures in Germany (Schneider and Wottrich 2017).

[8]For example, all caseworkers enquired about applicants' well-being, ensured them of confidentiality, explained the purpose of the interview and then asked a set of questions from a standardised questionnaire.

[9]These often contained formulaic questions required by law like 'What do you fear upon return to your home country?' and 'Were you able to communicate with the interpreter?' etc.

Scheffer 1998; see also the contributions in Part II of this volume). This is of particular relevance in the German case since interviews are not recorded. Again, caseworkers' routines were rather heterogeneous in this regard, with some working with a dictaphone only, others typing or taking handwritten notes, and yet others using voice recognition software. At the end of the substantive interview, applicants were asked whether they wished to have the protocol translated back to them. In most cases I observed they declined and left.[10] Presumably, this would have been different had they been accompanied by a legal representative.

After the interview, caseworkers need to use powers of practical judgement in order to assess and decide each case on an individual basis. In their decisions, they are asked to observe and apply legally binding rules and norms which, however, can in themselves be contradictory and in need of explication. A large share of the organisation's steering effort goes into the development of tools and aids that are meant to ensure a uniform application of the office's policy. At the same time, output-oriented practices of controlling and steering played an important role in life at the office during the time of fieldwork. Instruments such as 'MARiS', the agency's document- and workflow-management-system, and 'OrAs', an internal quota-system that specified productivity norms, introduced a logic of calculability and countability into the asylum decision-making process: via automatons, the completion of particular steps of the procedure was counted and entered the Board's statistics, which, on the one hand, were one of the most important means by which the organisation's performance was measured in terms of legitimacy and efficiency, and, on the other hand, also one of the prime instruments of control that the organisation exercised over its staff. The number of asylum interviews conducted and decisions written was important in the assessment of caseworkers' performance and could be consequential regarding promotions or their eventual appointment as tenured civil servants. What was counted and what was not affected the ways in which caseworkers perceived asylum applicants and their own work. Some interviewees talked about applicants only as workloads to be processed, and cases were described as difficult or easy depending on the anticipated time it was going to take to close the file (Schittenhelm 2015; Schittenhelm and Schneider 2017). Depending on organisational prioritisation and individual coping strategies, some cases were treated more quickly than others. Since

---

[10]Some caseworkers did, however, have the interpreter translate the protocol back block by block during the actual interview.

'MARiS' supports a kind of file-management that can render some cases very clearly visible and others nearly invisible (through various types of hold-files), it simultaneously enabled an emotional detachment from such differential treatment and from the fact that there were always more cases than one could possibly process. Taken together, the ways in which asylum casework was structured contributed to an administrative setting which was characterised by spatial, temporal and emotional distance between caseworkers and clients (for similar tendencies in the UK-context, see Gill 2016). As I will show below, the training was geared at counteracting the potential dangers resulting from this setting.

"Don't Turn Your Heart into a Den of Thieves and Murderers"

The vignettes presented in the following stem from field-notes taken during a five-day basic introductory course for asylum caseworkers. Of the ten participants, six were recently recruited staff with one to five months work experience whereas four had been ordered to re-enter the asylum unit in the context of rising application numbers after they had worked in other parts of the organisation for a number of years. Regarding gender, the group was split evenly. The units that are of particular interest here—interviewing and drafting-and-decision-making—were delivered jointly by headquarter staff responsible for quality assurance and experienced caseworkers from branch offices. Both units began with an input in the form of a lecture and then proceeded with a workshop unit during which trainees participated more actively and more practical issues were discussed.

Learning How to Interview

The first part of the session on interviewing techniques consisted of a lecture delivered jointly by BAMF staff and a representative from UNHCR. The overarching goal of asylum interviews was formulated as clarifying all questions relevant for decision-making in a fair and efficient manner. Particular ways of conducting interviews were discredited and trainers called on caseworkers to be empathetic, fair, loyal, sensitive, and open. To create a respectful interview atmosphere, they were advised to greet applicants in their own language, to enquire about their well-being, to offer water, to have tissues at their disposal etc. Ultimately, these recommendations aimed at transforming interviewing practices from 'police style' to 'dialogic communication' (Schneider and Wottrich 2017). They also indicated the desired emotional stance that caseworkers should take towards applicants, namely one of friendly neutrality. After the UNHCR representative had left, the workshop unit on interviewing techniques began. It started out with an input on credibility assessment by one of the trainers:

> A handout containing a list of 'reality criteria'[11] based on forensic psychology is distributed. Trainer B emphasises that this is a summary of the state of the art at the end of the 1990s when the office had commissioned a very expensive workshop by a highly acclaimed forensic psychologist for all decision-makers. He says he doesn't know whether much has changed in this regard since then. However, he says, the office now knows that a lack of reality criteria is not necessarily indicative of a lie. […] Trainer says it is a difficult topic. However, 'I still work like [professor X] told us'. He says he knows this is far from perfect but that he couldn't offer anything else at the moment. The office was going to update the material and introduce new methods for credibility assessment that he was curious to see but this was going to take another while. […] After having presented the different criteria in detail, the trainer recommends using the handout like a "blueprint" to lay over the written protocol of the asylum interview. He mentions non-verbal information gathered during the face-to-face-interaction and growing experience as a caseworker as additional helpful ingredients in determining credibility. His colleague quickly adds that non-verbal information and impressions should be noted in the written protocol so that third parties could relate to it, too.

The fact that the workshop unit on interviewing began with credibility assessment already shows how closely linked interviewing and decision-making are. While the input lecture centrally revolved around applicants' right to be heard and around caseworkers' duties regarding transparency and proper treatment of applicants what caseworkers apparently *really* need to learn is how to tell a truth from a lie. This is fundamental in maintaining the *illusio* that the asylum-bureaucratic game is worth playing. If everything were to be taken at face-value, there would be no need for a decision, no need for caseworkers, no need for an asylum authority at all. The vignette

---

[11]For example, logical consistency of statements, and unstructured and detailed narrations that include descriptions of interactions, one's own emotions, complications in the course of action etc.

above illustrates how concepts from the world of academia may be imported and used to endow administrative practices with an aura of authority, however outdated they might be. In the form of check-lists, they are turned into useful tools for handling the complexities of credibility assessments (for comparison, see Sorgoni, this volume).

After this opening, trainers asked participants to jot down any questions they might have concerning the asylum interview. Interestingly, the ensuing discussion quickly moved away from the question of credibility and truth and focused instead on issues of personal security, health and well-being. Caseworkers were concerned, e.g., about how to react when an applicant was infected with dysentery, critiqued the lack of security measures within the office, and one person made a sarcastic comment on how his main concern was that the bucket (to puke into) wasn't at hand in time. This initial discussion showed how caseworkers used the training above all as a space to voice concerns and to exchange personal experiences of their daily work with colleagues in a safe and closed environment. The frequent reference to the body, to issues associated with fear and/or disgust, were indicative of the emotional aspects of their daily work.[12] Trainers related to these concerns in an empathetic way but also emphasised that asylum interviews were no more dangerous than riding the tram and that all applicants underwent a prior health-check. Concerning security, they argued that the situation at BAMF was different from that at local foreigners' authorities (who are responsible for enforcing deportations) since caseworkers first of all had something to offer to applicants.[13] Differences in power and status, the division of labour and the various forms of organisational distancing described above were thus used to alleviate feelings of insecurity, threat and disgust.

Later on, the group returned to discuss questions of credibility assessment. Questions revolved around how to deal with doubts concerning the truthfulness of statements during the interview in general and around credibility assessments concerning religious conversion and sexual orientation in particular:

> One of the older participants asks how one could possibly get to the bottom of such things. He would consider this to be very very difficult considering that applicants could prepare in advance. Trainer A answers that such things should

---

[12]On the role of disgust in organisations, see Klatetzki (2016).
[13]Trainers contrasted this with the situation in Sweden where caseworkers had to personally communicate negative decisions to applicants.

always be considered in light of the country-specific guidelines. Questioner replies that these would not help him to know whether the applicant had really converted to Christianity. This was very difficult for him because these were things taking place inside the applicant.

Questions like these illustrate how caseworkers were thankful for expertise, tools and 'tricks of the trade' to help them cope with uncertainties. However, eventual hopes of receiving clear guidance were frequently frustrated:

> Trainer B goes on to say that, regarding homosexuality, sometimes there are very moving stories that need to be transported, too. 'There, I want to feel the vibrations' […]. After a discussion about the situation in a particular country of origin, the questioner again insists: There I have guidelines on how to decide. But my question was whether I believe him or not. Trainer A reacts, 'well, that's your job', 'that's why this is so highly qualified', 'that's something you have to bite yourself through', 'there are no hard and fast rules'. A participant sitting close to me whispers, 'Very helpful indeed'.

Against the backdrop of a huge apparatus of written rules, guidelines and databases, caseworkers were thus thrown back on their 'emotional intelligence' as human beings (see also Kobelinsky and Liodden, both this volume). Importantly, this concerned not only the type of emotional display that was required of caseworkers during the interaction with applicants which might be considered a form of emotional labour (Hochschild 2003). It also involved using their bodies' sensorimotor systems to decipher applicants' emotional displays, that is, as a kind of lie-detector. And furthermore, when all else failed, trainers appealed to caseworkers' pride and implicitly urged them to develop a habitus comparable to a judge[14]—a conception that is deeply entrenched in the organisational history of BAMF, where for a long time caseworkers used to act independently from directives, bound only by law and their 'intimate conviction' (see also Kobelinsky, this volume). The latter is a notion of central relevance in the German legal tradition and requires that decision-makers be inwardly convinced about the certainty and truthfulness of the information before them (on the difference between inquisitorial and adversarial asylum procedures, see Staffans 2008). Caseworkers were asked to enter into a kind of self-dialogue, to constantly monitor their own emotions and use them as guidance in situations of uncertainty. During the subsequent discussion of a protocol of an exemplary

---

[14]During the other training courses I observed, similar statements included "that's what you're here for, you just have to decide", "you are the decision-maker".

substantive interview, participants were asked to use the list of reality criteria to assess the credibility of the statements. Although the majority, including trainers, agreed that the overall story was coherent and plausible, two of the participants remained unconvinced:

> Trainer B recommends paying attention to the reality criteria in the course of the interview and states that apparently participants used different standards. He suggests taking the time to go over the protocol in an unburdened way, maybe using a highlighter, and to then see what outweighs. He says, 'at the end of the day, I can't write a rejection if I think he told me the truth', 'don't turn your heart into a den of thieves and murderers', 'don't act against your own conviction'.

Appeals like these may be considered as efforts to insert or reintroduce the sentient bureaucrat—conceived as a 'good' person—as a means to combat practices that are seen as being too entrenched in (individual or branch-specific) routines and as having, in a sense, become irrational.[15] The quote above gives us an idea of the direction this irrationality might take, namely that applications are rejected *in spite* of caseworkers' conviction of the truthfulness of the account. While remaining implicit, this points to the possibility that frontline-practices might become dominated by the 'wrong' emotions, either in the sense of moral indifference or even 'negative' emotions towards applicants. The list and the highlighter are turned into tools compensating for such an alleged lack of emotional reflexivity (Burkitt 2012).

Learning How to Write Decisions

The workshop unit on drafting decisions centrally revolved around the ways in which caseworkers should handle the written guidelines and templates for decision-making. During the training, trainers stressed how these functioned to safeguard transparency, efficiency, uniformity and lawfulness of decision-making practices. They also emphasised, however, that the flipside consists in the danger of not treating cases individually. A lot of effort was put into exposing and counteracting the dysfunctionalities of an excessive use of templates. The operative part of the decision was portrayed as the

---

[15] That is, they constitute efforts to maintain the status of asylum decision-making as a moral enterprise (Fassin and Kobelinsky 2012).

"core of the administrative act" and the statement of the facts of the case deemed a "high art". The written decision was likened to BAMF's "business card" and instructors urged caseworkers to keep in mind that they sign it with their own name and personally stand for it, that it was thus also their own personal business card. The metaphorical language used by the trainer vividly refers to the relations between the world of the administration and the 'outside world'. The decision is that which leaves the organisation, which is handed over to external actors and which may be used as an indicator of the office's performance. At the same time, it connects the work of caseworkers to that of other actors within the organisation and may also be used as an indicator of their own individual performance. As such, it is closely linked to the emotions of pride and shame. What constitutes a 'good decision' was then further specified by the trainer:

> The pre-formulated paragraphs for decisions are beneficial for not having to start from scratch each time anew. They are a blessing, in the sense of making life easier and to make you feel secure, but also a curse since they may seduce one into using them alone. It is important, however, that you get the transitions right and that you include very personal, individual things.

To write a decision 'properly' is thus a skilful and creative undertaking. However, the creativity demanded of caseworkers is restricted to particular elements of the decision and depends on the addressee. The *operative part* of the decision is always well structured, in the sense of it being based on standardised, pre-formulated paragraphs which are available in a variety of languages. This part of the decision is something that caseworkers are not supposed to change. Its main addressee is the applicant. The elaboration of the *grounds* for (negative) decisions, in contrast, is above all addressed at potential judicial review and not translated into the applicant's language. The relations between courts and administration are structured according to the necessity of making the work going into the administrative decision accountable. From the trainers' perspective, this requires an active transformation of the tools and aids provided by the organisation. It is caseworkers' responsibility to argue each individual decision and to use the available templates only if and where they fit the individual case. In this sense, the elaboration of the grounds of the decision is—or rather should be—an ill structured element of the decision (on the back-and-forth between ill and well structured, see Star 2010). When aids and tools are used without taking account of the individuality of each claim, the decision can lose its status. It becomes a defective decision that as such may be rendered useless or even prove detrimental to the organisation's reputation.

If, why, and how decisions should be argued was a subject of recurrent discussion during this training session. The relative autonomy of the organisation would be challenged if all the elements that enter into the decision-making process were to be made transparent. In particular, this concerns grounds for *positive* decisions. These go into an internal note but do not enter the written decision handed over to applicants. During the training, caseworkers' reasoning revolved around the danger of providing future applicants with a blueprint for their statements during the substantive interview if the office's policy regarding specific countries of origin or specific case constellations were to be made public. In this regard, writing decisions is always a work of immunisation, too.

What becomes obvious, then, is that next to its interpretative flexibility (a decision means something different to a caseworker, a quality supervisor, a head of a branch unit, a lawyer, an asylum applicant) the written decision constitutes a shared space between the asylum administrative authority and the wider social world and enables a kind of cooperation without consensus between a variety of different actors (Star 2010: 602). A lot of this cooperation rests on the invisible work done in caseworkers' offices (Star and Strauss 1999). While the organisational setting in which this work is done induces more standardisation, trainers are at pains to emphasise that particular elements of the decision *need* to be ill structured. The dilemma that characterises the decision-making process from the perspective of caseworkers can thus be formulated as a situation in which they are subject to major, even excessive, regulation through the organisation and the Ministry of the Interior, on the one hand, but are held personally accountable for the quality of decisions, on the other.

Conclusions and Outlook

Bureaucracy, in the Weberian ideal-typical characterisation, is geared to the efficient and effective implementation of rules. These rules should be applied in a rational, objective, fair, and impersonal manner. As a source of legitimacy, this model has come under increasing attack. In the literature, the general shift to procedural justice and proximity to citizens as new sources of legitimacy has been associated with more personal, even empathetic styles of executing bureaucratic tasks (Englert and Sondermann 2013). Within the German asylum administration, this shift takes on a particular twist. In the course of the training, the bifurcation of rational application of rules and more intuitive, emotionally based approaches to casework were both challenged and reinforced. An analysis of the processual character of casework is helpful in explaining this apparent paradox.

While the emotions that inform the process of decision-making do not appear on the surface of the written end-product, they are central at several moments of the procedure. As the vignettes illustrate, the face-to-face interaction between caseworkers and applicants may be infused with emotions like pity, fear, and disgust. Here, caseworkers are expected to engage in emotional labour by developing a neutral, yet empathetic stance towards applicants. Given working conditions on the ground, this is something that must be actively and consciously cultivated. Artefacts like the glass of water on the table may function as potential symbolic substitutes for such emotion work. In the discussions surrounding credibility assessments, in contrast, emotional appraisals were presented as being useful both as 'lie-detectors' and as 'moral compasses'. They are important in linking the situation of interviewing with writing the decision. Here, emotions are not so much something to be suppressed, controlled or managed but rather form part of more implicit ways of knowing-how, of intuiting situations and deciding which course of action to take. Trainers' rather awkward reactions to participants' questions illustrate the difficulties they are having in explicating this type of knowledge. Where they get the impression that emotional appraisals point participants into the 'wrong' direction, they refer caseworkers to tools like the list and the highlighter.

Finally, the workshop unit on writing decisions was infused with references to pride and shame, arguably the social emotion per se (Scheff 2000). In this context, remnants of the former autonomy of caseworkers formed an important point of reference for trainers' appeals to caseworkers' sense of responsibility. Symbolically, this found expression in the fact that it was still individual decision-makers who signed the decision with their own name. The subjectification of responsibility was legitimated and further reinforced by the organisational narrative of the decision-maker as a quasi-judge—i.e., a professional who is expected to act according to the letter of the law and according to her own work-ethos—but without the merits that used to go along with that: the power and autonomy to defend decisions departing from political or organisational expectations with reference to one's 'intimate conviction'. Given working conditions on the ground, appeals to caseworkers' pride and their capacities for empathy and emotional reflexivity are potentially offset by the fact that it is output rather than quality that is positively sanctioned. In this context, the various artefacts meant to decrease the complexities of work (the list, the guideline, the template) might not reduce but rather displace them (Star and Strauss 1999: 25)—to the detriment of both caseworkers and applicants.

Since casework revolves around the written decision as the one central object linking the world of the administration with the wider social world, the various ways in which emotions and materialities are linked during the different steps in the production of this object are deeply political. Amongst others, they influence which elements of the decision-making process are made transparent or rendered opaque and thus have consequences for the ways in which bureaucratic work is demarcated and shielded from external influences. In the current situation, the sovereign act of deciding on asylum cases is performed by a diverse group of actors with often limited and insecure employment contracts. Tasks and responsibilities have become more differentiated. Cases become categorised and streamlined before they even reach case officers' desks, and an even greater focus is put on numbers and outputs. Future research will have to enquire into possible implications of these changes for the realities of work and work cultures within BAMF. It seems fair to expect that any recognition of the individual case and/or the applicant will now require an even greater individual effort on the part of caseworkers. Being a decision-maker in Germany might be "a lonely business", as one interviewee put it, but this loneliness is populated by artefacts, symbols, and emotions indicative of conflictual social relations.

Acknowledgements I would like to thank the editors Nick Gill and Anthony Good for helpful comments and suggestions on an earlier version of this paper. Christian Lahusen also provided valuable feedback for which I am grateful.

References

Affolter, L. (2017). Asyl-Verwaltung kraft Wissen: Die Herstellung von Entscheidungswissen in einer Schweizer Asylbehörde. In C. Lahusen & S. Schneider (Eds.), *Asyl verwalten: Zur bürokratischen Bearbeitung eines gesellschaftlichen Problems* (pp. 145–171). Bielefeld: transcript.

Bohnsack, R. (2010). *Rekonstruktive Sozialforschung.* 8. Aufl. Stuttgart, [s.l.]: UTB GmbH: Barbara Budrich.

Bourdieu, P. (1989). Social Space and Symbolic Power. *Sociological Theory, 7*(1), 14–25.

Bourdieu, P. (1994). Rethinking the State: Genesis and Structure of the Bureaucratic Field. *Sociological Theory, 12*(1), 1–18.

Bourdieu, P. (1998). *Praktische Vernunft. Zur Theorie des Handels*. Frankfurt am Main: Suhrkamp.
Bourdieu, P., & Wacquant, L. J. D. (2013). *Reflexive Anthropologie*. Frankfurt am Main: Suhrkamp.
Bowker, G. C., & Star, S. L. (1999). *Sorting Things Out: Classification and Its Consequences*. Cambridge, MA and London: The MIT Press.
Bundesamt für Migration und Flüchtlinge. (2016). *Das Bundesamt in Zahlen 2015: Asyl, Migration und Integration*. Nuremberg.
Burkitt, I. (2012). Emotional Reflexivity. Feeling, Emotion and Imagination in Reflexive Dialogues. *Sociology, 46*, 458–472.
Clarke, A. E. (2003). Situational Analyses: Grounded Theory Mapping After the Postmodern Turn. *Symbolic Interaction, 26*(4), 553–576.
Clarke, A. E. (2012). *Situationsanalyse: Grounded theory nach dem Postmodern Turn* (Interdisziplinäre Diskursforschung). Wiesbaden: Springer VS.
Dahlvik, J. (2014a). *Administering Asylum Applications*. Dissertation, University of Wien.
Dahlvik, J. (2014b). Institutionelle Einsichten: Die Bedeutsamkeit von Schriftlichkeit und Dokumenten im Prozess der Bearbeitung von Asylanträgen. In J. Dahlvik, C. Reinprecht, & W. Sievers (Eds.), *Migration and Integration Research: Jahrbuch 2/2013* (pp. 301–317). Göttingen: V&R Unipress, Vienna University Press.
Deutscher Bundestag. (2014). *Antwort der Bundesregierung auf die Kleine Anfrage der Abgeordneten Ulla Jelpke, Jan Korte, Sevim Dağdelen, weiterer Abgeordneter und der Fraktion DIE LINKE. Ergänzende Informationen zur Asylstatistik für das Jahr 2013*. Drucksache 18/705.
Deutscher Bundestag. (2015). *Antwort der Bundesregierung auf die Kleine Anfrage der Abgeordneten Ulla Jelpke, Jan Korte, Sevim Dağdelen, weiterer Abgeordneter und der Fraktion DIE LINKE. Ergänzende Informationen zur Asylstatistik für das dritte Quartal 2015*. Drucksache 18/6860.
Deutscher Bundestag. (2016). *Antwort der Bundesregierung auf die Kleine Anfrage der Abgeordneten Luise Amtsberg, Volker Beck (Köln), Britta Haßelmann, weiterer Abgeordneter und der Fraktion BÜNDNIS 90/DIE GRÜNEN. Personalgewinnung beim Bundesamt für Migration und Flüchtlinge*. Drucksache 18/9895.
Englert, K., & Sondermann, A. (2013). "Ich versuch hier auch immer so dieses Amtliche irgendwie noch 'n bisschen zu überspielen." Emotions- und Gefühlsarbeit in der öffentlichen Verwaltung als Ausdruck von Staatlichkeit im Wandel. *Österreichische Zeitschrift für Soziologie, 38*(2), 131–147.
Fassin, D., & Kobelinsky, C. (2012). Comment on juge l'asile. *Revue française de sociologie, 53*(4), 657.
Gieryn, T. F. (1983). Boundary-Work and the Demarcation of Science from Non-Science: Strains and Interests in Professional Ideologies of Scientists. *American Sociological Review, 48*(6), 781–795.

Gill, N. (2016). *Nothing Personal? Geographies of Governing and Activism in the British Asylum System*. Oxford: Wiley-Blackwell.

Good, A. (2015). 'The Benefit of the Doubt' in British Asylum Claims and International Cricket. In D. Berti, A. Good, & G. Tarabout (Eds.), *Of Doubt and Proof: Ritual and Legal Practices of Judgment* (pp. 119–140). Farnham: Ashgate.

Hochschild, A. R. (2003). *The Managed Heart: Commercialization of Human Feeling* (20th anniversary ed.). Berkeley: University of California Press.

Jubany, O. (2011). Constructing Truths in a Culture of Disbelief: Understanding Asylum Screening from Within. *International Sociology, 26*(1), 74–94.

Klatetzki, T. (2016). Disgust and the Institutions of Cleanliness and Purity in Organizations. In E. Weik & P. Walgenbach (Eds.), *Institutions Inc* (pp. 30–62). London: Palgrave Macmillan.

Kreienbrink, A. (2013). 60 Jahre Bundesamt für Migration und Flüchtlinge im Kontext der deutschen Migrationspolitik. *Zeitschrift für Ausländerrecht und Ausländerpolitik, 33*(11–12), 397–448.

Mannheim, K. (2013 [1936]). *Ideology and Utopia: Collected Works of Karl Mannheim* (Vol. 1). Hoboken: Routledge.

Moore, S. F. (1972). Law and Social Change: The Semi-autonomous Social Field as an Appropriate Subject of Study. *Law and Society Review, 7*, 719–746.

Nohl, A. M. (2012). *Interview und dokumentarische Methode: Anleitungen für die Forschungspraxis* (4th ed.). Wiesbaden: VS Verlag für Sozialwissenschaften.

Probst, J. (2012). *Instruire la demande d'asile: Étude comparative du processus décisionnel au sein de l'administration allemande et française*. Dissertation, Université de Strasbourg and Philipps-University Marburg.

Scheff, T. J. (2000). Shame and the Social Bond: A Sociological Theory. *Sociological Theory, 18*, 84–99.

Scheffer, T. (1998). Übergänge von Wort und Schrift: zur Genese und Gestaltung von Anhörungsprotokollen im Asylverfahren. *Zeitschrift für Rechtssoziologie, 20*(2), 230–265.

Scheffer, T. (2001). *Asylgewährung. Eine ethnographische Verfahrensanalyse*. Stuttgart: Lucius and Lucius.

Schittenhelm, K. (2015). Asylsuchende im Blickfeld der Behörde. Explizites und implizites Wissen in der Herstellung von Asylbescheiden in Deutschland. *Soziale Probleme, 26*(2), 137–150.

Schittenhelm, K., & Schneider, S. (2017). Official Standards and Local Knowledge in Asylum Procedures: Decision-Making in Germany's Asylum System. *Journal of Ethnic and Migration Studies, 43*(10), 1696–1713.

Schmidt, R., & Volbers, J. (2011). Siting Praxeology. The Methodological Significance of "Public" in Theories of Social Practices. *Journal for the Theory of Social Behaviour, 41*(4), 419–440.

Schneider, S., & Wottrich, K. (2017). 'Ohne 'ne ordentliche Anhörung kann ich keine ordentliche Entscheidung machen…' – Zur Organisation von

Anhörungen in deutschen und schwedischen Asylbehörden. In C. Lahusen & S. Schneider (Eds.), *Asyl verwalten: Zur bürokratischen Bearbeitung eines gesellschaftlichen Problems* (pp. 81–115). Bielefeld: transcript.

Staffans, I. (2008). Evidentiary Standards of Inquisitorial Versus Adversarial Asylum Procedures in the Light of Harmonization. *European Public Law, 14*(4), 615–641.

Star, S. L. (2010). This is Not a Boundary Object: Reflections on the Origin of a Concept. *Science, Technology and Human Values, 35*(5), 601–617.

Star, S. L., & Griesemer, J. R. (1989). Institutional Ecology, 'Translations' and Boundary Objects: Amateurs and Professionals in Berkeley's Museum of Vertebrate Zoology, 1907–39. *Social Studies of Science, 19,* 387–420.

Star, S. L., & Strauss, A. (1999). Layers of Silence, Arenas of Voice: The Ecology of Visible and Invisible Work. *Computer Supported Cooperative Work, 8,* 9–30.

Thränhardt, D. (2014). Europäische Abschottung und deutscher Asylstau: Gibt es Wege aus dem Dilemma? *Zeitschrift für Ausländerrecht und Ausländerpolitik, 34*(5–6), 177–181.

Unabhängige Kommission 'Zuwanderung'. (2001). *Zuwanderung gestalten – Integration fördern: Bericht der Unabhängigen Kommission 'Zuwanderung'.*

Weber, R. (1998). *Extremtraumatisierte Flüchtlinge in Deutschland: Asylrecht und Asylverfahren.* Frankfurt and New York: Campus-Verlag.

Wettergren, Å., & Wikström, H. (2014). Who Is a Refugee? Political Subjectivity and the Categorisation of Somali Asylum Seekers in Sweden. *Journal of Ethnic and Migration Studies, 40*(4), 566–583.

Whyte, Z. (2015). In Doubt: Documents as Fetishes in the Danish Asylum System. In D. Berti, A. Good, & G. Tarabout (Eds.), *Of Doubt and Proof: Ritual and Legal Practices of Judgment.* Farnham: Ashgate.

Wikström, H., & Johansson, T. (2013). Credibility Assessments as 'Normative Leakage': Asylum Applications, Gender and Class. *Social Inclusion, 1*(2), 92–101.

Open Access This chapter is distributed under the terms of the Creative Commons Attribution 4.0 International License (http://creativecommons.org/licenses/by/4.0/), which permits use, duplication, adaptation, distribution and reproduction in any medium or format, as long as you give appropriate credit to the original author(s) and the source, a link is provided to the Creative Commons license and any changes made are indicated.

The images or other third party material in this chapter are included in the work's Creative Commons license, unless indicated otherwise in the credit line; if such material is not included in the work's Creative Commons license and the respective action is not permitted by statutory regulation, users will need to obtain permission from the license holder to duplicate, adapt or reproduce the material.

15

Conclusion

Nick Gill

The country coverage of this volume is by no means exhaustive. The ten European countries that form the basis of the ethnographic case studies reported are not intended to be representative of Europe in any statistical sense, especially considering the absence of former communist countries located in Eastern Europe. The selection reflects a number of factors, including the location of ethnographic projects that examine asylum determination and have been carried out in Europe, the editors' knowledge of these projects and abilities to attract responses to calls for chapter contributions to the volume, and the access to asylum determination systems that ethnographic work requires. Rather than positing that the volume explores the full extent of the variety of everyday practices that are bound up in asylum determination in Europe then, it is perhaps more accurate to claim that the book is suggestive of the extent of that variety.

One consequence of this is that the volume clearly highlights the importance of further research into the sorts of issues that have been raised. Hopefully therefore, the book will stimulate and encourage work that ethnographically explores further aspects of asylum determination, both thematically and in countries not discussed in this volume. Thematically, aspects of the determination process that deserve closer scrutiny include the exceptional 'fast track' processes that many European countries implement

N. Gill (✉)
University of Exeter, Exeter, UK
e-mail: n.m.gill@exeter.ac.uk

alongside their regular procedures; the differing interpretations—not only in legal doctrine but also on the ground—of key terms like 'vulnerability' that often serve to regulate entry to fast-track procedures; the means of progression of some cases to the higher courts as well as the role of strategic litigation in facilitating this progression; and the sociology and economy surrounding the generation of 'knowledge' about source countries, for example through country guidance information.

In terms of countries, certain states periodically distinguish themselves in the treatment of asylum seekers and refugees. Sweden, for example, accepted a very high number of Syrian refugees in 2015 and 2016 in relation to its population whilst Hungary and other Eastern European countries were far less accommodating. The Hungarian government's continuing aggressive stance towards NGOs that are deemed to be supporting migration make maintaining academic scrutiny of these issues paramount (EU Observer 2018). Moreover, Turkey has been deployed as part of Europe's remote control asylum strategy since 2015 via the EU-Turkey deal, raising grave concerns about human rights violations not only within Turkey but also on the Greek islands which have become places of routine detention and deportation (Amnesty International 2017). Given that the Turkey deal emerged at a time in which Europe as a whole was seen to be struggling to cope with the numbers of migrants arriving, this development reflects the central role of failure itself in the justification, production and development of systems of governance, including those of asylum (Foucault 1991; see also Vianelli 2018).

Further outside Europe, the volume begs the question of how to compare Europe's asylum determination processes with those in other developed countries, as well as in developing country contexts. Making comparisons with the ways refugee law is experienced and implemented in Australia, Canada, New Zealand and the US, for example, would allow a general picture to be formed of the degree to which international refugee law functions to practically protect, or exclude, refugee populations in developed countries. And given that the overwhelming majority of the world's population displaced by violent conflict are located in developing countries, further work and commentary that places the insights presented here in conversation with analyses of developing countries would be particularly welcome.

Notwithstanding the limitations of the sample of countries included in the volume, it makes two primary contributions. Firstly, it offers key insights into the messy, contingent, discretionary, unreliable, inconsistent and unjust processes through which legal doctrine is translated into bureaucratic practice in the context of large scale, international asylum decision making systems. And secondly, the volume illustrates the effectiveness of meticulous ethnographic research into asylum determination. In particular, it is the quality of the volume's ethnographic contributions that, I hope, will form the criteria upon which it is judged.

In his contribution to this volume, Robert Gibb (drawing on Willis and Trondman 2000), gives us a clear sense of what ethnography is. More than just another method, ethnography can involve multiple methodologies that facilitate a direct and sustained encounter with research subjects. Ethnography also involves a rich written account that represents more than just a report of findings. How, though, can we recognise excellent ethnography? Although 'it is impossible to fix a single standard for deciding the good and right purposes, forms, and practices of ethnography' (Bochner 2000: 268) scholars have provided us with some clues about how to sense and appreciate good ethnographic method in practice (see Muecke 1994). We might expect excellent ethnography to be about a 'worthy and interesting' topic, for example, to be 'sincere' and to bring to a chaotic or poorly understood arena new insights and 'meaningful coherence' (Tracy 2010). We want it to be 'evocative', 'engaging' and 'imaginative' (Crang and Cook 2007: 2005). It should also display 'abundant, concrete detail' (Bochner 2000: 270). We expect 'aesthetic merit', 'reflexivity' and even—ironically enough given the subject matter of many of the preceding chapters of this volume—'credibility' (Richardson 2000: 254). Perhaps most importantly though, we want a story (Bochner 2000). Something that moves us, affects us and calls us 'to action' (Richardson 2000: 254). For Bochner (2000: 271) this is something that hits 'my heart and belly as well as my head [...] that doesn't just refer to subjective life, but instead acts it out in ways that show me what life feels like now and what it can mean'.

The ethnographies in this volume describe and partake in perhaps the central drama of contemporary society: the struggle between globalisation and territorial control, flow and stasis (Bauman 1998). Often however, the way that refugees' role in this drama is discussed—in academic work, in newspapers and via social media—is either in dry and empty numerical terms or in ways that are trauma-heavy, pitying and condescending. Both these ways of talking about human displacement delete individual experience from the account: the quantitative fetish distils experience to numbers, targets and metrics which lend themselves to shrill and panicked talk of crises (Cohen 2002; see also Chapter 1, this volume); while the trauma fetish obscures the fact that displaced individuals are always more than refugees and have characters and life histories that precede and outlive displacement events. One of the primary achievements of the contributions in this volume, by contrast, is their poise: resisting the temptation to either simplify or sensationalise the stories they recount and the systems they describe.

The ethnographies in this volume are also distinctively *legal* ethnographies, although this does not mean that they are solely concerned with the law. As Laura Nader (2016: 191) asserts, legal anthropologists should not set out to study *only* the law, and indeed they would find it difficult to do so, since 'anthropologists are almost bound to be relationally orientated' (Good 2007: 30) which implies that the social, cultural and geographic context of the operation of the law is bound up in their approach to it. Rather, what is distinctive about a legal ethnography is its ability to cast legal concepts and processes in a new light, and in so doing challenge legal blindspots and habits of thought. '[A] legal anthropological perspective challenges conventional, doctrinal approaches to law that present it as a concept, universal across time and space … that represents a system of law that is coherent and uniform' (Benda-Beckmann et al. 2009: 3). Ethnography's innately 'anti-hegemonic' character (Blommaert 2009: 438) allows legal ethnography to be capable of detecting and representing the 'anarchic atmosphere' (Flood 2005: 34) of social systems by peering underneath the projected, but often synthetic, veneer of order that such systems, including legal ones, portray. These investigative abilities to discern the anarchism lurking beneath legal systems have fundamental implications for the law itself. It is the ethnographer's 'close attention to places, forms of life, conditions of speech and all those minor details', Latour (2010: 199) writes, that, 'little by little, by minor brushstrokes, allow one to redefine … [the] law.'

What this challenge to the projected universality, uniformity and coherence of the law produces is a heightened sensitivity to the contradictions and internal tensions within legal systems. This is more than simply a product of the 'emphasis on differences' (Bochner 2000: 268) that new ethnographies have adopted in response to the realism of traditional ethnographic approaches. It refers to 'basic differences between how lawyers and anthropologists think' (Good 2007: 29). Doctrinal legal scholars and legal practitioners tend to be much more concerned with attributing individual blame or responsibility than anthropologists and other social scientists, and consequently tend to assume that there is a single cause responsible for most observable phenomena, rather than multiple causes. They also tend to be more prescriptive while social scientists using ethnographic methods are more descriptive, albeit seeking to provide 'thick' descriptions (Geertz 1973). These differences can be associated with a penchant for deductive reasoning among lawyers and inductive reasoning among anthropologists (Conley and O'Barr 1998).

Perhaps the most fundamental distinction between the two, however, concerns their different imaginations of how the law relates to society, which 'divide fairly sharply into two distinct perspectives, the instrumental and the constitutive' (Sarat and Kearns 1993: 21). The instrumental view sees law as affecting society by 'imposing external sanctions and inducements' (ibid.: 21) while the constitutive view sees law as more active in terms of 'shaping internal meanings and creating new statuses' (ibid.: 21). What is at stake here is the separateness of the law from social processes. Not only, for Sarat and Kearns, are the law and social life mutually constitutive, but there is also an antagonism between them that the law, if taken at face value, effectively conceals. 'Law seeks to colonise everyday life and give it substance' they argue (Sarat and Kearns 1993: 7), drawing in part on Henri Lefebvre (1991), but 'law can never capture or organise everyday life… [l]aw does not descend on the everyday as an all-powerful outsider without encountering a lively resistance' (Sarat and Kearns 1993: 8).

Of all the social scientific methodologies, this couplet of antagonism and resistance has been made most visible through legal ethnography. This has, unsurprisingly, occasionally led to disagreement. At times for instance, the type of knowledge generated by ethnographers can prove incomprehensible, even irksome, to the doctrinal legal mind. Good (2007), for example, describes situations in which ethnographic evidence has been rejected by judges as 'not evidence of fact' (ibid.: 145), but more akin to 'commentary' (ibid.: 145), a frustration related to a commonly stated complaint about ethnography that 'we cannot learn anything beyond the details of the story told' (Flood 2005: 48). On the other hand, the juxtaposition of the different registers of legal and ethnographic perspectives, the latter affording a unique insight into the complex blend of co-constitution and antagonism between legal and social systems that doctrinal law tends to occlude, can also be highly productive. 'When our ways of looking are incommensurable' Bochner (2000: 266) writes, 'we can look in the same places, at the same things, and see them differently'. For Griffiths and Kandel (2009: 153) for instance, 'observations are important because they reveal […] multivocality'. What is most telling about their analysis is that the mutlivocality of social systems, including the voices of marginalised groups, is not easily accommodated by legal systems themselves. If legal systems cannot detect the voices of the marginalised independently then ethnography becomes a crucial means to improve access to justice. Additionally, the inductive approach that legal ethnography employs promises theoretical innovation. 'Ethnography is constant surprise' Flood writes (2005: 46) '[i]t gives rise to fresh theoretical insights as it evolves'.

It is in this spirit that, in closing, I identify two key antagonisms that the ethnographies contained within this volume have illuminated. They pertain to tensions not only within the legal systems of asylum determination that our contributors have studied, but across the socio-legal divide that these systems span. In each case, they give a flavour of the multiple contradictions between legal systems and everyday social life which are often influential, and sometimes decisively determinant, of both the experiences and outcomes of the law.

Fairness and Efficiency

The first antagonism concerns the tension between the administrative pressure to be efficient and the legal and moral pressure to be fair or just. Bureaucracies by their nature exert a certain amount of 'quantitative' pressure (Affolter et al., this volume) over decision making systems, and it is well known that tribunals, which occupy a contested position between formal law and administrative bureaucracy, often find themselves compromised, 'caught between administration and adjudication' (Hambly, this volume; see also Thomas 2011). Of particular concern is when national governments that have a degree of control over the workloads of those operating within the determination system, also have a vested interest in the outcomes reached - as is generally the case in administrative law. In the context of asylum determination, this has led to various concerns (Taylor 2007), including that the speeding through of decisions can introduce unacceptable levels of chance to the process, and privilege the state as a repeat player in the system (Burridge and Gill 2017).

The contributions in this volume reveal at least three further facets of this tension. The first is the complex emotionality that is bound up in it. Decision makers involved in asylum determination in Europe find themselves at the fulcrum of the passions and dramas of the global stage: not only are they required to determine the legal identities of the displaced (are they 'deserving' refugees or 'bogus' imposters?), but also, as a collective, and by degrees, they determine the very identity of Europe itself (is it welcoming? compassionate? coherent? chaotic?). As a result, the role of determining asylum claims is deeply contested in emotional terms. On the one hand, individual decision makers are subjected to an intricate form of emotional governance (Hunter 2015; Jupp et al. 2016) that seeks to induce from them '[t]he proper type of emotional involvement' (Schneider, this volume; see also Gill 2009). On the other hand, this governance is by no means failsafe: a range of influences vie for the 'allegiance' of decision makers—from the judgement of other professionals (will I be viewed as a 'softy'? Affolter et al., this volume) to the different office cultures that are often to be found in close proximity even within countries.

Second, the speed of processing decisions can warp the importance of certain events within the legal process. Under tight time constraints decision makers in many facets of social life, not just legal decision making, rely upon heuristics in the making of decisions (Thaler and Sunstein 2009; for a discussion in the legal field see Bone 2007). These are simple, efficient rules that help decision makers to reach a decision but that abstract markedly from the complexity of that decision by focusing on one aspect of it and giving less attention to other aspects. We know already that decision making on asylum applications rests too heavily on apparent inconsistencies in details of applicants' stories that are peripheral to the overall account (Herlihy and Turner 2006). But in the presence of acute time pressure, single misplaced words or phrases can exert an even more disproportionate influence if they activate the triggers that decision makers have chosen to employ in order to simplify their work. This effect is vividly illustrated in Sorgoni's account (this volume) of the 20-minute hearing at which the appellant lost their claim by uttering a few ill-chosen words at the end.

Third, the imperative for efficiency can result in a perception of 'intrusion' (Hambly, this volume) among decision makers: the administration's need for efficiency is seen to impinge upon decision makers' abilities to determine cases fairly and in good time. They may become resentful and defensive - 'we are not a statistically driven conveyor belt' one senior British judge has declared (Hambly, this volume; although see Burridge and Gill 2017). What results is a sort of insularity. Beset by the media, national governments and supra-national laws, a siege mentality can descend upon the offices and courts of asylum decision makers in practice (see also Campbell's discussion of government legal representatives in Britain - so-called HOPOs - this volume). Such sentiments can be especially keenly felt because there is often no verifiable evidence to help determine asylum claims, and individual decision-makers are only too aware of the gravity of making potentially life-threatening or life-saving decisions. What all this produces is the disproportionate importance of *the practice of co-workers and colleagues* in the determination of one's own approach to cases (Liodden, this volume). The combination of high levels of discretion, insularity, the gravity of cases, and a lack of verifiable evidence means that localised office and court cultures are particularly influential in asylum determination in Europe—arguably more so than in equivalent jurisdictions that are neither so emotionally and politically charged, legally plural or discretionary. To understand and to change asylum decision making in Europe then, an approach that takes seriously occupational cultures in the sites at which decisions are undertaken is vital.

Consistency and Variety

A second antagonism concerns the relationship between consistency and variety. In the context of asylum determination this antagonism usually surfaces in the form of discussion of inconsistent *decisions*. These are discernible in the variance of grant rates of asylum claims from ostensibly equivalent claimants. For example, claimants from the same country, making claims based on the fear of the same forms of persecution, have been shown to have highly divergent chances of success, according to which country their claim is heard in, which regions within countries their claim is considered at, which offices within regions consider their claim, and which particular judges within offices deal with their case (Gill and Good, this volume; see also Neumayer 2005; Rehaag 2012; Ramji-Nogales et al. 2009). What the contributions in this volume illustrate, however, is the importance of considering the breadth and variety of qualitative inconsistencies in processes alongside numeric differences in the rate of asylum claims granted.

Between states, although the Procedure Directive of the Common European Asylum System is an attempt to secure 'common' processes across Europe (Craig and Zwaan, this volume), the contributions in this volume demonstrate that there is still an extremely long way to go before we can talk about genuinely common procedures. Processual variety results from the overlapping legal regimes produced by international and national legal pluralism, the extensive discretion afforded to individual states with respect to the burden and standard of proof that they require, as well as the different legal traditions of European countries (ibid.). This can lead to considerable differences, such as allowing more appeals against negative decisions as a matter of course in some countries and not in others (see Sorgoni, this volume, for a discussion of Italy in this respect). Added to this, different states are also subject to different cultural influences, linguistic norms and media pressures, which can result in divergent interpretations of international law (Giannopoulou and Gill, this volume).

Within states, the contributions in this volume have revealed additional localised forms of inconsistency. Discrepancies in the linguistic registers of decision makers and applicants can be decisive in asylum claim determination, especially in the context of the linguistic complexities introduced when the internet is relied upon for information about origin countries (Spotti, this volume; see also Blommaert 2010). The places in which law is enacted can also make a considerable difference (Gibb, this volume). Alongside marked cultural differences between work teams in different courts and centres (Liodden, this volume) the micro-geographies of proximity between applicants and the other actors involved, lines of sight and the internal arrangements of corridors, rooms and buildings can all exert an influence over the communicative practices that take place (Gibb, this volume, see also Rock 1993; Mulcahy 2007). Added to this, the characters of individual actors within the system can play a pivotal role in legal systems. Judges sometimes diverge from conventions, as illustrated by Campbell's example (this volume) of the judge who decided to ask an extraordinary amount of questions and then deliver their judgement at the end of the hearing rather than the usual method of sending the decision by post. More fundamentally, so imbricated are legal processes by the 'conviction' of the judge that it has proven impossible to separate them in law, creating what Kobelinsky (this volume) calls a suspicion economy according to which cases that are not apparently legally watertight can be ushered through on the basis of shared liberal notions of compassion, whilst others attract scepticism on spurious grounds, like not 'look[ing] gay at all'. Caseworkers can also differ markedly in their approaches to their work, often depending upon whether or not they have a legal background (Affolter et al., this volume). Even those without a decision-making role can affect the visibility and transparency of the determination process as Sorgoni's example (this volume) of the archivist who tightly controls access to the records of Italian appeal procedures illustrates.

In short, the asylum determination system is riddled with a raft of different forms of qualitative inconsistency that the usual focus on consistency of outcomes misses, but that an ethnographic approach is well suited to reveal (see Gill et al. 2018). One of the consequences of the existence of this level and diversity of inconsistency is the development of double standards in the determination of asylum claims. As Craig and Zwaan remind us (this volume) asylum seekers are expected to show 'effort' and 'coherence' during the claim making process. When they fail to do so to the satisfaction of the authorities, as both Sorgoni and Danstrøm & Whyte demonstrate in their contributions, the result can be a rejected asylum claim. Ironically however, the asylum system itself would not satisfy its own criteria, since it embodies multiple forms of incoherence as well as a lack of timeliness in several respects.

Given the Herculean task of generating a genuinely common European asylum system in practice, one must ask what function the law serves in this area. While the law is conventionally viewed as regulatory in a practical sense, the stubborn resistance and infinite variety of the everyday contexts in which the laws relating to asylum determination in Europe are applied makes it difficult to accept that they achieve this objective in practice. Rather, it may be better to view the law in this area as essentially a statement of intent. If this view is adopted, then various alternative interpretations of the function of the law come into view. Optimistically, this statement of intent can be viewed as aspirational—an ideal that Europe is striving towards and that, by degrees, it is gradually realising, even if progress is slow and geographically highly uneven. Pessimistically however, the existence of a statement of intent that diverges dramatically from reality runs the risk of obscuring important features of the law as it is practised and of therefore appearing hypocritical. This divergence is especially costly when attempting to build trust with displaced people who are often vulnerable and traumatised. Once the system of determination becomes distrusted by its subjects, the very conditions of possibility for its effective and fair operation are undermined, as asylum seekers withhold and distort their own stories as a result (Danstrøm and Whyte this volume, Giannopoulou and Gill, this volume). According to this view, the notion of a common European asylum system is not only at odds with what the contributors to this volume have discovered, but could also act to exacerbate the practical difficulties of asylum determination in Europe.

Needless to say, regardless of which of these two views is taken, finding ways to close the gap between the formal body of doctrinal law that is embodied in such systems as the Common European Asylum System and the everyday reality of asylum determination in practice will be paramount in the years to come. If the ethnographies contained in this volume can help to achieve this, they will be excellent indeed.

References

Amnesty International. (2017). Greece: A Blueprint for Despair. Human Rights Impact of the EU-Turkey deal. Available at: https://www.amnesty.org/en/documents/eur25/5664/2017/en/. Accessed 5 Mar 2018.

Bauman, Z. (1998). *Globalization: The Human Consequences*. New York: Columbia University Press.

Benda-Beckmann, F. von, Benda-Beckmann, K. von, & Griffiths, A. (2009). Introduction: The Power of Law. In F. von Benda-Beckmann, K. von Benda-Beckmann, & A. Griffiths (Eds.). *The Power of Law in a Transnational World: Anthropological Enquiries*. New York: Berghahn Books.

Blommaert, J. (2009). Language. *Asylum and the National Order Current Anthropology, 50*(4), 415–441.

Blommaert, J. (2010). *The Sociolinguistics of Globalization*. Cambridge: Cambridge University Press.

Bochner, A. P. (2000). *Criteria Against Ourselves. Qualitative Inquiry, 6*(2), 266–272.

Bone, R. (2007). Who Decides? A Critical Look at Procedural Discretion. *Cardozo Law Review, 28,* 1061–2007.

Burridge, A., & Gill, N. (2017). Conveyor-Belt Justice: Precarity, Access to Justice, and Uneven Geographies of Legal Aid in UK Asylum Appeals. *Antipode, 49*(1), 23–42.

Crang, M., & Cook, I. (2007). *Doing Ethnographies.* London: Sage.

Cohen, S. (2002). *Folk Devils and Moral Panics: The Creation of the Mods and Rockers* (3rd ed.). London and New York: Routledge.

Conley, J. M., & O'Barr, W. M. (1998). *Just Words: Law, Language and Power.* Chicago: Chicago University Press.

EU Observer. (2018). Hungary Plans to Paralyse NGOs Dealing with Migration. https://euobserver.com/beyond-brussels/140990. Accessed 5 Mar 2018.

Flood, J. (2005). Socio-legal Ethnography. In R. Banakar & M. Travers (Eds.), *Theory and Method in Socio-Legal Research* (pp. 33–48). Portland, OR: Hart.

Foucault, M. (1991). *Discipline and Punish: The Birth of the Prison.* London: Penguin (Original work published 1975).

Geertz, C. (1973). *The Interpretation of Cultures.* New York: Basic Books.

Gill, N. (2009). Presentational State Power: Temporal and Spatial Influences Over Asylum Sector Decision Makers. *Transactions of the Institute of British Geographers, 34*(2), 215–233.

Gill, N., Rotter, R., Burridge, A., & Allsopp, J. (2018). The Limits of Procedural Discretion: Unequal Treatment and Vulnerability in Britain's Asylum Appeals. *Social & Legal Studies, 27*(1), 49–78.

Good, A. (2007). *Anthropology and Expertise in the Asylum Courts.* London: Routledge.

Griffiths, A., & Kandel, R. (2009). The Myth of the Transparent Table: Reconstructing Space and Legal Interventions in Scottish Children's Hearings. In F. von Benda-Beckmann, K. von Benda-Beckmann, & A. Griffiths (Eds.), *Spatializing Law: An Anthropological Geography of Law in Society* (pp. 157–176). Farnham, Surrey: Ashgate.

Herlihy, J., & Turner, S. (2006). Should Discrepant Accounts Given by Asylum Seekers Be Taken as Proof of Deceit? *Torture, 16*(2), 81–92.

Hunter, S. (2015). *Power, Politics and the Emotions: Impossible Governance?* Oxford: Routledge.

Jupp, E., Pykett, J., & Smith, F. M. (Eds.). (2016). *Emotional States: Sites and Spaces of Affective Governance.* London: Taylor and Francis.

Latour, B. (2010). *The Making of Law: An Ethnography of the Conseil d'État.* Cambridge: Polity.

Lefebvre, H. (1991). *Critique of Everyday Life (Volume II): Foundations for a Sociology of the Everyday* (J. Moore, Trans.). London: Verso.

Muecke, M. A. (1994). On the Evaluation of Ethnographies. In J. Morse (Ed.), *Critical Issues in Qualitative Research Methods* (pp. 187–209). London: Sage.

Mulcahy, L. (2007). Architects of Justice: The Politics of Courtroom Design. *Social and Legal Studies, 16*(3), 383–403.

Nader, L. (2016). Moving On—Comprehending Anthropologies of Law. In J. Starr & M. Goodale (Eds.), *Practicing Ethnography in Law: New Dialogues, Enduring Methods* (pp. 190–201). Springer.

Neumayer, E. (2005). Bogus Refugees? The Determinants of Asylum Migration to Western Europe. *International Studies Quarterly, 49*(3), 389–409.

Ramji-Nogales, J., Schoenholtz, A., & Schrag, P. (2009). *Refugee Roulette: Disparities in Asylum Adjudication and Proposals for Reform*. New York and London: New York University Press.

Rehaag, S. (2012). Judicial Review of Refugee Determinations: The Luck of the Draw? *Queen's Law Journal, 38*(1), 1–58.

Richardson, L. (2000). Evaluating Ethnography. *Qualitative Inquiry, 6*(2), 253–255.

Rock, P. (1993). *The Social World of an English Crown Court: Witnesses and Professionals in the Crown Court Centre at Wood Green*. Oxford: Claredon Press.

Sarat, A., & Kearns, T. R. (Eds.). (1993). *Law in Everyday Life*. University of Michigan Press.

Taylor, M. (2007). Refugee Roulette in an Administrative Law Context: The de´ja` vu of Decisional Disparities in Agency Adjudication. *Stanford Law Review, 60*(2), 475–501.

Thaler, R., & Sunstein, C. (2009). *Nudge: Improving Decisions About Health, Wealth and Happiness*. London: Penguin.

Thomas, R. (2011). *Administrative Justice and Asylum Appeals: A Study of Tribunal Adjudication*. Oxford and Portland, Oregon: Hart Publishing.

Tracy, S. J. (2010). Qualitative Quality: Eight "big-tent" Criteria for Excellent Qualitative Research. *Qualitative Inquiry, 16*(10), 837–851.

Vianelli, L. (2018). Governing Asylum Seekers: Logistics, Differentiation, and Failure in the European Union's Reception Regime. Ph.D. Thesis, University of Warwick.

Willis, P., & Trondman, M. (2000). Manifesto for Ethnography. *Ethnography, 1*(1), 5–16.

Open Access This chapter is distributed under the terms of the Creative Commons Attribution 4.0 International License (http://creativecommons.org/licenses/by/4.0/), which permits use, duplication, adaptation, distribution and reproduction in any medium or format, as long as you give appropriate credit to the original author(s) and the source, a link is provided to the Creative Commons license and any changes made are indicated.

The images or other third party material in this chapter are included in the work's Creative Commons license, unless indicated otherwise in the credit line; if such material is not included in the work's Creative Commons license and the respective action is not permitted by statutory regulation, users will need to obtain permission from the license holder to duplicate, adapt or reproduce the material.

Index

A

Accuracy. *See* asylum decision-making processes, accuracy of
actors, in asylum process 15, 18–19, 21, 28, 34–37, 46, 53–129, 134n, 136, 143, 150, 169, 176–178, 183, 195–196, 198, 200, 202, 204, 207–210, 214, 223, 266, 285, 287, 299–300, 302, 315. *See also* agency
adjudication 43, 53–56, 58, 60, 61, 64–66, 74, 176, 180, 183, 188–190, 195, 196, 198, 199, 202, 205, 208, 214, 312
Administrative Court (Germany) 291
administrative justice. *See* justice
administrative procedures. *See* asylum decision-making processes
admissibility 73, 114, 160, 291
admissibility interviews. *See* interviews
adversarial system, *See* asylum appeals, adversarial
advocates, asylum 19, 95, 96, 100n, 101, 102, 159, 161, 162, 171, 196, 198, 199, 200, 201, 202, 203, 204–214

Affolter, L. xi, 21, 28, 42, 263–283, 286, 302, 312, 313, 315
Afghanistan 12, 36, 43n, 75, 76, 118, 119, 123, 125, 183, 187, 190
agency 19, 20, 111, 117, 149, 187. *See also* actors, in asylum process
Amnesty International 121, 127, 195, 215, 235n, 237, 308, 316
Anderson, B. 23, 86, 88
APPAs (Switzerland) 269, 270
appellants 44, 96, 98–102, 104–107, 161, 162, 171, 197–199, 206, 214, 223–227, 230, 232, 233, 236, 313
appeals. *See* asylum appeals
Asilo in Europa (Italy) 226n, 227, 230, 232, 235n, 237
assesseur de l'Administration (France) 59, 63, 161–162
assesseur HCR (France) 59, 63, 161–162, 168
Asyl- und Wegweisungspraxis. See APPAs
asylum
positive valuation of 5, 64–66
schizophrenic response towards 2

320   Index

asylum appeals 8, 9–10, 13, 14, 19, 29, 33, 35, 44–45, 314. *See also* appellants; asylum decision-making processes; Common European Asylum System
  adversarial 92, 107, 204, 210, 297
  first instance 9, 11, 91, 98–100, 223
  inquisitorial 297
  non-suspensive 44, 137, 181, 233
  second instance 91, 100–105
  suspensive 12, 33, 44
Asylum and Immigration Tribunal (AIT) (UK). *See* tribunals
asylum applicants. *See* asylum seekers
asylum applications 2, 6, 8–14, 18–21, 32–35, 38, 40–43, 55, 62, 72–75, 113, 114, 136, 159, 179, 181, 197, 267, 270, 278, 288, 294
  numbers of xvii, 2, 7–11, 160, 228, 289
  sur place 98, 100, 104
asylum courts. *See Cour nationale du droit d'asile*; tribunals
asylum crisis. *See* crisis, asylum as
asylum decision-makers 10, 11, 15, 19, 21, 28, 34–37, 41, 105, 107, 134–136, 161, 166, 172, 180, 201, 230, 231, 242–249, 250–253, 255–259, 263, 265–268, 277, 286, 315. *See also* discretion; Home Office Presenting Officers; Immigration Judges; judges
  Austria 137–141
  cynicism of 281
  Denmark 176, 178–181, 183, 186, 188
  difficulties and dilemmas faced by 19, 21, 41, 43, 53, 242, 243, 263, 264, 270, 272, 274, 286, 300
  expertise of 276, 277, 297
  France 159–172
  Germany 285–302
  Norway 241–243, 245–258
  productivity of 21, 57, 73, 94, 96, 162, 250, 252, 266, 271, 279, 293
  security of. *See* security
  subjectivity of 234, 259, 272, 274, 280, 301, 312. *See also* disbelief; *intime conviction*; volitional allegiance
  Switzerland 263–283
  training of. *See* training
  UK 93n, 97
  use of discretion. *See* discretion
  well-being of 296
asylum decision-making processes 3, 6, 8, 9, 12–14, 17, 18, 25, 20, 21, 28, 29, 33–35, 37–39, 40, 41, 43, 44, 60, 61, 66, 72, 113, 133, 134, 196, 197, 218–305, 308, 312, 314. *See also* asylum appeals; *Asylum Procedures Directive*; Common European Asylum System; fast-track procedures
  accuracy of 57, 80, 163, 200, 225, 244, 245, 247, 250, 252, 255–257, 259
  Austria 133–138, 141–144, 146, 149–51
  Belgium 69–71, 73–78, 87, 88
  credibility assessment in. *See* credibility
  Denmark 21, 28, 175–183, 185–191
  discretion in. *See* discretion
  efficiency of 4, 6, 28, 29, 33, 96, 97, 113, 202, 209, 214, 244, 245, 249, 251, 252, 270, 271, 279, 286, 293, 294, 298, 300, 312–314
  flaws in 32
  France 25, 53–66, 155–174, 234n

Germany 21, 285–305
Greece 113, 114, 119, 121, 126, 235
interpreter's role in 13, 20, 37, 106, 110, 133–154, 160–162, 164–166, 167, 168, 169, 171, 181, 183, 186, 188, 224, 235, 291, 292, 293n
Italy 21, 221–235, 313, 315
Norway 21, 28, 241–62
outcomes of xvii, 8, 10, 36, 44, 56, 96–97, 104, 114, 179, 199–201, 214, 227, 229, 230, 253. *See also* asylum decisions
role of staff interaction in 156, 169, 170, 172, 246, 250, 274, 313
routinisation in 62, 249
social and legal context of 107, 196, 203. *See also* context
Switzerland vii, 28, 263–283
transparency of. *See* transparency
UK 21, 28, 35, 91–98, 100–102, 106, 107, 156, 195–217, 221, 234n
first tier 91, 98–100
second tier 91, 100–105
variations in xvii, 12–14, 18, 28, 203–205, 245, 246
asylum decisions 6, 9, 10, 11
appeals against. *See* asylum decisions, reconsideration of
consistency of 59, 245, 249–250, 290, 313, 314
correctness of 65, 150, 245–247, 250–252, 264, 266, 268, 271, 276–279. *See also* asylum decision–making processes, accuracy of
disparities in 59, 198, 274–278, 280–281
drafting of 57, 63, 75, 94n, 104, 293, 294, 298–300

fairness of 40, 96, 97, 235, 244, 264, 266, 272, 274, 276, 277
final 8, 9, 11, 73, 291
first instance 8–14, 18, 36, 59–60, 73, 96–100, 137, 159, 161, 162, 198, 222, 226n, 292n
first and second order 254
as 'good enough' 251
justness of 21, 241, 244–247, 255, 264–268, 273–278, 280
legitimation of 55, 273
negative 35, 44, 114, 158, 198, 221, 225, 229, 256, 258, 269, 272, 290, 296n, 299, 314
objectivity of 35, 59
positive xvii, 8, 9, 10–12, 56, 179, 185, 197, 269, 272, 280, 290n, 300
quality of 101, 106, 107, 236, 241, 251, 270, 271, 299, 300
reasons for 34, 35, 182, 227, 230, 247
reconsideration of 92n, 95, 97, 100–105, 137, 161, 162, 180, 198, 222, 223
timeliness of 10, 73, 185, 244, 250, 251
volume of 9–11, 12n, 114, 227
asylum determinations. *See* asylum decisions
asylum discourse. *See* discourse
asylum hearings. *See* asylum decision-making processes
asylum interviews. *See* interviews
asylum motive 175–178, 181–185, 187–191. *See also* narrative, asylum
asylum policies 1, 4, 6, 7n, 56, 61, 70, 114, 116, 201, 203, 210, 227, 229, 230, 236, 246, 247, 255, 258, 270, 293, 300. *See also* immigration policies

Index

Asylum Policy Instructions (APIs) (UK) 93, 94
asylum procedures. *See* asylum decision-making processes
asylum seekers 'bogus' 2, 55, 124, 203, 241, 273, 312. *See also* migrants, economic; refugees 'genuine'
Austria 12, 20, 133–154
authorities, state 12–14, 28, 34–35, 37–38, 44–45, 69–75, 77, 79–80, 84–87, 136–138, 159, 179, 185–187, 225, 229, 241, 257, 286–290, 296, 300, 315
authority, legal 16, 45, 202, 247
avocats (France). *See* advocates, asylum

B

Baillot, H. 195, 215, 252, 259
BAMF. *See* Federal Office for Migration and Refugees (Germany)
Bangladesh 76, 124n, 278
barristers (UK). *See* advocates, asylum
Bauman, Z. 1, 22, 256, 259, 309, 316
Belgium 12n, 32n, 36n, 38n, 69–89
von Benda-Beckmann, F. 16, 22, 310, 316, 317
benefit of the doubt 41, 42, 243, 274n
benefit fraud 2, 125, 203
Bigo, D. 5, 22, 70, 88
Blommaert, J. 20, 22, 72, 74, 75, 85, 88, 89, 157, 158, 170, 173, 178, 181, 192, 234n, 237, 310, 314, 317
Bohmer, C. 55, 67, 72, 86, 88, 175, 177, 192
border control. *See* immigration control
Boswell, C. 6, 22, 242, 260
boundary work 134, 285, 287
Bourdieu, P. 60, 67, 134, 196, 213, 215–217, 286, 287, 302, 303
Brexit 18, 23, 31
Bulgaria 12, 12n

burden of proof. *See* proof
bureaucracy 18, 36–37, 43, 56, 64, 71, 87, 122, 177–178, 183, 185, 202, 214, 242, 244, 249, 256–257, 286, 290, 295, 298, 300, 302, 308, 312
emotional 62
ethos of 247
street level 258, 264, 279
bureaucrats 3, 5, 15, 21, 59
Burridge, A. 97, 108, 128, 152, 198, 215, 216, 312, 313, 317

C

Cabot, H. 222, 226n, 234n, 237
camp 7, 20, 109n, 111, 118, 119, 121–124, 176–179, 184–188, 190, 191
Campbell, J.R. xi, 19, 44, 91–108, 198, 208, 209, 234n, 238, 313, 315
caseworkers. *See* asylum decision-makers; training
Centre for Identification and Expulsion (CIE) (Italy) 227, 233
Cherubini, F. 15, 23, 232, 238
childhood 111, 116–118, 120–123, 126
children 14, 30, 85. *See also* dependency discourse
asylum seeking 14, 18, 20, 32, 35–37, 111, 116–126, 142, 147, 246, 256, 258
best interests of 35
detention of 109, 110
protection of 119, 121, 122
rights of 35, 117, 126
unaccompanied minors 14, 33–35, 37n, 76, 78, 109–129
civil tribunal (Italy). *See* tribunals
civil law systems 38, 222

civil servants 57, 92, 113, 197, 198, 209, 235, 293
civil war 7, 118, 236
Code of Criminal Procedure (France) 53, 54
Coffey, G. 222n, 238, 254, 260
Cohen, S. 1, 2, 23, 309, 317
coherence. *See* narrative, asylum
Commissariaat General voor de Vluchtelingen en de Staatslozen (CGVS) (Belgium) 73, 77–82, 84, 86
Common European Asylum System (CEAS) 14, 16, 18, 27–33, 35, 36, 45, 222, 230–232, 314, 315
  opt-outs from 28, 31
common law 15, 54
communication 20, 21, 36–38, 79, 133–217
  breakdown of 74, 140, 148–149, 166–167
  electronically mediated 72, 74, 164–166
  intercultural 36, 74, 243, 289
  interpreter's role in 110, 133, 137, 140, 144, 145, 149–151. *See also* interpreters; interpretation
  management of 136, 143, 145, 150
  spatial aspects of 156, 168–171
communicative practices 156–159, 166, 167, 170, 172, 315
communities of interpretation 265, 266, 269, 276–281
communities of practice. *See* practice(s), communities of
compassion 63, 121, 264, 265, 272, 273, 276, 312, 315
'complaint'. *See* asylum appeals, Austria
Conley, J.M. 195, 215, 310, 317
conseils (France). *See* advocates, asylum
Conseil d'Etat (France) 59
Consistency. *See also* inconsistency; narrative, asylum
  in asylum decision-making 14, 209, 245, 250, 315
constructivism 6, 55, 85, 122, 196, 201
context
  administrative and bureaucratic 36, 134, 147, 151, 201, 244, 246, 251, 258, 308
  communicative 37, 156, 158, 159, 166
  humanitarian 116–118, 134, 136
  of interaction 156–159, 163, 166, 167, 169, 171, 172
  legal 94, 107, 133, 134, 178–181, 232, 235, 242n
  narrative 176–179, 183–184, 190–191
  political 5, 9, 31, 66
  socio-cultural 16, 20, 111, 117, 187, 196, 202, 213, 310
'context-free' 222
contextual disambiguation 231
contextualisation 21, 172
Convention reasons 11, 30, 101, 200, 214
conseil (advocate) (France) 161
Conseil d'État (France) 59, 222, 226n, 310
corridors, interactions in 156, 158, 159, 163, 169–171, 172, 207, 208, 315
corroboration 41, 72, 81, 186, 243, 253
country of origin information (COI) 98, 113, 232, 311
  COIS reports 98, 231
Cour nationale du droit d'asile (CNDA) (France) 53–68, 159–163, 167–169, 170, 171, 173, 174
Court of Appeal (Italy) 221, 226, 229
Court of Appeal (UK) 98n, 105, 198
Court of Justice of the European Union (CJEU) 29, 31–32, 36n, 42–43, 45, 49
Court of Session (Scotland) 198

324 Index

Cowan, D. 46, 195, 196, 217
Cowan, S. 195, 215, 252, 259
Craig, S. xi, 18, 27–49, 61, 71, 113, 230, 314, 315
credibility. *See also* narrative, asylum
  assessment of 19–21, 42–44, 65–66, 103–106, 147, 149, 160n, 175–177, 181–183, 189, 191, 195, 200, 221–240, 243, 245, 249, 250, 253–254, 256, 259, 270–271, 273, 278, 290, 295–296, 298, 301
  internal 175, 182, 231. *See also* consistency
  external 231, 243. *See also* country of origin information
  general 40n, 41, 230
Crépeau, F. 259–261
crisis, asylum as 2–5, 7–14, 115, 223, 229, 235–236
Croatia 12n
cross-examination 93, 99, 102, 206, 211, 212
Crown Court (England) 156, 172, 200
cultural sensitivity 14, 276
culture 5, 19, 37, 76, 142, 189, 225, 234, 236, 243, 278, 289. *See also* communication, intercultural; context, sociocultural; disbelief, culture of; intercultural encounters
  administrative and legal 11, 204, 209, 248, 249, 302, 310, 313–315
'culture of disbelief'. *See* disbelief
Cyprus 12n

D

Dahlvik, J. xii, 20, 134–154, 166, 181, 183, 186, 247, 252, 260, 286, 292, 303
Daniel, E.V. 55, 67, 177, 192

Danish Immigration Service (DIS) (Denmark) 179–184, 188
Danish Refugee Council (DRC) (Denmark) 179, 180
Danstrøm, M.S. xii, 20, 69, 175–193, 234, 315, 316
De Genova, N. 223, 236, 238, 240
Democratic Republic of Congo (DRC) 58, 62, 66, 76
Denmark 20, 175–193
  opt-outs by 28, 31, 32n
dependency discourse. *See* discourse
deportation 3, 6, 9, 12–13, 93, 96, 101, 105, 113, 124n, 137, 255n, 258, 288, 296, 308
  appeals against 12n, 36, 101, 137, 203, 233
detachment 43, 58, 291–294. *See also* distance
detention 30, 93, 107, 109, 113, 114n, 137, 227, 258, 308. *See also* children, detention of
  centres 16, 124–125, 166. *See also* waiting zone
determinations. *See* asylum decisions
D'Halluin(-Mabillot), E. 55, 67, 155, 174, 281, 282
Directorate of Immigration (UDI) (Norway) 241, 242, 248, 250–254
disbelief 55, 182, 256
  culture of 42, 203, 286
discourse 64–66, 72, 75
  asylum 3, 19, 110–111, 115–117, 125–126, 271
  dependency 122, 123
  circulation 181
discrepancies. *See* narrative, asylum
discretion, legal 15, 39, 195, 242–244, 248, 250, 256, 308, 313, 314
  absence of 94, 97, 211
  use by asylum decision-makers 15, 138, 195, 242–244, 247, 248, 254, 256, 258

use by judges 21, 99
distance
  emotional 291, 294
  intellectual 58, 116, 267, 276, 277, 291
  spatial 116, 184, 291, 294
distrust 4, 55, 117, 121, 123, 126, 177, 182, 185, 190, 257, 316. *See also* trust
divergencies. *See* narrative, asylum
documents 32, 40, 77, 187, 226n, 235, 287. *See also* evidence; texts
Doornbos, N. 36, 46, 265, 282
Doubt 44, 54, 58, 80, 84, 104, 224, 252, 259, 263, 296. *See also* benefit of the doubt; uncertainty
Dublin régime. *See Dublin II Regulation*; *Dublin III Regulation*; trust
duty, professional 15, 43, 65, 209, 210, 225n

E

Eastmond, M. 117, 128, 175, 177, 189, 192
economic migration. *See* migration
efficiency. *See* asylum decision-making processes
emotion
  display of 19, 125, 188, 297
  role of, in asylum decision-making 55–56, 58, 62–64, 66, 177, 246–247, 258, 272, 285–287, 291, 294–299, 301, 302, 312, 313
empathy 58, 63, 301
ENA (North African Emergency) (Italy) 227–230, 236
entextualisation. *See* texts
Eritrea 95, 98, 99, 101–105, 179, 288n
ethics
  deontological 234n
  professional 20, 134–136, 143, 144, 150, 151, 275
ethnicity 30, 70, 76, 78, 92, 116, 185, 242
ethnographic methods 15, 16, 18–22, 55, 69, 71, 73, 75–76, 111, 119, 155–157, 159, 167, 172, 176, 178, 179, 223, 267, 307, 310, 311
  compared to legal approaches 15–18, 310, 311
  value of 15, 155, 156, 168–171, 309, 311, 315, 316
ethnography 15, 16, 124, 135, 149, 156, 157, 200, 268, 307–318
European Asylum Support Office (EASO) 28, 114, 235n
European Court of Human Rights (ECtHR) 29–32, 36, 38, 43–45, 49
European Union (EU) xvii, 4, 7, 8, 12–15, 18, 22, 27–49, 70, 73, 113–114, 136–137, 151n, 179, 197, 229–230, 235–236, 308
evidence 33, 34, 39–42, 54, 57, 60–62, 64, 66, 77, 86, 96, 98, 99, 101–107, 113, 186, 197, 210, 212, 230, 231, 254, 264n, 265, 271, 311, 313. *See also* country of origin information; narrative, asylum; Statement of Evidence Form
  absence of 21, 41, 58
  assessment of 30n, 39–43, 54, 245
  documentary 39, 40, 57, 60, 61, 64, 105, 187, 224–226, 231, 232, 254
  expert 14, 18, 19, 44, 98, 100, 101, 103, 105, 107, 136, 138, 141, 147, 163, 231. *See also* winesses
  linguistic 44
  of nationality 44, 77

'objective' 39, 100, 104
    of sexuality 61, 62
    state's duty to obtain 42, 43, 71
'expertise trap' 16n

F

fairness, in asylum decision-making 28, 29, 33, 37, 40, 46, 96, 97, 106, 114, 196, 211, 233–236, 264–266, 272, 274, 276–278, 294, 312, 313
    procedural 101, 149–151, 182, 202, 205, 208, 209, 212, 214, 229, 234, 244, 246, 300, 316
Fassin, D. 55, 62, 67, 121, 127, 234n, 238, 263, 264, 273, 281, 282, 298n, 303
fast-track procedures 12–14, 162n, 197n, 307, 308
Federal Administrative Court (Austria) 136, 137
Federal Administrative Tribunal (Switzerland). *See* tribunals
Federal Asylum Office (FAO) (Austria) 20, 135, 136
Federal Constitutional Court (Germany) 291
Federal Office for Immigration and Asylum (FOIA) (Austria) 20, 135–137
Federal Office for Migration and Refugees (*Bundesamt für Migration und Flüchtlinge*, BAMF) (Germany) 287–290, 294, 296, 297, 299, 302, 303
Federführung (Switzerland) 269n, 270, 277
first instance decisions. *See* asylum decisions, first instance

First Tier Tribunal (Immigration and Asylum Chamber) (UK). *See* tribunals
Flood, J. 157, 167, 174, 310, 311, 317
formal and informal processes, formalism 16, 17, 37, 110, 116, 125, 126, 139, 168, 170, 201, 204–205, 211, 236, 244–246, 248, 272, 273, 275, 312, 316
France 2, 12, 19, 20, 44n, 53–68, 94, 121–122, 155–174, 200, 228, 234n, 264, 278
French (language) 75, 77, 79–81, 83, 84, 86, 125, 159, 164, 267n
French National Court of Asylum. *See* Cour nationale du droit d'asile

G

Garelli, G. 14, 25, 129
gender 28n, 37n, 61, 64, 110, 141, 185, 234, 294
German (language) 139, 140, 151n, 267n, 270n, 288
Germany 5, 10n, 21, 36, 113, 123, 124, 285–305
Ghana 228–230
Giannopoulou, C. xii, 14, 19, 36, 109–129, 314, 316
Gibb, R. xii, xiii, 20, 60, 110, 127, 135, 152, 155–174, 181, 186, 192, 200, 225, 234, 238, 243, 260, 265, 282, 309, 315
Gill, N. xii, 1–26, 36, 44, 76, 88, 95, 97, 109–129, 139, 149–152, 155, 195, 196, 198, 214–216, 222, 230, 238, 256, 264, 265, 270, 276, 280, 282, 287, 294, 302, 304, 307–318
Giordano, C. 183, 192, 236, 238
globalisation 20, 69–70, 75, 309
Goffman, E. 87, 89, 158, 174

Index

Good, A. xii, xiii, 1–26, 44, 68, 110, 111, 127, 135, 139, 150, 152, 153, 155, 156, 163, 174, 175, 177, 182, 183, 186, 192, 193, 195, 196, 214, 216, 222, 225, 230, 234n, 238, 243, 260, 262, 265, 282, 286, 287, 302, 304, 305, 310, 311, 314, 317
Goodwin-Gill, G. 2, 23, 113, 128, 245, 260
Greece 12–14, 20, 31, 32n, 36, 38n, 109–129, 222, 234n, 235, 308
Griffiths, A. 311, 316, 317
Griffiths, J. 16, 18, 23
Griffiths, M. 185, 193, 203, 216
Guild, E. 15, 23, 31, 46

H

Hambly, J. xiii, 21, 28, 42, 44, 195–217, 312, 313
harmonisation, of procedures 14, 29, 32, 222, 290n
Hawkins, K. 196, 201, 216, 243, 244, 249, 254, 261
hearing centres (UK) 92, 94, 198–200, 203–208, 214, 315
  differences between 198n, 203–205, 207
Herlihy, J. 243, 261, 313, 317
High Court (England) 197n
Higher Administrative Court (Austria) 137
Home Office (UK) xiii, 19, 34, 35, 91–107, 197, 198, 202, 205–213
homosexuality. *See* sexual orientation
HOPO (Home Office Presenting Officer) (UK) 19, 34, 35, 91–108, 198, 204, 205, 207–213
hotspots 14, 116, 235
human rights vii, 2, 29, 30, 32, 33n, 36, 39, 45, 99, 114, 115, 151, 162n, 179, 197, 229, 237, 242, 258. *See also* rights
  appeals 93, 100
  political management of 229–230
  violations of 7, 28, 30, 36, 110–111, 113, 137, 308
Human Rights Watch 109, 110, 126
humanitarianism 7, 116, 122
humanitarian protection 8, 11, 29, 32–34, 38, 40, 57, 73, 137, 162, 179, 180, 197, 224n, 227–230, 243, 256
Hungary 2, 12, 36, 308
Huysmans, J. 6, 24, 72, 89

I

identity 40, 61, 72, 74, 77, 80, 81, 84, 88, 161, 181, 230, 291
  construction of 246, 258
  misrecognition of 19, 69, 71, 86, 87
  refugees as threat to national identity 6, 115, 116, 236, 312
immigration. *See also* migration
  control of 2–4, 6–9, 18, 70, 94, 196–197, 214, 230, 236n, 242, 263, 308, 309
  legislation 17, 40n, 57n, 73, 92, 93, 100, 107, 111, 203, 290
  policies 1–6, 19, 93, 118, 202, 210, 222. *See also* asylum policies
Immigration Appeals Board (UNE) (Norway) 252–254, 257
Immigration Judges (IJ) (UK) 91, 94–97, 105, 107, 197, 198, 200–214, 313
  Designated, (DIJ) (UK) 95, 101, 106n
Immigration Rules (UK) xvii, 17, 40n, 93–94, 97, 107, 210, 214
inarticulateness 84–85
inconsistency. *See also* consistency
  in asylum decision-making 8, 11–12, 21, 195, 206, 231, 245, 259, 314, 315
  procedural 12, 308

indefinite leave to remain (ILR) (UK) 98, 197n
Inghilleri, M. 74, 89, 135, 140, 153
Injustice 88, 252–256. *See also* justice
inner belief. *See intime conviction*
intercultural encounters 71, 135, 276, 278. *See also* interpreters; interpretation
interpreters 18, 34, 36, 37, 55n, 106, 110, 120, 133–155, 159, 161, 162, 167–169, 175, 181, 188, 223, 224, 291–293. *See also* training
  absence of 79, 110, 125
  agency of 134–136, 142–146, 149
  as experts 136, 138, 141–142, 147, 149
  availability of 13, 36–38, 44, 74, 235
  certification of 138
  cooperation with officials 140–145
  neutrality of 135, 140–141
  power of 20, 134, 142
  professionalism of 20, 134, 144, 147–151, 186
interpretation, legal 15, 29, 43, 94, 107, 201, 230, 243, 248, 254, 265, 308, 314, 316
interpretation, linguistic
  limitations of 20, 106, 181, 225
  verbatim 150
  via telephone 160, 164–166, 172
intertextuality. *See* texts
interviews. *See also* interpreters; interpretation; video-conferencing
  admissibility 156, 159–160, 163–166, 172
  asylum 14, 20, 33, 36–37, 57, 72–75, 77–80, 84–86, 101, 110, 134–137, 140–149, 156, 158–162, 166–168, 171, 181–183, 188, 197, 200, 223, 225–226, 233, 236, 251, 264, 267–269, 271, 277–278, 286, 290–293, 294–298, 300, 301
  power relations in 20, 158
  screening 98, 101, 181, 197, 267, 291
  transcripts of 75, 77, 86, 135, 137–139, 145, 150, 162n, 163, 167, 226n
intime conviction 53–56, 58–60, 62–66, 248
Iran 123, 190, 257
Ireland 12n, 30n, 32n, 33n
Italy 7, 10, 12, 31, 36, 121, 221–240, 314

J

Jacquemet, M. 72, 74–75, 89, 234n, 239
Jubany, O. 195, 203, 216, 248, 261, 265, 282, 286, 304
Judges 15, 18–19, 21, 28, 34–35, 44–45, 136, 138, 159, 195, 200, 297, 301, 311, 314–315. *See also* Immigration Judges; *président*
  Danish 178, 180
  French 53–68, 159, 161–162, 169, 171
  Italian 221, 223–227, 230, 232, 234–237
judgment (judgement)
  by decision-makers 36n, 43, 144, 175–178, 181–183, 188–189, 191, 248, 270, 290, 293, 297, 301, 315
  by interpreters 146, 147, 149
judicial remedy 43–44, 299
judicial scrutiny 8, 29, 35
judicialisation 198
justice 20–21, 46, 55, 87, 96, 196, 204, 209, 212, 241–242, 244–246, 250, 252,

258–259, 271–275. *See also* injustice
  access to 44, 107, 311
  deferred 252
  procedural 300

K

Kälin, W. 36, 47, 178, 193, 278, 282
Kandel, R.F. 15, 24, 311, 317
Kelly, T. 281–282
Kobelinsky, C. xiii, 19, 28, 42, 44, 53–68, 94, 155, 174, 176–177, 186, 193, 234n, 238, 263, 264–265, 273, 282, 297, 298n, 303, 315
Kritzer, H.M. 195, 204, 216

L

linguistic register 71, 84–87, 314
Latour, B. 134, 222, 226n, 239, 310, 317
lawyer-client relationship 159, 171, 182–183, 188–190, 201, 207–210, 225
lawyers, role of 37, 59, 63, 107, 162, 171, 176, 178, 182–183, 188–191, 195–217, 223–226
legal aid 13, 38, 59n, 107, 110, 181, 198, 212, 223n
legal consciousness 18, 46
legal pluralism 16–18, 111, 116, 126, 196, 313
legal representation 44, 106, 122, 190, 197, 212, 214
  regulation of 199
Libya 7, 227–230, 233
lies/lying 104, 188, 190–191, 203, 295, 297, 301
Liodden, T.M. xiii, 21, 28, 44, 241–262, 266, 297, 313, 315
Lipsky, M. 196, 216, 244, 250, 252, 261, 264, 279, 282

M

Malkki, L. 122–123, 128
Malta 12n
manifestly unfounded. *See* unfounded claims
Maryns (Marijns), K. 72, 85, 89, 135, 139, 153, 181, 193, 234n, 239, 265, 282
media 3–4, 34, 62, 115, 122, 125, 133, 203, 222, 236, 241, 255–258, 270, 313–314
  social 72, 199, 309
mental health 5, 10, 14, 185
Merry, S.E. 18, 24, 46, 125, 128
Miaz, J. xiii, 21, 28, 42, 263–283, 312, 313, 315
misrecognition. *See* identity, misrecognition of
migrants, economic 3, 30, 55, 195, 225, 230, 232n, 235
migration viii, x, xi, 7, 14, 18, 55, 69–72, 196. *See also* immigration
  clandestine 110, 116, 126
  forced 120, 177
  policies. *See* asylum policies; immigration policies
Moore, S.F. 16–17, 24, 196, 203, 213, 217, 287, 304
moral certainty 54, 65, 66. *See also* proof, moral
moral economy 56, 273
moral panic 1–3, 9
morality, asylum and 22, 55, 66, 125, 190, 234n, 236, 258, 264–266, 272, 274–275, 285, 298, 301, 312
Moreno-Lax, V. 7, 9, 24
Mountz, A. 5, 25, 116, 128, 264, 283
Munro, V.E. 195, 215, 252, 259
mutual trust principle 31, 113

N

naming practices 69, 71–72, 84–85. *See also* linguistic register
narrative, asylum 20, 37–40, 58–59, 62, 65–66, 69, 72, 74, 88, 119, 123, 161, 234, 292, 295n. *See also* asylum motive
  ascribed authorship of 175–178, 183
  coherence of 41, 57, 77, 175, 187, 189, 230, 233, 272, 298, 315
  consistency of 175, 182, 187, 189, 231, 295n, 313
  construction of 57, 175, 185
  credibility of 57, 58, 71, 77, 175, 177, 191, 230–232, 278
  discrepancies/divergencies in 57, 69, 106, 175, 178, 182, 183, 189, 211, 292
  performance of 21, 177, 178, 190
  self-experienced 175, 178, 182–183, 189–190
  styles of 85, 189
National Commission on Human Rights (EEDA) (Greece) 113, 114
Netherlands 12n, 123, 257
Noll, G. 46, 47, 282
'normal procedure' (Denmark) 179–180
norms, normativity 15–16, 116, 125, 149, 196–197, 222, 241–2, 256, 259, 266, 272, 293
  informal 116, 139, 205
  linguistic 72, 87, 116, 314
  procedural 19, 40, 138, 139
Norway 28, 31, 44, 113, 187, 241–262
Norwegian Directorate of Immigration (UDI) 241–242, 247–254, 260, 262

O

O'Barr, W.M. 195, 215, 310, 317
Office français de protection des réfugiés et apatrides (Office for the Protection of Refugees and Stateless Persons, OFPRA) (France) 55–57, 59–60, 159–164, 166–170, 172–174
offices, open plan 170
opt-outs. *See* Common European Asylum System; Denmark; UK

P

Painter, J. 14, 25, 116, 128
Pakistan 61–62, 66, 124n, 133n, 223–225, 232
Papada, E. 14, 25, 116, 128
Papoutsi, A. 14, 25, 116, 128
persecution 2, 5, 34, 39, 57, 61–62, 64–66, 200–201, 230, 250, 257, 263, 278, 314
  fear of 11, 30, 33, 38, 98n, 242–243. *See also* well-founded fear
  risk of 8, 11, 33, 38, 42, 243, 250
pity. *See* compassion
Poertner, E. xiv, 21, 28, 42, 263–283, 312, 313, 315
Pöllabauer, S. 135, 138, 145, 153, 186, 193
post-traumatic stress. *See* trauma
practice 6, 16, 35, 39, 135, 159, 177, 180, 189, 196, 198, 205, 210, 222, 244, 247, 253, 255–256, 259, 277, 285–287, 290, 295, 298. *See also* communicative practices; interpreters, practices of; naming practices
  administrative and bureaucratic 97, 268–270, 272, 288, 293, 296, 308, 313

communities of practice 200–202, 204, 208, 265n, 313
  daily 15, 19, 55, 266, 307
  legal 53, 183, 201, 203, 212, 247
Prefecture
  France 60, 160
  Greece 111
  Italy 223n
président (France) 75, 161
Presenting Officer. *See* HOPO
Probst, J. 265, 283, 286, 304
productivity. *See* asylum decision-makers
professional standards. *See* duty, professional; ethics, professional; interpreters, professionalism of
proof
  burden of 39, 42, 42n, 45, 61, 235, 314
  of identity 69, 71–72, 74, 81, 86, 232
  moral 54
  standard of 38–39, 42–43, 314

Q

quasi-legality 17, 113, 180, 196, 221, 301

R

Ramji-Nogales, J. 245, 259, 261, 314, 318
Rampton, B.J.M. 75, 89, 157, 158, 170, 173
rapporteurs (France) 55n, 57–59, 64–66, 169–171, 264
reasonable degree of likelihood 38
reasonable doubt. *See* doubt, reasonable
reasons for refusal letter (RFRL) (UK) 97–99, 101, 106

reception centres 19–20, 111, 118, 120, 123, 136, 155, 267, 269–270, 275–277
recognition rates 12, 179, 235
reconsideration. *See* asylum decisions, reconsideration of
Red Cross 179, 184
refoulement 8, 27, 32–33, 113
Refugee Appeals Board (RAB) (Denmark) 175–176, 178, 180–184, 188–191
refugee policies. *See* asylum policies
refugee status detemination procedures (RSDP). *See* asylum decision-making processes
refugees 'genuine' 232–233, 241, 245, 258. *See also* asylum seekers
Rehaag, S. 200, 217, 245, 259, 261, 314, 318
religious conversion 296
Richardson, L. 135, 154, 309, 318
right-wing populism 4, 115
rights. *See also* children, rights of; human rights
  of appeal 9, 33, 35, 44–45, 97, 100, 203, 221
  to asylum 7, 38, 61, 65, 66, 246
  of asylum seekers 17, 33, 151, 188, 229, 235, 270, 295
  civil and political 27n, 29, 33n, 34, 44
  of refugees 17, 32, 113–114, 117, 126, 179, 223, 242, 258
risk
  to children 110, 122, 126
  of detention 197
  in Mediterranean 7, 9, 228
  perceptions of 234, 250
  of persecution 28, 30, 32, 33, 38, 42, 98n, 99, 101, 104n, 225, 232, 242–243, 245, 249, 256. *See also* refoulement

Rock, P. 156, 172, 174, 200, 205, 212, 217, 315, 318
Roitman, J. 5, 25, 236, 239
Romania 12
Rotter, R. 152, 185, 193, 216
rules, legal 15–19, 27–29, 35, 54, 110, 116, 196, 202–203, 209, 212, 213. *See also* Common European Asylum System; Immigration Rules
  application to children 35
  procedural 18, 27–29, 32, 37, 39, 93–94, 97, 138–139, 150n, 213
Rycroft, R. 110, 129, 134–135, 150, 154

S

safe country 73, 112, 114, 126, 230
safe third country 36, 39, 127
Scheffer, D.T. 140, 145, 154, 265, 281, 283, 286, 293
Schneider, S. xiv, 21, 42, 43, 58, 203, 266, 285–305, 312
Schoenholtz, A.I. 245, 259, 261, 314, 318
Schrag, P.G. 245, 259, 261, 314, 318
Schuster, L. 5, 25, 55, 68
Secretary of State for the Home Department (SSHD) (UK) 40n, 92, 94–95, 97–98, 100, 105, 107, 210
security 3, 5, 28, 31, 45, 107, 242
  of caseworkers 296
  securitisation 6, 70, 236
semi-autonomous social fields 16–17, 196
Senegal 76, 80, 84, 123, 125, 232
Serbia 2, 12n, 102
serious harm 30, 33–34, 38, 42
sexual orientation 61–62, 297
Shah, P. 47, 129, 154, 203, 217

Shuman, A. 55, 67, 72, 86, 88, 175, 177, 192
skeleton argument 98, 210
Smith, D.E. 135, 154, 242, 261, 262
social security 288
solicitors (UK) 19, 98, 198–199, 204, 208
  regulation of 199
Sorgoni, B. xiv, 10, 21, 44, 105, 200, 221–240, 296, 313–315
Souter, J. 203, 217, 236, 240, 265, 283
Spain 12n
Spotti, M. xiv, 19, 69–89, 181, 234, 315
standard of proof. *See* proof
State Secretariat for Migration (SEM) (Switzerland) 266–268, 270–271, 276–277, 279, 280n
Statement of Evidence Form (SEF) (UK) 98, 101
'storying' 120
strangers 1, 116, 185
subsidiary protection. *See* humanitarian protection
super-diversity 70
Supreme Court (Italy) 222, 225n
Supreme Court (UK) 43n, 198
sur place applications. *See* asylum applications
Sweden 5, 12n, 121, 197, 288, 292n, 296n, 308
Switzerland 12n, 21, 28, 31, 36, 263–283
Syria 3–4, 7, 12, 114, 119, 124, 179, 233, 236, 288n, 308

T

targets, performance 96–97, 209, 270–271, 279, 309
Tazzioli, M. 14, 25, 129, 223, 236, 238, 240

Territorial Commission (TC) (Italy) 10, 221–225, 226n, 228–229, 232–233, 236
texts. *See also* documents
  authorship of 80, 87
  entextualisation 75, 77, 158, 167–168, 234
  intertextuality 85
  production of 71, 74–75
Thomas, R. 195, 198–200, 202, 217, 244–245, 262, 312, 318
trafficking 14, 110
training
  of asylum decision-makers 10, 35, 267–268, 279–280, 285–289, 294–301
  of HOPOs 91, 92–95, 106–107, 208–210
  of interpreters 136–139, 141, 143, 151
  of barristers 199, 204, 211–212
transparency
  apparent, of facts 225
  in asylum decision-making 286, 295, 298, 300, 302, 315
trauma 37–38, 309, 316
  post-traumatic stress (PTSD) 14, 243
tribunals 19, 312
  Asylum and Immigration Tribunal (AIT) (UK) 91–92, 95, 97–98, 101, 104
  civil tribunal (Italy) 221–224, 226–229, 231, 235
  Federal Administrative Tribunal (Switzerland) 266, 268n, 270
  First Tier Tribunal (Immigration and Asylum Chamber) (UK) 105n, 196, 198–200, 202–203, 210, 212–213
  social relations in 204–208, 214
  Upper Tribunal (UK) 100, 105, 198

Trust 205–208, 248, 254, 267n, 292, 316. *See also* distrust
truth 19, 54, 63–66, 87, 119, 186, 211–212, 225, 231, 234, 295–296
  'web–truths' 74
truthfulness 62, 69–72, 74, 80, 296–298
Turkey 5, 7, 12n, 14, 36n, 44n, 112–114, 116, 124, 133n, 308
Turner, S. 243, 261, 313, 317

U

UDI. *See* Norwegian Directorate of Immigration
unaccompanied minors. *See* children
uncertainty 21, 242–246, 251–252, 257–259, 285–286, 297. *See also* doubt
  of outcome 175–176, 184–187, 251–252
unfairness. *See* fairness
unfounded claims 100, 160, 179, 291
United Kingdom (UK) 12n, 16–17, 30, 32n, 33n, 35, 40n, 91–108, 113, 156, 163, 195–217, 234n, 244, 294
  opt-outs by 28, 31, 32n
United Kingdom Independence Party (UKIP) (UK) 4
United Nations High Commissioner for Refugees (UNHCR) 7, 16, 25–26, 30n, 42, 47, 59, 63, 72, 89, 113–114, 117n, 119, 129, 138, 151, 154, 161, 222n, 223n, 225n, 230, 237, 240, 273, 294–295
  UNHCR *Handbook* 11, 36, 38–39, 41, 43n, 47, 97, 108, 243, 258, 262
Upper Tribunal (UK). *See* tribunals

V

Vertovec, S. 1, 26, 70, 89
video conferencing 12–13, 160n
Vogl, A. 178, 182, 193
volitional allegiance 264–265, 273, 276, 281
Vradis, A. 14, 25, 116, 128
vulnerability 14, 22, 32, 38, 110, 120, 151, 200, 277, 308, 316
  of children 110, 126

W

Wadensjö, C. 134, 142, 153–154
waiting, in asylum process 176, 184–185, 187, 191
waiting zone 160, 163–166
'web-truths'. *See* truth
well-founded fear 10–12, 30, 33, 38, 56, 98n, 104, 242–243. *See also* persecution
Wenger, E. 201, 216, 265, 283
Wettergren, Å. 247, 262, 286, 305
Whyte, Z. xi, 20, 69, 175–193, 245–46, 262, 281, 283, 286, 305, 315–316
witnesses 34, 40, 99, 102–105, 156, 206, 213
  expert 14, 18–19, 44, 98, 100–101, 103, 105, 107, 138, 141, 163, 202, 231. *See also* evidence; interpreters
witness statement 98–99, 101

Y

Yeo, C. 203, 212, 217

Z

Zetter, R. 122, 129, 258, 282
zone d'attente (France). *See* waiting zone

Zwaan, K. xv, 18, 27–49, 61, 71, 113, 230, 314–315

Legislation

Asylum and Immigration Appeals Act 1993 (UK) 17
Asylum and Immigration (Treatment of Claimants, etc) Act 2004 (UK) 40n, 100
Asylum Procedures Directive (APD) 30n, 33–35, 37, 42, 44, 47
Charter of Fundamental Rights of the European Union 27n, 33n, 35
Danish Aliens Act (2016) (Denmark) 179
Dublin II Regulation 112–113
Dublin III Regulation 12, 28, 31, 32n, 73, 126, 136, 179, 197, 289–290
Eurodac Regulation 31, 45
European Convention on Human Rights and Fundamental Freedoms (ECHR) 27n, 29, 30, 32, 33n, 99, 179
Immigration Rules (UK) xiv, 17, 17n, 40n, 93, 99, 107, 210
Norwegian Immigration Act of 2008 (*Act of 15 May 2008: On the Entry of Foreign Nationals into the Kingdom of Norway and Their Stay in the Realm*) 242
Qualification Directive (QDI, QDII) 27n, 30n, 32, 33n, 34n, 35, 40–42, 48, 230n
Reception Conditions Directive (RCDI, RCDII) 31–32, 48
United Nations Convention Against Torture (UNCAT) 27n, 29, 32, 33n
United Nations Convention on Civil and Political Rights (UNCCPR) 27n, 29
United Nations Convention on the Rights of the Child (UNCRC) 35, 117

United Nations Convention Relating to the Status of Refugees (1951 Convention, 'Geneva Convention') 2, 8, 11, 17, 27, 29, 30n, 33, 39, 43, 53, 57, 65, 98n, 101, 112–113, 117, 137, 179, 200, 214, 242n, 268, 273

Case Law
Abdolkhani and Karimnia v. Turkey 30471/08 [2009] ECtHR 1336 44n
AH (Failed asylum seekers—involuntary returns) Eritrea CG [2006] UKAIT 00078 104
Danian [1999] INLR 533 98
DK (Serbia) [2006] EWCA Civ 1747 101
Gebremedhin v. France 25389/05 [2007] ECtHR 44n
Italian Supreme Court (*Suprema Corte di Cassazione*), Cass. S.U., no. 27310 225n

MA (Draft evaders; illegal departures; risk) Eritrea CG [2007] UKAIT 00059 103
MJ (Afghanistan) [2013] UKUT 253 (IAC) 43n
M.M. [2012] CJEU C-277/11 42n, 49n
M.S.S. v. Belgium and Greece 30696/09 [2011] ECtHR 108 32n, 36n, 38n, 49
N.S. and Others [2011] CJEU, joined cases C-411/10, C-493/10 32n, 36n, 49
R (on the application of Cart) and ors v. Upper Tribunal and ors [2011] UKSC 28 198
Tarakhel v. Switzerland, 29217/12 [2014] ECtHR 1435 36n, 49
TN and others (Afghanistan) [2015] UKSC 40 [73] 43n

The manufacturer's authorised representative in the EU is Springer Nature Customer Service Centre GmbH, Europaplatz 3, 69115 Heidelberg, Germany. If you have any concerns regarding our products, please contact ProductSafety@springernature.com

Printed and bound by CPI Group (UK) Ltd, Croydon, CR0 4YY

23/03/2026

02076663-0020